12-05

WRIGLEY FIELD'S LAST WORLD SERIES

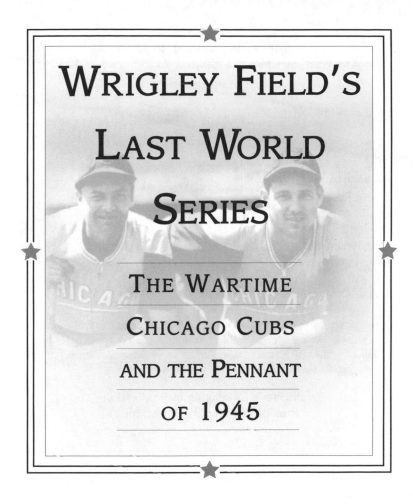

THE WARTIME
CHICAGO CUBS
AND THE PENNANT
OF 1945

BY CHARLES N. BILLINGTON

FOREWORD BY ANDY PAFKO

First Edition

www.lakeclaremont.com
Chicago

Wrigley Field's Last World Series:
The Wartime Chicago Cubs and the Pennant of 1945
Charles N. Billington

Published May 2005 by:

4650 North Rockwell Street
Chicago, Illinois 60625
773/583-7800
lcp@lakeclaremont.com
www.lakeclaremont.com

Publisher's Cataloging-in-Publication
(Provided by Quality Books, Inc.)

Billington, Charles N.
    Wrigley Field's last World Series: the wartime
Chicago Cubs and the pennant of 1945 / by Charles N.
Billington – 1st ed.
    p. cm.
    Includes bibliographical references and index.
    LCCN: 2004107983
    ISBN: 1-893121-45-3

    1. Chicago Cubs (Baseball team)–History–20th
century. 2. Baseball–United States–History–20th
century. 3. World Series (Baseball)–(1945) I. Title.

GV875.C6B55 2005   796.375'64'0977311
                          QBI05-800152

Printed in the United States of America
by United Graphics in Mattoon, Illinois.

10 09 08 07 06 05   10 9 8 7 6 5 4 3 2 1

*To Lieutenant Evans R. Billington and Captain George W. Barker,
who missed the baseball wars, fighting much bigger battles
in hostile, faraway lands*

CONTENTS

FOREWORD

In 1945 I was the 24-year-old starting center fielder for the Chicago Cubs, going to the World Series in my second full season in the major leagues. I was born and raised on a farm in Boyceville, Wisconsin, 25 miles away from Eau Claire, and when I came to Chicago to join the Cubs in September 1943, I had never set foot in a major league park in my life. It was a rainy, cold day, and I got a warm welcome from Stan Hack, the great Cubs third baseman. We had a game against the Philadelphia Phillies; only 314 fans were in the ballpark. Bill Lee, who was a great pitcher for the Cubs in previous years, was the Phillies' starter. Manager Jimmie Wilson put me in the lineup, and I got a double and drove in two runs my first time at bat. The second time I batted I got another hit and drove in two more runs. I played in 13 games for the Cubs in 1943 and hit .379. That success seemed to be a continuation of the great year I was having; before they called me up, I had won the batting title in the Pacific Coast League.

I played for the Cubs until the middle of the 1951 season. Chicago quickly became my new home. For several seasons I lived at the Sheridan Plaza Hotel, where many of the other players lived. I met my wife in Chicago, and at first we lived near Grand Avenue and Camerling Street. We bought a home in the Kelvyn Park neighborhood and lived there almost 20 years. Our last move was to suburban Mount Prospect.

I have a lot of friends and acquaintances in the Chicago area, and I am amazed and grateful that I am remembered so fondly. Baseball was very different when I first played in Chicago. Because of World War II, we had to have spring training at a resort in Indiana. All of the players and the front-office personnel worked with the clouds of war over their heads. The players were concerned about how long they would be able to play, and the front-office men had a hard time working around the war, trying to field a competitive team. The Cubs were one of the premier teams in the majors up through the war, a fact that surprises younger fans who were not around then. During the 1945 season we started kind of slowly, but we played great baseball through all of July and August. After that we cooled off a little bit but still had enough in us to hold off the St. Louis Cardinals. We did not hit a lot of home runs, but we were great at situation hitting and great at fielding, and our pitching staff was peerless. We did not know too much about the Detroit Tigers when the World Series started. They battled us tooth and nail, and we went at it for seven thrilling games. Their great pitcher Hal Newhouser proved to be a little too much for us, and they prevailed, winning four games to three. I still cannot believe the Cubs have not been back since.

My wife and I were very sad when I was traded to the Brooklyn Dodgers in 1951, but as I look back I had some great moments in Brooklyn and later on in Milwaukee with the Braves. I was fortunate enough to play in the World Series for the Dodgers in 1952 and twice with Milwaukee, in 1957 and 1958. We won the whole thing in 1957, and my last season as a player was in 1959. So I played 17 years in the major leagues and got to play in four World Series.

I have so many fond memories of the 1945 season, and this book does an excellent job of documenting that great year and describing organized baseball during the wartime era. For those who experienced the 1945 season, your recollections will be refreshed and you will gain many new insights as you read it. For everyone else, your knowledge of the game will be enhanced as you learn about a great period in baseball history.

—Andy Pafko

ACKNOWLEDGMENTS

I am indebted to many for the creation of this book. My first debt of gratitude goes to the "first editor" and chief source of encouragement, my wife, Cynthia. The piquant and persistent comments by my children, Sarah and Matthew, also prodded me along. Whatever writing ability I have came from Alice Gebhardt, Marion Olson, and Dr. R.G. Peterson. If I have mastered the ability to think instead of simply learn, Milton Nelson, Ronald Magnuson, Jack Schwandt, and Dr. Arthur Campbell are responsible. My respect for history and empathy for the past experiences of others came from my grandfather, C.M. Nelson, and my mother, Carol Billington. Writing about athletic endeavors is easier when one learns the determination, effort, and sacrifice that is involved; my thanks to four coaches, Ted Hedstrand, Dan McCarrell, Chuck Lunder, and Paul Quame.

The discussions and correspondence I had with Mrs. Hank Borowy, the late George Brace, the late Paul Erickson, Allen Higgins, Len Merullo, Melissa Nelson (granddaughter of catcher Dewey Williams), Andy Pafko, and the late Claude Passeau were all invaluable and central to the creation of this work. Mr. Merullo and Mr. Pafko in particular were extremely generous with their time and their rich memories of this era. The staff at the Chicago Historical Society Research Center, National Baseball Hall of Fame Library, and Northwestern University's Government Documents Department all made my research much easier. I am also appreciative of the insights about sports medicine, such as it was during those days, shared by Dr. Robert McMillan, orthopedic surgeon, and Dr. Steven Sholl, team physician for the Chicago Bulls.

I also want to thank Sharon Woodhouse and the staff at Lake Claremont Press, an organization that shares my interest and respect for the past. Their encouragement, enthusiasm, and ideas were most helpful and deeply appreciated.

ACKNOWLEDGMENTS

INTRODUCTION

As a youngster, my first exposure to baseball was through the medium of radio. In the mid-1950s, my father had a porch constructed behind our dining room. My father, a mechanical engineer, designed and built most of it by himself, but he hired a large older Swedish mason named Anders to lay the cement. Anders knew very little English and spoke Swedish, whether the individual he was addressing understood it or not. When he started the job, he had a black Ford Model T pickup truck with a crank starter underneath the radiator. I was very impressed with his truck, having seen such contraptions in the Our Gang Comedy shows and Laurel & Hardy films. Before the job was done, however, he had a new green Ford pickup, complete with cream-colored hubcaps. I remember being told that he got the new truck for free in exchange for the old one. The Ford Motor Company wanted old trucks like his for its own collection. I had never heard of such a thing before, but I was only seven years old at the time.

After his lunch, one of the first things Anders did was plug in a well-worn radio and listen to it. I did not pay too much attention to radio then, and most of my experiences with it came from listening to what my mother might have on during the day. I remember Alex Drier and the news, Arthur Godfrey—things like that. The shows elicited little emotional response from her, but occasionally she would sing along with a tune or perhaps whistle an accompaniment to what was playing. I remember her whistling bothering me; I tried whistling—in private, of course—and couldn't do it.

Anders listened to no such entertainment on his radio. His show had men talking, mentioning only other men's names, peppering their conversations with the names of cities and lots of numbers. Anders never whistled or broke into song while listening. What he did sometimes was a little more unsettling. When the men speaking on the radio got excited and talked faster, he would often momentarily stop what he was doing, listen intently, and then either respond with a pleasant grin and an exhortation or a look of displeasure with a scorning tone in his voice. One midafternoon when the men on the radio stopped sounding tense and sounded disappointed, he even threw his shovel down. I found all of this a little frightening but also fascinating, and I thought his responses might have something to do with him being Swedish. After all, he also talked differently than anybody I had ever heard before. I was very glad my mother never got so worked up over her radio shows; things about parents were hard enough to figure out at that age.

All of Anders's histrionics were my introduction to baseball. After seeing it on television every now and then, I got to slowly understand what the men on the radio were talking about. At this point, my friends and I were more interested in baseball as an activity than in knowing about any particular team. This changed, however, when my gang of fellows began the childhood ritual of hoarding baseball cards, matching those magic names with faces, and developing our own personal athletic icons. Before you ask, the answer is yes, my mother at some point later on threw out all the baseball cards, just like millions of other moms across America.

The following year, my lower front baby teeth remained firmly entrenched in my gums in spite of the relentless pushing of the permanent teeth coming in behind them. They had to be pulled, and my father told me that if I were brave during the procedure, he would take me to a baseball game. I put up with the ominous antiseptic smell of the Carlson Building in Evanston and the controlled trauma of having the teeth pulled and got to see the Cubs play the Cincinnati Reds on a very cloudy Saturday a few weeks later. The seats were in the third row behind the Cubs' dugout, reward indeed nowadays for a dental procedure, but in those days the futile Cubs averaged only about 8,000 fans per game.

When my father told me where the seats were, I decided I needed to bring my J.C. Higgins baseball glove. He heartily endorsed the idea, saying we would be sitting where foul balls sometimes land. I never thought of that, but upon hearing it, I could never tell anyone the real reason why I wanted to bring it. I had noticed in the games on television that many times most of the seats near the field were not completely filled. I thought to myself that if some of the people in the seats did not always show up, maybe there were days when some of the players did not show up. If my Saturday game was one of those days and I was in the third row with a glove, I reasoned, the players might ask me to join them so they would have enough guys to play.

Once we arrived at the park and settled into the seats, I was completely awed and a little intimidated by what I saw. These players were men, many of them big men, some of them very big men. They did not play catch before the game like my friends and I did. They threw very hard, all the time, and they never closed their eyes or turned their faces if the ball bounced directly in front of them; they just snatched it up, courageously ignoring a potential bad bounce to the face. Even though I knew it probably did not matter, I hid my glove under the seat, hoping none of the players would see it and get some ideas if all of their fellow players did not show up, and hoping even more fervently that they would show up. I suddenly lost all interest in doing anything but watching.

The most indelible memory of the game occurred in the early innings. Bobby Adams hit a single, triggering a short burst of loud enthusiasm and excitement from the crowd. I think Casey Wise batted next and struck out. The crowd emitted a quiet moan and irritated disgust that sounded vaguely familiar to me. The next hitter was Dale Long, whom I liked, because he batted left-handed like me. He became my ego ideal for many years a moment later, when he somehow hit the next pitch over the seats beyond right field, the ball bouncing against a billboard that said "Baby Ruth" on it. My young mind was dumbfounded as to how anybody could be strong enough to hit a ball thrown that fast that far. As he rounded third base, I noticed the Cincinnati pitcher glaring at him, walking off the mound a little bit toward him, and pointing at him with his index finger. His mouth was moving, but it was impossible to hear what he was saying. Long slowed down and looked at him, gesturing animatedly, and shook hands with his teammates, laughing while looking at the pitcher when he stepped on the plate.

At the crack of Long's bat, the old man sitting next to us dropped his program, stood up, and cheered with delight as Long jogged around the bases. I think it was at this moment that I realized that Anders's reaction to his radio show had nothing to do with him being Swedish.

WRIGLEY FIELD'S

LAST WORLD

SERIES

THE WARTIME

CHICAGO CUBS

AND THE PENNANT

OF 1945

CHAPTER 1

★ ★ ★ ★ ★ ★ ★ ★

FIVE DECADES OF SUCCESS,
FIVE DECADES OF FAILURE

To die-hard fans of the Chicago Cubs and to all followers of major league baseball, the word Cubs has become synonymous with failure. The rapid deterioration of the team following their last pennant (in 1945), the futile seasons in the 1950s and early '60s, and their rapid return to mediocrity and worse after the Leo Durocher years in the '70s and early '80s are all responsible for the Cubs' tarnished image. Yet an examination of the Chicago National League franchise in the first five decades of the twentieth century illustrates a stark contrast in the team's fortunes. In the first half of the century, few teams were as good as Chicago; in the second half, few teams were as bad. No other team in the major leagues went from being so dominant to so utterly futile as the Cubs did over the last half century.

Between 1900 and 1945, the Cubs won the National League pennant ten times. The only National League team with more World Series appearances was the New York Giants, with 13. During the first five decades of the twentieth century, the Cubs won at least one pennant every decade, something no other major league team was able to do. Not even the New York Yankees or the Philadelphia Athletics, the American League's most frequent champions, could match this feat. The Yankees won their first pennant in 1921, while the Athletics' last league championship occurred in 1931. Chicago also experienced the shortest dry spells between pennant-winning seasons through the World War II era, their longest hiatus lasting only from 1918 until 1929.

Yet in the 45 years following their last pennant, the Cubs finished first in their division only twice, in 1984 and 1989. Curiously, their most celebrated postwar season was 1969, when they finished second in their division. But even if they had been able to stay ahead of the New York Mets in 1969, they still would have had to win a playoff against the Atlanta Braves to capture the National League flag. The Mets did not deny Chicago a chance to win a pennant; they merely prevented them from winning a division. If the National League had not had a two-division format in 1969, the Cubs would have finished third, eight games behind New York and one game behind the 93–69 Atlanta Braves.

Finishing last, the exact opposite of winning the pennant, was what the Cubs accomplished with ease after the postwar era. Between 1946 and 1990, Chicago finished in the National League's basement nine times, with back-to-back last-place finishes in 1948–49 and 1980–81. During the first 45 years of the twentieth century, the team's only last-place finish came in 1925, but they quickly rebounded to go 82–72 the following year, for a 14-game improvement.

Between 1900 and 1945, Chicago, like the Cardinals, finished second six times, but both teams took fewer second-place finishes than the New York Giants, who had 12, and the Pittsburgh Pirates, who tallied 11. Between 1945 and 1969, when the National League divided into two divisions, the Cubs never finished second. Meanwhile, during the Durocher era, they finished second in their division three times: in 1969, 1970, and 1972. During the same period, they finished second to the bottom 11 times. The Cubs' only seventh-place finish through World War II came in 1921.

During the first half of the twentieth century, first-division finishes (ending the season in the top half of the league's final standings) were commonplace for Chicago. Through the World War II years, the Cubs finished in fourth place or better in 32 out of 45 seasons, a feat that in the National League only New York, with 34, and Pittsburgh, with 37, could eclipse. Only one American League team through 1945 could match such success: the New York Yankees, who matched the Cubs at 32. During the postwar years, however, the Cubs managed only three first-division finishes, when they finished third in 1946, 1967, and 1968. In 1969 the value of a first-division finish was greatly diminished when the two major leagues adopted a four-division format.

During the twentieth century's first five decades, Chicago also held the distinction of securing more first-division finishes than any other team in the National League. Between 1926 and 1939, the Cubs strung together 14 straight first-division finishes, with an additional 13 straight between 1903 and 1915. During roughly the same period, from 1901 to 1913, the Pittsburgh Pirates tallied 13 straight first-division finishes, and they garnered another 12 straight between 1918 and 1929. The New York Giants' records in this category were 12 straight (1903–14) and ten straight (1916–25). In the American League, the New York Yankees put together 20 straight first-division seasons from 1926 to 1945, while the Philadelphia Athletics were first-division for nine straight seasons, from 1925 to 1933. After World War II, however, first-division finishes by the Chicago Cubs were rarities.

In the years following 1945, the words *Cubs* and *second division* became virtually synonymous. If one waters down the divisional format instituted in 1969 and accepts the notion that a fourth-place finish in a six-team division is the equivalent of a second-division finish under the old format, Chicago finished in the bottom half of the league in 33 of the 45 seasons between World War II and 1990. The team's sorry record includes a stretch of 20 consecutive seasons in the second division, from 1947 through 1966, while the majors were still in a two-league format. The only season during that stretch when the team was not under .500 was 1952, when they finished fifth with a record of 77–77. As a means of comparison, through the end of World War II, Chicago finished in the second division only 13 times, and in seven of those seasons, they finished fifth.

Babyboomers growing up with the Cubs in the 1950s nostalgically recall the "cellar pennant" races that Chicago engaged in with the equally inept Philadelphia Phillies or Pittsburgh Pirates. From 1947 through 1962, last place in the National League was the exclusive domain of the Cubs, the Pirates, or the Phillies. In seven of those seasons, Pittsburgh finished last; Chicago claimed the cellar six times, and Philadelphia, four. In 1962 the newly formed New York Mets moved into the basement and spent the next four seasons there, but after the Mets vacated the premises in 1966, the Cubs moved right back in, shortly after new manager Leo Durocher embarrassed himself by boasting that "the Cubs aren't an eighth place team."

Although the Cubs, the Phillies, the Pirates, and the Mets cohabited in the nether regions of the National League during the first 20 years following World War II, only the Cubs are remembered for futility, because unlike the Cubs, the other three teams balanced their early postwar failures with success as the years progressed. In the years following World War II, the Phillies became a very good young team and actually won the pennant in 1950. During the latter part of the 1950s, they became weaker, and after the National League expanded in 1962, the Phillies were mired in mediocrity, never good enough to challenge the front-runners but managing to stay out of the cellar. By the mid-1970s, however, Philadelphia was once again a major league power. In 1983 they made it to the World Series, and in 1993 they won it with an entirely different team. Meanwhile, by the late 1950s, the Pirates had shed their futility, and in 1960 they won the World Series. In 1971 they repeated the feat, and they appeared in the play-offs several times thereafter. The Mets' level of incompetence was legendary when they first entered the league under manager Casey Stengel, but they permanently sealed Chicago's fate as an also-ran after 1969 and added some very successful seasons, including a World Series victory in 1986.

Attendance was another area in which the Cubs reigned supreme during the first half of the twentieth century. The Wrigley Field team was the first in the National League to draw more than a million fans, which they accomplished in 1927. Over the next 18 years, they repeated the feat six more times: in 1928, 1929, 1930, 1931, 1938, and 1945. In 1932 and 1938 they fell just short of that total. It would not be until 1941 that another National League team, the Brooklyn Dodgers, would draw a million in attendance. The Dodgers also hit the mark in 1942 and 1945, the same year the New York Giants attracted a million fans for the first time in their history. In the American League, the New York Yankees, after moving into Yankee Stadium, which dwarfed Wrigley Field in capacity, logged nine seasons at the million mark. The only other American League team to accomplish this feat in the first part of the century was the Detroit Tigers.

Any way you look at it, a study of the Chicago Cubs during the twentieth century is a study in contrasts, a history of notable success through World War II followed by a mirror image of unmatched failure in the postwar years. Throughout the twentieth century, no other team would follow ten pennants in a 45-year span with nine last-place finishes in the next 45 years. No other team would enjoy six second-place finishes and 32 years in the first division followed by 12 seasons with second-to-last finishes and 36 seasons in the second division. For the Chicago Cubs, the watershed year was 1945—the last season of their five decades of success, and the beginning of many decades of failure.

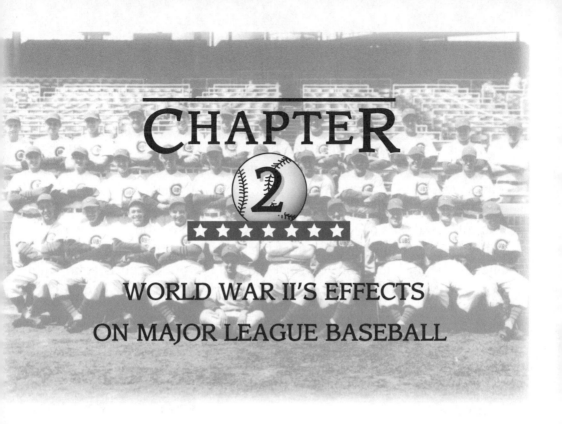

CHAPTER 2

WORLD WAR II'S EFFECTS
ON MAJOR LEAGUE BASEBALL

On the eve of World War II, baseball was truly the national pastime. In big city sandlots and rural open spaces, in high schools and colleges of all sizes, children and students played ball. When school was out, teenagers played on American Legion teams, while adults who still had an itch to play gravitated toward community leagues and, where talent warranted, the semipros. But even these outlets were not enough to satisfy Americans' passion for the sport; in addition to playing, they wanted to watch.

Americans' interest in baseball in the late 1930s was such that roughly 330 cities boasted professional minor league teams. Of these, 185 teams played in Class D leagues; 60 in Class C; 37 in Class B; and 24 each in Classes A and AA.[1] With 15 players to a team, or nearly 5,000 salaried players nationwide, the minor leagues were an important and viable industry, and their teams represented valuable community resources.

Atop the entire pyramid sat the major leagues. Composed of 16 teams in two leagues, they represented eight of the 15 largest metropolitan areas in the United States. New York City alone could boast of three teams: two in the National League and one in the American. Other cities with more than one team included Chicago, Philadelphia, Boston, and St. Louis; each of these cities fielded teams in both leagues. Rounding out the roster of major league cities were Pittsburgh and Cincinnati, with National League teams, and Detroit, Washington, D.C., and Cleveland, whose teams played in the American League.

On the eve of World War II, the location of the major league teams was still based on a city's size and its accessibility to other cities by rail. In spite of some teams' discreet investigations concerning moves to other cities, no team had relocated since Baltimore's American League team moved to New York City in 1903. A team's disinclination to move was based on several factors: for one thing, no team could move without every other team's consent; for another, the railways were still the most reliable means of transportation, thus, teams needed to remain close to the rail lines. In addition to these factors, the major league franchises felt a general reluctance to encroach upon minor league markets and territories.

Yet although baseball in 1940 was a favorite activity of American youth and a fixture of interscholastic sports nationwide, and although scores of cities boasted minor league teams, major league baseball was not the most popular spectator amusement by any stretch of the imagination. In the late 1930s, professional baseball at all levels generated approximately $17 million in revenue, while the motion picture industry pulled in $720 million, or more than 42 times that amount. Other popular amusements of the day included theater, opera, and classical music performances, which together accounted for $91 million of Americans' entertainment spending. Behind motion pictures and the performing arts was college football, the largest revenue-generating athletic activity, which brought in $37 million. After college football, Americans spent their entertainment dollars on nonprofit cultural events, such as community playhouse and civic orchestra performances, which accounted for $32 million of entertainment spending. Amateur athletic events—high school and college basketball and high school football—were fifth on the list, bringing in just over $20 million altogether. Behind professional baseball's $17 million in revenues came horse and dog racing ($12 million), professional ice hockey (almost $3.5 million), and professional football (just under $3 million).[2] Altogether, these entertainment spending figures would have some bearing upon the existence of professional baseball during the World War II era.

In its 65-year history, nothing changed the nature of professional baseball as drastically as the onset of World War II. Only twice in baseball's history had the United States gone to war, and neither previous war had required the kinds of sacrifices that World War II imposed on the sport. In 1898 the Spanish-American War had little effect on the baseball season because it did not require conscription, rationing, travel restrictions, or a military buildup.[3] Even World War I, with the intense sacrifices it demanded, brought about only two changes to the American and National leagues: the military's demands for manpower put 247 players in the service, and the federal government's "work or fight" edict ended the 1918 season one month early.[4] At the time, these were considered drastic measures, but they paled in comparison to the changes and hardships brought about by World War II.

Even after Franklin D. Roosevelt declared that professional baseball would continue in early 1942, World War II affected everything from player procurement to planning for the World Series. Blackouts and travel restrictions brought major scheduling changes, and as the war dragged on, attendance reflected those changes. Before the war was over, one season would feature two All-Star games, and another would see none. In 1943 even the composition of baseballs changed. With natural rubber no longer available for the ball's core, manufacturers experimented with substitute materials that produced a less resilient "dead" ball, and the result—predictably—was fewer hits and runs. But the earliest and most critical issue was whether baseball after the Pearl Harbor invasion would continue at all. By the end of the 1941 season, conscription had already claimed several major league baseball players, and haunted by memories of what World War I had done to the game, the lords of baseball wondered whether their sport would be a casualty of the war. The effects of World War I had given them good reason to worry.

After the United States entered the First World War in 1917, manpower shortages led eight of 20 minor leagues to cease operations.[5] In 1918 Secretary of War Newton D. Baker ruled that baseball did not deserve an "essential-to-the-war effort" classification, even though such status was granted to opera singers, professional musicians, stage actors, and movie actors. Later, American League President Ban Johnson declared the league would halt operations before the end of July, but at a formal meeting, representatives of both leagues voted to continue the season, potential player shortages notwithstanding. Then, somewhat unexpectedly, Secretary Baker softened his stance, granting the players military exemptions until September 1. Both leagues agreed to end the season at that time and to play a World Series, with 10 percent of the series revenues going to war-related charities. By season's end, however, few teams had completed the same number of games. The St. Louis Browns, with 123 contests under their belts, had played the fewest, while the St. Louis Cardinals and pennant-winning Chicago Cubs, with 131 apiece, had completed the most.

When the attack on Pearl Harbor brought the United States into the Second World War, baseball's executives understandably began to wonder what this war would do to their sport. But President Roosevelt allayed baseball's fears when he sent the famous "green light" letter to baseball commissioner Judge Kenesaw Mountain Landis on January 15, 1942. The letter read in part:

> I honestly feel that it would be best for the country to keep baseball going. There will be fewer people unemployed and everybody will work longer hours and harder than ever before. And that means they ought to have a change for recreation and for taking their minds off their work even more than before. . . . As to the players themselves I know you agree with me that individual players who are of active military or naval age should go, without question, into the services. Even if the actual quality of the teams is lowered by the greater use of older players, this will not dampen the popularity of the sport.[6]

Roosevelt also came out in favor of scheduling more games to accommodate the increasing number of American workers, opening a contentious issue for team owners to debate in the future.

On Armistice Day in November 1918, 247 major league baseball players were on active duty in the military. Two weeks after the attack on Pearl Harbor, Congress passed a law calling for conscription of all men between the ages of 20 and 45 and mandatory registration for all 18- and 19-year-old males. It was only because Congress feared the wrath of American mothers that it did not make the draft mandatory for the younger group. Older men between 45 and 64 were also required to register, and while they were welcome to try to enlist, the government declared it would not draft them.[7] Director of the Selective Service System General Lewis B. Hershey served in the same capacity he would occupy during the Vietnam War 24 years later. According to the rules established by Hershey's office, the following order for conscription would apply:

1. Single men with no dependents
2. Single men with collateral dependents (parents or minor siblings) but without jobs contributing to the war effort
3. Single men with collateral dependents and jobs contributing to the war effort
4. Married men without children and without jobs contributing to the war effort
5. Married men without children but with jobs contributing to the war effort
6. Married men with children but without jobs contributing to the war effort
7. Married men with children and jobs contributing to the war effort

The critical factor in determining marital status was when the wedding occurred; the critical factor regarding dependents was when a child was born. For marriages and births alike, December 7, 1941, was the cutoff date.

Once the order of conscription was established, the next step was to determine which jobs might qualify a person for military exemption under the contributing-to-the-war-effort clause. With so many Americans filling critical factory positions and taking up arms, General Hershey was extremely reluctant to declare that an individual playing baseball was contributing to the war effort. While seemingly at odds with FDR's green light edict, this stance was not really a contradiction. Roosevelt felt that the continuation of organized baseball at the minor and major league level was important and served the good of the nation. However, exemption from the draft for individuals participating in organized baseball was another matter. What mattered most to the government was that baseball, America's national pastime, be allowed to continue; who would actually play the game was not nearly as important. Obviously, baseball would lose a number of players, and the quality of play would suffer as the talent pool became thinner, but that was not the government's or the Selective Service System's concern.

Baseball's management soon learned the hard way that while the Selective Service System had spelled out the order of conscription at the national level, the teams were really at the mercy of local draft boards throughout the country. These boards could decide which jobs were important enough to qualify for the coveted "contributing-to-the-war-effort" designation, and as time went on, a player's exemption based on marriage, dependents, or off-season employment in a qualifying job was not always a good indicator of his draft risk. Because standards varied from draft board to draft board, and the number of men needed was a variable nobody could predict, some boards could meet their quotas by only taking single men, while others were required to go much further down the list. For the 1942 season, baseball went looking for promising youngsters who were too young to be drafted and for those whose physical infirmities kept them out of the military but did not prevent them from playing baseball. With more than 60 experienced players entering the armed services that year, more rookies were invited to spring training in 1942 than ever before. Teams with the most extensive farm systems, such as the St. Louis Cardinals and the New York Yankees, wielded an obvious advantage in the former category, but no team held an advantage over any other team when it came to finding ballplayers unfit for military service.

After the 1942 season, Congress changed the draft regulations in a way that made baseball adjust its thinking. In October, Washington had publicized its concern regarding a potential military manpower shortage and had begun efforts to enlist 7.5 million men by the end of 1943. In an effort to meet the goal, Congress in November approved the conscription of 18- and 19-year-olds; individuals still in high school were granted six months from their birthdays to complete their secondary education. One of the reasons for this change was that so many Americans aged 20 to 45 were found to be woefully unfit for service. The new reality forced the major leagues to completely rethink player procurement. Since 1942, teams had been stockpiling young players, some barely into high school, and now this strategy would be of no use. Under the new law, a player's desirability or value to a team was no longer his youthfulness but rather his marital and/or parental status prior to December 7, 1941. An additional change also inadvertently affected baseball: Anyone with an agricultural job anywhere in the country received an automatic deferral. As a result of this new wrinkle, the Brooklyn Dodgers and several other teams lost players who owned agricultural operations and found they could avoid the service by staying "down on the farm."[8]

With men older than 18 now being called to war, the major leagues could limp along, but the minors suffered badly. By 1943 only 62 of 330 teams remained. Of the 44 leagues, only nine were still in operation.[9] The

St. Louis Cardinals, with the most extensive and profitable farm system, took the unprecedented step of advertising for players.

At the end of the 1943 season, Washington gave baseball a scare when it decreed that fathers would be subjected to the draft. On December 19, however, baseball executives and some players got an early Christmas present when Congress ruled that fathers of children born before Pearl Harbor would be put at the bottom of the Selective Service System's draft eligibility list, regardless of their occupations.[10] This meant that local boards could not draft such men unless no one else was available. The change was an improvement, but not a panacea. For ballplayers from rural areas, where most men worked at exempt jobs in agriculture or coal mining, the change offered no guarantees. In addition, no one could predict how long the ruling would stand, as new rulings had already taken place twice during the previous year.

Although draft law changes were significant, the December ruling did not significantly change the composition of teams as they began spring training for the 1944 season. Some teams, like the Phillies and Dodgers, included a few extremely young players on their roster. Many teams, however, turned to older players, in some instances coaxing them out of retirement, and all teams carried an increased number of players with 4-F military classifications.

Much has been made of the "4-F ballplayer" during the World War II seasons, and it is often suggested that these players were responsible for a lower caliber of play during those years. A closer look at requirements for the 4-F classification indicates, however, that one could be an excellent baseball player but still have a physical anomaly or affliction that the armed forces chose to avoid. For instance, many 4-F players had high blood pressure or punctured eardrums, afflictions more common in the '30s and '40s than today. Individuals with osteomyelitis, a bone infection rare today but commonplace in the first four decades of the twentieth century before the widespread use of penicillin, were not drafted. During World War II, many skeletal disorders, some of which today would be considered minor, were deemed serious enough to interfere with the constant marching, crouching, and crawling expected of those inducted into the Army. While it is true that the wartime seasons were hurt when stars like Joe DiMaggio, Bob Feller, Hank Greenberg, and Stan Musial were drafted, many 4-F players excelled not only during the war years but also in the seasons before and after the war. Lou Boudreau, Phil Cavarretta, Marty Marion, Hal Newhouser, Ernie Lombardi, and Mort Cooper are just a few of the many excellent ballplayers with 4-F classifications.

By 1945 the unpredictability of the war threatened to change the scenario and force every baseball team into a mad scramble to fill its rosters. In the minor leagues that year, only 12 of the 44 minor leagues still existed.[11] Of the 607 active major league players in 1941, 358 were on active duty in the service. With the Allied powers engaged on both the European and Pacific fronts and the invasion of Japan looming, demands for conscripts intensified. In response, James Byrnes, head of the War Mobilization and Reconstruction Department, instructed General Hershey and the Selective Service System to reexamine all professional athletes classified 4-F, regardless of their sport.[12] The thinking was that if the professional athletes were truly unfit for military combat, they could do office work or fill occupations which contributed to the war effort, potentially freeing up others to fight the war. As William B. Mead points out in his work *Even the Browns*, about 60 percent of all players by this time were classified 4-F. Under the new decree, Philadelphia Phillies slugger Ron Northey was drafted even though he suffered from high blood pressure, a heart condition, and a punctured eardrum. Elsewhere, Boston Braves catcher Hugh Poland, who had earlier been rejected due to a deformed left foot, was drafted immediately once his occupation became known. Other inductees included the St. Louis Cardinals' Danny Litwhiler and Walker Cooper, who played only four games in 1945, and the Washington Senators' outfielder Stan Spence.

In March 1945, however, baseball welcomed two encouraging developments. On March 13, President Roosevelt reiterated that he was all in favor of baseball continuing and gave his blessing to an expanded number of night games. Then on March 21, Paul McNutt of the War Manpower Commission helped the game by ruling that individuals could leave their off-season, military-exempt jobs and return to baseball without fear of being reexposed to military induction. Almost every team carried several players fortunate enough to find off-season jobs in government or key industries that carried military exemptions with them; now they could report to spring training without worrying that they might be drafted.[13]

The next hurdle to clear was the Selective Service System's 4-F professional athlete ruling. This new policy did not sit well with baseball's establishment, but given the mood of the country, team owners and officials did not dare to go public with their indignation. Instead, they went to work quietly behind the scenes in Washington. The law was clearly on baseball's side: Suddenly a person's employment, regardless of his physical condition, could automatically trigger military induction. In the spring of 1945, Missouri Congressman C. Melvin Price and Kentucky Senator Albert B. "Happy" Chandler spearheaded a move in Congress to reverse the "professional athlete" draft ruling, and in May, soon after Germany's surrender, the edict was suspended. It must be noted that V-E Day had as much to do with the change as any sense of congressional fairness. Still, in the wake of the ruling, Senator Chandler became a favorite of baseball's ruling elite, and when Judge Landis died in November 1944, major league baseball owners named him commissioner.

By 1945, 384 major league baseball players had been drafted, but by 1946, only 22 were in the service.[14] This development pleased the baseball establishment, but key parts of the GI Bill of Rights, introduced in 1946, did not. The GI Bill required all employers to give returning veterans first crack at their old jobs, and the rule applied to the major leagues as well. In 1946 rosters were expanded to allow 30 players per team, but when spring training began in 1946, teams were still flooded with players. While some teams tried to circumvent the rule, most teams, unwilling to trigger lawsuits or negative publicity, complied. Still, more than a few players returning from the military were paid off in settlements or offered their old rate of pay at the minor league level.

In the decades following World War II, neither the Korean nor the Vietnam wars came close to affecting player availability as much as World War II did. During the Korean War, conscription was much more limited, drafted individuals rarely served more than two years, and most teams lost no more than two players. The Marine Corps, however, engaged in a general recall of its trained pilots during the Korean War. Consequently, the Boston Red Sox lost Ted Williams, who resumed his fighter pilot escapades, and the New York Yankees lost second baseman Jerry Coleman. When the 1964 Gulf of Tonkin conflict escalated American involvement in Vietnam, many ballplayers enlisted in military reserve programs, remaining stateside after completing basic training, attending monthly meetings, and spending two weeks per year on active duty. Among those who took this route were Kenny Holtzman, who pitched masterfully for the Cubs, albeit mostly on weekends, while in the reserves in the late 1960s, and Red Sox pitcher Jim Lonborg, who helped his team win the pennant in 1967, returning to play when his military passes would allow. In the late 1960s, a lottery system based on birth dates greatly lessened the likelihood of conscription for players who drew high numbers, and in 1973 the draft was eliminated entirely. No conflict—the Spanish-American War, World War I, the Korean War, or the Vietnam War—ever affected an athletic institution as much as World War II affected professional baseball. The baseball institution most affected, however, was spring training.

IN DECEMBER 1942, Director of the Office of Defense Transportation James Eastman became concerned about the burden on the nation's railroad industry as it struggled to meet the country's tremendous wartime needs. Eastman asked Commissioner Landis and the presidents of both leagues to come up with a plan to reduce the transportation requirements for baseball, and Landis ruled that spring training for the 1943 season would be planned to lessen rail travel as much as possible. As a result of Landis's ruling, all 16 major league teams were directed to find sites for spring training north of the Eastman–Landis Line, a border that roughly followed the Ohio and Potomac rivers.[15]

The biggest benefit to holding spring training in Florida or California, of course, was the warm, dry weather. Players traditionally used spring training not only to hone their baseball skills but also to get in shape; without the benefit of warm temperatures, outdoor conditioning options were limited. As a result of the new directive, suddenly the front offices of all 16 teams had a lot of work to do. The Boston Braves chose Choate, a preparatory school in Wallingford, Connecticut, for their camp, while Bear Mountain, New York, near West Point, became the new preseason home of the Brooklyn Dodgers. Farther west, the Chicago Cubs moved from California's Catalina Island to the resort community of French Lick, Indiana. About an hour away, Indiana University in Bloomington became the Cincinnati Reds' training facility. In New York, the Giants were a commuter's distance from the Polo Grounds in Lakewood, New Jersey, site of the *Hindenburg* disaster, while in Pennsylvania, the town of Hershey welcomed the Philadelphia Phillies. The Pittsburgh Pirates had to travel all the way to Muncie, Indiana, for their preseason warm-ups, but the Cardinals had only to travel to Cairo, Illinois, a short hop from St. Louis, to reach their new camp location.

In the American League, the Boston Red Sox stayed in their home state, setting up camp at Tufts College in Medford, Massachusetts, while the Chicago White Sox shared French Lick, Indiana, with the Cubs. Purdue University welcomed the Cleveland Indians, and another Indiana town, Evansville, became the spring training home of the Detroit Tigers. Like the Giants, the Yankees went to New Jersey, working out in Asbury Park. The Philadelphia Athletics stayed close to home, too, settling in Wilmington, Delaware. Meanwhile, Cape Girardeau, Missouri, 120 miles south of St. Louis on the Mississippi River, became the St. Louis Browns' training camp. Commissioner Landis had ruled that both St. Louis teams could train south of the Ohio River if they stayed relatively close to their homes. Another college campus, at the University of Maryland in College Park, became the preseason home of the Washington Senators. Given the limits imposed by federal transportation officials, teams could only compete on an intersquad basis or with other major league teams stationed relatively nearby. Baseball's annual spring training exodus to the Sunbelt would not resume until after World War II.

CHANGES IN TRAVEL

UNTIL THE EMERGENCE of nationwide airline travel, major league baseball was always one of the railway's best customers. While the Cincinnati Reds had experimented with air travel a few times in the 1930s, railroads were the overwhelming choice for a variety of reasons. One benefit was that teams could charter enough Pullman sleeping cars to give every player a semblance of privacy and normality while on the road, with a lower berth for each player and private rooms for managers. Another advantage was that in the 1940s, urban ballparks, like railroad depots, were located in the central parts of cities, rather than on the outskirts or in suburbs, as many are today. Thus, rail centers were ideally located and offered convenient, reliable, and comfortable service.

To play each of the other seven teams in the league 11 times at home and 11 times on the road, four trips to each city from April until the end of the season in September became the routine for each team. This was not a problem before the war, but as wartime demands forced the railroads to shoulder an increasing burden of passenger service, Judge Landis instituted changes to free up badly needed space on the nation's rails. First, instead of requiring travel to seven cities four times per season, the schedule was changed so that each team would make only three trips. This saved a tremendous number of passenger miles and, to further lighten loads, teams would occasionally take less than their full complement of players on the road.[16] Another change was that private rail cars were no longer available to the teams; as a result, players found themselves sharing slumber coaches or chair cars with military personnel and civilians. During spring training in 1944, when the Pittsburgh Pirates were not allowed onto an overcrowded Pennsylvania Railroad passenger train between Indianapolis and Terre Haute, Indiana, the entire team piled into the baggage car, along with their equipment.[17]

The increased need for passenger service quickly translated into equipment shortages. To meet the need, older, previously out-of-service cars were dusted off; not surprisingly, these were subject to breakdowns and were inherently less comfortable. With all the difficulties that rail travel presented, many teams began chartering buses for travel to nearby cities, and these soon became a common mode of travel in the East between New York, Philadelphia, and Boston and in the Midwest between Detroit and Cleveland. Other solutions emerged, too. The Chicago White Sox even took a steamship between Cleveland and Detroit in 1945.

CHANGES IN NIGHT GAMES

IN ADDITION TO travel complications, scheduling for night games was another headache during World War II. Night baseball had been an ongoing topic of disagreement among the mavens of baseball before the war. By the 1940s a majority of minor league games were scheduled at night. The Cincinnati Reds were the first team in the major leagues to install lights, and by 1941, ten of the 16 major league franchises were scheduling night games. Exceptions in the American League were the Red Sox, Tigers, and Yankees; in the National League, only the Braves and Cubs lacked lights. Cubs owner Philip K. Wrigley had actually purchased lights for his team at the end of the 1941 season, intending to install them for 1942. In January 1942, however, the nation's wartime needs prompted him to donate them to the Navy.

Teams with lights wanted to use them as much as possible because they drew more fans, and the teams generally made more money playing at night, too. William Mead in *Even the Browns* notes that the St. Louis team drew as many fans in 14 night games as they did in 63 day games during the 1939 season.[18] Yet the owners without lights—and, more important, Commissioner Landis—did not care for the concept. Baseball, they felt, was designed to be played in the sunshine. Schoolboys and impressionable youngsters made their way to day games, and their patronage, considered critical to baseball's continued popularity, was lost when night games were scheduled. Another objection was that playing at night kept the players up later, delaying but not necessarily eliminating nefarious postgame activities. Finally, the damp, cooler conditions were viewed as health and injury risks. Many observers viewed night baseball as a fad, an adult amusement that would eventually be replaced by more traditional forms of evening entertainment, and that if night games were promoted, attendance would diminish in the long run.

As he usually did, Landis got his way in 1940 and reduced the number of night games from 14 to seven per team, which hurt teams with weak attendance, such as the Phillies, Browns, and Senators. Seven night games per team remained the limit for the 1941 season as well.

A change was in the offing, however, after Pearl Harbor. President Roosevelt's green light letter of January 15, 1942, to Judge Landis had ended with the following sentence: "I hope that night games can be extended because it gives an opportunity to the day shift to see a game occasionally." The influence of Washington Senators owner Clark Griffith appeared to be all over this part of the missive. In 1940 Griffith and the brain trust of the St. Louis Browns had lobbied unsuccessfully to keep 14 night games per season after Landis had lowered the number to seven. At the time, the 16 major league team owners were split on the issue, and Landis had broken the tie. The commissioner, however, was loath to ignore a presidential "hope," especially one that would presumably make baseball more accessible to a patriotic, hardworking citizenry. Eventually, Landis relented and raised the night game quota back to 14 for every team except the Senators, who were allowed 21, because Washington's workforce consisted primarily of day-shift office workers.[19]

The fear that Pearl Harbor instilled in the country, however, affected how these night games would be scheduled, and blackouts and dimouts became commonplace after April 1942 on both coasts. The thinking was that illuminated skylines on the eastern seaboard could silhouette ships and make them even easier prey for the roaming German submarines and that any lights on the West Coast would help enemy planes attempting to stage an air raid. After July 1942, night baseball for all amateur, semipro, and professional contests was banned on the West Coast, as well as on some areas of the East Coast and Gulf of Mexico. The blackout order on the East Coast affected teams differently. Five eastern teams played in illuminated stadiums: the Dodgers and Giants in New York, the Philadelphia Athletics and Phillies, and the Washington Senators. Griffith Stadium in Washington and Philadelphia's Shibe Park, home to both the Phillies and Athletics after the Phillies abandoned Baker Bowl, were not considered close enough to any part of the coast to pose a security risk with night games. Illumination at the Polo Grounds and Ebbets Field, however, posed greater risks.

Problems with artificial lighting around New York City were considered enough of a security risk to severely limit night baseball in both stadiums. In the wake of the blackout order, Police Commissioner Louis Valentine and military officials announced that the ban would also apply to Coney Island and Times Square. Only 60 minutes of artificial light after sunset would be allowed at either facility. The teams were to play up to this time deadline; if a contest was not concluded, the final score would be the score at the end of the last completed inning. Not surprisingly, the policy proved problematic. Reluctant to lose the additional revenues that night games provided, both leagues began scheduling games two hours earlier, which still allowed most day-shift workers to attend. With daylight savings time in effect, the games started in daylight and ended under the lights in darkness, giving rise to the phenomenon of twi-night baseball. Dimout policies continued through the 1943 season but were eliminated before the end of the year. On May 23, 1944, night baseball returned to New York City in a game at Ebbets Field between the Giants and the Dodgers.[20]

CHANGES IN ATTENDANCE

DURING WORLD WAR II, it became common for major league teams to schedule exhibition games against armed forces teams from various military bases. Each team was required to have one such home game per season, with the proceeds going to the military relief charities established to provide funds for the families of men serving overseas. These games occurred in 1942, '43, and '44 and netted more than $1 million. In 1943, when Judge Landis decreed three road trips for each team instead of four, schedules changed again, as both home stands and road trips were lengthened. With all of the changes the baseball industry experienced with scheduling, however, attendance during World War II did not decline.

With millions of Americans fighting overseas and millions more at work on the home front, nobody would say that World War II was good for baseball attendance. Yet an examination of the figures and an analysis of the teams' profits and losses indicate that the World War II years, while not as lucrative as the 1920s, represented a time of significant financial recovery from the Depression. The war years were also a period during which the seeds for the unprecedented growth in the postwar 1940s were sown, with returning veterans swelling attendance figures. They were also partially responsible for baseball's attendance declines in the early 1950s, as the growth of suburbia diminished the sport's urban fan base. While the war brought hardships to many aspects of American life, its effect on major league attendance figures was minimal.

During the 1920s, major league teams made money in more than 80 percent of their seasons, but just less than half of their seasons were profitable between 1930 and 1939.[21] During the 1930s, the consolidated income of the American League showed a net loss in 1931; likewise, both the American League and the National League ended 1932, 1933, and 1934 with losses. Of the 96 major league teams' balance sheets filed between 1940 and 1945 (16 teams, six seasons), roughly 67 percent showed a profit, and 1943 was the only year that consolidated earnings for both leagues ended the season in the red.

Attendance totals also fluctuated, often widely, after the war started. During World War II, if a team improved, improvements in attendance usually followed, sometimes dramatically. Conversely, if a team disappointed, the results would be poorer attendance. While 1943 proved one of the weakest seasons for attendance in baseball's history, the World War II years ended with a very profitable 1945 season, which laid the foundation for unprecedented attendance and profits between 1946 and 1949.

During World War II, for the first time in history, four different teams eclipsed the 1 million attendance figure. In 1941, 1942, and 1945, the Brooklyn Dodgers drew more than a million paying customers, while the Cubs, Giants, and Tigers reached that milestone in 1945. What is even more impressive is that Chicago and Detroit accomplished this feat without the help of night games and that Chicago that season played two fewer home games than any other team. The 1945 season, in fact, set a record of 10,841,123 in total major league attendance, over 700,000 more than the old mark set in 1930. The following year, that record amount nearly doubled when major league attendance reached 18,523,288, and it increased even further in 1947 and 1948, as more than 20 million fans paid to see major league baseball each year, the two highest season totals for the 16-team era.

While World War II affected the attendance figures of major league baseball, it did not diminish the public's interest in the sport, and for all teams, actual attendance was higher than reported. As a gesture of support to America's military, uniformed servicemen were admitted free to all major league games during World War II.[22] This policy lowered attendance figures, because teams reported paid attendance and military attendance separately. Another factor in the attendance figure discrepancies was the fact that ordinary citizens could get in free to certain games by donating critical war materials. Throughout the war, various teams collected cigarettes, cooking grease, used rubber tires, and other badly needed materials. The most infamous collection drive occurred late in September 1942 at the Polo Grounds when the Giants granted free admission in a double header against the Boston Braves to youngsters under 16 donating scrap metal. The young Giants aficionados, their attention spans waning after 16 innings of end-of-the-season play between two teams completely out of a pennant race, charged the field in the eighth inning of the second game. Order could not be restored; the Giants, ahead at the time, forfeited to the Braves and their promising young lefty, rookie Warren Spahn, who went off to war the following season.

The turnstiles of the baseball world spun more frequently from 1941 through 1945 for nearly all teams than during the worst years of the Great

Depression. Attendance was weakest during the 1943 season, when 7,465,911 fans paid to see major league games. That season was hurt by greatly restricted night games, a dead ball that changed the nature of many of the contests, and no true pennant races in either league for most of the season. In addition, the increasing numbers of Americans employed in the war effort meant that workers had considerably less leisure time to devote to entertainment. In spite of these obstacles, the 1943 attendance figures eclipsed totals for every season from 1932 through 1935. When the limitation on night games was lifted in 1944, major league attendance increased almost 18 percent. In 1945, with pennant races under way in both leagues and with the war's end in sight, baseball's attendance figure shot 45 percent higher than in 1943. From 1941 to 1945, total major league attendance was approximately 45 million, far more than the 35.8 million during the early Depression years of 1931–35 and about the same as the 44.8 million in the late Depression seasons of 1936–40.

As World War II progressed, two other factors unique to this period in American history boosted baseball's attendance and popularity: widespread employment and gasoline rationing. With the nation emerging from the doldrums of the Depression and swiftly transitioning to nearly full wartime employment, Americans had more money to spend but less to spend it on. Production of consumer goods had nearly ground to a halt, while at the same time railroad and airline travel restrictions forced many to postpone travel and vacation plans. Gasoline and tire rationing meant that traditional escapes, like the Sunday drive to the country or weekend getaway, became impractical. The only diversions available to most Americans were entertainment options close to home or accessible by public transportation. In the 1940s, most major league stadiums were located in the metropolitan areas of major cities, with subways or elevated rail service providing easy access for thousands of fans. Urban areas with more than one team, like New York, Boston, Chicago, and St. Louis, offered multiple opportunities for major league entertainment. For many Americans in search of diversions, baseball was the logical choice.

As in other periods of baseball history, teams showing a dramatic improvement on the field during the 1940s almost always experienced a corresponding increase in their gate receipts. Between 1943 and 1944, the American League's St. Louis Browns climbed from sixth place to first, and the excitement generated a 137 percent increase at the box office. With attendance climbing from 214,392 to 508,644, the team's profit also soared, from $45,375 to $285,034.[23] Meanwhile, in the National League, a modest rise in the standings from eighth to seventh by the perennially weak Philadelphia Phillies netted that team a 103 percent improvement in attendance from 1942 to 1943. The team's $6,076 profit in 1943 marked the first time since 1936 that the franchise had not finished in the red. Such an increase was not the result of their modest improvement in the standings but was instead due to the dramatic improvement in their record; in 1943 they won an astounding 52 percent more games than in the previous season. So what if they only went from 42 to 64 victories?

Elsewhere in the Nationals, the Brooklyn Dodgers went from seventh to third place from 1944 to 1945 and along the way realized a 75 percent increase in their gate, edging out the pennant-winning Chicagoans with a league-leading 1,059,220 in paid attendance. The Dodgers' balance sheets reflected an even more dramatic improvement, as profits soared from $3,923 to $252,721. In Chicago the Cubs' 1945 attendance grew by 62 percent as the team drew 1,036,386 fans, even though they played two fewer home games than any of the other teams in the league, with bad weather forcing a transfer of two contests against the Pirates to Pittsburgh at the end of the season. In one year the Cubs managed to improve from a sub-.500 fourth-place finish to their pennant-winning season of 1945.

In the American League, Washington's Senators moved from seventh to third place from 1942 to 1943. This improvement netted the team's owners a 42 percent boost in gate receipts, with paid attendance at 574,694. The Boston Red Sox experienced a similar increase in fortunes in 1944, drawing 506,975 into Fenway Park as they moved from seventh place to fourth. It should be noted that two of these large increases were accomplished without the benefits of night baseball; neither the Cubs nor the Red Sox had lights during World War II. If a team made big improvements during World War II, their attendance and bottom line usually made a similar improvement.

The converse of this phenomenon also applied. Teams that experienced bad seasons on the heels of good suffered commensurately at the gate. The most glaring example was the Boston Red Sox. In 1943 the team slid from second place to seventh and saw their attendance plummet to 358,275, or only 49 percent of the previous year's 730,340. Their loss of $312,410 in 1943 was the worst loss for any team during World War II. In 1943 the New York Giants suffered a similar fate, falling into the National League cellar after finishing third the year before. Attendance likewise fell, from 779,621 to 466,095, a 40 percent decline. Over the same period, the Giants' $54,151 profit in '42 became a $248,973 loss the following year, the second highest total loss of the war years. Elsewhere, the Detroit Tigers, a team with strong attendance throughout World War II, fell from first place in 1940 to a fourth-place tie in 1941. That year attendance fell from 1,112,693 to 684,915, a reduction of 38 percent. The team's balance sheets reflected an equally steep decline, as their 1940 profit of $194,320 fell to a loss of $6,568 the following year. In Cincinnati the Reds endured two such seasons. Although they finished third in 1944 and were expected to mount a serious challenge for the pennant the following year, instead they suffered one of their worst seasons in history and finished in seventh place, with attendance falling 29 percent, from 409,567 to only 290,070. A few years earlier, a similar pattern had occurred in Cincinnati. After dominating the major leagues in 1939 and winning the series in 1940, Cincinnati only managed to finish third in 1941, and attendance fell 24 percent, from 850,180 to 643,513.

The appetites of a peaceful citizenry and hordes of returning veterans for baseball were even more voracious in 1946 than in the record-setting year of 1945. In 1946 total attendance soared to 18,523,288, as the Dodgers, Cubs, Cardinals, Giants, Phillies, Red Sox, Indians, Tigers, Yankees, and Senators each drew more than a million in paid attendance. Not far behind were Chicago's White Sox, who finished only 17,000 short of the million mark. Also, 1946 was the year that the Yankees became the first team in history to eclipse a gate of 2 million in one season. Total major league attendance in 1948 was almost 21 million, the highest total ever in the history of the major league's 16-team format, a record that would stand until 1962, when the major leagues expanded to 20 teams. Interestingly, the changes in player compensation did not parallel those in attendance and revenue during World War II.

CHANGES IN PLAYER COMPENSATION

AVERAGE BASEBALL SALARIES during the war years were actually lower than they had been before, but major league baseball players were still paid handsomely compared to the working population of the nation. In 1939 the average salary in the United States was approximately $1,269 for 12 months of work; in the major leagues, it was $7,306 for seven months' employment. In other words, even if they earned no additional income during the off-season, major league ballplayers made on average almost six times more than the average American worker. By 1943 a war-inflated economy had raised the average American worker's annual salary to $1,964, while the average major league salary was down to $6,423. Average major league salaries were now only a little over 3 times the average United States wage. Regardless of their salaries, all major league personnel received 10 percent of their pay in the form of war bonds. Almost all players supplemented their income with off-season work. Some even declined to play as the war progressed if they held positions deemed essential to the war and were thus eligible for the coveted military deferments these positions supplied.

During the 1940s, star players at the pinnacle of the sport were paid astronomically more than the average worker's salary, just as they are today. The year before he entered the military, the Cleveland Indians' star pitcher, Bob Feller, earned $50,000, while Hank Greenberg earned $55,000 from the Detroit Tigers before he enlisted as a $250-per-year soldier. Unlike today, baseball executives during the war years almost uniformly earned more than the players. During 1942 Larry MacPhail, general manager of the Brooklyn Dodgers, earned $70,000 per year,[24] while the Cardinals' Branch Rickey earned $80,000 plus a share of the team's profits.[25] Today most teams include players who earn more than their team's principals in guaranteed, multiyear salaries. Another difference between baseball salaries then and now is that in the 1940s, lucrative signing bonuses for promising amateurs or veteran professionals had not yet come into vogue. The first player to receive a significant signing bonus was the Detroit Tigers' Dick Wakefield, who received $52,000 and a new Packard for signing with the team in 1941. Signing bonuses were not given during World War II, because the military draft eliminated any guarantee that there would be a return on the investment.

At various stages, World War II exerted both downward and upward pressure on player compensation. Between 1941 and 1945, the average wage in the major leagues actually decreased because so many of the players were first- or second-year men. Another negative effect on player salaries was that in the early years of the war, owners took advantage of the mood of the country, cutting some players' salaries drastically. The owners correctly sensed that there would be no public relations backlash because the entire nation was sacrificing to further the war effort. Toward the end of 1942, Congress imposed salary and price controls throughout the country, and some baseball owners discreetly enquired whether they were free to cut their players' salaries further. Any cut in players' wages would represent a commensurate increase in profits and wages for the owners. Congress, however, ruled that no player could earn less for the 1943 season than the lowest paid player of the same team in 1942, and it further ruled that no player could receive a raise above the amount earned by the highest paid member of his team in 1942.[26] Players demanding more than the highest salary for the previous year's team were sometimes traded to teams that could meet their demands without exceeding their highest paid player's income.

By 1944, however, as teams struggled to obtain capable players, the tide turned, and ballplayers fortunate enough to be unconcerned about conscription began holding out for higher salaries. Team owners sometimes responded through the press, praising American citizens for their war-related sacrifices and pointing out how fortunate some were to be playing baseball instead of enduring combat. Still, as concerns about fielding competitive teams rose, salaries began to increase.

CHANGES WITH THE ALL-STAR GAME

IN AN ERA of wartime sacrifices, baseball's two showcase events—the All-Star Game and the World Series—were not exempt from the effects of the war. When the idea for the All-Star Game originated in 1933, the plan was to alternate play between American League and National League venues each season. Before the war was over, the program would see changes not only in venue but also in the number of contests and in player compensation. Even game revenues, normally reserved for the leagues, were at times designated for war relief funds.

With the1933 World's Fair drawing crowds to Chicago's lakefront at the site of the former Meigs Field, the White Sox's Comiskey Park, some three miles west of the fairgrounds, was a natural location for the first All-Star Game. In 1934 action shifted to New York and the Giants' home field at the Polo Grounds. Part of the public's fascination with All-Star contests stemmed from this second game, when local hero Carl Hubbell struck out Babe Ruth, Lou Gehrig, Jimmie Foxx, Al Simmons, and Joe Cronin in the game's opening minutes.

In 1942 the All-Star event was scheduled for the National League's Ebbets Field, home to the Brooklyn Dodgers, with game revenues earmarked for war relief funds. Capacity at Ebbets Field that year was 32,000, while the city's Polo Grounds could accommodate 56,000. With war relief a priority, tradition was cast aside, and the Giants became the first team to host a second All-Star Game. Miffed Dodgers fans stifled their indignation in the interests of patriotism. Unfortunately, the weather did not cooperate, and an inclement forecast and rain in the late morning held the crowd to 33,694, a total that Ebbets Field could have easily accommodated with only a smattering of standing room only patrons. The winning team in 1942 earned the right to play another "all-star game" against a lineup of major leaguers in the military.

The evening following the contest at the Polo Grounds, the victorious American League stars played the Service All Stars in the first-ever "second" all-star game, featuring hometown hero Bob Feller of the U.S. Navy on the mound in Cleveland. With 78,000 seats, Cleveland's Municipal Stadium was the largest park in the major leagues, and an enthusiastic crowd of 62,094 watched the American League knock Feller out in the second inning and beat the Service All Stars 5–0. The game brought in well over $300,000 in revenue for Army and Navy relief funds, the purchase of war bonds and stamps, and a fund to buy baseball equipment for military bases. The two All-Star Game format would not reappear again until 1959.

Changes for the 1943 All-Star Game were not nearly as extensive. One noticeable difference, however, was that 14 of the previous year's 50 participants were off fighting the war. The 1943 extravaganza was held on July 13 at Philadelphia's Shibe Park, home to the National League Phillies and the American League Athletics. With the country on an almost full-employment war footing, concerns about turnout made for another first. While baseball purists held their tongues, the first night game in the history of the All-Stars drew a sellout crowd of 31,938 to watch the American League overcome Pirate Vince DiMaggio's two home runs for a 5–3 finish. Even the rosters of this one-game-a-year event were not immune to the reality of the war, as 21-year-old Cardinal Howie Pollet, a southpaw with a sparkling 1.75 earned run average (ERA), was inducted into the Army Air Corps before he could even play.

During the 1944 All-Star contest, 29,589 fans enjoyed a rare 7–1 National League victory at the Pittsburgh Pirates' Forbes Field during the second night All-Star Game in history. A highlight of the evening was the performance of Chicago Cub Phil Cavarretta, who dazzled the crowd with a new All-Star on-base record of a triple, a single, and three walks. Also helping the National League to victory that night was teammate Bill Nicholson, who ignited a four-run rally with a pinch double. Revenues from the 1944 All-Star contest were earmarked for the war effort at such an unprecedented level that the players were not even paid in cash. Each American League participant instead received a $50 war bond for his efforts, while National League players received personalized mementos that varied according to the number of times they had been named to play in All-Star Games. The artifacts ranged from plaques for first- or second-time participants to an engraved, personalized cigarette case for 11th-time participant Mel Ott. Given the alternatives, the players were not about to complain. Already, 30 players from the 1942 and 1943 All-Star Games were in the military, and Uncle Sam's timing could not have been worse for one unlucky hurler, as the National League pitching staff was victimized again when Cardinals ace Red Munger packed up his belongings, his 11–3 record, and a league-best 1.34 ERA and left for the Army . . . on the morning of the game.

Ironically, in 1945, the year the war ended, major league baseball set the all-time attendance record, even though the All-Star Game had been cancelled. The decision to cancel was reached on March 11, 1945, when American League President Will Harridge met with National League President Ford Frick and Office of Defense Transportation head Colonel Monroe Johnson. At the meeting, the three men agreed to a 25 percent cut in all travel for the 1945 season. Eliminating the All-Star Game would make a significant contribution toward reaching their goal. The affair had been slated for the American League's Fenway Park in Boston, but because few players could get there without the railway or bus travel, and because the nation's passenger trains were already taxed to the limit, the three men decreed that the game would not be held, even though squads had already been selected and players listed in the record books. The nationwide jubilation over the war's termination overshadowed and silenced any public disappointment.

CHANGES WITH THE WORLD SERIES

COMPARED TO THE changes in the All-Star Game format, the World War II–era World Series underwent relatively minor changes. In 1942 some of baseball's executives, encouraged by the significant revenues raised for military causes during other games, toyed with putting the World Series on tour, sending each game to a different city, preferably those with the largest seating capacity, but the idea never came to fruition. Instead, the series ran as scheduled in St. Louis for the first two games and New York for the final three, with the Cardinals besting the Yankees, four games to one. Even though the touring idea flopped, the five-game classic still netted more than $360,000 for war-related charities and relief funds. One first for 1942 came when the series was broadcast overseas to the fighting men in Europe, who followed the action via shortwave radio. This service to those in the military overseas was a potent morale booster.

In the 1943 series, it was the Cardinals and Yankees once again, but the results were as different as they could be, with the Yankees sweeping the Cardinals by the same four-to-one margin. Sensitive to the demands the war had put on rail passenger traffic, baseball that year moved from the two-three-two format to a three-four arrangement, with the series opening with three games in New York and then moving to St. Louis for four. In order to accommodate the mandates of the War Transportation Board, however, both teams had to travel to St. Louis on the same train. To avoid chances for fraternization on the 24-hour journey, the league office arranged with the Pennsylvania Railroad to seat the Yankees in the front cars and the Cardinals at the rear of the 19-car special. Once again, both teams donated a portion of their revenues to military-related causes.

Travel restrictions would not be an issue for the World Series in 1944, as Sportsman's Park in St. Louis, home to both the pennant-winning Cardinals and Browns, played host for the entire series. For the

Cardinals, it was the third pennant in a row; for the Browns, it was a first. With the series confined to one stadium, St. Louis became the third city in baseball history to host the entire affair, which quickly became known as the Streetcar Series. Only Chicago in 1906 and New York in 1921, '22, '23, '36, '37, and '41 had ever hosted an entire series. Also, 1944 marked the third time in which every game of a series was played in the same stadium. The two previous occasions were in 1921 and '22, when the New York Yankees and Giants had shared a home at the Polo Grounds.

While the situation in St. Louis solved travel headaches for major league baseball and was a great event for the fans, it provided a unique inconvenience for the two managers, Luke Sewell and Billy Southworth. Like many large cities during World War II, St. Louis had a housing shortage, and since the Browns and Cardinals shared the same stadium, the two teams were never in St. Louis at the same time. During normal season play, Southworth settled into the Lindell Towers apartment when the Cardinals were at home, and Sewell did the same when the Browns were in town. Suddenly, now that both teams would be in town playing each other, one of them had to move, but as luck would have it, another tenant in the building was going out of town, and the accommodating owner made his apartment available. Sewell chose to move, because the newly available space was somewhat larger and he had invited his mother to stay with him and see the games. Revenues from the 1944 World Series earmarked for war-related relief efforts amounted to fully half of the winning Cardinals' and losing Browns' team shares.

Meanwhile, the war-induced crisis in railway travel required Draconian measures. After rail travel restrictions canceled the All-Star Game in 1945, it was necessary for management to at least consider canceling the World Series as well. Fortunately, they decided they did not have to, and the Tigers took the Cubs, four games to three, in a series that drew more than 330,000 fans, about 55 percent more than the St. Louis affair the year before. Even though the war had ended nearly two months before the series began, its lingering effects could still be felt in the fall of 1945. Because travel restrictions were still in effect, the first three games were played in Detroit and the next four in Chicago. But even before the first game in Detroit, the Cubs ran into wartime headaches when they learned that no hotel space was available. The initial plan to house the team on a D & C Lines steamship moored in the Detroit River met with fierce player resistance, and eventually the Cubs moved into the Book Cadillac Hotel in the central part of the city.

CHANGES WITH THE BASEBALL ITSELF

ONE OF THE most bizarre effects of World War II on major league baseball occurred during the 1943 season, when a shortage of critical baseball manufacturing material significantly altered the nature of the games themselves. By 1943, the A.G. Spalding Company, manufacturer of major league baseballs for the previous 66 years, was feeling the adverse effects of World War II. The German occupation in Belgium and France meant that shipments of the specialized European horsehide used for baseball covers could not be delivered. Meanwhile, the Japanese Empire controlled most of the rubber tree plantations in the Far East, a tremendous amount of the world's rubber supply. After much experimentation, a grade of domestic horsehide, subjected to a series of hit-and-miss tanning processes, was deemed suitable for the ball's cover. Getting the right substitute, however, for the high-grade cork in the ball's core proved a real problem. The Spalding Company finally settled upon an inner core consisting of balata and granulated cork, which was not a war-restricted material. The core was covered with an inner shell of black balata and an outer shell of red balata.

Balata, the saplike secretion of the bully tree, is found in the southern latitudes of North America. The material was not war-restricted and was relatively easy to obtain. Once cured, balata becomes extremely hard and durable. Spalding freely admitted that the balata was inferior to natural rubber and tried to compensate by winding the woolen yarn inside the baseballs more tightly. This proved to be no solution, however, and a new "dead-ball" era, featuring exceptionally low-scoring contests, began.[27]

The balata ball had an immediate impact on both leagues. In Chicago in 1943, the Cubs did not hit their first home run until their 33rd game. Final scores all over the league validated the dead-ball theory, with few runs scored anywhere. Of the first 29 major league games opening the season, 11 were shutouts. In 1942 pitchers had served up 1,071 home run pitches, but the figure for 1943 was only 905. Those 905 homers amounted to the lowest season total in the major leagues since 1926. Hitters complained that they had to hit the ball twice as hard to reach the fences.

To underscore the difference that the dead balls made, Cincinnati Reds general manager Warren Giles, a member of Commissioner Landis's baseball design committee, conducted a well-publicized but unscientific test at Crosley Field, dropping 12 balls from 1942 from the roof of the stadium to the sidewalk outside the park. He then dropped 12 newly formulated balata balls. The 1942 baseballs bounced an average of three and a half feet higher than the balata balls. More scientific tests at the Cooper Union Institute validated these results; the findings proved the balata ball was much less resilient than the ball used in 1942. Spalding representatives blamed the lack of hitting on cool spring weather and maintained that things would even out over the months of the season. Eventually, however, they recanted and explained that poor-quality rubber cement, which had prematurely hardened, was the cause of the "dead" balata balls.[28] With this explanation, the major leagues agreed to use the remaining stock of 1942 baseballs for the rest of the 1943 season. After 1943 cork and synthetic rubber were no longer restricted, thanks to the War Production Board. The Spalding Company was relieved, baseball's offensive production statistics rose, and what had raised the potential for World War II's most devastating effect upon baseball was no longer an issue.

BEFORE THE DEMOLITION of the Polo Grounds in 1963, a five-foot monument in front of the structure honored Eddie Grant, a former Giant who perished in the Argonne Forest one month before the Armistice. Grant became the first of three major leaguers to sacrifice their lives in World War I. In World War II, only two players, both with limited major league experience, perished: Catcher Harry O'Neill, whose career lasted one game with the Philadelphia Athletics, died at Iwo Jima, and Elmer Gedeon, an outfielder for five games with the Washington Senators, died when his fighter plane was shot down over occupied France on his birthday in 1944. Three major league managers lost aviator sons in World War II: They were the Detroit Tigers' Mickey Cochrane, the St. Louis Cardinals' Billy Southworth, and Jimmie Wilson, Cubs manager from 1941 through part of 1944.

Among the wounded in World War II were a dozen major leaguers, while a handful of others suffered illnesses or injuries that either ended or impaired the ability to play. But no other player suffered to the extent that Hall of Famer Christy Mathewson did. Gassed during the late stages of World War I, Mathewson never completely recovered, developed tuberculosis, and died in 1925. The most harrowing World War II injury came when the Washington Senators' Bert Shepard was shot down over Germany in 1944; he lost his injured leg to an amputation below the knee and then was taken prisoner. Shepard miraculously came back to pitch one game for the Senators in 1945 with his artificial limb and appeared in several other exhibition games, his efforts serving as an inspiration for other wounded veterans around the country. The effects of World War II on the players who served far overshadowed the tremendous effects it had on their chosen craft, as was also true for others who served.

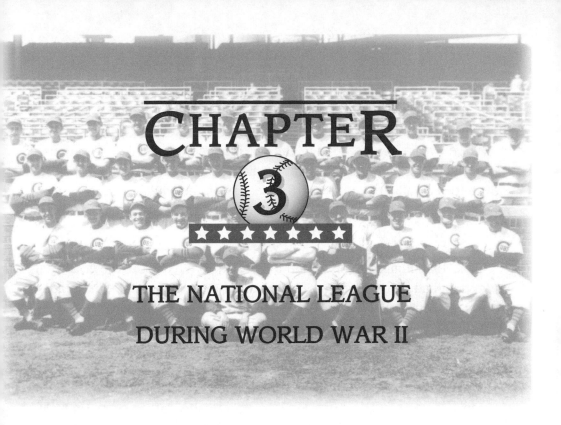

CHAPTER 3

THE NATIONAL LEAGUE
DURING WORLD WAR II

T he end of World War II marked a period of significant power shifts in the National League. Two teams that had been perennial doormats would begin a renaissance and were at the dawn of some of their best seasons in history, while three teams that experienced great success during the 1930s would begin a period of stagnation or failure. The two ball clubs that dominated the World War II seasons would go in different directions; one would continue to win and begin the most successful period in their history, while another would fall into an elongated period of mediocrity.

PHILADELPHIA PHILLIES

WHILE THE PHILADELPHIA Phillies were one of the two teams on the verge of ascendancy, they were just as inept during World War II as they had been for the previous 25 years. In five of the six seasons between 1940 and 1945, Philadelphia had finished in eighth place. In four of those six seasons, they had lost more than 100 games. The team boasted few player performances of any merit and played to very small crowds. When the franchise developed financial difficulties, the National League had to intervene and force the team's sale, and three different sets of owners were in charge over a two-year span. During this time, the Phillies also gained the distinction of becoming the first major league team to lose a rostered player to the military draft. Yet the seeds for the Phillies' success were reaching fruition by the end of World War II, and there was reason for hope.

1940

The 1940 Phillies—continuing their losing streak of the previous year, when they had lost 106 games and finished 50 games out of first place— wound up in the cellar with a record of 50–103. Baseball loyalists in the City of Brotherly Love suffered the indignity of seeing both the city's National and American league entries lose 100 or more games apiece in 1940. Phillies manager Doc Protho had little to rely upon. Two Phillies, pitchers Kirby Higbe and Hugh Mulcahy, were the only players to distinguish themselves among the league's leaders in any statistical category. Higbe led the National League in strikeouts with 137, finished second in fewest hits allowed per nine innings with an average of 7.70, was third in innings pitched with 283, and was fifth in strikeouts per nine innings with 4.36. The Phillies had paid dearly to acquire Higbe from the Chicago Cubs in 1939, giving up veteran pitcher Claude Passeau, but the rough-hewn South Carolina native was clearly the Phils' best pitcher during the 1940 campaign; he finished the season at 14–19 and completed 20 games with an earned run average (ERA) of 3.72. In addition, Higbe was named to the 1940 All-Star Game. Phillies pitcher Mulcahy led the major leagues with 22 losses but finished third in the National League in complete games with 21. The luckless Mulcahy went 13–22 in 1940 with the team's best ERA, 3.60. Mulcahy joined Higbe in the 1940 All-Star Game. As a group, the Phillies' pitching staff had the worst ERA in the National League, a paltry 4.40.

Philadelphia hitters fared only marginally better. Third baseman Pinky May of Laconia, Indiana, led the team in hitting with a .293 average, while left fielder Johnny Rizzo, acquired in a June trade with the Cincinnati Reds, led the team with 20 home runs and 53 runs batted in (RBIs). May's batting average with the Phillies was an equally respectable

.293. The only other Philadelphia hitter with a respectable offensive performance was center fielder Joe Marty, who batted .270, hit 13 home runs, and had 50 RBIs.

The Phillies posted the worst team batting average and the worst team slugging average in the National League during this sorry season. The team's stolen base total was a pathetic 25 (barely half of the next worst team's total, the New York Giants' 45), the team's fielding average was tied with Boston's as the league's worst, and the Phillies' ERA was the league's worst. A team this insufficient was not going to attract much of a following, and the Phillies averaged fewer than 2,700 fans per game. Their total attendance of 207,177 was not even half that of their in-town rivals, the Philadelphia Athletics, who drew 432,145, even though the Athletics also finished in last place (in the American League) and, like the Phillies, lost 100 or more games.

1941

As bad as 1940 was for Philadelphia, 1941 proved to be an even bigger disaster when the Phillies eclipsed their worst season in the twentieth century (1928, when they went 43–109) and went 43–111, 57 games behind the pennant-winning Brooklyn Dodgers. Before the year was over, Higbe was traded to the Brooklyn Dodgers for a badly needed $100,000 and three players: Vito Tamulis, Bill Crouch, and Mickey Livingston, the only legitimate major leaguer of the three. Later, Hugh Mulcahy became the first major leaguer to leave his team for the military, when he was drafted in March 1941, nine months before Pearl Harbor. Sadly, the promising right-hander's career ended with his conscription.[1]

While serving in the Philippines, Mulcahy contracted dysentery and lost a great deal of weight. In 1945 he rejoined the Phils but pitched in only 23 games before he was out of baseball for good in 1947. With the pitching staff gutted for the 1941 season, the only two Phillies hurlers who posted ERAs of less than 4.45 were Lee Grissom with 3.97 and Ike Pearson at 3.57. Meanwhile, the bespectacled Johnny Podgajny posted the team's best record at a dismal 9–12, and Cy Blanton, in spite of a 6–13 record with a 4.51 ERA, was named to the National League team for the All-Star Game. As in the previous season, Philadelphia's ERA of 4.50 was the worst in the National League.

Offensively, however, the Phillies showed some signs of coming to life in 1941. Rookie second baseman Danny Murtaugh, who would go on to managerial fame in later years with the Pittsburgh Pirates, led the league in stolen bases with 18, and outfielder Stan Benjamin was the league's second-best base stealer with 17. As a team, the Phillies stole 65 bases, only three fewer than Cincinnati, who topped the league in that category. At the plate, another rookie, left fielder Danny Litwhiler, gave long-suffering Philadelphia fans something to cheer about. Hitting .305 with a team-best 18 home runs, Litwhiler was third in the league in total hits with 180 and fourth in total bases with 275. The Ringtown, Pennsylvania, native was also named to the National League's All-Star team in 1942. Elsewhere, third-year man Nick Etten, finally getting a chance to start at first base, led the team with a .311 batting average and 79 RBIs.

These four individuals got little support from the others, however, as the Phillies posted the worst team batting and slugging averages in the National League and the second-worst fielding average. Even though attendance was up about 10 percent, at 231,401, it was still not even half of the Athletics' 528,894. At the end of the season, manager Doc Protho's three-year stint came to a close when he was fired. In his three years of managing the Phils, Protho had gone 138–320 for a dismal .301 winning percentage.

1942

For the 1942 season, 61-year-old Hans Lobert, who had managed the team to two defeats in 1938 after Jimmie Wilson's departure, came back to manage the Phillies, becoming the oldest "rookie" manager in history. During a 14-year career between 1903 and 1917, Lobert had played for the Pirates, Reds, Phillies, and Giants. In his day, he stole more than 40 bases in four different seasons and was considered one of the fastest runners in the game.[2] As in previous years, Philadelphia's opponents had their way with Lobert's charges. The Phillies reached their nadir in 1942, going 42–109 and finishing in the National League basement for a record fifth consecutive season. Not one Philadelphia player finished among the National League leaders in any individual category. The only bright spots were Danny Litwhiler, who led the team in hitting with nine home runs, 56 RBIs, and a .271 batting average and was named to the National League All-Star team, and pitcher Tommy Hughes, who in his last year before serving in World War II turned in the best year of his career and led Phillies pitchers, going 12–18 with a 3.06 ERA. Hughes would return to play for the Phillies in 1946 and ended his five-year major league career with Cincinnati in 1948. As a team, Philadelphia finished last in eight categories: stolen bases, home runs, runs produced, RBIs, opponents' runs allowed, errors committed, fielding average, and team ERA (for the third straight year). Altogether, the team's players produced only 354 RBIs in 1942, the fewest by any team since the dead-ball era.[3] Litwhiler was the RBI leader with only 56. He distinguished himself as the only regular in major league history to go through the entire season without making an error.

The team paid for their overall futility at the box office, averaging 2,988 customers per game, or 230,138 for the season. People not only avoided seeing the Phillies, they also stopped listening to them. In 1939 the team's revenue from radio broadcast rights was $46,500, more than the Braves, Cubs, Reds, and Cardinals received. With their poor showing, 1942 broadcast revenues were down 30 percent to only $32,800. At the end of the year, Philadelphia's balance sheet showed a loss of $56,251, the sixth consecutive season ending in red ink. The National League office decided to intervene.

Owner Gerry Nugent had a long history of selling good players to other teams to make ends meet. Since the 1930s, All-Stars such as Chuck Klein, Dick Bartell, Bucky Walters, Dolph Camilli, Claude Passeau, Kirby Higbe, Curt Davis, and Johnny Moore had been sold to other teams so that payroll, hotel bills, and spring training expenses could be met. The addition of night baseball games in 1939 did not provide any increases in profit; in 1939 the Phils lost almost $27,000 more than they had lost in 1938. Frightened by the overtures a young Bill Veeck was making to buy the team and stock it with star players from the Negro leagues,[4] the National League forced Nugent to sell, paying him $10 per share for 4,685 of the 5,000 outstanding shares of stock in the club.[5] The league in turn sold the team to 33-year-old William D. Cox, a wealthy New Yorker and a favorite of Ford Fricke, the president of the National League. The magnitude of this mistake would not be known until the 1943 season was well under way.

1943

The Phillies made a foolish trade with the Yankees in January before the 1943 season started. Nick Etten, their leading hitter in 1941, whose numbers were off in 1942, was thrilled to go to New York, where he started at first base for a team that won the World Series. The Phillies got a badly needed $10,000 and four players: infielder Ed Levy, catcher Tom Padden, and pitchers Al Gettel and Al Gerheauser. Only Gerheauser contributed much during the 1943 season. Another move by Cox was firing manager Hans Lobert (who would later resurface as a coach for the Cincinnati Reds), replacing him with Bucky Harris. The 47-year-old Harris had experienced a fair measure of success in his previous 19 managerial seasons, with one pennant and seven first-divisions finishes. With some good performances from the likes of outfielder Ron Northey and pitchers Dick Barrett, Ken Raffensberger, and Schoolboy Rowe, Harris had the Phillies off to a much-improved 38–52 record when Cox made a decision that eventually would cost him a career; he fired Harris and replaced him with Fred Fitzsimmons. The young owner had bitten off more than he could chew. Harris, furious about his release, complained to Commissioner Landis's office that Cox was betting on his own team's games.[6] This situation was not resolved until November, well after the Phillies' season ended.

Fitzsimmons did almost as well as Harris in piloting this improved Phillies team, going 26–38, yielding a seventh-place finish at 64–90, a remarkable improvement of 22 more victories and 19 fewer losses. Second-year man Northey, the pride of Mahanoy City, Pennsylvania, was the team's best hitter with a .278 average and 68 RBIs. His 16 home runs were good enough for third in the National League. Babe Dahlgren represented the Phillies in the All-Star Game. The versatile Dahlgren, acquired for Lloyd Waner and Al Glossop from the Brooklyn Dodgers a month before the season started, hit .287 with five home runs and 56 RBIs while playing first base, third base, shortstop, and even catcher for one game. Rowe went 14–8 with an excellent 2.94 ERA. The tall Texan led all National League hurlers in fewest walks allowed per nine innings. Rowe also became the first pitcher in history to hit a grand slam home run as both an American League and National League pitcher, when he accomplished the feat for the Phillies as a pinch hitter.[7] The newly acquired Gerheauser went 10–19 with a 3.60 ERA. The Phillies as a team finished third in the league in team home runs but continued to be the league's worst in stolen bases, fielding average, and errors committed. Nonetheless, the fans responded to this entertaining team and 1943 attendance doubled to almost 467,000. The Phillies outdrew their landlords, the Philadelphia Athletics, by almost 90,00 fans, the first time this had occurred since both teams began to play in Shibe Park in 1938.

After Kenesaw Mountain Landis settled the William D. Cox affair, the effects would be felt by the Philadelphia organization and its followers for decades to come. The young Cox was intimidated by Landis's reputation and his wrath. Thinking Landis might go easier on him in a public forum, Cox demanded an open hearing but probably regretted that his wish was granted. Landis invited the press to attend, but the tactic did not help Cox's situation whatsoever. Landis ruled that Cox, at the age of 33, could not hold any office or be employed by any baseball organization for life.[8] Robert Carpenter of Wilmington, Delaware, the head of the mammoth Dupont Company, bought the Philadelphia Phillies at this point for less than a half million dollars. Carpenter, with his family ties to Dupont, was one of the wealthiest men in baseball at that time. He put in his 28-year-old son, Robert Jr., as president. One of young Carpenter's first acts was to name ex-Boston Red Sox and New York Yankees great Herb Pennock the team's general manager.[9] The 49-year-old Pennock, who was a lifetime 241–162 left-hander with an amazing 5–0 record and 1.95 ERA in five World Series, had been running the minor league system of the Boston Red Sox at the time. He freely spent Carpenter's money and established a farm system; in all previous seasons, the Phils neither owned nor had an affiliation with a single minor league team. At a time when almost four out of every five minor league teams were either owned or locked into a contractual agreement with a major league team,[10] this marked a watershed change in how Philadelphia would procure and develop future talent. Their trip to the World Series just seven years after their farm system's establishment is a testimonial to Pennock's skill and success.

In an effort to change their losing image, the Phillies took the unprecedented step of conducting a fan contest to choose a new nickname. The winning entry was Blue Jays, submitted by a Mrs. Elizabeth Crooks, but the moniker never really took hold. The press and most fans continued to refer to them as the Phillies, and the "Blue Jay" label was abandoned altogether before the 1946 season.[11]

1944

Carpenter and Pennock kept Fitzsimmons as manager for the 1944 season and witnessed a year in which Philadelphia did not improve but the rest of the league got a little better. Perhaps thrilled with Cox's departure and the new direction of the franchise, the team won five straight in early May 1944 and for a brief period held on in second place. As the season progressed, they returned to their usual level, however, and finished with an almost identical record as they had in 1943, going 61–92, unfortunately landing them once again in the cellar. This time, however, they were only one and a half games behind seventh-place Brooklyn, three and a half behind sixth-place Boston, and five and a half behind fifth-place New York. Attendance for the season was 369,586, an average just less than 4,800 per game, and the team lost $136,669. The balance sheet, however, did not matter as much as it used to; the Phillies' front office had money and was building for the future. The seeds of the great Whiz Kids team of the late 1940s were being sown.

In spite of their record, the Phils featured some players who had very successful seasons in 1944. Northey established himself as one of the finest hitters in the National League in 1944, finishing third in home runs with 22, third in RBIs with 104, and fifth in total bases with 283. He and Chicago's Andy Pafko led all National League outfielders with 24 assists, and his .288 batting average was the Phillies' highest. First baseman Tony Lupien, acquired from the Boston Red Sox for a waiver price, proved to be a great bargain. The Chelmsford, Massachusetts, native hit a solid .283 and was second in the National League in stolen bases. The Phillies' pitching improved also, largely due to three individuals. Ken Raffensberger led the league in losses with 20, but that did not overshadow his 13 victories, his fourth-best strikeout total among all National League pitchers, and his third-best strikeouts per nine innings ratio. Raffensberger was also awarded the victory in the All-Star Game in July when the National League beat the American League 7–1. People marveled that a Philly played a significant role, let alone got the win, in an All-Star Game. Charley Shanz, the only pro ballplayer Anacortes, Washington, ever produced, had a good year on the mound, going 13–16 with a 3.22 ERA, as did Dick "Kewpie" Barrett at 12–18. The Phillies finished last because, after Northey, Lupien, and center fielder Buster

Adams, they simply had no offense. Only the Boston Braves had a lower team batting average than the Phillies in 1944, and no team had a worse slugging average. Every team scored more runs than the Phils, and only Cincinnati (which still finished third) had fewer home runs. The Phils also had the lowest stolen base total in baseball; if it were not for Lupien, the number would have been an abysmal 14.

Undeterred, Carpenter and Pennock stayed the course and continued to concentrate on the younger talent in the organization. During the season, they brought up two 16-year-old infielders, Putsy Caballero and Granny Hamner. Few teenagers brought up during World War II amounted to much, but Caballero went on to be a reserve infielder for eight years, and Hamner became a fixture on the Whiz Kids teams and enjoyed a 17-year career.

1945

When the Phillies opened training camp for their 1945 season in Wilmington, Delaware, the *Official Baseball 1945* published by A.S. Barnes and Company listed no fewer than 38 Phillies on an "Honor Roll" of major leaguers still active in the military.[12] Significant baseball names like Del Ennis, Lee Grissom, Ernie Koy, Joe Marty, Pinky May, Hugh Mulcahy, Danny Murtaugh, and Schoolboy Rowe dotted the list. Unfortunately, the controversial "professional athlete" draft early in 1945 added the names of Philadelphia's two biggest stars in 1944. Ken Raffensberger, the ace of their pitching staff, was inducted on April 30, putting a big hole in the rotation. Raffensberger returned in 1946 for Philadelphia and was traded to Cincinnati in 1947. He had his best years with the Reds, winning 18 games in 1949 and going 17–13 with a 2.81 ERA in 1952. He retired and ended his successful 15-year career in Cincinnati after the 1954 season. The other big name on the list was the Phils' best hitter, Ron Northey. Northey carried a 4-F classification for years due to a punctured eardrum, a heart condition, and high blood pressure, yet he was one of the unlucky ballplayers called for a new physical early in 1945. To avoid going into the Army, he tried enlisting in the Navy but was turned down due to the three aforementioned afflictions. Incredibly, soon after that rejection, the Army examined him and he was inducted.[13] The muscular outfielder returned to start for Philadelphia in 1946; his productive 12-year career included tours of duty with the Cardinals, Reds, Cubs, White

Sox, and again with the Phillies in 1957, after which he retired. His son Scott was born in October 1946 and played briefly with the Kansas City Royals in 1969.

The Phillies picked up two able veterans to shore up some of their losses. They signed ex-Giants catcher Gus Mancuso to anchor a now shaky pitching staff. To fill the void left by Northey, they traded pitcher Al Gerheauser to Pittsburgh for center fielder Vince DiMaggio, who at the time was considered one of the premier defensive players in the game. DiMaggio spent much of the 1944 season irritated with the Pittsburgh front office, one reason being the low sum the players received for meals.[14] He played very little the last half of the 1944 season in Pittsburgh and asked to be traded.

While the Phillies did not expect to challenge for the National League pennant in 1945 and the loss of two of their best players to the service was a severe blow, the organization hoped to avoid a last-place finish in a season where their primary goal was to have their promising young players gain more experience and playing time. Some very decent players, both established veterans and untested prospects in their improving farm system, would be returning after the war. There was a sense of anticipation that the youth movement would start paying off. The dividends, however, were still a few years away.

BOSTON BRAVES

THE BOSTON BRAVES were the other team that suffered through the World War II years and the decades before but rose to prominence once the war was over. The Braves never ended a season above sixth place during the war years, and in their best season in the six-year stretch, they finished 17 games below .500. Managing the Braves through the 1944 season was Casey Stengel, years away from his American League fame and never appreciated by the local press and fandom. The reality was that Stengel had little to work with and the Braves had limited resources during his tenure. Between 1930 and 1945, the team reported a profit in only four seasons. Their attendance totals often rivaled those of the Philadelphia Phillies and St. Louis Browns for the smallest crowds in baseball, and Boston had the lowest total attendance in the National League between 1940 and 1945.

1940

The conclusion of the 1940 season, the first of three consecutive seventh-place finishes, found the Braves with a record of 65–87. Buddy Hassett gave Braves fans something to cheer about when he managed ten straight base hits. In spite of this remarkable achievement, Hassett hit only .234 for the season and committed 21 errors, more than any other first baseman in the league. Johnny Cooney, 39 years old at the start of the 1940 season, led the team in hitting with a .318 average, third best in the National League; Chet Ross bested his teammates in home runs (17) and RBIs (89). His 14 triples was the second-highest total in the league. Left fielder Max West (batting .261 with seven homers and 72 RBIs) was named to the National League All-Star team in 1940, along with shortstop Eddie Miller, a .276 hitter with 14 home runs and the best fielding average of any National League shortstop in 1940. West distinguished himself by hitting the only home run in the contest, helping his National League teammates defeat the American League at Sportsman's Park in St. Louis. As a team, however, the Braves lacked power, finishing last in the National League with only 59 home runs. With the sparkling Miller at shortstop, the Braves topped the league in double plays. Dick Errickson led Boston pitchers with a 12–13 record, and Manny Salvo posted the best ERA, 3.08. Salvo also had more shutouts (five) than any other National League pitcher for the season. The Braves made a $7,309 profit, drawing only 241,000 for the season—barely one-third that of their crosstown rivals, the Red Sox. Only the Philadelphia Phillies drew fewer fans in the National League during the 1940 season.

1941

The 1941 season was almost a repeat of 1940, with the Braves going 62–92 and again finishing in seventh place. Johnny Cooney led the team with a .319 average, second best in the league. Max West hit a team-high 12 homers, and Eddie Miller tied West for the team lead in RBIs with 68. Once again, the Braves had a severe power shortage, hitting a National League–worst 48 home runs. Miller led all National League shortstops in fielding average, as he had done in 1940, and once again was placed on the National League All-Star squad. Jim "Abba Dabba" Tobin was the team's best pitcher, despite a lackluster 12–12 record; his 20 complete games were third best in the National League. Tom Early had the Braves' best ERA, 2.53. While the Red Sox once again drew more than 700,000 fans, the Braves managed only 263,680, less than every team but the Philadelphia Phillies.

1942

Seventh-place monotony continued in 1942, but two new names graced the Boston Braves' roster during this season—a pair of rookies who would figure prominently in the Braves' rise to power before the decade was over: Warren Spahn and Johnny Sain. Spahn debuted for the Braves on April 19, 1942. The future Hall of Famer appeared in four games that year, ending the season with a record of no wins and no losses and an ERA of 5.74. Sain debuted five days later than Spahn. He appeared in 40 games during 1942, went 4–7, and had a 3.98 ERA. World War II claimed both of them after this season, and they returned in 1946, leading the Braves to fourth place that year, third the following one, and a pennant in 1948. For a seventh-place team, the Braves had quite a few players with distinguished seasons in 1942. Future Hall of Famer Ernie Lombardi, toward the end of his brilliant career, came to the Braves and won the batting title with a .330 average; he also was fifth in the National League in slugging percentage and named to his sixth All-Star team. Third baseman Nanny Fernandez was the league's second-best base stealer with 15. Slick-fielding shortstop Eddie Miller was once again named to the All-Star team. Max West led the team in the power departments with 16 home runs and 56 RBIs. His home run total was fifth best in the National League. Pitcher Al Javery, a local boy from Worchester, Massachusetts, came into his own in 1942, his third season in the majors, going only 12–16 but tying for second in the league in shutouts with five. Javery's 3.03 ERA matched Manny Salvo's for the team's best in the 1942 season. Jim Tobin continued his mound mastery in everything but avoiding losses. His 12–21 record was the most losses in the National League, but he was first in the league in innings pitched with 288 and first in complete games with 28. Tobin also distinguished himself by hitting an amazing three home runs in one game against the Chicago Cubs, an incredible feat for a pitcher, and went on to hit six homers for the season, tying the season record for pitchers at that time. Tobin's home run production was almost a tenth of the Braves' home run total for that year (68). As in the other two seasons, the Braves were second to last in attendance, drawing just over 285,000 fans, some 455,000 fewer than the Red Sox.

1943

Things looked bleak for the Braves when the 1943 season began. World War II claimed Nanny Fernandez, Warren Spahn, and Johnny Sain, and in December 1942, All-Star shortstop Eddie Miller was traded to the Cincinnati Reds for Eddie Joost, Nate Andrews, and a badly needed $25,000. Boston's team payroll in 1943 sunk to $138,000, the lowest in major league baseball. At the start of the season on April 20, manager Casey Stengel was hit by an automobile and was out for two months.[15] A Boston sportswriter cynically nominated the cabdriver for Local Sportsman of the Year. In spite of these developments, the collapse of the New York Giants helped Boston move up to sixth place, as Stengel came back to guide the team to a 68–85 record. Johnny McCarthy was the team's best hitter with a .304 average, while Chuck Workman, the best ballplayer Leeton, Missouri, ever produced, hit ten home runs and had 67 RBIs to lead the power categories. Al Javery and Nate Andrews led all Boston pitchers. Javery was 17–16 and was first in the National League in innings pitched and third in strikeouts. Only four other National League hurlers won more games that season, and Javery was named to the 1943 All-Star team. Andrews posted the most losses in the National League while finishing with a 14–20 record, but he was third in innings pitched and posted a sixth-best ERA in the National League, 2.57. If the Braves could have hit that season, they would have been much better. Their run production, team batting average, home run total, on-base percentage, and slugging average were the worst in the National League. Workman alone hit more than a quarter of the team's home runs, ten out of a paltry total of 39. Big changes, however, were on the horizon—changes that would rather quickly improve the team's fortunes but ultimately result in a huge loss for the city.

1944

In January 1944, the Boston Braves were sold to three of the team's minority stockholders. Lou Perini, Guido Rugo, and Joseph Maney were construction moguls who had flourished with wartime construction contracts and provided the franchise with financially sound ownership. They were affectionately nicknamed the Three Little Steamshovels, after the characters in a children's book. Perini became the head of the franchise.[16] They all stayed away from the baseball decisions, naming Bob Quinn the head of player development and his son John general manager. One of the Steamshovels' first moves was to remove the unpopular Stengel and replace him with coach Bob Coleman for the upcoming season. The season got off to a great start when Jim Tobin no-hit the Brooklyn Dodgers 2–0 on April 27 in Boston. Tobin gave up two walks in the game, both to the aging Hall of Famer Paul Waner. He became the first pitcher in history to hit a home run while throwing a no-hitter. Another pitching highlight came in August, when Red Barrett threw just 58 pitches, setting a major league record, and shut out the Cincinnati Reds 2–0. Coleman, however, could only lead the team to another sixth-place finish, ahead of Brooklyn and Philadelphia, with a record of 65–89. The most notable performances for Boston in 1944 came from center fielder Tommy Holmes. Plucked from the New York Yankees' minor league system before having the chance to crack into their major league roster, Holmes started with the Braves in 1942. In 1944 the 26-year-old native of Brooklyn hit .309 with 13 home runs and 73 RBIs. Holmes's 195 hits were third in the National League, as were his 288 total bases. His strong showing was but a prelude of what he would do the following year, with one of the best offensive displays in National League history. Tobin, Andrews, and Javery dominated the Braves' pitching categories and were named to the National League All-Star team for their efforts, one of the few times three pitchers from the same team were All-Stars. Tobin went 18–19 with a team-best 3.01 ERA. His 18 victories were fifth highest in the league; he also finished second in innings pitched and first in complete games with an amazing 28. Andrews went 16–15 with a 3.22 ERA. Javery won ten but lost 19; his strikeout total, however, was third best in the National League, and his strikeout-per-game ratio was second best. Significant contributions from others, however, were few and far between. While the team's home run production rose from 39 to 79 (thanks in part to Butch Nieman's team-leading 16), the Braves still had the worst team batting average, slugging average, and on-base percentage. Attendance dropped to 208,000 for the season, the National League's lowest figure by more than 160,000 and the team's lowest since 1924. Financially, the team lost a whopping $133,022, but with the change in ownership, the pockets were much deeper than before; by the end of the 1944 season, the Boston Braves were turning a corner.

1945

When the Braves opened their 1945 spring training camp at the Choate Preparatory School in Wallingford, Connecticut, they welcomed pitcher Lefty Wallace back from the war but had few other new faces in camp. Boston's "Honor Roll" of players still engaged in World War II had 29 names at the start of the season, including key contributors like Manny Fernandez, Bama Rowell, Connie Ryan, Johnny Sain, Sibby Sisti, Warren Spahn, and Max West.[18] The 1945 season began with the Braves' pennant hopes still in the military, but with starting pitchers like Nate Andrews, Red Barrett, Al Javery, and Jim Tobin and the uncertainties most of the other teams had with their rosters, it was plausible for Braves fans to hope for the best.

NEW YORK GIANTS

THE NEW YORK Giants, the premier franchise of the National League during the first half of the twentieth century, had one of the least successful periods in their history during World War II. Three of their great players from the 1930s, all destined for the Hall of Fame, played a prominent role with the team throughout World War II, but their magic was missing. Carl Hubbell won 11 games in 1940, 1941, and 1942 but went 4–4 in 1943, the last year of his brilliant 16-year career. Bill Terry and Mel Ott both played and managed during World War II, but their successes on the field were not duplicated in their managerial capacities. Between 1940 and 1945, they each managed only one first-division finish and only one winning season. Unfortunately for the Giants, this was also a period when the Yankees continued to dominate the American League, and the Dodgers began to emerge as a significant National League power. There was not one season between 1940 and 1945 in which the Giants finished above the other New York City franchises in season attendance.

1940

Bill Terry managed the Giants in 1940 to a lackluster sixth-place finish with a record of 72–80. Center fielder Frank Demaree, a mainstay in the powerful Chicago Cubs pennant-winning squads of the 1930s, led the team in hitting with a .302 average; Mel Ott paced the squad with 19 home runs; and first baseman Babe Young drove in 101 runs, fifth best in the National League. Master Melvin was second in the league in total walks with an even 100, and only one National Leaguer topped his .407 on-base percentage: Elbie Fletcher of the Pirates. Catcher Harry Danning hit .300 with 13 homers and 91 RBIs. Ott and Danning were named to the National League All-Star team, as were left fielder Jo-Jo Moore (the pride of Gause, Texas) and shortstop Billy Jurges. Hal Schumacher paced Giants pitchers with a 13–13 record and also had the best ERA, 3.25. Bill Lohrman went 10–15 but tied for the National League lead in shutouts with five. Walt "Jumbo" Brown, all six feet, four inches and 295 pounds of him, had seven saves—good enough to be the highest total in the league along with Johnny Beggs of the Reds and Mace Brown of the Pirates. Carl Hubbell went 11–12 with a 3.65 ERA but was the only Giants pitcher named to the All-Star Game. The Giants put lights in the Polo Grounds and beat the Boston Braves 8–1 in front of 22,260 fans in their first night engagement, on May 24, 1940. In New York City at that time, the Dodgers already had lights in Ebbets Field, but the Yankees were still adamantly against them. The Giants drew just under 750,000 fans that year, an increase of 50,000 from 1939. Yet in spite of the new lights, the Giants were outdrawn in 1940 by both the Dodgers, who finished second, and the Yankees, who finished third.

1941

The Giants' story was much the same in 1941, when they won two more games and lost one less, going 74–79, this time good enough for fifth place, trading places with a weakened Chicago Cubs team. Mel Ott found his Hall of Fame batting eye in 1941 and led the team with 27 home runs, achieving the second-best home run percentage in the league, and drew 100 walks for the second straight year, which in 1941 was good enough for third in the National League. Third baseman Dick Bartell hit .303, and Babe Young once again drove in more than 100 runs, a league-second 104. Young was fifth in the league in total bases, and center fielder Johnny Rucker finished third in doubles. Second baseman Billy Jurges thrilled Giants fans by getting nine straight hits during the 1941 season. Backstop Harry Danning dropped off offensively to a .244 average with seven homers and 56 RBIs, but the great catcher was nonetheless placed on the All-Star team for the fourth straight year. Jumbo Brown led all National League pitchers with eight saves, Hal Schumacher went 12–10, and Cliff "Mountain Music" Melton paced the staff with a 3.01 ERA. Carl Hubbell (11–9, 3.57 ERA) once again was named to the National League's pitching staff for the All-Star Game. No discussion of the Giants' pitching staff in 1941 would be complete without a mention of Tom "Lefty" Sunkel. The pride of Paris, Illinois, was mistakenly classified 1-A by his draft board in spite of a significant handicap: He was blind in his left eye.[19] Sunkel, one of the few major leaguers in history with such an affliction, was previously with the Cardinals. He spent three years with New York and ended his career after the 1944 season, when he pitched for the Dodgers. Admirably overcoming his handicap, Sunkel walked 133 batters in 230 innings during his six-season career and even managed a batting average of .212.

As a team, the Giants' performances were commensurate with their finish in the standings, with the exception of home runs, in which they finished third. The Giants drew about 763,000 fans in 1941, approximately 16,000 more than in 1940 and a half million less than the pennant-winning Dodgers and 200,000 less than the World Champion Yankees. For the year, the Giants posted a modest profit of $46,000.

1942

Shortly after the 1941 season, changes were made to shore up the team for the next season. Bill Terry was replaced by Mel Ott to manage the team, a move enthusiastically embraced by Giants followers. Soon after the managerial switch, the Giants traded Ken O'Dea, Bill Lohrman, Johnny McCarthy, and $50,000 to the St. Louis Cardinals for the storied slugger and future Hall of Famer Johnny Mize. In May 1942, the Giants reacquired Lohrman from the Cardinals for cash. Mize had dipped to only 16 home runs in 1941 but had two home run titles to his name and was one of the most respected hitters in the National League at the time. In spite of mediocre pitching, the hard-hitting Giants, who led the National League in team home runs and ended the season tied with Brooklyn for the fewest errors and best fielding average, finished in third place, a distant 20 games away from the first-place Cardinals, with a very respectable record of 85–67. The effectiveness of the Giants' one-two punch with the two future Hall of Famers in the middle of their lineup is apparent in almost every hitting category. Ott won the home run title with 30, and Mize was close behind him, second in the league with 26. Mize finished first in slugging average, and Ott was second. Mize was first in the National League in RBIs with 110, and Ott was fifth with 93. Ott won his last National League home run title in 1942 and was first in home run percentage, Mize finishing third in that latter category. Mize was second in total bases, and Ott was fourth. Once again, Ott finished first in most walks, drawing more than 100 for the seventh consecutive year, a new National League record. He was also first in runs scored and second in on-base percentage. Mize finished third in the National League in runs scored. Both players were named to the National League All-Star team. If the pitching in 1942 had been as effective as the hitting and fielding, the Giants might have challenged more seriously for the pennant. Bill Lohrman proved invaluable, going 13–4 with a 2.56 ERA to pace the Giants. He finished second in the National League in fewest walks per nine innings, a category in which Carl Hubbell finished third. Ace Adams led the league in games pitched and finished second in total saves. Cliff Melton (11–5, 2.63) and Hubbell were placed on the All-Star team, joining Mize and Ott. The Giants drew 779,000 fans with their improved efforts, less than the first-place Yankees by 143,000 and less than the second-place Dodgers, who were hotly engaged with St. Louis throughout the season in the pennant race, by 258,000.

1943

The bottom fell out in 1943. The war claimed four starters; All-Star catcher Harry Danning, outfielder Babe Young, center fielder Willard Marshall, and first baseman Johnny Mize were all in the military. A great many of their minor league organizations ceased operations as well. The Giants finished in last place for only the third time since 1900, going 55–98. Their 30-game turnaround in victory totals was one of the worst in National League history. Player-manager Mel Ott led the team with 18 home runs, good enough for second in the National League, and his on-base percentage was .423, topped by only Stan Musial. Second baseman Mickey Witek led the team with a respectable .314 average, also pacing the Giants with his 55 RBIs, a paltry total for a team leader. The great Ernie Lombardi was acquired just after the season started from the Boston Braves for catcher Hugh Poland and promising second baseman

Connie Ryan. "The Schnozz" came through for the Giants with his usual great year at the plate, hitting .305 with ten homers and 51 RBIs at the age of 35 and being placed on his seventh All-Star team. Ace Adams paced the pitching staff, going 11–7 with a league-second nine saves and a 2.82 ERA, becoming the first pitcher to appear in 60 or more games in two consecutive seasons. Adams's efforts earned him a spot on the National League All-Star team. Carl Hubbell, at 40, pitching in the last season of his career, went a tired 4–4 with an uncharacteristically obese 4.91 ERA in 12 appearances. On June 5, however, King Carl thrilled the fans with a brilliant one-hitter against the Pittsburgh Pirates, one of the few bright spots in the Giants' season. Four years later, he entered the Hall of Fame. The Giants' fielding fell off precipitously; the pitching staff gave up the most walks in the National League and also had the highest ERA. The old adage that pitching and fielding win ball games was borne out by the Giants in 1943; the last-place Giants led the league in home runs but still lost 98 games. Giants fans avoided this team in droves. Season attendance, at 466,000, was the lowest since the Depression season of 1932 and far below the season attendance of the Dodgers and Yankees. Their team payroll of $201,661 was third highest in the league that year. Only Brooklyn and Chicago had higher payrolls in 1943. Like so many teams before them, the Giants learned the hard way that a high payroll and a low finish in the standings are a recipe for financial disaster. For only the fifth time since 1920, the Giants finished in red ink, losing $248,973, the biggest deficit any National League team had ever experienced up to that time since the league's inception.

1944

New York's fortunes improved somewhat in the 1944 season, going from eighth to fifth with a record of 67–87. A 13-game losing streak cost them a chance to crack into the first division. Phil Weintraub, who had not been on a major league roster since he played 100 games for the Phillies in 1938, had the highest batting average on the team, .316. Mel Ott, however, led the Giants in every other major offensive statistic. Ott hit 26 home runs, second best in the National League, with the league's highest home run percentage. He was third in the league in slugging average and also in drawing walks. His 82 RBIs were the highest total for the Giants.

Carl Hubbell retired after the 1943 season, but Bill Voiselle more than picked up the slack. The young fireballer went 21–16 with a 3.02 ERA. He led the National League in strikeouts and innings pitched (313, an unusually high number for a rookie) and was third in complete games. Voiselle was named to the All-Star team in 1944 and won the Chicago Baseball Writers' of America Rookie of the Year Award. Ace Adams had another productive year, leading the league in saves with 13 and appearing in more games than any other National League pitcher. Attendance was up more than 200,000 from the previous season to 674,000, still a great deal less than the Yankees' but more than the Dodgers' totals for the season and good enough for the club to make a tidy $53,489 profit, badly needed after 1943's financial disaster.

1945

The Giants opened spring training at the Rockefeller estate in Lakewood, New Jersey, with players like Bartell, Danning, Marshall, Mize, and Young still in the service. The pitching staff was bolstered by the return of Van Lingle Mungo, recently discharged from the service. The mellifluously named Mungo, who tied a record by striking out seven consecutive hitters in 1936, clearly had his best years behind him but was still one of the most feared pitchers in the game. Mungo was virtually guaranteed a starting role for the 1945 season. Teaming Mungo with his fellow South Carolinian Bill Voiselle and reliever Ace Adams, the Giants would open the season with a very respectable pitching staff. Their staff also included one of baseball's most fascinating curiosities, the tallest pitcher in baseball history up to that time, Johnny Gee. Gee, who in true baseball fashion received a nickname, Whiz, was one of the few major leaguers avoiding military conscription because of his height, six feet, nine inches. Gee came via a trade with the Pittsburgh Pirates in 1944, in what was strictly a player-for-cash transaction, and the Giants were hoping he could make an impact.

Chicago Cubs

LIKE THE NEW York Giants, the Chicago Cubs' domination of the National League declined during the World War II years. After finishing in the first division in every season since 1925 and going through their "every three year" pennant stretch in 1929, '32, '35, and '38, the Cubs finished in the second division from 1940 through 1943, made an improved fourth-place finish in 1944, and captured the last pennant in their history (as of this writing) in 1945. A big part of the reason for the franchise's decline was changes in the front office. Boots Weber was the Cubs' successful general manager from 1934 through 1940. The Cubs had no farm system at this time, and Weber had a knack of picking up promising minor leaguers and making very successful trades; his personnel moves engineered the pennants of 1935 and 1938. Leading the players from 1932 through 1938 was manager Charlie Grimm. The banjo-playing Grimm was very much a "player's manager," being demonstrative with his respect and affection for his players. Owner Philip K. Wrigley openly stated in 1944, when he rehired the affable Missourian, that Grimm was the best manager the team ever had.

Weber's replacement in 1940 as general manager was ex-*Chicago Herald-American* sportswriter Jim Gallagher. Wrigley was impressed by both the praise and criticism that flowed from Gallagher's pen over the years, and he undoubtedly recalled that his father had called upon a sportswriter in another era to run the team, when William Wrigley hired William Veeck Sr. for the job in 1919. Gallagher engineered a five-year plan for the organization that included the development of a modified farm system. The success of this venture was mixed. Many of the players on the pennant-winning 1945 squad developed under this system, but for the most part, World War II and its drain on baseball talent doomed Gallagher's plans to failure. Gallagher's biggest failings were the trades he made with other major league teams. Many of his deals, especially involving the Brooklyn Dodgers, were shortsighted failures.

Managing the Cubs during most of the war years was Jimmie Wilson. Wilson was perceived as a tough guy with a no-nonsense attitude. Wrigley and Weber were impressed with his efforts during the 1940 World Series. Wilson was a coach for the Cincinnati Reds and took over the catching duties in the fall classic when the great Ernie Lombardi got injured. During that series, he hit .353, had the Reds' only stolen base, and guided the Reds' fabled pitching staff while they went on the win the World Series—all at the age of 40.

Wilson's flaws, however, became apparent during his tenure with the Cubs. Starring for a team in a World Series is very different than managing.

Wilson was an unpopular and unsuccessful manager with the Philadelphia Phillies from 1934 through 1938. He never piloted the Phils above seventh place and finished in the cellar twice. Wilson's best year in Philadelphia was his second, when they finished seventh with a 64–89 record for a .418 winning percentage. He quit the Phillies before the end of the 1938 season, complaining about his players' poor abilities—a "player's manager" he was not. When one examines the lineup the Cubs fielded during Wilson's years, it is apparent that they should have been much more successful.

1940

The 1940 season was a big disappointment. Player-manager Gabby Hartnett had the team in third place in May, but the Cubs went on to lose 31 games by one run and finish in fifth place at 75–79. This was their first second-division finish since 1925. Like Bill Terry and Mel Ott with the Giants, Hartnett was an example of a peerless Hall of Fame player who found less success managing a team. He angered easily, and his disputes with two pitchers, the washed-up Dizzy Dean and Clay Bryant, a mainstay of the 1938 pennant team, added to his problems.

Third baseman Stan Hack led Cubs hitters with a .317 average and set a record by scoring 100 runs for the fifth consecutive season. Hack also tied Cincinnati's Frank McCormick for most hits in the National League with 191 and was second in stolen bases with 21. His .395 on-base percentage was fifth best in the league. Right fielder Bill Nicholson came into his own in 1940 also, leading the Cubs in home runs (25) and RBIs (98). Nicholson finished second in the National League in home runs and slugging average and third in home run percentage, and he was named to the 1940 All-Star Game. Left fielder Jimmy Gleeson hit .313 and finished third in the league with 39 doubles. Center fielder Hank Leiber also distinguished himself at the plate, hitting .302 with 17 home runs and 86 RBIs.

On the mound, Claude Passeau, acquired in 1939 from the Phillies for Kirby Higbe, Joe Marty, and Ray Harrell, had the kind of dominant season that would characterize many of the seasons in his 13-year career. Passeau went 20–13 in 1940 for a sub-.500 team with a 2.50 ERA, second best in the National League. He was also third in the league in strikeouts and games pitched and fourth in saves and complete games. For the 1940 season, the Cubs drew 534,878 fans. The only National League teams outdrawing them were Brooklyn, World Champion Cincinnati, and New York. They were also outdrawn by their crosstown rivals, the White Sox, who finished in a surprising tie for fourth place. The Cubs lost $182,019, more than any team in baseball that year, but losses on the balance sheet were usually a secondary concern of owner Philip K. Wrigley. Wrigley often stated that his mission was to keep the team as a legacy to his father; that and his desire to maintain the team's winning tradition were more important than how much money the team made.[20]

1941

In 1941 the Cubs, eager to develop their own talent but not invest as heavily in a farm system as other teams had, greatly expanded the number of teams with which they had contractual agreements and first refusal for top players. They already owned the Los Angeles Angels in the Pacific Coast League but added five more clubs to their minor league portfolio: Tulsa of the Class AA Texas League; Macon of the Class A South Atlantic—the "Sally"—League; Muskogee of the Class C Western Association; and finally, two Class C teams, Lake Charles of the Evangeline League and Janesville in the Wisconsin State League. While the new organization paled in comparison to the minor league network of teams like the Cleveland Indians, New York Yankees, and St. Louis Cardinals, independent minor league teams were becoming a rarity by the 1940s, and the move was a necessity.

Hartnett was dismissed after the 1940 season, his playing contract being sold to the New York Giants. For manager, the Cubs replaced the best catcher in their history with Wilson. In Wilson's first year, the Cubs were never in contention and slipped to sixth place with a 70–84 record. With Gallagher and Wilson running the team, better results were expected, but two trades backfired. Jimmy Gleeson went to Cincinnati for their World Series shortstop Billy Myers; Myers had a bust of a season and appeared in only 24 games. Gallagher also inexcusably sent future Hall of Famer Billy Herman, their All-Star second baseman in three-pennant winning seasons, to the Brooklyn Dodgers for Johnny Hudson, Jimmy Gilbert, and $65,000. This could have been the worst trade Gallagher ever made, and the rationale behind it is unclear. Apparently, Wilson was uncomfortable with Herman being around, knowing the team's penchant for putting in established stars as player-managers and feeling that such a change might be too convenient for the Cubs with the popular and successful Herman around if the team continued to falter again under his direction. Another Gallagher mistake was releasing the popular Augie Galan, who quickly signed with Brooklyn. Galan, a mainstay on the Cubs since 1934 and one of the most solid left fielders in baseball, was injured and played only sparingly in 1940. Herman's and Galan's contributions at Brooklyn would haunt the Cubs throughout the World War II seasons.

During the 1941 season, Stan Hack continued his offensive magic, hitting .317, topped by only three other National League hitters. He led the league with 186 hits and finished second with 111 runs scored and second in on-base percentage with .417. Bill Nicholson's 26 home runs were good enough for third in the league, and his RBI total at 98 was fifth best. Only two other National League sluggers posted a better home run percentage in 1941. The Cubs lost the hitting prowess of Hank Leiber early in the season, when he was hit in the head and suffered a brain concussion. Sadly, Leiber never regained his skills after he returned to baseball; without Leiber's bat and with Galan off to Brooklyn, Dom Dallessandro filled in at left and turned out to be a pleasant surprise, driving in 85 runs. As a team, the Cubs hit 99 home runs, two less than Brooklyn, which led the league in that category. Hack and Nicholson were named to the National League All-Star team for the 1941 season.

Joining them as an All-Star was Claude Passeau, with a 14–14 record and a 3.15 ERA. Passeau finished second in fewest walks per nine innings and fourth in complete games. Vern Olsen was also a factor on the mound, going 10–8 with a 3.15 ERA. In 1941 Chicago became the first team to install an organ in their stadium for the enjoyment of the fans; over the years, this would become a standard fixture in organized baseball. Their attendance was 545,159, fifth in the league and more than 130,000 less than the rival White Sox, who had a surprising third-place finish but played only .500 baseball. The team's bottom line was $157,846 in the red.

1942

Gallagher had some ideas in 1942. To add some power at the plate, he picked up future Hall of Famer Jimmie Foxx, released on waivers by the Boston Red Sox. With Leiber gone, the Cubs needed some power, and with luck this would have been a quick fix. Gallagher also brought 20 pitchers to spring training; Wilson relied on many of them until Memorial Day. But things did not work out well in 1942; the Cubs finished a poor 68–86 (which, amazingly, was good enough for sixth place) and were not in contention during the entire season. Foxx hit three home runs in 205 at bats with a .205 average. He was replaced by Lou "thc Mad Russian" Novikoff in left field. Novikoff and Hack shared batting honors on the team, both of them hitting .300. Hack had a bit of an off year, ranking among National League leaders in only two categories. He finished third in doubles with 36 and fourth in on-base percentage with a .402 average. Bill Nicholson had another big year at the plate; he was second in triples (11), third in total bases, second in hits (173), and fourth in home runs (21). Passeau, the only Cubs All-Star in 1942, was fourth in the league with 19 wins, posting a 2.68 ERA to go along with a 19–14 record. Passeau finished second in complete games and third in total innings pitched.

Had it not been for World War II, Chicago would have had night games for the 1942 season, but in January, three months before Opening Day, owner Philip K. Wrigley realized the military had a better use for them. Attendance was still up compared to 1941, however, as the Cubs drew 590,972 fans, more than every other team in the league exccpt the Dodgers and Giants. Attendance issues were back to normal locally as well, with the Cubs outdrawing the White Sox by more than 165,000. Financially, the Cubs almost broke even, losing only $7,188 for the 1942 season.

1943

World War II caught up with the Cubs' roster before the start of the 1943 season as six players left for the service: starting second baseman Lou Stringer, reserve catcher Bob Scheffing, reserve second baseman Bobby Sturgeon, promising first baseman Eddie Waitkus, and pitchers Vern Olsen and Johnny Schmitz. Stringer returned in 1946 but did not start and retired from the Boston Red Sox in 1950 after a six-year career. Scheffing also returned in 1946, quit playing after the 1951 season with the St. Louis Cardinals, and went on to manage the Cubs from 1957 to 1959 and the Detroit Tigers from 1961 to 1963. Sturgeon shared the starting shortstop position for the Cubs in 1946 along with the aging Billy Jurges, eventually ending a six-year major league career with the Boston Braves in 1948. Waitkus started at first base in 1946, moving Phil Cavarretta to right field, and played well enough to be the National League Rookie of the Year. Tragedy interrupted Waitkus's distinguished career when he suffered a bullet wound at the hands of a deranged female admirer, who shot him in her Edgewater Beach Hotel room in Chicago while he was with the Phillies. Waitkus, the pride of Boston Latin High School, ended a successful 11-year career with the Phils in 1955. Olsen appeared in five Cubs games in 1946 and then left baseball. Schmitz was back in 1946, eventually becoming the ace of the staff when he went 18–13 for the last-place Cubs in 1948, and retired after 13 years of playing in 1956. In 1943 Jimmie Wilson, despite becoming increasingly unpopular with the fans and the media, got a vote of confidence from Wrigley after the Cubs started the season with a 9–21 record. Because they went 65–58 the rest of the season, one could assume that the team began to respond to their controversial leader, but in fact, the real reason was the play of three young newcomers: Eddie Stanky, Peanuts Lowrey, and Hi Bithorn.

Eddie Stanky came to the Cubs from Milwaukee's minor league team, the Brewers, reportedly packing a handgun when he arrived.[21] Stanky played an effective second base and was a pesky offensive threat. The diminutive Peanuts Lowrey, former child movie star, hit a strong .292; his 13 stolen bases were second best in the league, and his 12 triples tied him for third in that category. Hi Bithorn, in his second season in the majors, unseated Passeau as the ace of the staff, going 18–12 with a 2.60 ERA. His seven shutouts were the most in the National League; his 18 wins were the fourth-highest total; his winning percentage, fifth best. Bithorn, of Puerto Rican and Danish extraction, was the first Latino player to have an impact on the Cubs. The fiery competitor could be unpredictable also; tired of the heckling about his heritage he received in a game against the Dodgers, he angrily threw his fastball into the Dodgers' dugout at Leo Durocher's head. Bithorn joined the Navy after the 1943 season, was not as effective upon his return in 1946, and died in mysterious circumstances in Mexico City in 1952. Bithorn Stadium in San Juan, Puerto Rico, is named in his honor.

In spite of the dissatisfaction with Wilson and the Cubs' lackluster performances on the field, the beginnings of the pennant-winning 1945 squad were in evidence in 1943. Gallagher wisely picked up Paul

Derringer, the storied right-hander from Cincinnati, for cash. In 1943 Derringer went 10–14 but was second in the league in fewest walks allowed. Also, Hank Wyse, in his second year in the majors, went 9–7 with a respectable 2.94 ERA. Passeau went 15–12 with a 2.91 ERA. After a slow start, Bill Nicholson regained his customary form, leading the league in home runs with 29, RBIs with 129, and home run percentage; he was also second in total bases and third in runs scored. Nicholson and Passeau were named to the 1943 All-Star team.

Cubs attendance fell to 508,247, below only the pennant-chasing Dodgers and Cardinals, in a season in which major league attendance was down more than 12 percent. The White Sox finished a surprising fourth and drew exactly 647 more fans than the Cubs in 1943. The team posted a profit of $33,000, even though their $251,026 payroll was second only to Brooklyn's in the National League and they received only $41,000, less than the major league average, for broadcasting rights. Historically, the Cubs did not get all they could from radio coverage, partly because Wrigley felt the real payoff was in the publicity and promotion inherent in having games on the air.[22] Helping the team's bottom line were the tremendous concession sales, $121,145, dwarfing the amounts received by other teams.

1944

The press and the fandom were upset with the team, however, and much of the off-season was spent with Cubs loyalists demanding Wilson's immediate departure. The team had too much talent to languish so long under his leadership. In addition to the Cubs losing their best pitcher to the Navy before the 1944 season, Uncle Sam also cost them a starting outfielder, a starting catcher, and a most promising reserve: Peanuts Lowrey, first-string backstop Clyde McCullough, and catcher Mickey Livingston. Lowrey managed to be one of the draftees able to return to the majors for the 1945 season and went on to a successful 13-year career, after which he became a major league coach. McCullough was back in time to dress for the 1945 World Series; he batted once and struck out in a pinch-hitting role. In 1946 he was starting behind the plate once again and hitting a respectable .287. Livingston, like Lowrey, also returned for the 1945 season, and he ended a ten-year career with the Brooklyn Dodgers in 1951. The Cubs lost Paul Derringer for much of the season when he injured his ankle during spring training in snowy French Lick, Indiana. Gallagher needed more pitching in 1944, and Bob Chipman, the Dodgers' left-hander, was available after the 1944 season started. The price was high; promising Eddie Stanky was sent to Brooklyn, but Gallagher had confidence in second baseman Don Johnson, a late-season call-up in 1943. The intense Stanky had not been happy in Chicago and had discussed the possibility of wanting to be traded with Charlie Grimm early in the 1944 season.[23] Stan Hack did not report for spring training and did not intend on returning to the team. Gallagher prayed that 33-year-old Tony York, the pride of Hillsboro, Texas, could pick up some of the slack.

But two new infielders and an added lefty on the staff were not enough to prevent manager Jimmie Wilson from giving the fans their wish. When the team started the 1944 season with a 1–9 record, Gallagher and Wrigley had enough and fired Wilson. A good coach and player, Wilson could simply not succeed when he had to lead. Concerned about the safety of his son, who was serving as a bomber pilot in World War II, Wilson seemed impatient and intolerant of the younger players who had the good fortune of playing baseball during those years. His son, a promising athlete in his own right, died when his bomber crashed over India in the winter of 1944, just before the birth of his first child, Wilson's grandson.[24] After his dismissal from Chicago, Wilson was immediately rehired by Cincinnati as a coach. Three years later, he died unexpectedly, two months short of his 47th birthday.

Wrigley wanted his favorite, Jolly Cholly Grimm, to come back and manage the team, regretting that he had ever let him go. After Grimm arrived, "Smilin' Stan" Hack returned to the team, ending his "retirement." Grimm's Cubs went 74–69 to finish the season at 75–79 (coach Roy Johnson managed one game, a Cubs loss, prior to Grimm's arrival), for a rare fourth-place finish with a sub-.500 record. Winning and losing streaks highlighted the Cubs' season. The Cubs were 1–10 when Grimm arrived and 1–13 after his first three games, the 13-game losing streak being one of the worst in their history. Chicago managed to win seven straight toward the end of May and finally climbed out of the cellar by the Fourth of July. A bad July slump followed, but the month ended with an 11-game winning streak. The Cubs' August, however, included losing streaks of five and seven games. A strong September, which included a six- and a four-game winning streak, sealed their finish in the first division.

The players took to the popular Grimm immediately, some of them remembering playing for him back in 1938. Buoyed by slugger Bill Nicholson's greatest season, the team was permeated by a different attitude. Nicholson finished first in home runs (33), runs scored (122), RBIs (116), and total bases (317). He was second in slugging average, walks, and home run percentage, and he also finished second in voting for the Most Valuable Player Award, which was won by St. Louis glove magician Marty Marion. Nicholson hit four home runs in a doubleheader on July 23, when Giants manager Mel Ott paid him the ultimate compliment; with the bases loaded, Ott ordered Nicholson walked intentionally, forcing in a run instead of affording him the chance to do even more damage. Phil Cavarretta led the team with a .321 batting average, fifth best in the league, and was third in triples with 15. Newcomer Roy Hughes's 16 stolen bases were topped by only two other National Leaguers. Another rookie, Andy Pafko, started in center field and tied Ron Northey to lead all National League outfielders with 24 assists. Dom Dallessandro filled in nicely for Lowrey, who was in the military, hitting .304 with 74 RBIs. Three position players were named to the All-Star team: Cavarretta, Johnson, and Nicholson. Cavarretta spearheaded the rare National League victory at Pittsburgh's Forbes Field, setting a record by reaching base five consecutive times, with a triple, a single, and three walks.

On the mound, Hank Wyse went 16–15 and Claude Passeau went 15–9 with a 2.89 ERA. The only National League team to outdraw the rejuvenated Cubs in 1944 was the New York Giants. The Cubs' total of 640,110 was almost 80,000 more than the White Sox, who finished a disappointing seventh in the American League. For the year, the Cubs posted a profit of $69,660, their best showing since 1937.

PITTSBURGH PIRATES

THE PITTSBURGH PIRATES' fortunes during the World War II era mirrored their performance during the first half of the twentieth century, with five first-division finishes and one fifth-place finish between 1940 and 1945. The baseball magic that Pie Traynor, Honus Wagner, Arky Vaughn, Lloyd Waner, and Paul Waner brought to Pittsburgh came to an end during the war years. While the new faces who replaced them never won a pennant, only St. Louis, Brooklyn, and Cincinnati could best or match Pittsburgh's accomplishments during World War II, and both Cincinnati and Brooklyn had seventh-place finishes while the Pirates never finished worse than fifth.

1940

The changing of the guard was most significant in 1940. Frankie Frisch replaced Pie Traynor as the field manager. Frisch, nicknamed the Fordham Flash, managed the St. Louis Cardinals with success from 1933 through 1938, and when the Pirates got Vince DiMaggio from Cincinnati for starting left fielder Johnny Rizzo, the changes began. Lloyd Waner and Paul Waner, two baseball fixtures in Pittsburgh, went from center field and right field to the bench, replaced by DiMaggio and promising second-year man Bob Elliott. Rizzo's departure meant another comparative newcomer, Maurice Van Robays, would start in left field. The move paid off; DiMaggio led the team in home runs with 19, and Van Robays's 116 RBIs were third best in the National League. Elliott hit a solid .292 in his first full season. The biggest offensive surprise, however, came from a reserve third baseman in the eighth year of a nondescript 12-year career, little Debs Garms. Garms, standing only five feet, eight inches tall, won the National League batting title hitting .355, qualifying with only 358 at bats. Arky Vaughn put in another stellar year at the plate, hitting .300; he also finished first in the league in triples and runs scored, second in doubles, and fifth in total bases. Vaughn was the only Pirate on the 1940 All-Star team. First baseman Elbie Fletcher also had a fine season, leading the National League in bases on balls (119) and on-base percentage (.418), having a fourth-best 104 RBIs, hitting 16 home runs, and batting .273. As a team, the Pirates had the league's highest batting average and led the National League in doubles and runs scored.

They would have finished higher in the standings if their fielding and pitching were anywhere near as good as their hitting. No team had a lower fielding percentage or committed more errors, 217 in 154 games, 100 more errors than pennant-winning Cincinnati. The pitching staff's ERA of 4.36 was only slightly ahead of the league's worst, Philadelphia's 4.40. Rip Sewell went 16–5 with a 2.80 ERA, third best in the league, and his winning percentage was the league's second best. Fastball specialist Mace Brown, known best in baseball history as the pitcher who gave up

Gabby Hartnett's famous "homer in the gloamin'" in 1938, tied for the league lead in saves with seven and was second in total games pitched. The rest of the pitching staff was a virtual disaster. On June 4, 1940, the Pirates beat Boston 14–2 in the first night game held in Forbes Field, in front of 20,319 fans. For the entire season, the Pirates drew 507,934, the fifth-highest total in the National League, and lost $14,954 for the season.

1941

The 1941 season was almost identical to 1940, with the Pirates again finishing fourth but winning three more games for a record of 81–73. Before the season began, they experienced the distinction of being one of the first teams to lose a player to the military when little-used pitcher Oad Swigart, who had appeared in seven games in 1940, was drafted. Swigart never returned to major league baseball. The team did not hit quite as well as they had in 1940, but both fielding and pitching improved. Arky Vaughn led the team with a .316 batting average, while Vince DiMaggio hit 21 home runs and drove in 100 runs, the third-highest RBI total in the league for 1941. Elbie Fletcher led the league in drawing walks with 118, was the league's toughest out with a .421 on-base percentage, and was second in triples with 17. Third baseman Lee Handley finished the season with 16 stolen bases, third best in the league. Catcher Al Lopez, Bob Elliott, and Arky Vaughn made the 1941 National League All-Star team; Vaughn became the first player to hit two home runs in an All-Star contest, going long with a two-run blast in the seventh off Washington's Sid Hudson and duplicating the feat in the ninth off Chicago White Sox hurler Edgar Smith.

Max Butcher emerged as the ace of the pitching staff, going 17–12 with a 3.05 ERA. His 19 complete games were fifth best in the National League. Rip Sewell had an off year, going 14–17, suffering more defeats than any other pitcher in the league in 1941. As a team, the Pirates fell to third in team batting average, but their team fielding was better and the pitching staff's ERA was greatly improved, down almost one run per game to 3.48, fourth best in the league.

On August 19, manager Frankie Frisch emerged with an umbrella from the visitors' dugout at Ebbets Field to let umpire Jocko Conlon know what he thought of the rainy conditions. Hoping to get the game called with his team ahead, Frisch instead got thrown out by the irritated Conlon, the occurrence later immortalized in a famous *Saturday Evening Post* cover by Norman Rockwell. The Pirates drew 482,241 fans in 1941; only Philadelphia and Boston had a smaller gate that season; in spite of the low attendance Pittsburgh ended the year with a $19,615 profit.

1942

World War II claimed the second Pittsburgh Pirate before the 1942 season when infielder Burgess Whitehead was drafted; he returned to play in 55 games in 1946, the last season of his nine-year career. Pittsburgh's most dismal year during the World War II era was 1942, the only season in which they had a losing record. The Pirates only slipped to fifth place, but they had a negative swing of 15 games in the victory column, falling to 66–81. Bob Elliott led the team in hitting with a comparatively low .296 average and was the sole Pirate in the 1942 All-Star Game. Vince DiMaggio's 15 home runs and 78 RBIs paced a greatly weakened Pirates attack. Elbie Fletcher was the only Pirate ranking among National League offensive leaders, once again finishing first, with a .417 on-base percentage, and drawing a second-best 105 walks. Rip Sewell returned to previous form, pacing the pitching staff with a 17–5 record, while Max Butcher's 2.93 ERA was the team's best. The Pirates finished in the middle of the league in hitting, fielding, and pitching; their attendance fell to 448,897; and the team lost almost $34,000. Attendance was lower throughout all of major league baseball in 1942, with the increased number of individuals in the military and people generally having less leisure time with industrial production intensified for the war effort.

1943

Pirates efforts and fortunes improved dramatically, however, in the 1943 season, a year in which they had a positive swing of 14 games in the victory column. They improved at the plate and on the mound enough to move to fourth place, going 80–74. Bob Elliott and Vince DiMaggio paced the Pirates at the plate. Elliott hit .315, fourth best in the National League, and led the Pirates with 101 RBIs, second only to the Cubs' Bill Nicholson. Elliott was third in triples with 12 and fourth in slugging average as well. Fletcher, after leading the National League in on-base percentage the previous three seasons, finished fourth in 1943 at .395. DiMaggio's 15 home runs were also good enough to be fourth best in the league. Frankie Gustine and Jimmy Russell both had 12 stolen bases, the third-highest totals in the National League. Pirates pitcher Rip Sewell perfected his dew-drop ball (also known as an eephus pitch) during the '43 season. The path of Sewell's unusual offering was a slow, blooping arc, which many batters cursed as unhittable. Sewell tied Cincinnati's Elmer Riddle for the most wins in the season, going 21–9 with a 2.54 ERA. His winning percentage was the second best in the league, and his 25 complete games were the best in the majors. Sewell, DiMaggio, and Fletcher represented the Pirates in the 1943 All-Star Game.

Team speed was a hallmark for the 1943 Pirates; they were first in triples with 73 and led the league in stolen bases with 64. The pitching staff's ERA was down to 3.06, topped only by the World Champion Cardinals. Another reason for their success in 1943 was because the Pirates lost few key players to the military, certainly fewer than most other teams. Missing the 1943 season and entering World War II were Ken Heintzelman, Billy Cox, and Lefty Wilkie. Heintzelman returned in 1946 but went to Philadelphia in 1947, posting a 1.16 ERA for the Whiz Kids in the 1949 World Series and ending a 13-year career in 1952. Cox also returned to Pittsburgh in 1946 but achieved his greatest fame later with another team. His 11-year career ended in 1955, but not before he had big years with the Brooklyn Dodgers and appeared in three World Series. Wilkie returned to the Pirates in 1946 for seven games, posted a 10.57 ERA, and then was out of the majors. In 1943 more fans appeared to see this exciting team. Attendance was up to 498,740, fourth highest in the National League. With the second-lowest payroll in the league ($158,000), the Pirates posted a $56,160 profit.

1944

More success came to Frankie Frisch's charges in 1944, despite the loss of two important players to the war, starting first baseman Elbie Fletcher and outfielder Maurice Van Robays. Both returned in 1946, Fletcher ending a successful 12-year career with the Boston Braves in 1949 and Van Robays ending six years in the majors after appearing in 59 games that year. In 1944 Pittsburgh had their best season since 1927, going 90–63, the first time in 16 years that the team reached 90 victories and their first second-place finish since 1938. Over their last 59 games, the team played .678 baseball, better than any team in the majors, going 40–19, doing even better than the pennant-winning Cardinals, who had run away with first place long before the Pirates made their move. This latter part of the Pirates' season included a winning streak of 11 games and a remarkable stretch in which they went 17–1. With all their success, they still finished a distant 14 games behind St. Louis, who won the pennant at 105–49. Once again, hitting, pitching, and team speed were the Pirates' strengths, which more than made up for some very mediocre fielding.

Third baseman Bob Elliott and new first baseman Babe Dahlgren, acquired in December 1943 for Babe Phelps and cash from Philadelphia, led the Pirates' attack. Elliott batted .297 with 108 RBIs, good enough for second in the league, as were his 16 triples. Elliott was also third in runs scored with 109. Dahlgren's offensive numbers were .289, a team-high 12 homers, and 101 RBIs. Right fielder Johnny Barrett set the league's base-stealing standard with 28, and Jimmy Russell finished third in runs scored with 109. Vince DiMaggio and Bob Elliott made the National League All-Star team, playing in front of a partisan crowd in their home, Forbes Field. DiMaggio soured on the Pirates during the season, however, and played very little during the second half.

Rip Sewell continued his mound mastery, going 21–12 with a 3.18 ERA. He was third in the league in wins and innings pitched, fourth in complete games with 24, and fifth in winning percentage. Sewell made the All-Star team for the second straight year. Nick Strincevich was a huge pitching asset for the Pirates in 1944 as well, going 14–7 with a 3.08 ERA and allowing only 1.75 walks per game, the second-lowest ratio in the league. Relief pitcher Xavier Rescigno, the pride of Manhattan College, had five saves, second best in the league, and appeared in 48 games, a total eclipsed by only two National League hurlers. As a team, the Bucs led in triples and stolen bases; were second in slugging average, runs scored, and walks allowed; and were third in team batting average and ERA. Major league baseball attendance was up in 1944 compared to 1943, and the Pirates enjoyed an increase of more than 100,000, drawing 604,278, their highest total since 1938. The team also made a profit of $111,112, for their best year financially since 1938. Only the Cardinals, Tigers, and Yankees made more money than Pittsburgh in 1944.

On the strength of their 1944 performance, Pittsburgh was expected to mount a serious challenge for the National League pennant in 1945, and there was a good deal of optimism when they opened their spring training camp in Muncie, Indiana. While the Pirates' "Honor Roll" of players still serving in the military included 31 names, only three of them, Elbie Fletcher, Ken Heintzelman, and Maurice Van Robays, had been regulars during previous seasons.[25] Pittsburgh also had the good fortune of not losing any players to the military during the off-season. On March 31, they traded the unhappy Vince DiMaggio for promising lefthander Al Gerheauser, strengthening their starting rotation. As opening day approached, the Pirates felt better about their chances in the 1945 season than they had in many years.

CINCINNATI REDS

THE CINCINNATI REDS, on the strength of a pennant-winning season in 1939 and a victorious trip to the World Series in 1940, entered the World War II era as the most dominant franchise in the National League. By 1940 the man most responsible for their ascension was working for the Brooklyn Dodgers: Larry MacPhail. MacPhail was a premier front-office man, perhaps less remembered today than Bill Veeck or Branch Rickey, but the Reds were the first of three franchises—the others being the Brooklyn Dodgers and New York Yankees—that he shepherded to greatness. His innovations at Cincinnati were as remarkable as the teams he assembled. The Reds were the first team to offer season tickets (1934),[26] the first to play night baseball (1935), the first to travel by airplane (St. Louis to Chicago, 1935), and the first to broadcast their games on radio (1934). During the war years, the Reds' manager was Bill McKechnie, one of the most successful managers of the twentieth century. McKechnie had previously led the Pirates and Cardinals to the World Series, and after his achievements in Cincinnati were completed, he was enshrined in the Hall of Fame.

1940

The Reds were favored to win the pennant in 1940 after finishing first in the National League in 1939 with 97 wins. They lived up to expectations, going 100–53 during the regular season and winning the pennant by 12 games, the largest National League bulge since 1931. They beat the Detroit Tigers, four games to three, in one of the more thrilling World Series to date. Outstanding pitching, the best fielding in the league, and the hitting of first baseman Frank McCormick and catcher Ernie Lombardi were the hallmarks of this excellent team. McCormick paced the Reds' offensive attack, and he won the Most Valuable Player Award over the slugging Cardinal first baseman Johnny Mize. The six–foot, four-inch McCormick was one of the best clutch hitters in the league in 1940 and finished first in doubles (44), tied with Stan Hack for first in hits (191), second in RBIs (127), and second in total bases (298). McCormick also led the Reds with 19 home runs. Lombardi, the only catcher to win two batting titles, hit .319 with 14 home runs and 74 RBIs. Both of them also led the league in fielding at their respective positions and were named to the 1940 National League All-Star team. Second baseman Lonnie Frey led the National League in stolen bases with 22, and third baseman Billy Werber, batting in front of McCormick and Lombardi, was third in runs scored with 105.

The pitching staff of the 1940 Reds, however, was the reason the team dominated so completely. The starting rotation was one of the best in baseball history. Bucky Walters, whom MacPhail had picked up from the Philadelphia Phillies in 1938 for Spud Davis, Al Hollingsworth, and $50,000, was the ace of the staff. The converted third baseman went 22–10 with a 2.48 ERA. Walters led the National League in the following categories: wins, ERA, innings pitched (305), complete games (29), and fewest hits per game (7.11). Walters was also third in winning percentage and tied teammate Paul Derringer for fifth-highest strikeout total with 115. Paul Derringer, the eight-year mainstay of the Reds' staff since 1933, when MacPhail got him from the Cardinals for shortstop Leo Durocher, almost matched Walters's remarkable performance. Derringer went 20–12 with a 3.06 ERA, finishing first in fewest walks per game (1.46). Derringer finished second in the National League, trailing only Walters, in the following categories: wins (20), innings pitched (297), and complete games (26). Both Walters and Derringer earned spots on the 1940 National League All-Star team. Derringer was also fifth in the league in winning percentage. Junior Thompson went 16–9 with a 3.32 ERA, finishing third in the league in fewest hits allowed per game and fourth in winning percentage. Jim Turner went 14–7 with the league's fifth-best ERA, 2.89. Complementing this staff was Joe Beggs, the best relief pitcher in baseball in 1940, with seven saves, a 12–3 record, and a 2.00 ERA. Walters won both his starts in the World Series, posting a 1.50 ERA and allowing only eight hits in 18 innings of work. He threw two complete game victories: the first a three-hitter and the second a shutout in which he himself hit a home run. Derringer won two World Series games and lost one; his loss was the first game in the series and his second victory was in game seven. A special championship laurel, however, went to Reds coach Jimmie Wilson. Wilson was forced into catching duties when Ernie Lombardi got injured in the first game, after the team had already tragically lost second string catcher Willard Hershberger earlier in the season. Wilson caught six of the seven games, hit .353 (6-for-17), and at the age of 40 stole the only base of the 1940 World Series. His efforts were rewarded after the season when Cubs owner Philip K. Wrigley, impressed by his performance, named him Chicago's new manager.

The Reds' need for Wilson is one of the most tragic stories in the annals of baseball and the only dark spot on Cincinnati's brilliant season. Their backup catcher during the year was 33-year-old Willard Hershberger, a third-year backstop with an excellent .316 lifetime batting average. In spite of his abilities, Hershberger was his own worst critic and felt immense pressure and responsibility shepherding the best pitching staff in baseball in the heat of a pennant race. After catching a game against the Giants in which Bucky Walters relinquished a 4–1 lead in the ninth inning and lost the game following two New York home runs, Hershberger could not forgive himself. When the Reds checked into Boston for their next series, Hershberger slashed his throat while alone in his room at the Copley Plaza Hotel on August 3, 1940.[27] Perhaps the greatest tribute to Bill McKechnie and the remarkable Reds of 1940 was that they could endure this tragedy and still prevail. This tragedy set the stage for Jimmie Wilson's World Series heroics.

In the National League, only the Brooklyn Dodgers drew more attendance than the Reds' total of 850,180. Their profit of $270,240 was by far the highest in the major leagues in 1940 and would be eclipsed by only one team in professional baseball during the wartime era, the St. Louis Browns in 1944.

1941

Fresh from their World Championship in October 1940, the Reds remained virtually intact for the 1941 season. The only significant change was the addition of Jimmy Gleeson from the Cubs to replace the injured Ival Goodman in right field. The excellent fielding and pitching the Reds exhibited in 1940 continued, but Cincinnati suffered a serious letdown in all offensive departments. The strength of the Brooklyn Dodgers and St. Louis Cardinals were too much, and Cincinnati fell to third place with a record of 88–66, which put them 12 games behind pennant-winning St. Louis.

The only Red among league leaders in any offensive category in 1941 was Lonnie Frey, whose 16 stolen bases tied him for third in the National League. Left fielder Mike McCormick, no relation to first baseman Frank, led the team in batting with a .287 average; Frank McCormick's 19 home runs and 97 RBIs paced the Reds in the power departments. Both Frank McCormick and Frey earned spots on the 1941 National League All-Star team. The pitching staff, however, was another story. Third-year man Elmer Riddle supplanted Bucky Walters as the ace of the staff. His 19–4 record yielded the best winning percentage (.826) in the league, and his sparkling 2.24 ERA was the league's best as well. Only two other National League pitchers won more than Riddle's 19 games: Brooklyn's Kirby Higbe and Whitlow Wyatt, each finishing with 22. Johnny Vander Meer, "the Dutch Master," returned after two off years with a flourish. Vander Meer went 16–13 with an ERA of 2.82, fourth best in the league. Vander Meer dominated as the strikeout king of the early 1940s, and the '41 season was no exception. He led the league with 202 strikeouts in 226 innings, averaging 8.03 strikeouts per game, tops in the majors. As a means of comparison, Bob Feller averaged 6.82 strikeouts per game in 1941. Vander Meer also allowed the fewest hits per game (6.84) and had the second-highest shutout total (six). Vander Meer's only shortcoming was his wildness, a problem that plagued him throughout his career. Against many hitters, however, even this shortcoming was an advantage. His episodic lack of control coupled with his blinding speed intimidated many hitters. Walters continued his mound domination in 1941 as well, going 19–15 with the fifth-best ERA in the league, 2.83, almost identical to Vander Meer's. Walters finished first in the National League in complete games (27) and innings pitched (302), third in strikeouts (129), fourth in wins, and fifth in shutouts (five). Johnny Beggs finished second in saves with five.

As a team, the Reds were first in fewest opponents' runs allowed, stolen bases, fewest errors, best fielding average, and most complete games, and a very close second in team ERA, 3.17 to Brooklyn's 3.14. Their woeful offense, however, turned out to be the 12-game difference between them and the pennant-winning Cardinals. Cincinnati finished sixth in runs scored, home runs, and slugging average; seventh in doubles and team batting average, in front of only Philadelphia; and last in triples. Attendance was down by more than 200,000 to 643,513, fourth best in the league but a steep decline in a season in which the National League attendance overall was up almost nine percent. Pittsburgh was the only other National League franchise to experience a drop in attendance from 1940 to 1941. Even with this reduction at the gate, the Reds posted a profit of $123,025, third highest in the National League.

1942

In 1941 the Reds won 12 fewer games than they had in 1940. In 1942 they won 12 fewer than they had in 1941, going 76–76 for a rare fourth-place finish with a .500 record, 29 games behind the champion St. Louis Cardinals. Six new faces made their debuts in the Reds' lineup. Ray Lamanno replaced Ernie Lombardi, traded in February 1942 to the Boston Braves for cash, behind the plate. Bert Haas took Bill Werber's spot at third after Werber was traded for cash to New York. Max Marshall, Gee Walker, and Eric Tipton came in to play right, center, and left, replacing Jimmy Gleeson, Harry Craft, and Mike McCormick. Gleeson and Craft left the majors, but McCormick simply lost his starting outfield position and remained with the Reds.

The Reds continued to have major problems with hitting and their fielding average fell, but their pitching remained respectable. Frank McCormick led the team at the plate with a .277 average, a meager 13 home runs, and 89 RBIs. Lamanno was the only other Red with double-digit home runs, hitting 12. Johnny Vander Meer paced the pitching staff with an 18–12 record, posting the National League's fourth-best ERA, 2.43. Once again he led the league in strikeouts (186) and strikeouts per game (6.86). The Dutch Master was also second in hits allowed per game (6.93) and fifth in wins and complete games (21), tying teammate Bucky Walters in the latter category. Relief pitcher Johnny Beggs finished third in saves with eight.

While the Reds as a team had the second-best ERA in the National League at 2.82 and ten more complete games than their nearest competitors in that category (St. Louis), team hitting statistics and fielding statistics fell off a great deal compared to 1941. The Reds were fifth in stolen bases, sixth in runs scored, seventh in slugging average, and last in team batting average, a paltry .231. While new catcher Ray Lamanno hit a respectable .264, the recently discarded Ernie Lombardi won the batting title for the Boston Braves. Five teams committed fewer errors than Cincinnati, and five had a better fielding average. While major league attendance was down 10 percent for the 1942 season, the Reds' gate was down more than a third; only 427,031 fans came to see this disappointing, weak-hitting team, with Boston and Philadelphia being the only National League franchises that year with a smaller gate. The team barely broke even, posting a $4,916 profit.

1943

Fortunes changed for the Cincinnati franchise in 1943, however. With All-Star Eddie Miller coming over from Boston to replace Eddie Joost at shortstop, Steve Mesner replacing Bert Haas at third, and Ray Mueller replacing Ray Lamanno behind the plate, the Reds' defense improved dramatically. In spite of the balata ball, the Reds' hitting improved, and perhaps because of the balata ball, their pitching was even more effective. These factors added up to an 87–67 record, good enough for second place, yet a distant 18 games behind the front-running Cardinals.

World War II hit the Cincinnati squad hard before the 1943 season; the team lost six players, two of them starters. Mike McCormick went from the outfield to the Army. He returned in 1946 for 23 games and was subsequently traded to Boston, finishing a ten-year career in 1951 with the Washington Senators. Starting catcher Ray Lamanno was also lost, returning in 1946 and retiring from baseball in 1948, ending a five-year career. Promising Ewell Blackwell left for the service, returning for only nine games in 1946 but going 22–8 for the Reds in 1947. He was traded to the Yankees in 1952, participated in several World Series, and ended a successful ten-year career in 1955 with the Kansas City Athletics. No less a hitter than Andy Pafko said that Blackwell, in his prime, was the toughest pitcher in the National League.[28] Local boy Clyde Vollmer was drafted and returned to the Reds in 1946. In 1948 he was traded to the Washington Senators and left baseball in 1954 after a ten-year career. Second baseman Benny Zientara was also drafted and returned to play half of the 1946 season for the Reds, ending his four-year career in

Cincinnati in 1948. Rookie Bobby Adams was also drafted, getting his discharge in 1946 and ending a 14-year career after the 1959 season with the Chicago Cubs. Adams was one of the few players in history who had both a brother (Dick, one year his senior) and son (Mike, born in 1948) who played in the major leagues. The biggest Reds story regarding the war, however, concerned coach Hank Gowdy. Gowdy, a 17-year major league veteran between 1910 and 1930, was the first major leaguer to enlist in World War I. In a display of unselfish patriotism at the age of 54, Gowdy reenlisted in 1943, was immediately commissioned as a captain, and was discharged in time to return to the Reds as a coach in the 1945 season.[29]

Mike Marshall replaced Mike McCormick in right, and Ray Mueller took over from Lamanno behind the plate. Mueller matched Lamanno's performance at the plate and led all National League catchers with 100 assists; Marshall, however, proved to be a disappointment, hitting only .236, a big drop from the previous season.

The Reds' offensive leaders in 1943 were Frank McCormick, who upped his average to .303; Eric Tipton, with a paltry nine home runs; and shortstop Eddie Miller, with 71 RBIs. Miller's total was respectable for a shortstop but extremely low for a team leader. During the '43 season, Reds fans enjoyed an exciting offensive display put on by reserve infielder Woody Williams, who played in just 30 games but tied a National League record with ten straight hits. The only Cincinnati hitter to finish among the National League offensive leaders was Tipton, whose .395 on-base percentage was fifth best in the league. Defensively, shortstop Miller and second baseman Lonnie Frey had the best fielding averages (.979 and .985, respectively) in the league at their positions. McCormick, Miller, and Frey all participated in the 1943 All-Star Game.

Cincinnati's pitching in 1943 was very effective. Elmer Riddle emerged as the new ace of the staff. Riddle went 21–11 with a 2.63 ERA, tying St. Louis's Mort Cooper and Pittsburgh's Rip Sewell for the most wins in the league and finishing with the fourth-highest winning percentage. Vander Meer fell to 15–16 but proved to be unhittable when he had good control. He led all National League pitchers with 174 strikeouts, had the best strikeout-per-game ratio at 5.42, was second in innings pitched with 289, was third in hits per game at 7.10, and was fifth in complete games with 21. Bucky Walters went 15–15 and tied Vander

Meer with 21 complete games. Clyde Shoun went 14–10 with seven saves, the third-best total in the league. Vander Meer was the only Reds pitcher named to the 1943 All-Star team.

As a team, the Reds hit only 43 balata balls for home runs, the fifth-highest total in the league, and the team batting average was .256, also fifth best. They led the National League in fewest errors, most double plays, and team fielding average. Their staff ERA of 3.13 was third best, behind Pittsburgh (3.06) and St. Louis (2.57). Major league baseball experienced a 13 percent drop in attendance during 1943, and the Reds were no exception, drawing 379,122, about 11 percent less than in 1942. Their team payroll was $196,329, and they received $45,000 for radio broadcast rights, both amounts being close to the league average. Concession sales only totaled $61,501, worse than every team except Boston and Philadelphia; yet profits for the year, at $16,503, were up from the year before.

1944

The demands of World War II were hard on the Cincinnati roster again before the start of the 1944 season. All-Star second baseman Lonnie Frey, a married 32-year-old with three children,[30] was drafted and replaced at second by Woody Williams. Frey returned to the Reds in 1946 but then went on to the Cubs, Yankees, and Giants before ending a successful 14-year career in 1948. Versatile Bert Haas, who played both infield and outfield for the '43 Reds, was also lost to the service. He, too, returned briefly in 1946 and played later with the Phillies, Giants, and White Sox, retiring in 1951. His nine-year career culminated in being selected for the National League All-Star team in 1947. Promising young Hank Sauer was drafted but returned in 1945 to play 31 games for the Reds. Sauer's big break came in 1949, when he was traded to the Chicago Cubs, engendering such a loyal following among Cubs fans that he earned the nickname the Mayor of Wrigley Field. He ended a 288–home run, 15-year career with the San Francisco Giants in 1959. The pitching staff made a supreme sacrifice to the war effort by bidding adieu to Johnny Vander Meer. The Dutch Master returned in 1946 but was not the same after the war. He remained with the Reds until 1950, when he was traded to the Cubs, and ended his career with the Cleveland Indians in 1951 after 13 seasons in the majors.

In spite of these losses, the Reds improved their successful 1943 season by two games, finishing 89–65 in 1944, a game and a half behind second-place Pittsburgh but 16 behind the eventual World Champion Cardinals.

The 1944 campaign got off to a good start and culminated when reliever Clyde Shoun got a rare start and tossed a no-hitter against the Boston Braves, winning 1–0 over the Braves' Abba Dabba Tobin.[31] The season unfolded with no team ever catching the St. Louis Cardinals and the rest of the league never catching Cincinnati and Pittsburgh. The Reds and Pirates held their own battle for second place, far ahead of the rest of the league. After Labor Day, Cincinnati finished the season with a 20–9 record, the strongest finish in the league.

Frank McCormick once again led the Reds in every important hitting category, batting .305 with 20 home runs and 102 RBIs; his home run and RBI totals were good enough for fourth in the National League. McCormick once again was named to the All-Star team, joined by catcher Ray Mueller, who set a catching record appearing in 154 games, while hitting .286 with ten homers and 73 RBIs. The individual most responsible for the successes of 1944, however, was Bucky Walters. Walters went 23–8, leading the majors in victories and fewest hits per nine innings (7.36). He was second in ERA (2.40), shutouts (six), and complete games (27) and fourth in winning percentage. His All-Star performance, however, was topped in one category by Ed Heusser, who went 13–11 but had the best National League ERA at 2.38.

As a team, the Reds were second in fewest opponents' runs allowed, first in complete games and fewest walks (the latter category enhanced by Vander Meer's departure), second in team ERA, a distant seventh in total runs scored, and last in home runs with a measly 51. The crippling effects of the war on baseball's rosters became glaringly apparent for the Reds on June 10, when the war-depleted Reds sent teenage phenom Joe Nuxhall, two months short of his 16th birthday and a month away from pitching in a junior high school game, to mop up in a lopsided 18–0 loss to the Cardinals. Nuxhall initially did well, retiring the first two Cards he faced, but then the significance of his surroundings got to him and he gave up five walks, a wild pitch, and singles to Emil Verban and Stan Musial. The youngest player in major league history spent the next seven years in the minors before embarking on a 135-victory, 15-year career with the Reds in 1952.

Major league attendance was up in 1944, and the Reds experienced an increase also, drawing 409,567, an increase of more than 30,000 over their 1943 attendance. They almost doubled the profit they made the previous season, making $30,611.

Cincinnati opened its spring training facility at Indiana University in Bloomington, full of hope, on the eve of the 1945 season. No fewer than 37 Reds were still in the military, and the list included valuable players like Frey, Lamanno, Vander Meer, and a new inductee, pitcher Clyde Shoun.[32] Shoun would return in 1946, going 1–6, and finished his 14-year career in 1949, after leaving Cincinnati for the Boston Braves and Chicago White Sox. Little did the Reds know that Shoun's departure, among other problems, would affect them so adversely during the 1945 season.

1945

A shortage of talent forced the Reds to get very creative with several spots on their spring training roster. Cincinnati gave Dick Sipek, the third deaf player in major league history (one of the other two being his father, New York Giants pitcher Luther "Dummy" Taylor, who played for nine years and won 21 games in 1904), an outfield spot. The 22-year-old Sipek was an athlete with legendary accomplishments at the Illinois School for the Deaf.[33] He distinguished himself and earned a spring training roster spot by hitting .318 with 85 RBIs in 1944 at Birmingham in the Southern Association. Three teenagers—18-year-old infielder Ralph Kraus, 18-year-old pitcher Herm Wehmeier, and 19-year-old infielder Ray Medeiros—joined Joe Nuxhall as the youngest members of the spring training squad. At the other end of the chronological spectrum, 47-year-old Hod Lisenbee and 44-year-old Guy Bush appeared on the pitching staff.[34] Bush broke into the major leagues and started his excellent career with the Chicago Cubs in 1923, several years before any of the teenaged aspirants were born. The Cincinnati Reds' 1945 roster encapsulated the travails of major league baseball during World War II.

BROOKLYN DODGERS

LARRY MACPHAIL, THE same individual responsible for the Cincinnati Reds' ascendancy at the close of the 1930s and into the World War II years, was also responsible for the rise of the Brooklyn Dodgers in the 1940s. From

1940 through 1945, only the St. Louis Cardinals eclipsed the Dodgers' successful seasons, which consisted of five first-division finishes, including a pennant in 1941, and one year in seventh place. The fruits of MacPhail's labors were evident at the beginning of the 1940 season. Starting shortstop was Pee Wee Reese, one of the most famous Dodgers of all time; MacPhail got him for a pittance from the Boston Red Sox farm system. At first base was the slugging Dolph Camilli, obtained from the cash-strapped Phillies for $50,000. Outfielder Dixie Walker, a fan favorite and perennial All-Star, came from the Detroit Tigers. Pete Reiser was acquired from the Cardinals' organization for next to nothing. Reiser was one of the baseball prizes Commissioner Landis granted free agency in March 1938 when he intervened to "reform" the Cardinals' farm system practices.[35] In June 1940 he traded for another slugger to put Brooklyn over the top in their challenge with pennant-winning Cincinnati.

1940

On June 12, 1940 MacPhail strengthened the Dodgers, getting Joe "Ducky" Medwick and pitcher Curt Davis from St. Louis for $125,000 and four players, a steep price to pay in those days, especially in light of Medwick's near-tragic destiny in a Brooklyn uniform. Davis was a first-class pitcher who went 22–16 and hit an amazing .381 in an All-Star season for the Cardinals in 1939. Medwick, however, was the key to the deal and things did not turn out to the Dodgers' liking. Brooklyn started the season on a high note when pitcher Tex Carlton threw a no-hitter against the Cincinnati Reds on April 30.[36] In June 1940, Dodgers manager Leo Durocher, an ex-Cardinal and heckler without peer, teamed with Medwick to taunt and belittle Cardinals pitcher Bob Bowman in the Cardinals' hotel when they were in New York for an early season series. Bowman and Medwick had been teammates in St. Louis, and bad blood existed between Bowman and Durocher. Bowman got his revenge when Medwick faced him at the plate. On June 19, one week after Medwick had joined the Dodgers, Bowman drilled the new Brooklyn slugger in the head with a fastball, sending him to the hospital for a week. An enraged MacPhail left the stands and charged the mound, challenging Bowman to a fight.[37] Later, he unsuccessfully asked for an attempted murder charge from legal authorities, and Durocher, to no avail, asked the commissioner to ban Bowman from baseball for life. Medwick had some successful years after the head injury but was not the same feared game-breaker he had been. In some ways, this event typified the roustabout, always on-the-edge "Durocher Dodgers" and proved to be quite a backdrop to a successful 1940 campaign. Brooklyn finished in second place, 88–65, four games ahead of the despised Cardinals but 12 behind the World Champion Reds.

Dolph Camilli and Pee Wee Reese led the offensive charge for the Dodgers in 1940. Camilli finished third in the league in slugging average (.529), third in bases on balls (89), and fourth in on-base percentage (.397). His 23 home runs and 271 total bases were the fourth-best National League totals. Reese finished fifth in the league in stolen bases with 15 and hit .272 with five homers.

Walker (batting .308 with six homers and 66 RBIs) and the healed Medwick (batting .300 with 14 homers and 66 RBIs) were also important spokes in Brooklyn's offensive wheel. On the mound, 40-year-old Freddie Fitzsimmons paced the pitching staff, going 16–2 for the highest winning percentage in the league (.889) with a fourth-best 2.81 ERA. Whitlow Wyatt, in his second season since being acquired by MacPhail from the Cleveland Indians, almost matched Fitzsimmons, going 15–4 with a 3.46 ERA. Wyatt finished second in the National League in strikeouts (124) and also strikeouts per game (4.66); he tied for the National League lead in shutouts with five. As a team, the Dodgers were first in triples with 70 and second in home runs with 93; their pitching staff led the National League in strikeouts and fewest walks and was second in team ERA and fewest opponents' runs allowed. Six Dodgers were named to the All-Star team in 1940: Wyatt, Durocher, Medwick, third baseman Cookie Lavagetto, second baseman Pete Coscarart, and catcher Babe Phelps. Brooklyn led the National League in attendance during 1940, drawing 975,978, a slight increase from 1939, a year in which attendance for the league was down about 7 percent. The Dodgers also posted a profit of $125,221, an amount topped only by pennant-winning Cincinnati.

1941

Prior to the start of the 1941 season, Brooklyn lost their first rostered major leaguer to the military, the seldom-used outfielder Joe "Muscles" Gallagher, who was drafted into the Army. Gallagher never played again in the majors after his conscription. MacPhail's skill at trading perhaps reached its apex in 1941. He gave the Cardinals catcher Gus Mancuso, minor league pitcher Joe Pintar, and $65,000 for catcher Mickey Owen. He completely fleeced the Chicago Cubs by talking their general manager, Jim Gallagher, into parting with perennial All-Star, fan favorite, and lifetime .300 hitter Billy Herman for two unknowns—reserve shortstop Johnny Hudson and seldom-used, baby-faced outfielder Charlie Gilbert—and $65,000. In fairness to Gallagher, Cubs manager Jimmie Wilson may have lobbied Gallagher to get rid of Herman. Floundering teams in those days often put esteemed veterans in as player-managers. The affable and trusted Herman would be a logical choice if Wilson were unsuccessful, and his departure could have made Wilson feel more secure. Another star MacPhail plucked from Chicago was Augie Galan, an excellent outfielder who had led the National League in stolen bases twice while playing with the Cubs. The Dodgers demoted right fielder Joe Vosmick to the bench, moved Dixie Walker to right, and inserted young phenom "Pistol Pete" Reiser in center field. These changes, along with the addition of pitching ace Kirby Higbe, put Brooklyn over the top as they won their first pennant in 21 years, going 100–54 to edge out the Cardinals by two and a half games.

A trade MacPhail made for Higbe proved to be the blockbuster, resembling the previous year's transaction for Medwick. MacPhail sent Vito Tamulis, Bill Crouch, and Mickey Livingston (who would later prove his value to the Cubs in 1945), along with the princely sum of $100,000, to the cash-starved Phillies to get Higbe. The Columbia, South Carolina, native had led the National League in strikeouts the year before and was one of the most promising pitchers in the game at that time. The colorful, hard-drinking Higbe had a seventh-grade education and an incredible pitching repertoire. Higbe's biography, *The High Hard One*, a colorful depiction of the major leagues in the late 1930s and '40s, includes an entire chapter devoted to the Dodgers' exploits with Ernest Hemingway during their spring training in Havana. Higbe, Hugh Casey, Curt Davis, Billy Herman, Augie Galan, and many others would join Hemingway in activities ranging from dove shooting to boxing in Hemingway's living room. Whatever the endeavor, hard drinking was always a part of it.

With a record of 100–54, Brooklyn won the pennant for the first time since 1920, finishing two and a half games in front of the Cardinals. Reiser, Camilli, and Medwick paced the Brooklynites at the plate. Reiser, only 22 years old, became the youngest player to ever win a batting title, hitting a robust .343 and finishing 24 points ahead of his nearest rival, the Braves' Johnny Cooney. The young center fielder was also first in slugging average (.588), total bases (299), doubles (39), triples (17), and runs scored (117). His .406 on-base percentage was the fourth best in the league. Reiser also excelled in the field, committing only seven errors in 363 chances. For his magnificent efforts, Reiser won the Chicago Baseball Writers' Association of America Rookie of the Year award and was second in the voting for the National League's Most Valuable Player Award. Camilli's 34 homers and 120 RBIs were both tops in the National League, as was his home run percentage, 6.4. Also, the slugging first baseman was second in slugging average (.566), walks (104), and total bases (294). Camilli proved to be the third toughest out in the National League, with an on-base percentage of .407. Medwick, in what would be his last big year at the plate, hit .318 with 18 home runs and 88 RBIs. His batting average was third best in the league, as were his total bases (278) and runs scored (117). Medwick's .517 slugging average was good enough for fourth best in the National League. In a rare occurrence of offensive domination by one team, Reiser, Camilli, and Medwick were first, second, and fourth in the National League in slugging percentage. Following two serious beanings experienced by Pete Reiser and Pee Wee Reese during the season and remembering Medwick's similar experience the year before, all Dodgers hitters began to wear liners inside their hats while batting.[38]

Kirby Higbe did not disappoint, pacing Dodgers mounds men by finishing 22–9 with a 3.14 ERA. He tied for best in the league in victories and games pitched (48), was second in winning percentage (.710) and innings pitched, was fourth in strikeouts (121), and was fifth in complete games (19). Nearly matching him was Whitlow Wyatt at 22–10 with a 2.34 ERA. Wyatt was the National League's best hurler for total shutouts and tied Higbe for most wins. He was second in ERA, strikeouts (176), hits per game (6.96), and complete games (23); third in innings pitched (288); and fourth in winning percentage (.688). Curt Davis also had an excellent season, finishing first in fewest walks per nine innings (1.57) and third in shutouts (five) while cruising to a 13–7, 2.97 ERA season. Fourth starter Hugh Casey went 14–11 with a 3.89 ERA and appeared in 45 games, the third highest total in the league. Camilli, Medwick, Reiser, Lavagetto, Wyatt, catcher Mickey Owen, and new second baseman Billy Herman were named to the All-Star team; surprisingly, Higbe was overlooked.

Camilli was named the National League's Most Valuable Player, with Reiser second, Wyatt third, Higbe seventh, Dixie Walker tenth, and Herman 11th in the balloting, making for six Dodgers among the top 11 vote getters—an unprecedented domination by one team of that honor.

As a team, the Dodgers ran the table in almost every offensive category, finishing first in runs scored (800), doubles, triples, home runs, batting average, and slugging average but tying for last in stolen bases with only 36. Why risk a steal with all that power? They were second in fewest opponents' runs allowed (581) and also fielding average, while the pitching staff had the highest number of saves and the lowest team ERA (3.14). Their World Series matchup against the crosstown Yankees was a disappointment, with the Dodgers going down 4–1. In the third game, with the series tied at a game apiece and Brooklyn leading 1–0, Yankees pitcher Marius Russo drove a liner off Freddie Fitzsimmons's kneecap, fracturing it, knocking him out of the game. The Yanks got two runs off Casey and took control of the series. While Mickey Owen's dropped third strike in game four is often cited as costing the Dodgers the series, the real reason is that their hitting completely failed, as Yankees pitchers held them to a paltry .182 batting average with only one home run (by Reiser in game four).

With their enthusiastic, loyal fandom, a pennant race against the hated Cardinals, and an upcoming "City Series" against the rival Yankees, Brooklyn's attendance was up almost 25 percent in 1941, to 1,214,910. This was far and away the highest attendance total in the majors that season, the Yankees being a distant second with 964,722. It was the first million draw in Brooklyn history and the first in the National League since Chicago reached the milestone in 1931. The team turned a profit of $146,794.

The Dodgers lost All-Star third baseman Cookie Lavagetto and reserve catcher Don Padgett to the war before the start of the 1942 season. Lavagetto returned to the Dodgers in 1946 and had a minor role with the team through 1947, when he retired. Most people remember him, however, as the manager of the Washington Senators/Minnesota Twins from 1957 through 1961. Padgett also returned in 1946 but was traded to the Boston Braves; he played there and briefly with the Phillies before ending an eight-year career in 1948. MacPhail wasted no time in filling the gaping hole the war effort caused at third base. In December 1941, he traded Pete Coscarart (a former All-Star now expendable with the acquisition of Billy Herman), the reliable Babe Phelps (who went on to have a better year behind the plate than Owen), Luke Hamlin, and outfielder Jimmy Wasdell to Pittsburgh for legendary Pirates shortstop Arky Vaughn.

1942

Brooklyn got off to an extraordinary start in 1942 and was 71–29 after their first 100 games. They barely cooled off, playing .600 ball the rest of the season, and finished with a record of 104–50, four games better than the year before. They finished with the best second-place record since the 1909 Chicago Cubs. They finished second because the Cardinals recorded the best record since the 1909 Pittsburgh Pirates, winning 106 and losing only 48. In July the Dodgers had a ten-game lead, and Pete Reiser was flirting with a .400 batting average when he fractured his skull, crashing into the unforgiving center field wall at St. Louis's Sportsman's Park in a futile attempt to flag down an 11th-inning Enos Slaughter blast. His absence, coupled with St. Louis's amazing 21–5 record during the final month of the season, cost them the pennant. Durocher hurried Reiser back into the lineup, perhaps prematurely, as Reiser finished the season at .310, fourth best in the National League, and was the National League's base-stealing champion in 1942 with 20. Camilli had another peerless season, finishing second in the league in home run percentage (5.0) and RBIs (109), third in home runs (26) and walks (97), and fifth in total bases (247). Medwick contributed with a .300 average and only four home runs, but his 37 doubles were second best in the league, and his 96 RBIs were fourth best. Wyatt went 19–7 on the mound, the league's third-highest win total and the fourth-best winning percentage. Curt Davis, 15–6, sported a 2.36 ERA (third best in the league), had the second-best shutout total with five, and was fifth best in winning percentage. Kirby Higbe went 16–11 with a 3.25 ERA, finishing third in the league for giving up the fewest hits per nine innings, 7.31. Hugh Casey was second in games pitched with 50 and first in saves with 13. The big surprise, however, was a waiver pickup by MacPhail the previous August (as insurance for the 1941 pennant race), Larry French. French was one of the winningest lefties in the majors throughout the 1930s and was a keystone in the Chicago Cubs' pitching staff through most of his career, but the

Cubs gave up on him late in 1941 and MacPhail helped himself to the classy lefty. All he did for the Dodgers in 1942 was go 15–4 with a 1.83 ERA, the best winning percentage in the league and the second-best (by 0.05) ERA. The only positions on the 1942 National League All-Star team without one Dodger able to play it were left and right field. The infield from first to third featured Medwick, Herman, Reese, and Vaughn; Mickey Owen was behind the plate; and Pete Reiser played center field. Pitcher Whitlow Wyatt also made the squad. Owen distinguished himself by hitting his only home run of the season in the game. Brooklyn once again dominated major league baseball in attendance, drawing 1,037,765, their second consecutive year with more than a million fans; by contrast, the World Champion Cardinals drew only 553,552. Brooklyn outdrew the Yankees by more than 100,000 and the Giants by almost 258,000; their profits in 1942 totaled $155,451, more than twice the profit of any other team in the league.

1943

No team in baseball lost as many individuals to World War II as the Dodgers did before the 1943 season. The most significant loss was the departure of MacPhail himself. MacPhail, who had served in World War I, took an officer's commission and would return after the war as a New York Yankees executive, in spite of the protestations of the Brooklyn organization. He was replaced by Branch Rickey, the architect of the St. Louis farm system and their rise to prominence. Nine rostered players and two promising minor leaguers also entered the service: pitchers Hugh Casey, Larry French, and Joe Hatten (a minor leaguer); catchers Cliff Dapper and Herman Franks; shortstops Pee Wee Reese and Stan Rojek; third baseman Lew Riggs; outfielders Pete Reiser, Johnny Rizzo, and Carl Furillo (a minor leaguer). Hugh Casey returned to Brooklyn for the 1946 season, was unhittable and almost single-handedly stopped the Yankees in the 1947 World Series, and was obtained by MacPhail to pitch for the Yankees in 1949. Casey, the most effective National League relief pitcher of the 1940s, lost his stuff and was sent down to the minors thereafter. The crafty right-hander's story ended sadly. After failing in a comeback attempt in the 1951 season, he took his own life. Apparently despondent about his marital breakup, he shot himself in an Atlanta hotel on July 3, 1951, eerily foreshadowing the death of his good friend Hemingway.[39] Larry French never pitched in the majors again after World War II, but he went out in style. The last game he pitched for the Dodgers before entering the Navy was a superb one-hit victory. Joe Hatten returned in 1946 and went 14–11 for the Dodgers, eventually retiring with the Cubs in 1952, when he ended his seven-year career. Cliff Dapper, who had appeared in only eight games for the Dodgers in 1942, never returned to baseball. Herman Franks came back in 1947 with the Philadelphia Athletics, ending his playing days in 1949 with the Giants. He managed the San Francisco Giants from 1965 through 1968 and the Chicago Cubs from 1977 until 1979. Pee Wee Reese was able to continue his Hall of Fame career in 1946. Becoming one of the most popular Dodgers in history, he retired in 1958 after playing 16 years. Stan Rojek also returned in 1946, retiring with the St. Louis Browns in 1952 after an eight-year career. Lew Riggs played one game in 1946, his tenth season in the big leagues, and retired. Pete Reiser returned in 1946, hit only .277 and was out of baseball in 1952 after playing with the Cleveland Indians. Johnny Rizzo never returned to the majors, his five-year career ending with his military induction. Carl Furillo became the Dodgers' starting center fielder in 1946 and went on to great success and popularity in Brooklyn, starring in the legendary Pafko-Snider-Furillo outfield in 1952, appearing in seven World Series, and ending a 15-year, all-Dodgers career with a .299 batting average in 1960.

Needless to say, with all the losses, the Dodgers had holes to fill. Veteran Arky Vaughn moved from third to shortstop to fill the void left by Reese's departure. Diminutive Frenchy Bordargary was picked off the Yankees' roster and played third base. Center field was given to ex-Cubs veteran Augie Galan, and Luis Olmo, the pride of Areca, Puerto Rico, won the left field job. A spot was found for the 18-year-old fireballing pitcher Rex Barney, who appeared in nine games, went 2–2, and had an overly generous 6.35 ERA. While the Dodgers experienced a negative 23-game swing, their 81–72 record was good enough for third place, albeit light-years behind the champion Cardinals and their 105 victories. Many Dodgers also had problems getting along with skipper Leo Durocher, who created a near-mutiny in midseason. An argument with Bobo Newsome, at the time the staff's ace with nine wins, about how to pitch to certain hitters angered the squad and incensed Arky Vaughn. Branch Rickey brought peace by trading Newsome to baseball purgatory, the St. Louis Browns, which did not go over well with the team.[40]

Yet for all their internal troubles, Brooklyn's offense could not be faulted in 1943. Billy Herman hit .330, second only to Stan Musial in the National League, and finished third best in the league in RBIs (100), hits (193), and doubles (41). Vaughn's 20 stolen bases and 112 runs scored were tops in the league. Herman, Vaughn (.305), Olmo (.303), Bordargary (.302), and Dixie Walker (.302) gave Brooklyn five starters who batted higher than .300 for the season, a rare accomplishment. Galan hit nine balata balls out of the park to lead the team in homers, and his .412 on-base percentage was second best in the National League. Camilli slumped, hitting only .246 with six home runs. As a team, Brooklyn was first in doubles and runs scored and second in team batting average and stolen bases. Herman, Galan, Walker, and Owen were named to the National League All-Star team.

The Dodgers did not fare so well on the mound, the loss of French and Casey being too much to overcome. Fitzsimmons appeared in only nine games, went 3–4, and retired at the age of 43 after the season. Wyatt paced the staff with a 14–5 record, the highest winning percentage in the league (.736), and had the fourth-best ERA at 2.49. Higbe fell to 13–10 with a league fifth-best 108 strikeouts. Les Webber and Ed Head attempted to make up for Casey's absence. Webber led the league in saves with ten; Head was fourth in that category with six. Only New York's Ace Adams topped Webber's 54 game appearances, and Head's 47 game appearances were third highest in the league. But team statistics in 1943 proved that Dodgers pitching was much weaker than their hitting. Their ERA at 3.88 was worse than every other National League team in this dead-ball year except last-place New York's, and only New York and Philadelphia gave up more runs than the Dodgers. With no pennant race, player losses, and a fandom much busier with the war effort than in 1942, Brooklyn's attendance fell a precipitous 36 percent to 661,739 in a season in which all of baseball's attendance was down over 12 percent. In spite of this drop, no team in the major leagues outdrew the Dodgers in 1943, the Yankees being the closest with 618,330 paid admissions. Brooklyn received $150,000 from the 50,000 watt station WOR for radio broadcasting rights, almost three times the league average, but their $271,424 payroll was larger than any other team except the Yankees, and their minor league affiliates lost an incredible $93,551. The Dodgers posted a consolidated loss of $62,719 for the season, the first time they were in the red since 1938.

1944

As the 1944 season began, the Dodgers lost five more players, four to the war effort. Higbe was drafted and would not return until 1946, when he was 17–8, picking up right where he left off. He was traded to Pittsburgh in 1947 and to the New York Giants in 1950, ending a successful 12-year major league career. He hung on in the minor leagues for years after that, hoping for one more chance, before becoming a prison guard after serving time himself for passing bad checks.[41] Nineteen-year-old Rex Barney was also lost to the war effort, coming back in 1946 to appear in 16 games. He played in both the 1947 and 1949 World Series for the Dodgers and won 15 games in 1948. His six-year major league career ended in 1950. Outfielder Gene Hermanski came out of the service in 1946, contributing largely as a fourth outfielder until 1951, when he was traded to Chicago. He ended his nine-year career in 1953 with the Pittsburgh Pirates, a career highlighted by appearances in seven World Series games in 1947 and four in 1949. But the losses of Billy Herman and Arky Vaughn cost the Dodgers their two most productive hitters and one of the best keystone combinations in the game. Herman returned in 1946 but was traded to the Boston Braves before the season was half over. At the end of the season, he was traded to Pittsburgh, where owners John Galbreath and Bing Crosby named him manager in 1947. Vaughn decided to stay on his farm in 1944 instead of playing for Leo Durocher; he came back to Brooklyn in 1947, hitting .325 in 64 games, after Burt Shotton replaced the volatile Durocher as the Dodgers' manager.

These losses opened the roster to a bevy of youngsters. Twenty-one-year-old infielder Eddie Basinski, a professional violinist in the off-season, played in 39 games. Four teenagers dotted the spring training roster. 16-year-old shortstop Tommy Brown appeared in 46 games. Eighteen-year-old shortstop Gene Mauch played in five games. Another 18-year-old, Cal McLish, joined the bull pen and appeared in 23 games, going 3–10 with an astronomical 7.82 ERA.[42] McLish, the pride of Anadarko, Oklahoma, was an ambidextrous pitcher in the minors, sometimes pitching lefty and sometimes righty. He only pitched right-handed in the majors, outlasting all his young teammates, playing 15 years with the Dodgers, Pirates, Cubs, Indians, Reds, and Phillies. Tommy Warren, age 17, pitched in 22 games but never pitched another season in the majors due to injuries he suffered in World War II after he was drafted. Twenty-one-year-old Howie "Steeple" Schultz also made the squad and played in 45 games. Brooklyn became the first team to offer a contract to a returning World War II veteran. Red Durrett, discharged from the Marine Corps after being shell-shocked in the battle for Guadalcanal, played 11 games in the outfield.[43]

The Dodgers experienced a negative 18 game turnabout, avoiding the cellar by one and a half games, with a seventh-place 63–91 record, 42 games behind the World Champion Cardinals. They ended a late June home stand after a five-game winning streak helped them reach third place, their high water mark for the season, but their fate was sealed when they lost 15 consecutive games during a long western road trip.

Replacing Herman and Vaughn up the middle initially was the 18-year-old Gene Mauch at shortstop and manager Leo Durocher at second, but Mauch lasted only six games and the 38-year-old Durocher got injured. Brooklyn got so desperate for infield help that they called up the fuzzy-cheeked Tommy Brown. Brown, a native of Brooklyn, would make baseball history the following year. Eddie Miksis, age 17, played infield in 26 games. The Dodgers finally settled on the young and fiery Eddie Stanky, obtained from the Cubs for pitcher Bob Chipman, and journeyman shortstop Bobby Bragan, obtained from the Phillies in 1943 for pitcher Tex "Texas Jack" Kraus. Howie "Steeple" Schultz replaced Camilli at first base. At six feet, six inches, Schultz was one of the few major leaguers exempt from the military because of his height. A basketball star at Hamline University, the St. Paul native was also a pioneering player in the National Basketball Association, playing for Anderson, Fort Wayne, and Minneapolis between 1946 and 1953. Dixie Walker and Augie Galan were the only bright spots in this dismal season. Walker won the batting title in the National League, hitting .357, ten points ahead of Stan Musial. He was second in on-base percentage (.434), fourth in slugging percentage (.529), and fourth in total bases (283). Walker earned the Outstanding Player of the Year Award, later named the Sid Mercer Award, by the admiring local New York sportswriters. Galan hit .318 with 12 homers and 93 RBIs. He was also first in the National League in bases on balls with 101, second in doubles with 43, and third in on-base percentage at .426. Galan, Walker, and Owen were once again named to the National League All-Star team.

Curt Davis led the pitching staff with a weak 10–11 record and a 3.34 ERA. Davis was third best in the league in fewest walks per game (1.81) and tied for fourth in total saves with four. Les Webber appeared in 48 games; the only National League pitcher with more appearances was the Giants' Ace Adams. As a team, the Dodgers still finished second in team batting average (.269), but they were last in opponents' runs allowed, errors committed, fielding average, ERA (an astronomical 4.68), and walks allowed. In a year in which major league baseball saw a 17 percent increase in attendance, the Dodgers experienced an 8 percent decline to 640,110. As a testimonial to their popularity and loyal following, however, only the Cubs and Giants outdrew the Dodgers in spite of their 91 losses that season. Financially, they barely broke even in 1944, posting a $3,923 profit.

1945

Brooklyn, with 34 players still active in the armed services,[44] did not have high expectations when they opened their 1945 spring training camp in Bear Mountain, New York. Branch Rickey reached into the minors for two more pitchers and invited 19-year-old Ralph Branca and Leroy Pfund, the pride of Wheaton College, to spring training.[45] In March he dispatched veteran pitching mainstay Whitlow Wyatt to the Philadelphia Phillies for $20,000. Augie Galan replaced Howie Schultz at first, young Eddie Basinski came up from the minors for good to replace Bobby Bragan at shortstop, and veteran minor leaguer Goody Rosen, who appeared sparingly with the Dodgers in 1944, came in to play center field. In spite of Rickey's youth movement, there was room on the roster for 42-year-old Babe Herman, who had been out of the majors since 1937. The lifetime .324 hitter appeared in 37 games, batted .265, and hit the last home run (the 181st) of his career during the 1945 season.

ST. LOUIS CARDINALS

THE ST. LOUIS Cardinals were the most successful franchise in the National League during the World War II era. Between 1940 and 1945, the Cardinals finished third once, second twice, and first three times, winning the World Series in 1942 and 1944. The only other team in the majors with six first-division finishes during that period was the New York Yankees, and their three pennants, two third-place finishes, and one fourth-place finish did not match St. Louis's success. In spite of sharing the second-smallest National League market with an American League franchise, the Cardinals' domination stemmed from their farm system, the largest and best developed in baseball. The man most responsible for their organization and success was their general manager, Branch Rickey.

By 1940 Rickey was in his third decade as vice president and business manager of the Cardinals. In his early years running the team, the Cardinals could not generate the revenue their competitors could and consequently could not buy the contracts of the top players in the minor leagues. Rickey envisioned a graduated baseball organization with the Cardinals on the top and "feeder teams" underneath. In 1919 the team bought a half interest in a minor league team in Fort Smith, Arkansas, and by 1930 they gained control of four other teams. When the Depression hit, many minor league teams were struggling financially. Their economic woes opened the door for Rickey to expand the teams under the Cardinals' control. St. Louis would take on the team's economic risks in consideration for exclusive rights to the players. By 1940 the Cardinals controlled 32 teams and had contractual agreements with eight others.[46]

To fill these rosters, the Cardinals relied on the largest scouting system in the major leagues, along with extensive contacts with college programs. Rickey was also a great believer in open tryout camps; even if no players were signed, the publicity and exposure were well worth the effort. Because they had so many teams, the Cardinals were not as hesitant as other teams were to take a chance on a marginal young ballplayer. While teams like Cleveland and the New York Yankees had well-run farm systems, neither team's system compared with Rickey's in sheer size. Immediately before World War II, many teams, such as the Philadelphia Phillies, Pittsburgh Pirates, and St. Louis Browns, did not even have working agreements with one minor league squad. Until 1941 the Chicago Cubs had one team: the Los Angeles Angels. The Cardinals had more than 600 minor leaguers contractually bound to them in the early 1940s before the United States entered World War II—almost one out of every six players in the minors.

With a surplus of talent and more players capable of playing major league–caliber baseball than they had major league roster spots for, the

Cardinals' minor league teams were usually successful as well. Their winning led to a loyal following and good attendance, especially since baseball was more of a local pastime in that era, with no television and little extended radio coverage of major league contests. The Cardinals enjoyed a profitable, consistent revenue stream from their minor league franchises and sometimes would take pains to foster their support. The Cardinals' organization was known, for instance, to apologize to the fans in a minor league city if they called up one of the team's star players to join their major league roster.

One might think that this commitment to minor league success would potentially frustrate and disillusion the promising young ballplayer who may have had a faster track to the majors if he had signed with another team. Rickey would often avoid this problem by structuring salaries based on how many years a player was in the organization instead of what level he had attained. For example, if a player was in his fourth year in the Cardinals' organization, he probably had a contract specifying what his salary would be that year, whether he was playing in the low minors or the high minors. If the player reached maximum potential well short of a higher level, his contract would simply not be renewed. In some ways, this arrangement benefited the player, but in many more ways, it benefited the Cardinals.[47] The player benefited in that he had a guarantee of earning a decent wage regardless of what level in the minors he was playing. To a young high school prospect from a family struggling with the Depression, this was a tremendously important factor. The lowest paid minor leaguer toiling on a Class D team in 1940 made approximately $85 a month; the average monthly wage for all industries in the United States in that year was roughly $105. Few prewar jobs paid 80 percent of the average American wage to someone barely out of high school.[48]

The Cardinals, however, benefited even more. They made more money than any other team selling off players because they had so many available. They did not suffer a financial drain from buying players' contracts from minor league teams like many of their competitors did. Their salary structure served to keep their major league payroll low also. Most first- or second-year Cardinals were making the same money as their counterparts in the minors who had the same number of years in the organization.

This procedure also allowed Rickey to handle his major league roster to his best financial advantage. When a successful Cardinal was reaching what Rickey considered a top-level major league salary, he would often trade or sell that player to another team. In April 1938, Rickey sold Cardinal great Dizzy Dean to the Cubs for $185,000; Dean was washed up with a sore arm, and Rickey managed to get pitching mainstays Curt Davis and Clyde Shoun, along with outfielder Tuck Stainback, as part of the deal. In June 1940, Rickey sold an aging Ducky Medwick to the Brooklyn Dodgers for four players and $125,000. Between 1939 and 1942, the Cardinals received more than a half million dollars by selling the contracts of established but aging players to other clubs, replacing them with the much lower-paid youngsters up from the minors. With profitable minor league teams, having a lower pay scale for younger players, replacing high-salaried, established players with those less expensive younger ones, and having a knack of getting other teams to overpay for those established players, Rickey and the Cardinals had a very effective and profitable organization. No wonder that this franchise, whose highest attendance between 1930 and 1945 was 633,645 during an era when the Cubs, Dodgers, Giants, Tigers, and Yankees would often approach or exceed 1 million per season, was usually the most profitable team in baseball.

These practices also proved to be extremely lucrative for Rickey himself. His contract called for him to receive 20 percent of the team's total profits every season over and above his reported $80,000 salary. His high compensation, in stark contrast to the team's low payroll, alienated and embittered many of the players. It also was a factor in his downfall in St. Louis.

In 1938 Judge Landis earned the nickname the Great Emancipator by granting free agency to about 100 Cardinals minor leaguers because of what he considered to be nefarious contractual player personnel practices by the Cardinals organization, particularly singling out Rickey for criticism. Cardinals owner Sam Breadon was hurt by this development and did not renew Rickey's contract with the Cardinals when it ended in 1942. At that time, the Brooklyn Dodgers lured him, eager to fill the spot of their departed Larry MacPhail.

1940

In the 1940 season, the Cardinals went through two managers before settling on Billy Southworth to lead them to an 84–69 record, good enough for third place but a distant 16 games behind the World Champion Reds.

Ray Blades was at the helm for the first 38 games of the season but was unable to inspire the troops past a poor 14–24 record. Mike Gonzalez filled in for an interim period, but the team went 1–5 under his direction for six games. So, with the team barely playing .333 ball at 15–29, Southworth came in, engineering a remarkable .633 winning percentage as the team went 69–40 under his direction for the remainder of the season. Southworth is often overlooked today, but he was one of the greatest managers of his era. While Durocher, Grimm, McKechnie, and Stengel are names more familiar in the annals of managing, Southworth, who had an impeccable record as a minor league manager in the Cardinals' organization, won two World Series and four pennants, had 11 first-division finishes in 13 years of managing, and went 1,064–729 for a .593 winning percentage during his major league managerial career.

Johnny Mize finished second in the Most Valuable Player voting after hitting .314 with 43 home runs and 137 RBIs, leading the league in both of the latter two categories. Mize also finished first in slugging percentage (.635, which was 100 points higher than his nearest competitor, Chicago's Bill Nicholson), total bases (368), and home run percentage (7.4). Rookie right fielder Enos "Country" Slaughter, a big reason why Rickey chose to trade Ducky Medwick to Brooklyn in June 1940, hit an excellent .307 with 17 homers and 73 RBIs. Center fielder Terry Moore almost matched Slaughter's production, hitting .304 with 17 home runs and 64 RBIs. Moore's 18 stolen bases were the third-highest total in the league. Medwick was traded after only 37 games, hitting .304 in 158 plate appearances. Left fielder Ernie Koy, obtained from the Dodgers in the Medwick deal, rounded out the Cardinals' offense hitting .310 with eight homers and 52 RBIs. Moore, Mize, and Cardinal–Dodger Medwick were named to the 1940 All-Star team.

Ex-Cubs pitching mainstay Lon Warneke, "the Arkansas Hummingbird," paced the staff with a 16–10 record and a 3.14 ERA. Fiddler Bill McGee, the pride of Batchtown, Illinois, also went 16–10, but with a softer 3.80 mark. Clyde Shoun, one of the players obtained in the Dizzy Dean deal with the Cubs, led the league in game appearances with 54, and his five saves were the fourth-highest total in the National League.

As a team, the Cardinals were first in home runs (hitting 119, which was 26 more than their nearest competitor in this category, Brooklyn) and slugging percentage, second in total runs scored, and second in team batting average. As was customary, the Cardinals outdrew their crosstown rivals, the Browns, but their extremely thin attendance total of 324,078 represented a 19 percent drop from the year before. Major league baseball as a whole experienced a 10 percent increase between 1939 and 1940. In spite of their strong third-place finish, every National League team except the Boston Braves and the Philadelphia Phillies outdrew the Cardinals in 1940. They still posted a profit of $68,190, higher than every National League team except for Brooklyn and Cincinnati.

1941

The Cardinals improved even more in 1941. Rickey was busy between seasons making roster changes that resulted in new faces at four positions. Second baseman Joe Orengo was dispatched to the New York Giants for cash in November 1940. The following month, Stu Martin went to Pittsburgh for cash. Also in December, starting catcher Mickey Owen was traded to Brooklyn for catcher Gus Mancuso, minor league hurler Joe Pintar, and $65,000. Owen would be a cog in the Dodgers' machine that won the National League pennant in the 1941 season but would become the goat in the World Series with his famous dropped third strike against the Yankees. Cash was also the compensation when left fielder Ernie Koy left for the Cincinnati Reds in May 1941. The last major transaction involved the Cardinals and New York Giants. Fiddler Bill McGee went to New York in exchange for pitcher Harry Gumbert, pitcher Paul Dean, and a small sum of money.

Replacing Orengo at second was the 23-year-old pride of Florissant, Missouri, Frank "Creepy" Crespi. Jimmy Brown replaced Martin at shortstop, and Nebraskan Johnny Hopp became the starting left fielder. Mancuso replaced Owen behind the plate.

These changes worked well, as the Cardinals notched an impressive 13-game improvement to 97–56 for the third-best record in the major leagues that season. Unfortunately, the Brooklyn Dodgers went 100–54 to win the pennant. The Cardinals were in the race throughout the season but missed the pennant by two and a half games. Johnny Mize led all St. Louis hitters in 1941 with a .317 batting average, 16 home runs, and 100 RBIs. Mize finished first in the league in doubles with 39 and third in slugging percentage with a lusty .535. His RBI total was also third highest in the league, and only three National Leaguers hit for a higher average. Hopp responded well to his starting job, hitting .303, posting the third-highest number of triples (11) in the league, and finishing fifth in stolen bases with 15. Enos Slaughter experienced no sophomore slump whatsoever, hitting .311 with a slugging percentage of .496, fifth highest in the league. Mize, Slaughter, and center fielder Terry Moore earned spots on the National League All-Star squad.

Cardinal pitchers distinguished themselves as well during the 1941 season. Ernie White went 17–7, posting the third-best winning percentage in the league, and had the league's third-best ERA, 2.40. Lon Warneke went 17–9, a .654 winning percentage, fifth best in the league. The highlight of Warneke's season was a no-hitter on August 30 against the Cincinnati Reds.[49] Howie Krist set a new National League record by winning ten games without a loss, in spite of an elevated 4.03 ERA. Mort Cooper's 118 strikeouts were surpassed by only four National League hurlers, and his average of 5.69 strikeouts per game was second best in the league. Freddy Hutchinson's five saves tied him for fifth place in that statistic. No Cardinal pitchers earned trips to the All-Star Game, however.

As a team, the Cards tied for the best batting average at .272 and were second only to Brooklyn in runs scored. Their pitching staff was first in strikeouts with 659, a full 56 more than their nearest competitors in that category, the Dodgers. Their team ERA was third in the league at 3.19, the league's third best, very close behind Cincinnati (3.17) and the pennant-winning Dodgers (3.14). Cardinal attendance soared in 1941 to 633,645, an amazing 96 percent improvement. While they drew almost four fans for every one that showed up to see the St. Louis Browns, three National League teams and five in the American League had higher totals at the gate. The Cardinals' profit of $154,557 topped the National League.

1942

St. Louis added some impressive new faces in the lineup for 1942, and one of them came to symbolize the team in the postwar era. They lost only one player to the military before the start of the season, pitcher Johnny Grodzicki. His right leg, wounded in combat, never completely healed, and he lost his effectiveness when he returned in 1946. He made postwar pitching appearances in three games in 1946 and sixteen in '47, totaling only 23 innings of work. He left baseball after the 1947 season. Howie Pollet and Johnny Beazley joined the pitching staff, Whitey Kurowski earned the starting job at third base, star pitcher Mort Cooper's younger brother Walker became the starting catcher, and a lithe left-handed hitter with an unusual batting stance and one of the most beautiful swings in history earned the left field job: Stan Musial, of Donora, Pennsylvania. Pollet and Beazley pitched so well that general manager Branch Rickey took the bold step of releasing one of 1941's 17-game winners, Lon Warneke. Warneke returned to the Chicago Cubs in July, a cash deal netting St. Louis the princely sum of $75,000. Veteran catcher Gus Mancuso, on the bubble with a high salary and the arrival of Walker Cooper, was sold to the New York Giants in a cash transaction. The Cardinals went on to dominate like no other team had in 35 years, winning 106 games while losing 48, crowning their achievement with a comparatively easy conquest of the New York Yankees in the World Series. The Cardinals won–lost record was the best in the National League since the Chicago Cubs went 107–45 in 1907.

If only winning the pennant had been as easy as taking the World Series. Another New York team, the Dodgers, was in a heated race with St. Louis throughout and was actually in first place for most of season. Brooklyn won 71 of their first 100 games, and the Cards were ten games out of first place in early August. But as Brooklyn faded with the loss of Pete Reiser and Durocher being reluctant to rest his regulars, the Cardinals went an amazing 30–6 in the final five weeks of the season. St. Louis moved into first place on September 13 and won the pennant by two and a half games. Enos "Country" Slaughter, the pride of Roxboro, North Carolina, emerged as one of the premier players in baseball. No National Leaguer topped his 292 total bases, 188 base hits, and 17 triples. His team-leading .318 batting average and 100 runs scored were both second best in the league. Slaughter was third in slugging average (.494), on-base percentage (.412), and RBIs (98, which also led the team). No Cardinal hit more than Slaughter's modest 13 home runs. Slaughter, however, became embittered in the off-season due to the Cardinals' penurious salary offer. Stan Musial broke in with a very impressive season for a rookie. The Donora Greyhound's .315 batting average and ten triples were both good enough for third in the league. Shortstop Marty Marion led the league in doubles with 38; Johnny Hopp again finished among the league's top five base stealers with 14. Slaughter, catcher Walker Cooper (batting .281 with seven homers and 65 RBIs), all-purpose infielder Jimmy Brown, and center field defensive standout Terry Moore (batting .288 with six homers and 49 RBIs) all earned All-Star spots. Moore's gravity-defying leaping catch over a lunging Stan Musial to rob Joe DiMaggio of extra bases was a defining moment in the World Series and, according to Cards manager Southworth, the greatest catch he ever saw.[50]

The Cardinals' pitching was just as dominant as their hitting. Their team ERA of 2.55 was the lowest for any team since 1919, when the Cincinnati Reds' staff posted a 2.23 team ERA in the dead-ball era. Mort Cooper anchored the staff with a 22–7 record and a spellbinding 1.78 ERA over 279 innings. His victory total, ERA, and ten shutouts were the highest in the league. Cooper, aided by his brother Walker working behind the plate, was second in innings pitched, strikeouts (152), and strikeouts per game (4.91); he also had 22 complete games, third best in the league. Cooper won the National League Most Valuable Player Award in 1942. Johnny Beazley proved that Rickey's hunch to sell Warneke was correct. The Rookie of the Year went 21–6 with a 2.13 ERA, both figures being second best in the league. He also appeared in 43 games, a total surpassed only by Brooklyn's Hugh Casey and New York's Ace Adams. Warneke appeared in only 15 games for Chicago and went 5–7. Beazley became the first rookie in history to defeat the New York Yankees in a World Series game, and he had two complete game victories in the series to emerge as the newest of St. Louis's many heroes. Howie Krist went 13–3 for the World Champs, giving him a record of 23–3 (an .885 winning percentage) over two seasons. Mort Cooper made the National League All-Star pitching staff, which inexplicably overlooked Beazley.

As a team, the Cardinals were first in the following categories: runs scored, fewest opponents' runs allowed, doubles, triples, batting average, slugging average, pitchers' strikeouts, shutouts, and team ERA. They were second in stolen bases, fewest walks allowed, and saves. The sole team weakness was hitting the long ball; only the Pittsburgh Pirates and Philadelphia Phillies hit fewer home runs. Amazingly, three teams (Brooklyn, New York, and Chicago) had a higher paid attendance total than the juggernaut 1942 Cardinals. Only 553,552 fans paid to see one of the most dominant teams in baseball history play during the regular season. Cardinals profits were down as a result, with the team clearing $63,552, an amount, however, that only Brooklyn surpassed. The 1942 season would be the last in which Branch Rickey would run the organization. Owner Sam Breadon did not renew Rickey's contract after the 1942 season, still smarting from Commissioner Landis's rebuke over the farm system issues several years earlier. The Brooklyn Dodgers saw to it that Rickey's unemployment was very brief.

1943

World War II caused many teams to lose players to conscription before the 1943 season, and the Cardinals—losing three All-Stars, two pitchers, and two reserves—were no exception. Enos Slaughter went into the Army Air Corps. Jimmy Brown, Johnny Beazley, Johnny Blattner, Creepy Crespi, and Terry Moore were also drafted. In July, Howie Pollet, in the middle of a brilliant season, was inducted into the Army Air Corps. At the time, he had an 8–4 record with a sterling 1.75 ERA.

Enos Slaughter would return to the starting Cardinals lineup in 1946. His 19-year career ended in 1959 with the Milwaukee Braves, where he was traded from the Yankees. Slaughter was a never-quit ballplayer who retired with a career .300 batting average and a .291 average in five different World Series, two with the Cardinals and three with New York. His Hall of Fame induction occurred in 1985. Terry Moore returned to St. Louis in 1946 and ended his successful 11-year career after the 1948 season. A four-time All-Star, Moore managed the Philadelphia Phillies for 77 games in 1954. He is still remembered as one of the most outstanding defensive outfielders in history. Johnny Beazley's fate was more unfortunate. He, too, returned in 1946 but was not the same. Overused and sometimes under orders to pitch in service games even though his arm was injured, Beazley developed chronic arm trouble and went 7–6 in three seasons after World War II, retiring from baseball in 1949. Creepy Crespi never played again in the major leagues, the reason perhaps being more comical than tragic. Confined to a wheelchair after breaking his leg in a service game, Crespi decided to enter a wheelchair race. He could not stop in time and collided with a wall, refracturing the still healing limb, and never played ball again.[51] Johnny Blattner was destined for a kinder fate. Released by the Cardinals after his discharge from the military but signed by the New York Giants, Blattner played regularly in 1946, '47, and '48. He was traded to the Phillies in 1949 and retired after that season. Jimmy Brown, 36 years old after his military discharge, played in 79 games for the Pittsburgh Pirates and retired after the 1946 season. At age 25, Howie Pollet came back to go 21–10 for the Cardinals in 1946 after he left the service. Pollet retired after the 1956 season, having won 131 games in his career, which included nine years with the Cardinals as well as several seasons with the Pirates, Cubs, and White Sox.

With all these losses, the Cardinals had huge holes to fill in center field, right field, and second base, along with the second spot in their pitching rotation, as the 1943 season began. Musial moved from left to right field, and the Cardinals sent Buster Adams, Coaker Triplett, and Dain Clay to the Philadelphia Phillies for Danny Litwhiler and Earl Naylor. Litwhiler, with a new lease on life after going from a last-place team to a World Champion, started in left field. Harry "the Hat" Walker was promoted from his reserve status to the center field position. Rookie Lou Klein won the starting job at second base. Max Lanier, Harry Brecheen, Harry Gumbert, Murry Dickson, George Munger, and Howie Pollet (before his midseason conscription) all took turns as effective starters. The only lineup change not dictated by World War II was at first base, where Ray Sanders beat out Johnny Hopp. As a testimonial to the strength of their organization and the managerial skill of Southworth, the Cardinals did not miss a beat in spite of all the personnel changes. They went 105–49, winning another pennant, this time in a breeze. The Cincinnati Reds finished second, a distant 18 games behind, and the hated Dodgers were in third, almost a month (23 games) behind.

Stan Musial won the Most Valuable Player Award, and teammate Walker Cooper was second in the voting. Musial's offensive statistics were astonishing; he finished first in seven of the 12 major hitting categories. Musial won the batting title with a .357 average and finished first in several other categories as well: slugging average at .562, on-base average at .425, hits with 220, doubles with 48, triples with an astounding 20, and total bases with 347. He struck out only 18 times in 617 at bats. Stan the Man finished behind only Arky Vaughn for most runs scored in the National League and tied with teammate Walker Cooper for fifth in RBIs. Cooper had the league's third-best batting average (.318), tied for the third-highest slugging percentage (.463), and tied for fifth in RBIs with Musial at 81. Once again, almost every change in the lineup paid off for Southworth, a testimonial to the incredible depth of the Cardinals' entire organization. Rookie second baseman Lou Klein hit .287 with seven home runs and 62 RBIs and had the league's fourth-highest total bases, 257. Harry Walker hit .294 and had 14 assists playing center field. Shortstop Marty Marion, third baseman Whitey Kurowski, Cooper, Musial, and Walker all earned spots on the All-Star team.

Cardinals pitchers more than held their own in 1943. Mort Cooper went 21–8, tying Elmer Riddle for the most wins in the National League. He finished second in strikeouts with 141 and shutouts with six, and his ERA of 2.30 was surpassed by only two National League pitchers, both of whom were teammates. Southpaw Max Lanier was one of those two. The best player Denton, North Carolina, ever produced came upon his craft in an interesting fashion. He broke his right arm as a youngster and became so impatient waiting for it to heal that he simply taught himself to throw left-handed. His son Hal was an infielder with the San Francisco Giants and New York Yankees for ten years (1964–73). In 1943 Lanier went 15–7 for the third-best winning percentage in the league. He struck out 5.19 batters per nine innings, second best in the league, and had a fourth-highest strikeout total of 123. Lanier's sparkling ERA, 1.91, was second in the league, right behind teammate Howie Pollet, perhaps the most dominating pitcher in 1943 for the 118 innings he pitched. Pollet was first in fewest hits allowed per nine innings at 6.31, his 1.75 ERA was one of the lowest in years, and he finished third in most strikeouts per nine innings, 4.64. Harry Gumbert went 10–5 and Howie Krist 11–5, giving him a record of 34–8 (an .809 winning percentage) over three years. Harry Brecheen was 9–6, Murry Dickson 8–2, and George Munger 9–5. Cooper, Lanier, and Pollet all made the National League All-Star pitching staff. Cooper and his brother Walker finished fifth and second, respectively, in the voting for the 1943 Most Valuable Player Award. No brother combination in history had ever achieved such recognition.

The pitching of many teams benefited with the balata ball in 1943, but the Cardinals were one of the few teams that did not suffer because of it at the plate. As a team, St. Louis was first in batting average and slugging average, second in home runs to the last-place New York Giants, and second in triples, hitting 72 of them, one less than the Pittsburgh Pirates. They led the league in fewest opponents' runs allowed, complete games, strikeouts, shutouts, and team ERA (an extremely low 2.57). Only the second-place Cincinnati Reds had a better fielding average. The World Series was another story, however, as the New York Yankees this time had the upper hand, 4–1.

The great Cardinals hitters slumped badly, scoring nine runs in the five games and hitting a paltry .224. Perhaps the biggest Cardinals story in the series occurred before the second game. Mort Cooper was slated to pitch with brother Walker behind the plate. The brothers learned that their father, a mail carrier in Atherton, Missouri, had died unexpectedly the night before; Southworth let them decide if they still wanted to play. They dedicated the game to their father, and the Cooper battery put away the Yankees on six hits for St. Louis's only World Series victory.

Like 11 of the 16 major league teams, the Cardinals experienced an attendance decline in 1943, drawing 517,135 for the regular season, a seven percent decline compared with a 12 percent dip for the rest of major league baseball. Their profit of $105,791, again highest in the league, was almost twice that of Pittsburgh, the second-most profitable club that season. An examination of their balance sheet in 1943 explains why. Their $195,597 payroll was only $3,000 more than the team payroll in 1939 and $24,000 less than it was in 1929. In spite of their complete domination of the National League that season, only three teams had lower payrolls: Philadelphia, Pittsburgh, and Boston. The Cardinals' payroll was only $10,000 more than Philadelphia's in 1943. While their radio broadcast revenues of $39,200 were nearly the league's lowest, the team earned more than $100,000 from concession sales and an unheard-of $94,242 from playing exhibition games. The team with the second-highest exhibition game revenue in 1943 was the Chicago Cubs, which at $11,695 had little more than a tenth of St. Louis's total.

1944

Few player transactions occurred before the 1944 season, and the Cardinals had to reload the roster as five more players answered Uncle Sam's call. Starting center fielder Harry Walker and four pitchers—Al Brazle,

Murry Dickson, Howie Krist, and Ernie White—all left for World War II. Walker returned in 1946 when he had an off year but won the National League batting title in 1947 with a lusty .363 average after being traded early in the season to the Philadelphia Phillies. He also played for the Cubs and Reds before ending his playing career back in St. Louis in 1955. That same year, he started his managerial career, being named skipper of the Cardinals. Walker also managed in Pittsburgh and Houston, guiding his teams to first-division finishes five times in nine seasons. Brazle, the pride of Loyal, Oklahoma, returned to help the Cardinals win the World Series in 1946 and ended a ten-year career, all in St. Louis, after 1954, compiling an impressive 97–64 record. Dickson led the National League in winning percentage after his military discharge in 1946, going 15–6. One of the few players to pitch in three different decades, Dickson broke into the majors in 1939 and retired after 1959, pitching in Pittsburgh, Philadelphia, Kansas City, and New York (with the Yankees) before ending his career. Krist never regained his effectiveness, pitched 18 innings after he left the service in 1946, and left the majors after that season. White, the best pitcher to ever call Pacolet Mills, South Carolina, his hometown, hung on through the 1948 season after he left the service in late 1945. White's arm was worn out, and he never regained the magic he had in 1941. He hooked up with the Boston Braves for the 1946, '47, and '48 seasons and appeared in only 28 games after World War II. Johnny Hopp came back to the starting lineup to fill the void left by Walker. Emil Verban replaced Lou Klein at second base. Ted Wilks came up from the minors, pitching brilliantly. Rookies Freddy Schmidt and Al Jurisich also joined the pitching staff. Pepper Martin, one of the original members of the "Gashouse Gang" Cardinals teams in the early 1930s, came out of retirement at the age of 40, playing 40 games in the outfield. He hit the last two homers of his career and with a respectable .279 batting average in 1944. Once again, the Cardinals breezed through the National League with a record of 105–49, winning more than 100 games for the third consecutive season. They were out of first place only four days during the entire season and went into first permanently on May 7, never to relinquish it. Their record on Labor Day was 91–30, but they went 14–19 after that, at one point losing eight straight to second-place Pittsburgh. In spite of the Cardinals' stumble in September and Pittsburgh's peerless play the last two months of the season, the Pirates still finished 14 games behind. St. Louis crowned their 1944 achievements with a victory in the fabled Streetcar Series over their landlords, the St. Louis Browns.

Stan Musial, Walker Cooper, Whitey Kurowski, Ray Sanders, and Johnny Hopp paced the potent St. Louis offense. Musial led the league in slugging average (.549), on-base percentage (.440), and doubles (51) and tied Chicago's Phil Cavarretta for the most hits (197). His .347 batting average was second best in the National League, as were his 312 total bases and 112 runs scored. Becoming more patient at the plate, the young Musial walked 90 times, the fourth-highest total in the league. Hopp made up for the loss of Harry Walker in center field, posting the fourth-best batting average in the league, .336, along with a fourth-best 15 stolen bases. Kurowski's 20 homers paced the Cardinals; only four National Leaguers had more in 1944. Sanders hit .295 with 12 homers and 102 RBIs, the team's highest RBI total and the fourth best in the league. Besides shepherding the best pitching staff in baseball, Cooper hit .317 with 13 homers and 72 RBIs. Marty Marion won the Most Valuable Player Award, leading all major league shortstops in fielding average. Cooper, Kurowski, Marion, and Musial were named to the 1944 National League All-Star team.

The depth of the St. Louis farm system proved itself once again as newcomers capably replaced Cardinals pitchers off to war. Mort Cooper paced the staff with a 22–7 record, the second-highest victory total in the league, good enough for the third-highest winning percentage. Only Ed Heusser and Bucky Walters had a better ERA than Cooper's 2.46. He also finished fifth in strikeouts and complete games. Rookie Ted Wilks had one of the best seasons of any rookie in history, going 17–4 with a 2.65 ERA. Wilks had the best winning percentage in the league, allowed the fewest hits per nine innings, and tied teammate Max Lanier for the fourth-best National League ERA. Lanier also matched Wilks's victory total, going 17–12, with the National League's second-highest strikeout total, 141. Brecheen went 16–5, for the league's second-highest winning percentage. Munger went 11–3 with a 1.34 ERA in 130 innings, Schmidt was 7–3, and Jurisich went 7–9. Lanier and Munger were on the National League staff in the 1944 All-Star Game at Forbes Field.

Few teams in history dominated team statistical categories like the 1944 St. Louis Cardinals. They were first in the following categories: runs scored, fewest opponents' runs allowed, doubles, home runs, batting average, slugging average, fewest errors, most double plays, fielding average, most strikeouts, shutouts, and team ERA. They were second in triples and complete games. If they had a weakness, it was in stolen bases; only the moribund Philadelphia Phillies had fewer than the Cards' total of 37. They won the Streetcar Series four games to two, but the Browns gave them a much more difficult time than most people thought they would. Incredibly, four National League teams—New York, Chicago, Brooklyn, and Pittsburgh—had higher regular season paid attendance in 1944. Even their rivals the Browns outdrew the Cardinals, with a paid attendance total about 10 percent higher than the Cards' total of 461,968. Once again the most profitable team in the National League, the Cardinals cleared $146,417 in their championship season.

The Cardinals became the fifth team in major league history to win three consecutive pennants, joining the Chicago Cubs, Pittsburgh Pirates, New York Giants, and New York Yankees in the achievement. Observations that the Cardinals' organization would not recover from the departure of Branch Rickey, much to the regret of the rest of the league, seemed badly mistaken. The wartime Cardinals were also one of several teams giving lie to the theory that somehow all 4-F ballplayers were inferior ones. Mort Cooper's and Marty Marion's knee problems kept them out of the war. Part of the treatment for Whitey Kurowski's childhood bout with osteomyelitis was the removal of part of the bone in his right arm, and the subsequent asymmetry of his two limbs left him with a 4-F classification. Harry Brecheen, Ted Wilks, and Ray Sanders were also not draftable due to physical problems. The seasons these "4-F" players had, not only during World War II but also before and after the war, gives testimony to their skills.

1945

World War II cast a pall over the Cardinals before the 1945 season began when manager Billy Southworth's son, a promising minor leaguer before he enlisted in the Army Air Corps, perished in a military flight between New York and Florida on February 15, 1945.[52] Before the 1945 season started, St. Louis knew that the one player they could not afford to lose was the seemingly undraftable Stan Musial. Stan the Man worked in a defense plant in the off-season, was married, had a son born before

Pearl Harbor, and was the sole support of his parents. Musial's father could no longer work, having contracted black lung disease in the mines of Pennsylvania. There was only one problem—the draft board serving Musial's Donora, Pennsylvania, area did not have enough bodies to meet their quota, and thus the Cardinals lost the best young player in the league for the 1945 season.[53] Unfortunately, he was not the only important player called to serve. The U.S. Army drafted two other starters and two pitchers as well; no other team was decimated by the comparatively light draft in 1945 as much as the Cardinals were. Walker Cooper, Max Lanier, Danny Litwhiler, and Freddy Schmidt were also called up to serve at the end of World War II. Cooper and Litwhiler were victimized by the infamous "professional athlete" draft that took Ron Northey of the Phillies and Stan Spence of the Washington Senators. Cooper's conscription occurred after he had played in four games and posted a .389 batting average.

Cooper was discharged in time to play in 1946, but the Cardinals sold his contract to the New York Giants for a tidy $175,000 in January 1946. He went on to have an 18-year career, retiring after 1957 at the age of 42, after playing with the Cardinals, Giants, Reds, Braves, Pirates, and Cubs. Lanier came back and went 6–0 to help the Cardinals win the pennant in 1946 and ended his 14-year career after the 1953 season. Litwhiler played only six games for the Cards in 1946 and was traded to the Boston Braves. His successful 11-year career ended after his 1951 season in Cincinnati. Pitcher Freddy Schmidt also returned to St. Louis in 1946 but left the majors after 1947, ending a three-year career that included postwar stints with the Philadelphia Phillies and Chicago Cubs. Musial's postwar activities became legendary. He returned to play every game for the World Champion Cardinals in 1946, won seven batting titles over 22 seasons, retired in 1963 at age 43, and entered the Hall of Fame as one of the best left-handed hitters in history.

As the Cardinals opened their 1945 spring training camp in Cairo, Illinois, they were beset with other personnel problems as well. Walker and Mort Cooper held out for $17,500 before the 1945 season. The widely held belief was that they would be the highest salaried players on the team, but owner Sam Breadon offered them less. Marty Marion had just won the Most Valuable Player Award and was probably the best shortstop in baseball, and he rightfully insisted on a raise as well. Irritated at the salary demands but cognizant that the three were the nucleus of the team, especially with Musial and Slaughter out, Breadon eventually gave them all $15,000 contracts. Marion reluctantly signed, but the Cooper brothers became salary holdouts. A $15,000 salary in 1945 could be considered standard pay for a proven, successful veteran, and most teams had perhaps a half dozen players compensated as such. League leaders and high-achieving World Series stars, however, commanded more. Walker Cooper's holdout became moot when he went into the service four games into the season. But on May 16, with the season barely one month old, Mort left the team to prove his point. Breadon, weary of the situation but determined to hold the line on the payroll, traded him to the Boston Braves for their ace right-hander, Red Barrett, and $60,000. Whether it was simply good fortune or good scouting, St. Louis lucked out again; Barrett led the league in wins, and Cooper's best years, it turned out, were all behind him.

In an attempt to fill the 29 holes the military put in their roster during World War II, St. Louis got Buster Adams back from Philadelphia, where they had traded him in 1943 as part of the Danny Litwhiler deal, in exchange for John Antonelli and Glenn Crawford. With Musial's absence, Adams was penciled in at center field, Hopp moved to right, and promising rookie Red Schoendienst, a switch-hitter, came in to start in left. Another rookie, catcher Del Rice, took Cooper's spot, but the starting job went to veteran Ken O'Dea. Up from the minors with hopes to bolster the pitching staff were big Kenny Burkhardt, Jack Creel, and the pride of Chicopee Falls, Massachusetts, lefty Stan Partenheimer. St. Louis had a confident outlook throughout spring training that the deepest roster of talented minor leaguers would pull them through to success once again in the 1945 season.

CHAPTER 4

MARCH 1945: SPRING TRAINING
AT THE FRENCH LICK SPRINGS HOTEL

The Chicago Cubs, like all other teams, experienced their share of difficulties as World War II continued to impose sacrifices on the sacred ritual of spring training. For the third year in a row, the Cubs, dutifully adhering to the Eastman–Landis Line, had set up preseason camp 50 miles northwest of Louisville, Kentucky, in the resort town of French Lick, Indiana, but in 1945 the war's effects were such that only nine players reported for the camp's opening. By the second week, the team was so desperate for players that they welcomed two semipros from Pennsylvania who wanted to practice with them. Until more players showed up, the Cubs would be forced to play two of their more agile catchers at shortstop. For third base, they relied on a 53-year-old coach. To make matters worse, a creek so insignificant that it did not appear on many Indiana maps continually overflowed, forcing the team to practice indoors—sometimes in the meeting hall of their hotel.

Legitimate competition for spring training in 1945 consisted of only four games against Cincinnati and two games against a minor league squad. Like the Cubs, Cincinnati was affected by wartime shortages. Listed on the Reds' roster were a high school junior who was only available on weekends and two pitchers well into their 40s. Meanwhile, the Cubs continued to fret over key players who had failed to show up. In addition to players who did not dare leave their militarily exempt off-season jobs, there were the salary holdouts. When the Cubs finally got to play Cincinnati, they had to borrow two of their opponent's pitchers to fill in for the absences and injuries on their own staff.

COACHES SMITH, JOHNSON, AND STOCK

On March 1 the Cubs announced that Red Smith would rejoin manager Charley Grimm as the team's third coach. Grimm had relied heavily on the 41-year-old Smith during four seasons with the Milwaukee Brewers in the American Association. The Wisconsin native had also served as line coach for the New York (football) Giants in the fall of 1944 and in previous years had held the same position with the Green Bay Packers.[1] Smith, whose major league career consisted of pitching one game for the New York Giants in 1927, was slated as a bull pen coach and a scout in this, his first major league coaching assignment.

Smith joined a coaching staff that included Roy "Hardrock" Johnson and Milt Stock. The 50-year-old Johnson had pitched one season for the Philadelphia Athletics in 1918 and had served on the Cubs' staff with Grimm between 1935 and 1939 and again in 1944. From 1940 until 1942, as manager of the Tulsa Oilers in the Class AA Texas League, he had mentored seven future Cubs, all now on the team's roster: Cy Block, Paul Erickson, Paul Gillespie, Don Johnson, Peanuts Lowrey, Len Merullo, and Hank Wyse.[2]

Meanwhile, Stock, a 53-year-old Chicago native, had tallied 14 years in the majors, playing for the Giants, Phillies, Cardinals, and Dodgers, and had ended his career in 1926 with a .289 batting average. Before joining the Cubs in 1944, he had managed the organization's Macon affiliate in the Class A South Atlantic (Sally) League. One of the future major leaguers Stock had developed in Macon was Eddie Stanky, who in 1942 had married Stock's daughter to form what may have been baseball's first manager and shortstop, father and son-in-law combinations.[3]

CAMP OPENS

ON SATURDAY, MARCH 3, Grimm, Smith, and trainer Andy Lotshaw rode the Monon Railroad train out of Chicago's Dearborn Station and headed for French Lick. When they arrived, they received an introduction to the spring rains and flooding that would complicate the team's practice over the following days. After making their way from the station to the resort on roads that were nearly impassable, they discovered that surging waters from the nearby Lost River had flooded the team's golf course practice area. The next day, the three men, along with Wrigley Field groundskeeper Bobby Dorr, worked all day on the vast expanse of green near the eighth hole. Given how aggravating the conditions that greeted them were, the men were grateful that the players were not expected to report until early Thursday morning. By that time, they fully expected to have the playing conditions under control.

Prior to the group's departure, traveling secretary Bob Lewis had made reservations for 16 players on the Monon Special for Wednesday, March 7. At 9:15 p.m., when the train left Dearborn Station, Lewis was accompanied by only six players: Cubs pitcher Ed Hanyzewski, ex-New York Giants catcher Joe Stephenson, minor league pitcher George Hennessey, semipro pitcher Al Nusser, and two hopefuls who had played for the Los Angeles Angels in 1944, outfielder Virgil "Rabbit" Garriott and infielder Johnny Ostrowski. The nine others Lewis was expecting, including seven regulars from the 1944 season, never showed up. But waiting for the Monon express as it pulled into Greencastle, Indiana, were Cubs catcher Mickey Livingston and pitcher Mack Stewart. Both had somehow managed to catch up with the group after making numerous rail connections from their respective hometowns of Perry, South Carolina, and Macon, Georgia. The group did not travel much farther before flooding forced them to detrain at Orleans. Arriving in French Lick at 7:00 a.m. on Thursday, three hours later than planned, the players negotiated the hilly and rain-soaked 18-mile route to their hotel. Later that morning, two more coaches, Milt Stock and Hardrock Johnson, arrived, along with outfielder Frank Secory.

ONCE THESE EARLY arrivals had assembled in the hotel, the team received a telegram informing them that Dom Dallessandro, at .305 the second-best hitter on the 1944 team, had been inducted by his Reading,

Pennsylvania, draft board. Then general manager Jim Gallagher admitted for the first time that 11 players on the active roster had not been heard from in more than two months. These updates put a damper on the strange and lonesome indoor workout at the French Lick resort's massive assembly hall. Only one month earlier, the team had filed a spring training roster listing five catchers, 16 pitchers, 11 infielders, and six outfielders.[4]

Things became more encouraging the next morning, when 1944's All-Star second baseman Don Johnson and first-string catcher Dewey Williams showed up in time for the Chicagoans' first outdoor workout. To save wear and tear on the few bodies in camp, Grimm offered himself, coach Johnson, and coach Smith to pitch batting practice. The next day (Saturday, March 10), first baseman Heinz Becker, who had delivered big years with Grimm when both were with the Milwaukee Brewers, settled in to camp, along with two curious characters from Greensboro, Pennsylvania: Walter Watson and Glen Cox. The pair, a couple of self-described "ballplayers" with military deferments for punctured eardrums, had learned the Cubs were short of players and had driven to the resort to offer their services. Incredibly, Grimm agreed to the arrangement and got them a room in the resort. In several spring training contests, Watson and the left-handed Cox played in the outfield.

The team held its first three-hour drill on Sunday and then learned that Ostrowski, despite his 4-F draft status, had been ordered back to Chicago for a preinduction physical. Ostrowski was not the kind of high-profile, physically perfect professional athlete whom draft boards were fond of scrutinizing. Ear problems and a missing kidney had earned him a 4-F rating all through the war, and he had, in fact, only appeared in eight games with the Cubs.[5] If a player like Ostrowski could be recalled for a review, then who might be next, the players wondered. If Uncle Sam needed Ostrowski, the players not yet in camp who were clinging to their draft-exempt civilian jobs might never give them up.

LATE ARRIVALS AND SOME REAL PRACTICE

IN SPITE OF the team's worries and manpower shortages, real baseball finally began on Tuesday, March 13. While the players were glad to see live action, the lineups gave them pause and a sense of how much World

War II had affected the game. Playing for the A team were Garriott in center field, the often-injured but strong-armed right-handed pitcher Hanyzewski in right, coach Smith in left, and outfielder Secory at shortstop. Mercifully, the team could rely on Becker, Johnson, Ostrowski, Livingston, and Nusser where they belonged, at first, second, third, catcher, and pitcher, respectively. For the B team, the lineup was even stranger. Filling in as leadoff man and at center was Pennsylvania walk-on Cox; elsewhere on the field, the 47-year-old Grimm covered first, 50-year-old coach Johnson manned second, and catcher Williams handled shortstop and batted cleanup. The rest of the lineup consisted of Watson, the other Pennsylvania walk-on, in left field; coach Stock at third; Stephenson, where he belonged, at catcher; and Hanyzewski, vacating his right field slot on the A squad to serve as the pitcher for the B team. Just to get two camp teams going, the Cubs had to rely on two amateur walk-ons, two coaches over 50, one coach and one manager in their 40s, five players out of position, and a hurler with a history of arm trouble playing both right field and pitcher. To complete the picture, trainer Lotshaw and traveling secretary Lewis served as umpires. Eyeballing the lineups, Grimm and general manager Jim Gallagher asked the press if they had heard "how things were going" in other teams' camps. Their curiosity seemed an indication of how poorly things were going for Chicago.

At least Hanyzewski and Secory could smile through their aches the next day when Paul Derringer arrived, increasing their meager pitching staff to three. The arrival of shortstop Roy Hughes cheered the team further. With Hughes's arrival, Secory could move back to left field, where he belonged, and Smith could retreat to the safety of the sidelines.

ROY HUGHES

The 34-year-old Hughes was an amazing comeback story. Born January 11, 1911 (1/11/11), he broke in with the Cleveland Indians in 1935. In 1938 Cleveland traded him to the St. Louis Browns, and from there he went to the Philadelphia Phillies in 1939. In 1940, however, he slipped to the minors and was playing for Montreal when a base runner sliding into second landed on his right shoulder. Hughes heard a popping sound and afterward could not raise his arm. Doctors told him his career was finished. That winter, Hughes was further injured when a can of tar he was attempting to thaw exploded, showering him with the hot, sticky material. The 30-year-old spent weeks in the hospital, but then, to his amazement, Hughes learned that the heat of the tar had welded together the injured shoulder muscles. With his arm back, Hughes returned to Montreal and then played two extremely successful seasons for the minor league Los Angeles Angels in 1942 and '43. In 1944 he moved up to the Cubs, filling the infield hole left by Stan Hack's retirement. By late August, he was leading the team in hitting and finished the year with a .287 average that included 16 doubles and 16 stolen bases.[6]

While he was one of the fastest base runners in the National League, Hughes was also extremely intelligent on the base paths. In 1944, for instance, he was tagged out only once in 17 attempted steals. Hughes was also a lithe, graceful infielder with exceptionally soft hands. What he lacked in arm strength, he more than made up for in accuracy. His arrival at French Lick in the spring of '45 was postponed by his dying father's illness, but Grimm was pleased to see the willowy infielder show up in opening-day form. Hughes made arrangements to be with the club until he was called back to his father's bedside.

PAUL DERRINGER

If Grimm was pleased to see Hughes arrive in opening-day trim, he was even more gratified to note that the same was true of Paul Derringer. The 38-year-old pitching legend had arrived carrying only 230 pounds on his six-foot, four-inch frame—the best shape the Cubs had ever seen him in. Perhaps Derringer had finally realized what an asset he could be to the team if he regained the form that had brought him such fame in Cincinnati and St. Louis.

With 207 victories in 14 seasons, Derringer entered the 1945 season as the second winningest active pitcher in the majors, surpassed only by Red Ruffing, who had tallied 258 wins over 18 campaigns. A more impressive statistic at the start of 1945 season was Derringer's 3,432 total innings pitched for an average of 245 innings per season. When he was on his game, the big Kentuckian would show hitters the highest kick in the majors—over six feet, according to Ed Burns of the *Chicago Tribune*—and then deliver a jug-handled curve or blazing fastball with pinpoint control, earning him 1,421 strikeouts and only 710 walks up to this time. The only problem was that since the Cubs had signed him in January 1943, Derringer had not been on his game, and his career record in Chicago was a paltry 17–27.

In two years at Rochester in the International League before his 1931 debut with the St. Louis Cardinals, Derringer had amassed a record of 40 wins and 23 losses. Yet all he managed in his first year in the National League was a record of 18–8. The following year, he slipped even further, and in May 1933, Derringer and Leo Durocher were the featured players in a six-player swap between the Cardinals and the Reds. In his stint with the Reds, Derringer labored 248 innings and tallied a respectable 3.30 ERA, but the team as a whole won only 58 games and finished dead last. Afterward, however, both Derringer and the Reds began their ascent. A 22–13 record in 1935 landed Derringer on the All-Star team. His 25–7 record in 1939 put him there again, and that year the Reds won the pennant. When Derringer followed with a 20–12 All-Star season in 1941, the Reds went on to win the World Series. Two average seasons followed, however, and the Reds sold him to the Cubs.

Aside from two mediocre years following the World Championship, Cincinnati found Derringer expendable because of his volatility. On an early road trip to New York in 1939, Derringer had punched out a man in the Reds' New York hotel and then never bothered to go to court. After the court issued a warrant and judgment for more than $8,000, Derringer avoided the state until the team finally paid the judgment, an amount well above the average major league player's salary that year.[7] Only then was it safe for Derringer to play in New York. But after a tense 2–1 loss to the Yankees in game one of the 1939 World Series, Derringer's temper got the better of him again. A locker room tantrum over All-Star Ival Goodman's botched outfield play ended when Goodman, 40 pounds lighter and six inches shorter, punched him solidly and squarely on the jaw.[8]

With the big salary that Derringer commanded through most of his baseball career, he had amassed the most expensive wardrobe of anyone on the Cubs. Referred to as a "Beau Brummel" by J.G. Taylor Spink of the *Sporting News*, Derringer always sought out the best food and creature comforts available.[9] The big right-hander was the only one on the team who relaxed by smoking a pipe in the clubhouse.

In Chicago in 1943 and 1944, Derringer's weight had increased, and a badly sprained ankle in snowy French Lick during spring training in 1944 cast further doubts on Derringer's ability to deliver for the Cubs. Chicago, starting spring training in 1945 pitifully thin in the pitching department, needed a big year from Derringer, the winningest career pitcher in the National League, more than they ever did before.

ON THURSDAY, MARCH 15, the team's prospects brightened as Andy Pafko reported to camp, and the Cubs added another badly needed pitcher, 28-year-old George Woodend, to their roster. But hopes sank later that day when the Office of Defense Transportation announced more travel restrictions for the majors. Under the new rules, all preseason exhibition games involving "side trips" were canceled. Preseason games between two teams training in the same city were still permissible, as were contests against the military, provided the military provided the transportation, and any games a team could arrange on its way home from camp. But because the Cubs would not travel through any other team's area on their return to Chicago, the new rules did not seem to offer them any new opportunities for play. The Cubs' only hope for preseason major league competition lay in the fact that the Reds, training in Bloomington, Indiana, would have to travel through French Lick on their return to Cincinnati. As a result, both teams began planning for extended spring training games in French Lick and in the Louisville–Fort Knox area.[10]

IN THE CUBS' first intraclub game, Grimm's B team easily handled the A team's Nusser for a 7–0 victory. On Saturday, March 17, the camp breathed a collective sigh of relief as Phil Cavarretta checked in, and later the club welcomed a fourth catcher, Paul Gillespie, who had been with the team a short time in 1944 following his military discharge. Also on the 17th, Gallagher notified Grimm that he expected third baseman Stan Hack and pitcher Hank Wyse would arrive shortly. Aside from Wyse, five pitchers from the 1944 staff—Bob Chipman, Paul Erickson, Japhet "Red" Lynn, Claude Passeau, and Hy Vandenberg—were still missing. A greater mystery was the whereabouts of rookie Jorge Comellas, a Havana native with 18 wins and a 2.61 ERA for the Los Angeles Angels in the Pacific Coast League in 1944. Not only had Gallagher not heard from Comellas, but he had no idea where he was.

HACK, WHO HAD "retired" the year before until the Cubs had replaced manager Jimmie Wilson with Grimm, managed to arrive three months earlier for the 1945 season than he did in 1944 and was in time for

Sunday's intraclub game. One of the game's greatest contact hitters, Hack rifled his second pitch for a double. On Monday, March 19, shortstop Lennie Merullo checked in, with Grimm promising opportunities for more play than in 1944. Later that day, traveling secretary Lewis and concessions chief Ray Kniep drove to Louisville to meet with officials at the Louisville Slugger Bat Corporation to see what could be done about the impending baseball bat shortage. With the war's tremendous demand for hardwood, decent white ash was becoming increasingly difficult to obtain. On Tuesday, March 20, Chipman reported. The Cubs' most successful left-hander in 1944 was an important addition to the French Lick contingent. With a 12–10 record the previous season, he added strength and depth to the pitching staff. Meanwhile, Grimm's concerns over Nicholson continued. The absence of the major league's premier power hitter for the last two years had hurt the Cubs' offense, but it affected defensive play as well. With Nicholson out, Grimm decided to play strong-armed Pafko in right field, moved Cavarretta from first to center, and put Becker, a favorite from the Brewers, at first. Becker, plagued with foot problems, would be a liability at first over an entire season, but he was a respectable .326 hitter with eight triples and 22 doubles in 101 games for Grimm in 1944.

THE MOST IMPORTANT news for spring training in 1945 came on Wednesday, March 21, when Paul McNutt, head of the War Manpower Commission, ruled that players could leave their off-season, military-exempt jobs and return to professional baseball without reexposure to the draft. In the wake of his decree, teams all over the majors announced the return of countless players whose status had previously been uncertain. The news brightened a dreary day in the Cubs' camp. After the initial rainy weather, the team had enjoyed ten days of sunny, 70-degree spring weather when flooding rains once again drove the players indoors. With no other choice, the players transformed the caucus room in the resort's main building into a pitching workout room, while the huge auditorium swallowed ground balls. As the players did calisthenics, Grimm accompanied them with jitterbug tunes on the hotel piano.

THE FIRST CUB to contact general manager Gallagher following the manpower ruling was the player all of Cubdom was the most concerned about, Bill Nicholson. The preeminent National League slugger of the

World War II years reported that he was pleased with his contract, still working at a war plant near his hometown of Chestertown, Maryland, trying to get some batting practice in five times a week, and fully expected to be in right field against the Cardinals at Wrigley Field on Opening Day, April 17. More good news arrived Thursday in the form of starting right-hander Hank Wyse. Four days later, on Sunday March 25, Claude Passeau left his tung oil farm in Mississippi and checked into the French Lick Springs Hotel. Passeau had led the team's pitchers the previous season with a 2.89 ERA, while Wyse had led with 257 innings pitched. Together, they accounted for 31 of the team's 75 victories, Wyse with a record of 16–15 and Passeau going 15–9. Finally, on the 19th day of spring training, Chicago had its five starters—Wyse, Passeau, Derringer, Chipman, and Hanyzewski—all together in camp.

WITH THEIR STARTING five in camp and relievers Hennessey, Stewart, and Woodend looking strong, the Cubs' brass did less hand-wringing about holdouts Erickson and Vandenberg and started thinning their active roster. Red Lynn, who had gone 5–4 in 22 games the previous season, was given an outright release. Lynn had never reported to training camp, choosing instead to hold on to his job as a railroad brakeman for the Santa Fe Lines in his native Texas. Two other players, optioned out to the Los Angeles Angels, were 23-year-old right-hander Dwight Adams and infielder "Piccolo" Pete Elko. Elko, who had played for the Angels, Nashville, and the Cubs in 1944 and had also logged nine games with the Cubs in 1943, had been given permission to train in Los Angeles with the Angels. That decision may have hurt him: The excellent play of Johnny Ostrowski, one of the original six Cubs to open camp back on March 8, may have persuaded Gallagher and Grimm that Elko was expendable.

MORE COMPLICATIONS

AS THE CUBS readied themselves for their six-game spring training series against Cincinnati, they learned that the Pittsburgh Pirates, winners of 90 games the previous season and a team that many expected would challenge the World Champion Cardinals, had strengthened their pitching staff, trading center fielder Vince DiMaggio to the Phillies for left-hander

Al Gerheauser. Gerheauser had gone 8–16 for the last-place Phillies the previous season but had given the Cubs fits in 1943 with his 3–0 record against them. DiMaggio, regarded as one of the best fielders in baseball, had irritated Pirates management by complaining about the $4.50 meal allowance. By midseason he was on the bench more than the field and was asking to be traded.

THE CUBS' FIRST contest, scheduled for Monday, April 2, against Cincinnati, was rained out. Health issues made a dreary day worse for the Chicagoans, who saw three established players leave camp to return to Chicago: Cavarretta, who was summoned back to Evanston due to his wife's illness; Ostrowski, who faced military reclassification following an Army physical; and worst of all, Passeau, slated by many to start the season against the Cardinals on April 17, who was sent back to Chicago for tests to see why his right arm was sore for the first time in his 14-year career. Taking Passeau's place was Len Rice, freshly arrived from Los Angeles, where he had worked out with the Cubs' blessing at the Angels' training camp. Rice's arrival fueled sportswriters' speculation over why he would report without pitcher Ray Prim and outfielders Ed Sauer and Peanuts Lowrey. Those three were considered much more valuable than another catcher, and their absence at French Lick led Edgar Munzel of the *Chicago Sun* to conclude that Prim, Sauer, and Lowrey were holding out, something general manager Gallagher was loathe to admit.

WET WEATHER AGAIN forced a cancellation for the game rescheduled for April 3, but this time both teams were able to get in some outdoor practice. With another workday gone and no game to cover, the Chicago media, much to Grimm and Gallagher's dismay, began wondering how many holdouts the Cubs were actually dealing with. The number they came up with was eight: one outfielder, two infielders, and five pitchers. Outfielder Lowrey had held out before, so he seemed an obvious candidate. Infielders Charlie Brewster and Bill Schuster, both of whom played for the Cubs in 1944, were thought to be holdouts because of management's evasive explanations regarding their absence from camp. Meanwhile, the three suspected pitching holdouts—Paul Erickson, Charlie Gassaway, and Hy Vandenberg—had all served on the Cubs' staff in 1944. While Gassaway had appeared in only two games, Vandenberg had gone

7–4 with a three-hit victory over the Phillies in July and a combined three-hit effort with Derringer over the second-place Pirates in September. Erickson, who worked as a milkman in Chicago during the off-season, had been less successful at 5–9 but had managed to pitch a two-hitter in May against the Pirates and a three-hitter against the Cardinals in September. The other two pitchers were the gems of the Cubs' minor league system in 1944: Prim and Comellas, 22–10 and 18–14, respectively, for the Los Angeles Angels. These pitching absences were more serious now that Passeau's arm had become a big question mark and the oft-injured Hanyzewski had just come up lame with more arm trouble. However, outfielder Sauer reported to camp the next day and brought word that Prim, with whom he had been training in Los Angeles, was on his way east also.[11]

THE MEDICAL REPORT on Passeau reached camp on Wednesday, April 4, the same day wet weather forced a cancellation of the third contest against the Reds. X-rays revealed a chipped humerus, most likely the result of a high school football injury 19 years earlier, and doctors recommended up to four days of x-ray therapy.[12] Meanwhile, Jimmie Wilson, fired after two weeks as a Cubs manager in 1944 and now coaching for the visiting Reds, expounded on the Cubs' chances to the press. Interestingly, the writers' views seemed to reflect their opinions of general manager Jim Gallagher. Writing for the morning *Tribune*, Edward Burns, a Gallagher critic, noted that Wilson had judged the team improved in several areas but still too weak in pitching to challenge St. Louis for the National League pennant. Later that day, Gallagher advocate John Carmichael, writing for the afternoon *Chicago Daily News*, criticized Burns for misquoting Wilson and taking his statements out of context. According to Carmichael, Wilson declared, "The Cubs should finish one-two-three in the National League this year." It really was getting time for the scribes to start covering baseball.[13]

THE GAMES BEGIN

THE TIME FINALLY came on Thursday, when the Cubs, borrowing two pitchers from the visiting Cincinnati Reds, trounced their guests in French Lick 5–0. With the team already suffering from pitcher injuries, Grimm did not want to risk any more arms in the game, so the Reds loaned the Cubs 42-year-old ex-Cub Guy Bush and 44-year-old Hod Lisenbee. Both men hoped to capitalize on the extreme pitching shortage in the majors, and both would end up pitching for Cincinnati during the 1945 season. In 1929 and again in 1932, Bush had been a mainstay on the Cubs' pennant-winning teams, and between 1928 and 1934, he had racked up 121 wins for Chicago. In spite of his success with the North Siders, though, he was perhaps best known for his role as bench jockey and Babe Ruth's chief antagonist in the 1932 World Series game at Wrigley Field, when Ruth pointed out and hit his fabled "called shot" home run.

The Reds gave the Cubs their two older hurlers and kept for themselves 17-year-old Herman Wehmeier, a high school junior and phenom in the Cincinnati American Legion. The Reds were interested in seeing what Wehmeier could do, and because he had to be back in class on Monday, they did not have a lot of time to check. Wehmeier was understandably nervous and gave up all five runs in the first inning. His pitching line, however, showed four strikeouts, two walks, and four hits allowed in three innings of work. The youngster was actually on a fast track to the majors, coming up to the Reds for good in 1947 and enjoying a 14-year career with the Reds, Phillies, and Cardinals. For the game on Friday, April 6, the two teams traveled to Fort Knox, where 7,000 soldiers gave them a taste of major league crowds as the Reds rallied late in the game off Cubs reliever Stewart to secure a 5–4 win despite two home runs by Cubs catcher Gillespie. The appreciative Fort Knox officials treated all the players to tank rides before both teams left for nearby Louisville.

For Saturday, April 7, the Cubs scheduled a doubleheader; they defeated the Louisville Colonels of the Class AA American Association 9–6 on their home field in the first game but lost 19–4 to Cincinnati in the second game. Chipman and Wyse got their innings in and did well against the Colonels, but after Grimm took Derringer out of the second game, the Reds had their way with the Cubs and scored nine runs late in the game off Hennessey.

The next day, however, tables were turned as the Reds led off the Parkway Field festivities before a crowd of almost 6,000. Following the Cubs' example, they won their first game against the Colonels, the score this time being 8–6, but when the dust settled in the second game, the Cubs had drubbed the Reds 19–5, with Hughes going 5-for-5 and Prim getting his first Cubs spring training action, striking out seven and giving up only one hit in four innings.

On Monday, April 9, both teams returned to French Lick, but before the game, the Cubs trimmed their roster to 31 players, releasing pitcher Gassaway to the Milwaukee Brewers and shortstop Brewster to Los Angeles. Neither had reported to spring training or contacted Gallagher. In their final French Lick spring tune-up, the Cubs beat Cincinnati 6–5; all proceeds from the game were donated to the American Red Cross. As the Cubs prepared to break camp, the long-absent Comellas arrived from his home in Havana, Cuba, while holdout Vandenberg began negotiating through the press. Vandenberg declared to a *Chicago Daily News* reporter that he would stay in his Minneapolis home and play park district baseball in the Twin Cities before he threw a pitch for the salary that Gallagher had offered him. The big right-hander claimed he had been working out with the University of Minnesota baseball team, "wearing out their catchers," and could pitch four innings on a moment's notice.[14] Vandenberg's contractual posturing, Passeau's sore elbow, and Hanyzewski's arm trouble may have been the chief reasons that the Cubs decided to take Comellas with them to Chicago after seeing him throw on April 10, the day before they broke camp.

BACK TO CHICAGO

IN CHICAGO ON Wednesday, April 11, Passeau reported that his elbow was feeling better, and the team welcomed shortstop Bill Schuster, who signed his contract and then joined Passeau for a workout in Wrigley Field. Later that day, most of the Cubs joined the team, settling into the city for the start of the season after the weekend's annual exhibition series against the White Sox.

A small crowd of 2,554 sat anywhere they pleased in frigid Comiskey Park on Thursday, April 12, as the Cubs and the Sox squared off in the annual city exhibition series. Those who stuck it out saw the Cubs knock Sox hurler Thornton Lee around at will and easily handle their South Side rivals for a 15–3 finish. Game stats included 13 hits in four innings for the North Siders and a 15-run lead before the Sox scored twice in the sixth. Derringer confounded the Sox hitters for five innings, giving up only two hits and striking out three, and Wyse proved almost as stingy the rest of the game. The only hitch for the Cubs was the loss of starting right fielder Secory, who left the game with a badly pulled leg muscle.

The Cubs were eagerly anticipating another opportunity to best their crosstown rivals the next day when word came from Washington that President Franklin D. Roosevelt had died. With the war-weary nation in mourning, Friday's and Saturday's games were canceled. The two teams made plans to finish the series at Wrigley Field on Sunday, April 15, but 40-degree temperatures canceled the game, and Grimm put the team through a two-hour practice after team photographs were taken. A surprise participant was outfielder Peanuts Lowrey, who had ended his holdout, signed his contract, and shown up for pictures and practice. Grimm made it clear, however, that because he had not been at spring training, he would not see much action in the near future. The press, meanwhile, was led to believe that Lowrey had been part of the contingent given permission to work out in Los Angeles with the Angels and that because Lowrey had chosen not to come under contract, he had been barred from the workouts.

WITH THE SEASON under way, the media indulged in its long-standing tradition of making predictions. Weighing in early was the April 5 *Sporting News*, whose writers saw St. Louis taking first, followed by Pittsburgh, Cincinnati, New York, Chicago, Boston, Brooklyn, and Philadelphia. The following week, they revised their forecast, moving Chicago up to fourth place and New York down to fifth, most likely with an eye toward Passeau's encouraging medical report and the presence of promising rookies Prim and Comellas. In the American League, meanwhile, the *Sporting News* put St. Louis in first, followed by New York, Detroit, Cleveland, Boston, Philadelphia, Chicago, and Washington. At the *Chicago Herald-American*, veteran sportswriter Leo Fischer was more optimistic for Chicagoans on both sides of town. His National League predictions put the Cubs second behind St. Louis, followed by Pittsburgh, Cincinnati, Boston, New York, Philadelphia, and Brooklyn. In the American League, Fischer felt good enough about the White Sox to put them in sixth ahead of Boston and Washington and behind St. Louis, Detroit, Philadelphia, Cleveland, and New York. Meanwhile, the *Chicago Sun's* legendary sports columnist Warren Brown, in his widely read column So They Tell Me, sketched out his thoughts on how the National League would go, declaring the Cubs and Giants greatly improved but noting that, unfortunately for Cubs fans, the Cardinals were still in the National League. Brown argued that even though Musial was in the service and the outfield was weak, the team nevertheless had the Cooper brothers and the best infield in all of baseball.

Perhaps the most important prediction on a national level in this pre–Las Vegas era came from James J. Carroll, the betting commissioner of St. Louis. Carroll gave the Cardinals 4 to 5 odds for appearing in a World Series championship. His odds for the Pirates were 3 to 1; for the Reds, 4 to 1; for the Cubs and Giants, 10 to 1; and for the Braves, Dodgers, and Phillies, a near hopeless 25 to 1. In the American League, the St. Louis Browns had the best odds of winning the pennant at 8 to 5, followed by the Detroit Tigers at 2 to 1, the Yankees at 4 to 1, and the Philadelphia Athletics at 5 to 1. Farther down the list were the Cleveland Indians, who faced 10 to 1 odds like the Cubs; the Boston Red Sox, whose odds were 15 to 1; and the White Sox and Senators, who were 25 to 1.

One Chicago daily, however, printed the predictions of two veteran sportswriters whose forecasts proved uncannily accurate. Columnist John P. Carmichael, in his Barber Shop offering on Thursday, April 12, predicted the Cubs would win the pennant if they were able to get the pitching they hoped for. Carmichael reasoned that catching, which had been a glaring weakness in 1944, was much stronger this year, and he called the Cubs a great offensive club that could lead the league in hitting. Although the team's pitching seemed questionable, Carmichael's predictions were the Cardinals, Cubs, Pirates, Giants, Braves, Dodgers, Reds, and, lastly, Phillies. Even more optimistic was Carmichael's colleague Francis J. Powers, the dean of all Chicago sportswriters in 1945, who boldly predicted that the Cubs would win the pennant if Hanyzewski and Passeau were available all season, if Bill Nicholson was not drafted, and if Lowrey signed and regained his form in left field. If the two pitchers did not come through, third place would be a good finish by Chicago, Powers predicted, but he added that they might fall as far as fifth. Overall, Powers envisioned a season-long, four-team race in the National League between Chicago, St. Louis, Pittsburgh, and Cincinnati. Lofty expectations, to be sure!

CHICAGO IN THE SPRING OF 1945

SETTLING INTO THEIR Chicago quarters for the long season, the Cubs couldn't help noting that at least some writers—and no doubt a number of eager fans—held them in high regard. In addition, the April 1945 Cubs fans—and Americans everywhere—felt something more intense than the usual rush of spring's arrival, something that was not deadened by Roosevelt's passing. With a sense that the nation's long-anticipated victory was at hand, Cubs fans rejoiced and turned their attention to a season that seemed as full of promise as the victorious war news from Europe.

IN 1945 MOST Cubs lived very close to Wrigley Field at one of two hotels, both of which are still standing and look much the same today as they did then. The Sheridan Plaza, at the corner of Sheridan and Broadway, was less than a mile and a half from the ballpark and was home to almost all the players who were unmarried or did not have their wives with them for the season. The other hotel, the New Lawrence, at 1039 W. Lawrence, was smaller and homier than the Sheridan Plaza and served as home for a majority of players whose wives had come to Chicago for the season.[15] If a player wanted something of his own, he might find housing such as that offered in an ad in the *Chicago Herald-American* on April 15: small, rehabbed kitchenette apartments at 668 Sheridan, not far from Wrigley Field, for $52.50 per month with a two-year lease. Those desiring more opulent accommodations could look to the Gold Coast, where $300 per month secured an 11-room, six-bath apartment in the high-rise apartment built in 1928 at 1430 N. Lake Shore Drive. Rents for similar properties today are 20 times that amount.[16]

If a player felt his chances were good for remaining on the team, he might decide to go house hunting. In 1945 a five-room cottage with a four-room basement apartment and two-car garage at 2100 N. Orchard listed at $4,500, a little less than the average major leaguer's salary that year. For $7,000 a player could purchase a home in Evanston, where Cubs first baseman Cavarretta and team treasurer Earl W. Nelson lived. Farther up the shore in Glencoe, where Commissioner Kenesaw Landis was living when he died in November 1944 while tending to his Victory Garden, a seven-room, two-story stucco residence cost $9,000; larger homes on the lakefront started at about four times that amount.[17]

Automobiles were even more within the financial reach of the players, but with nationwide gasoline and tire rationing still in effect, few would bother with cars during the season. Still, for those who were interested, a 1936 Buick cost $275, while a 1938 Chevrolet with a radio and heater went for $575. The more established ballplayer who wanted to make a statement could buy a fully equipped 1940 Packard Model 120 four-door sedan for $1,000. If he wanted to research his purchase, he could just "Ask the Man Who Owns One." (This was Packard's famous slogan; Packard was the premier U.S. automobile from 1920–1950.) Finding a newer used car in 1945 posed more of a challenge; because it was unpredictable when newly manufactured vehicles might once again become available, most owners of 1941 or 1942 models made every effort to hang on to them.[18]

Most ballplayers, however, were more interested in entertainment, meals, movies, and companionship than houses or cars. Close to the New Lawrence was a popular restaurant called Tony's Place. The Sheridan Plaza tavern was another favorite, especially with the young women in the area. Other popular nightspots, such as the 5100 Club at 5100 N. Broadway, the Riviera Theatre, and the Aragon Theatre, offered floor shows and dancing and were within walking distance of both hotels. For players who wanted top-name entertainment, the Edgewater Beach Hotel was not far.[19] If the Boston Braves or New York Giants were in town, they could fraternize, because both teams roomed at the Edgewater during road trips in 1945.

Just up the block from the Edgewater was the Bryn Mawr Theatre, which was showing *When Our Hearts Were Young and Gay* the weekend before Opening Day. A few blocks north by elevated train, the Howard Theatre featured *Together Again* with Charles Boyer and Irene Dunne. Heading south, one could catch all the first-run movies downtown in Chicago's Loop. On the weekend before Opening Day, the State Lake Theater boasted Mickey Rooney and a young Elizabeth Taylor in *National Velvet*, while the United Artists Theatre offered *A Tree Grows in Brooklyn*. Other hits of 1945 included *The Lost Weekend, Twenty Seconds over Tokyo, Our Vines Had Tender Grapes*, and *Laura*. Movies in the 1940s were a favorite pastime for more than a few players.[20]

Few of them were likely to desire more culture than that which the movies offered, but if they did, Spanish pianist Jose Iturbi was playing at the Opera House, where the best seat for the recital was $3.60, or barely twice the amount of a Cubs box seat. Elsewhere in Chicago, Russian piano virtuoso Alexander Brailowsky was appearing at Orchestra Hall, where the Chicago Symphony Orchestra had about two months left in its 55th season. For the few players interested in drama, the Erlanger Theatre featured Paul Robeson and Jose Ferrer in Shakespeare's *Othello*. But regardless of which entertainment venues players visited to amuse themselves during their off-hours, the Cubs were the hottest ticket in town on Tuesday, April 17, when they took center stage in the outdoor theater known as Wrigley Field, to star with their guests, the World Champion St. Louis Cardinals.

CHAPTER 5

★ ★ ★ ★ ★ ★ ★ ★

APRIL THROUGH JUNE:
WIN SOME, LOSE SOME

I f the Chicago Cubs were going to do anything special in the 1945 season, they would first have to overcome a serious obstacle created by the major league office, which scheduled their first 17 games against the St. Louis Cardinals, Pittsburgh Pirates, and Cincinnati Reds. In the previous season, the Cardinals had finished first and then dusted off the St. Louis Browns, four games to two, to win the World Championship. Fourteen and a half games behind them that year were the second-place Pirates, who had won 90 and lost 63. One and a half games behind the Pirates was third-place Cincinnati. Optimists could note that the Cubs had rounded out the first division in 1944, finishing fourth, but they would be overlooking the fact that the Chicagoans had also finished the season at 75–79, four games under the .500 mark. In other words, the club had scored a rare first-division finish with a sub-.500 record, 30 games behind pennant-winning St. Louis. As if the grueling start to the 1945 season weren't enough, after the first 17 games were finished, Chicago could look forward to a four-city, 15-day road trip to Philadelphia, New York, Brooklyn, and Boston. If it were any consolation, at least they had gotten to open the season at home . . . albeit against the World Champion Cardinals.

CHARLIE GRIMM

An overlooked strength of this 1945 Cubs team was manager Charlie Grimm. The 47-year-old St. Louis native had debuted as a player on July 30, 1916, for the Philadelphia Athletics and later toiled for the Cardinals and Pirates before joining the Cubs in 1925. As a player, Grimm was a career .290 hitter and led all first basemen in fielding for seven of his 20 seasons. As manager of the Cubs (replacing the prickly Rogers Hornsby) from 1932 to 1938, Grimm had led the team to two pennant-winning seasons, in '32 and '35. Midway through the 1938 pennant season, Grimm was replaced by Gabby Hartnett. Nine games into the 1944 season, Grimm was summoned by owner Philip K. Wrigley to replace the unpopular Jimmie Wilson. Taking over the dispirited, cellar-dwelling Cubs team, Grimm led them to fourth place that season.

Grimm had an uncanny knack of identifying with the players; he knew which egos needed feeding and which needed limits, and perhaps more important, he knew when to meet those needs. While he prided himself on "leaving the whip to the lion tamer,"[1] he was never a pushover and he kept a doghouse, which some players occupied; yet with Grimm, the players always put themselves there, and he always gave them opportunities to work their way out. He was also an accomplished musician, not above cheering up the boys in the clubhouse with his banjo or serenading them in the hotel lobby at the piano. In his eight years of managing the Cubs, he finished fourth only once. He also finished third twice, second twice, won two pennants outright and had a hand in a third. Among all the great National League managers in 1945—Brooklyn's Leo Durocher, Cincinnati's Bill McKechnie, Pittsburgh's Frankie Frisch, and St. Louis's Billy Southworth—only McKechnie could match Grimm's record, and he had been practicing the craft 14 years longer. Grimm's players loved him, and Wrigley himself declared Jolly Cholly the best manager the Cubs ever had.[2]

OPENING DAY 1945

FANS ARRIVING FOR Opening Day 1945 had three seating choices at the same prices the club had charged in 1944: box seats for $1.80, grandstand seating for $1.25, and bleacher seats for $.60. Box seats in the lower level consisted of wood and steel folding chairs that could be moved anywhere within the "box," an area approximately six feet by eight feet marked off by gray metal railings. In 1932 Wrigley reduced the number of folding chairs in each box from eight to six, cutting into box office revenues but providing more comfort for fans. At the time, Wrigley Field's capacity was 38,396, the fourth highest in the National League, eclipsed by only Braves Field in Boston, Forbes Field in Pittsburgh, and the Polo Grounds in New York. Because of generous standing room only guidelines from Mayor Edward J. Kelly's people at city hall, however, Sunday and holiday games at Wrigley Field would commonly draw well over 41,000 people.

In 1945, for the first time in the park's history, no ushers were available for crowd control and customer assistance. Because of the severe manpower shortage that the last year of World War II imposed upon the nation, the ushers were replaced for the first time ever by usherettes. While the fans probably heard the national anthem before the opening game on April 17, the song was not sung at every game but was saved for special events. At the time, this was also the practice of the armed forces; the national anthem was performed only on special occasions, such as national holidays. "There is a difference between patriotism and commercialization," Wrigley would explain.[3] Instead, the talented Roy Nelson entertained the fans at the keyboard of Wrigley Field's electronic organ. In 1941, when Wrigley ordered its installation, no other major league park offered such entertainment. Nelson played before games, between innings, and after games but not between pitches.

In 1944 the nature of the park was changed when the seven-year-old scoreboard, the bleachers, and the large doors on the outfield wall were painted a low-luster, nonreflective dark green. For many years, they had been a muted reddish brown, and not every patron was used to the new color.[4] In 1945 Wrigley Field was the only park in the National League that did not have lights for night games. The baseball field's dimensions were identical to what they are today; the only difference was that the foul ball screen behind the plate started 19 inches in front of the short brick wall on the ground, not on top of the wall, like it does today.

Those not going to the game but intent on following the action could tune in radio station WIND, with the legendary Bert Wilson on play-by-play, assisted by Wayne Osborne. Wilson's trademark line was "I don't care who wins, as long as it's the Cubs!" The Cubs had been on the radio since 1925, and in 1945 they had only two sponsors, the Walgreen Drug Company and P. Lorillard Tobacco. To Wrigley, the benefit from broadcasts lay not in the revenue they generated but from the publicity they engendered.

Grimm put the following lineup on the field at Wrigley for the season opener on April 17:

> Stan Hack, third base
> Lennie Merullo, shortstop
> Phil Cavarretta, first base
> Bill Nicholson, right field
> Ed Sauer, left field
> Andy Pafko, center field
> Don Johnson, second base
> Mickey Livingston, catcher
> Paul Derringer, pitcher

The strengths of the team were at first, second, third, right, and center. In the previous season, first baseman Phil Cavarretta had hit .321, tied for most hits in the league, and starred in the 1944 All-Star Game. At second, Don Johnson had committed 47 errors in 1944 but had made the All-Star team on the strength of a league-leading 385 putouts, a .271 batting average, and 71 RBIs. The closest National League second baseman to Johnson in RBIs that year was St. Louis's Emil Verban, who had only 43. At third, Stan Hack had long been regarded as one of the best with a glove and was considered one of the most outstanding leadoff men in the majors as well. Like most of his teammates, however, Smilin' Stan hadn't cared for manager Jimmie Wilson, and he had announced his retirement before the 1944 season. He only reconsidered when Grimm became manager and convinced him to rejoin the team.

In right field, Bill Nicholson, who had missed winning the 1944 MVP award by one vote, had established himself as one of the top power hitters during World War II; his 33 home runs and 122 RBIs led the majors that year. At center, the young Andy Pafko had proved in his first full season (1944) that he could run, field, hit, and throw, and National League base runners quickly learned that year that they ran against Pafko's rifle arm at their own peril, as Pafko led the league with 24 assists.

Behind the plate, Mickey Livingston, back from the war, headed a quartet of catchers that included Dewey Williams, Paul Gillespie, and Len Rice. Each Cubs catcher in 1945 had specific strengths, but no one was clearly superior to the other three. Livingston had the most major league experience, was fair at hitting for average, and was the preferred battery mate of his roommate, pitcher Claude Passeau. Williams, who had started 79 games in 1944, when Livingston was in the military, was seen as the most assertive "field general" of the group and had the best arm by far. Gillespie, 25, discharged from the service like Livingston in late 1944, was the youngest catcher on the team, the best hitter among the catchers, and the only one of the four with legitimate power. At the start of the 1945 season, Gillespie had sported a .261 average in only 42 at bats, with a remarkable three homers and a double, and was one of the few players in history to homer during his first time up in the majors. Rice had appeared in only ten games for the Cubs in 1944 and had gone hitless in his four at bats. Considered to have a great throwing arm and to handle pitchers well by calling an excellent game, Rice was by far the fastest base runner of the four. It was rare at that time for a team to carry four catchers, but a rules change in 1945 allowed the customary 25-man roster to be expanded to include five servicemen, and both Gillespie and Livingston qualified as discharged veterans.

At shortstop, Lennie Merullo had a cannon for an arm and was a daring and intelligent base runner, but he had hit only .212 the previous year. Roy Hughes was a better hitter, and some thought Bill Schuster was more consistent in the field. The Cubs' left fielder on opening day was Ed Sauer, since Frank Secory was hurt the week before against the White Sox. Sauer also took advantage of Grimm's irritation with the newly discharged Peanuts Lowrey, who was holding out for a higher salary.

Salary holdouts not only affected the position in left but also caused problems on Grimm's pitching staff. By Opening Day, Hy Vandenberg and Paul Erickson had not yet reported. To make matters worse, Passeau, 15–9 in 1944, was suffering from painful bone chips in his pitching elbow and looked as though he might need surgery. That left Paul Derringer, the reliable Hank Wyse, lefty Bob Chipman, the fragile fireballer Ed

Hanyzewski, and two successful call-ups from the Cubs' Los Angeles Angels minor league squad: the aged Ray Prim and the mercurial Jorge Comellas. The Cubs entered the 1945 season short on pitching, and if Passeau were to be out any length of time, or if Prim or Comellas did not come through, the Cubs' prospects for 1945 were dim.

One difference between Opening Day 1945 and Opening Day 1944 was the number of major leaguers trickling back from the battlefront. In addition to Gillespie and Livingston, another Cub who enjoyed such good fortune was outfielder Peanuts Lowrey. Lowrey, who had been drafted in April 1944, had served as an MP and was discharged in October with two punctured eardrums. Gillespie's Coast Guard obligations, meanwhile, had ended in September 1944. Livingston's Army stint ran from March through November of the same year, but his World War II experiences were much more complicated and troubling than those of his two teammates.

MICKEY LIVINGSTON

In the summer of 1939, Thompson Orville (Mickey) Livingston had been a 22-year-old catcher playing for Springfield in the Eastern League, drawing all kinds of attention with his .360 batting average, a tremendous improvement on his .223 the previous year at Trenton. His play behind the plate was also much improved, as his fielding errors had dropped to eight from the previous season's 23. The future looked promising for Mickey Livingston, but a harsh encounter with an infield wall brought his ascent to a halt. In the middle of the season, he was chasing a routine foul pop-up behind the plate when a strong gust of wind suddenly pushed the ball. Livingston ran harder toward the stands, but before he could get underneath for the catch, he ran headfirst into the cement wall of the third base dugout. The result was a severe concussion. Treatment and time off provided no relief; one month after the injury, he underwent spinal taps to relieve pressure on the brain and to improve his eyesight.

For the rest of his career, Livingston's vision was affected, especially whenever he played in extremely hot weather. When he was finally cleared to play, he limped through the rest of the season, finishing with a .299 average. Livingston managed to play another year at Springfield and then was signed by the Brooklyn Dodgers. Soon afterward, on November 11, 1940, the Dodgers traded him along with Vito Tamulis, Bill Crouch, and $100,000 to the lowly Phillies for pitcher Kirby Higbe. It was a trade typical of the rich-get-richer deals that characterized the era, with the doormat Phillies trading the pitcher who had won a quarter of their victories the previous two seasons to a first-division team in exchange for three unknowns and some badly needed cash. Livingston stayed with the Phillies until August 1943, when Cubs catcher Clyde McCullough was drafted into the military and the Cubs gave Philadelphia their aging and inexpensive pitching star, Bill Lee, in exchange for Livingston.

The following year, Livingston's draft board in tiny Newberry, South Carolina, ran into difficulties filling its quotas. Naturally, board members began reexamining Livingston's status. Perhaps the neurological issues might not be such a big deal, they reasoned. He'd been playing baseball professionally, hadn't he? Predictably, Livingston was called for another physical, and on March 28, 1944, he left baseball for boot camp. During basic training, his experience hunting small game in South Carolina served him well; at the end of his training, he earned a marksman rating. Soon, however, Uncle Sam regretted taking Livingston's neurological issues so lightly. The pressure on his head from the web and strapping in his army helmet caused severe headaches. It also exacerbated the vision problems. In October, Livingston was reclassified and granted a medical discharge. Soon afterward, his company was sent to the Battle of the Bulge, where only 300 of its 5,000 members survived. Few players in baseball welcomed the chilly Opening Day in 1945 as much as the Cubs' starting catcher, Mickey Livingston.[5]

THE SEASON BEGINS

AS PLAY BEGAN on April 17, a crowd of 11,788 braved 40-degree temperatures at Wrigley Field to cheer on their heroes. Their loyalty was rewarded as the Cubs wrung maximum efficiency out of just four hits to defeat the World Champion Cardinals and reliever Bud Byerly 3–2. Derringer, who earned the Opening Day start on the strength of his spring training performance, went nine innings, evenly spreading out seven hits, walking only one, and striking out four. Cardinals starter Ted Wilks, coming off an incredible 17–4 season, baffled Cubs hitters for the six innings he pitched, though the Cubs caught a break in the second when

Bill Nicholson pounded a Wilks fastball against the screen behind the bleachers in right, giving the Cubs an early lead. Nicholson was again instrumental in the Cubs' victory in the ninth, coaxing a walk out of Byerly. Up next was Sauer, who bunted him to second; then Johnson singled him home after an intentional walk to Pafko. It was an encouraging win against the defending World Champs, powered by the most popular Cub of the World War II era, Bill Nicholson.

Bill Nicholson

Born on December 11, 1915, in Chestertown, Maryland, a small town on the peninsula between Chesapeake Bay and the south Jersey border, William Beck Nicholson sprang from a region of the country that would soon become famous for its contributions to baseball. Eight years before Nicholson's birth and just five miles away, Jimmie Foxx was born in Sudlersville. Twelve years earlier, in 1895, Babe Ruth was born across the bay in Baltimore. Nine years before Ruth, Home Run Baker entered the world in nearby Trapp. And Nicholson wasn't the last of Maryland's home run prodigies. One year after Nicholson's birth, in 1916, Charlie "King Kong" Keller began life in Middletown.[6] Continuing the home run leadership tradition of its native sons—Baker in the 1910s, Ruth in the '20s, and Foxx in the '30s—Nicholson's accomplishments at the plate during World War II secured this small area of upper Maryland as the cradle of power hitting in the first half of the twentieth century.

As a youth, Nicholson had aspired to a naval career but was spurned by nearby Annapolis because he was colorblind. He attended Washington College in his hometown instead, where he excelled at football and baseball. After graduation, Connie Mack signed the young Nicholson, but he hit a disappointing .197 his first year in the Texas League for Oklahoma City. Near the end of the season, Mack brought him up to the Athletics for 11 games, where Nicholson caught just one fly ball and went hitless in 12 at bats, striking out five times. Not surprisingly, Mack gave up on him, burying him in the minors, and for the next few seasons, Nicholson toiled at Williamsport, Portsmouth, and Chattanooga. In the minors, however, he found his groove, hitting well over .300 for all three teams and racking up 65 home runs and 273 RBIs in only 363 games. At Chattanooga, Nicholson's manager was ex-Cubs Hall of Famer Kiki Cuyler, who was instrumental in his becoming a Cub.

Mack's Athletics needed money. During the 1938 season, they were averaging barely 5,000 fans per game, ahead of only the Chicago White Sox and the St. Louis Browns. They would finish the 1938 season more than $50,000 in the red after not having posted a profit since 1932.[7] The Cubs, meanwhile, had only one legitimate power hitter that season, Hank Leiber, who finished with 24 home runs. Cuyler convinced the Cubs that Nicholson was for real, and the Cubs gave Mack $35,000. In his first game with the Cubs, on August 1, 1939, Nicholson homered, and the love affair with the fans was under way. It wasn't long before Braves manager Casey Stengel told Cubs skipper Jimmie Wilson that he would play eight men if Wilson would only take Nicholson out of the lineup. On another occasion, Nicholson banged out one of the longest right field homers in the park's history, just missing hitting the centerfield scoreboard. In 1943 and 1944, he led the National League in home runs and RBIs, tying records held by Ruth and Foxx.

Also in 1944, Nicholson led the league in runs scored and total bases and was second in walks and slugging average, finishing second for the MVP award. On July 23, 1944, he hit four consecutive home runs at the Polo Grounds against the New York Giants. When he came up for a fifth time, Giants manager Mel Ott ordered him intentionally walked with the bases loaded, conceding one run in fear of what Nicholson might do on his own. While this is a testimonial to how respected Nicholson was at the plate, it must also be pointed out that at the time, Ott was tied with Nicholson for the National League home run lead (Ott eventually ended the season seven home runs behind, finishing second with 26), so some selfish motives by the Giants' player-manager factored in Ott's decision making as well. Finally in 1944, to the eternal aggravation of White Sox fans, Nicholson hit 33 home runs—ten more than the entire Chicago White Sox team. Adding to Nicholson's popularity with Cubs fans was the fact that he and his wife lived in Chicago's Albany Park neighborhood during the baseball season. Nicholson's $18,000 salary was one of the highest on the Cubs' payroll that year, and by 1945, his continuing productivity was expected and deemed essential if the Cubs were to have any chance to contend for the pennant. As the season opened, there was nothing to indicate that 1945 would be the most difficult and frustrating year of his career.

THE CUBS CAME back to earth, and the Cardinals more closely resembled World Champions in the second game of the season, as Harry Brecheen of Broken Bow, Oklahoma, coasted to an 8–2 victory. Meanwhile, Livingston went 3-for-4 and Sauer hit a left field home run and a double off the wall, but the Cardinals had their way with starter Prim after the third inning and were successful against his three successors: Mack Stewart, Jorge Comellas, and George Hennessey.

OFF TO PITTSBURGH AND CINCINNATI

FOLLOWING THE CARDINALS series, the Cubs boarded their Pennsylvania Railroad overnight train at Union Station and headed for the Schenley Hotel and a four-game set against the Pittsburgh Pirates, whose home was Forbes Field. Built in 1909, the stadium was one of the larger parks in the National League, seating 40,000. The field was spacious as well, with the center field line 457 feet from home plate. Both power alleys were more than 400 feet, and the left field line was 365 feet. The only measurement hostile to pitchers was the right field line, only 300 feet from home plate to the fence, a welcome sight to left-handed Cubs hitters like Cavarretta and Nicholson. Home plate at Forbes Field was near the corner of Sennott and Boquet streets, and the Pittsburgh Park District's Schenley Park bordered the outfield fences.[8] The Schenley Hotel was just on the other side of Schenley Park, very close to Forbes Field, and because of its proximity every team in the National League stayed there in 1945.

WITH VETERAN PITCHER Hy Vandenberg ending his holdout and joining the team for this first road trip, manager Charlie Grimm was hoping he would not need a parade of relief pitchers in Pittsburgh games. Grimm undoubtedly hoped to see some hitting for a change as well, after Cavarretta, Hack, and Merullo went a combined 1-for-22 in the opening series against the Cardinals. However, the Cubs lost 5–4 in the Pirates' home opener on Friday, April 20, before a crowd of 9,449 Pirates faithful. With Wyse making his first start of the season, the Cubs could not hold leads of 1–0, 3–2, or 4–2. The game marked the 20th time in eight seasons that Pirates starter Rip Sewell had beaten the Cubs. The next day, the tables were turned when Derringer and Nicholson duplicated their Opening Day heroics against the Cardinals to hold off the Pirates 4–3. Derringer scattered 13 hits and pitched all nine innings but needed a game-saving throw by Nicholson in the ninth to gun down the potential game-tying Pirates runner at the plate. Nicholson, shortstop Roy Hughes, Cavarretta, Pafko, and Johnson all had two hits off Pirates starter Preacher Roe and reliever Nick Strincevich.

The series in Pittsburgh culminated with the Cubs' first doubleheader of the season, and the 27,690 fans, along with 427 uniformed servicemen admitted free, were so frustrated with the Cubs' two victories that their angry faces were photographed for the April 26 edition of *Life* magazine. In the first game, southpaw Bob Chipman threw a three-hit shutout to win 3–0, and Prim hung on in relief of Hanyzewski and Vandenberg to ensure a 5–2 victory in the second game. Sauer led the Cubs' offense with a triple and three singles in seven at bats, and Hughes, starting at shortstop, had four hits for the afternoon as well. Pittsburgh management issued seat cushions to the fans before the game, and before the end of the second game, the crowd expressed their displeasure by flinging most of the cushions onto the field, with a *Life* magazine photographer recording the gestures for posterity. The pitching of Prim, ineffective in his previous outing against St. Louis, and Vandenberg, appearing for the first time after ending his salary holdout, were most encouraging developments, but Chipman's success in game one made the day.

BOB CHIPMAN

In 1944 Robert Howard Chipman was a freckled, thin, lanky 25-year-old thrilled to be pitching in his hometown for the Brooklyn Dodgers, even if Leo Durocher had used him sparingly the previous year. The Cubs, however, were short of left-handers and had two quality second basemen: the older, more consistent Don Johnson and the younger, temperamental but talented Eddie Stanky. On June 8, 1944, the Cubs sent the volatile Stanky to the Dodgers for Chipman in an even swap. Johnson made the National League All-Star team, Chipman went 12–10 for the year, and Stanky, who would marry Cubs coach Milt Stock's daughter, went on to future success and notoriety in New York. The Cubs believed they had acquired their first quality left hander since the legendary Larry French was in his prime after Chipman, a soft-tossing, six–foot, three-inch lefty, won four straight victories in July 1944. In his first three years in the minors, Chipman had gone 48–20. In 1939 he had led the Sally League in winning percentage, and in 1941 he led the Southern Association in shutouts. While pitching for Savannah in 1940 (where he was 17–5), he contracted undulant fever, probably from contaminated dairy products, in the hot, humid Georgia climate. He recovered but was weaker and had less endurance. The only silver lining was that this malady supplied him two different 4-F classifications from his busy Brooklyn draft board.

In 1944 Chipman was finally cleared for military duty, but he was never called up. Durocher and the Dodgers used him in all of three games after his promotion to the majors in 1941 and 1942; in six innings of work, he gave up only four hits and no earned runs. Even though effective lefty hurlers were precious commodities during the war years, Durocher was not impressed with Chipman's thin build or with his health history, and he was considered expendable when someone like Stanky was available.[9] Chipman, who at times had bristled under Dodgers manager Durocher, began thriving under the guidance of Cubs manager Grimm. If Prim could come through this year, the Cubs would have two reliable lefty starters . . . a luxury for any team.

THE FOLLOWING MONDAY, the Cubs traveled to Cincinnati and checked into the Netherland Plaza Hotel for a three-game series against the Reds. The Reds' home since 1912 had been Crosley Field, named after their owner, industrialist Powel Crosley Jr. Located at the intersection of Findlay Street and Western Avenue, the park had a seating capacity of 30,210, which was the smallest in the National League in 1945, but the dimensions of the field were about average: center field was 387 feet from home plate, the right field line was 366 feet, and the left field line was a much cozier 328 feet. A unique feature of Crosley Field was a raised three-foot berm approximately nine feet from the outfield fence, which ran from foul line to foul line and served as a warning track to the outfielders.[10]

Cold, chilly rain canceled the games on Tuesday and Thursday, but on Wednesday, April 25, clutch hitting and more quality pitching led to another victory. Passeau, in his first start of the year, threw a five-hit shutout to beat Bucky Walters 4–0. Meanwhile, Hack, Cavarretta, and Lowrey each had two hits, as did pitching star Passeau. Passeau, one of the best hitting pitchers of his time, smashed the 11th home run of his career off Walters in the third inning and then singled later in the game. After opening the season against teams considered by many to be the three toughest in the league, the Cubs were 5–2, a half game behind the first-place New York Giants. Also on this day, they received the news that Derringer, off to his best start in years, was named the National League Player of the Week by the *Sporting News*.

The Chicagoans were feeling good about themselves, indeed, as they returned to Wrigley Field for another four-game series against Pittsburgh over the weekend. Manager Charlie Grimm was getting good production out of the lineup, and his decision to play Hughes at shortstop and Lowrey in center in place of Merullo and Pafko, respectively, looked very good at this point. The pitching matchups for the weekend were Paul Derringer against Rip Sewell on Friday, Hank Wyse against Max Butcher on Saturday, and Bob Chipman and Jorge Comellas against Preacher Roe and Nick Strincevich in the Sunday doubleheader. In the first game, on Friday, April 27, Derringer spread out eight hits and coasted to a complete game and a 7–3 victory. On Saturday, Wyse pitched a masterpiece and enjoyed the support of 14 Cubs hits, getting a one-hit shutout, with Bill Salkeld ruining the no-hit bid with one out in the eighth inning. Cavarretta had a perfect day at the plate and Hughes, Sauer, and Nicholson each had two hits.

HANK WYSE

Henry Washington Wyse was beginning what would become the greatest season of his career. A 26-year-old right-hander of Irish and Cherokee descent born in Lunsford, Arkansas, Wyse came from an extremely athletic family and claimed that his two brothers, who had never played organized baseball, were superior to him in ability. In 1940 Wyse broke in with Tulsa in the Texas League and later that year played at Moline, returning in 1941 to Tulsa, where the legendary Peaches Davis taught him his devastating sinker and a great curveball. In 1941 Wyse went 20–4, and in 1942 he was 20–11. At the end of the 1942 season, the Cubs called him up, and he made his debut on September 7.[11] Altogether Wyse appeared in four games for the '42 Cubs and went 2–1, posting an excellent 1.93 ERA. In the off-season, Wyse, who worked in the Oklahoma oil fields, had injured his back in a workplace accident that excluded him from the military draft. As a result of his injury, Wyse often wore a corset when he pitched. In 1944 Wyse emerged as the best young pitcher on the team, going 16–15 and gaining Grimm's trust. Nicknamed

Hooks in honor of his money pitch, Wyse's effectiveness came from his ability to consistently throw all the pitches in his repertoire for strikes, rarely giving up walks, and the tremendous movement on his curve, which he was confident throwing in any situation. In February, two months before the start of the 1945 season, he married Doris Ann Burns. Before it was over, 1945 would be a year he would never forget.[12]

CLOUDY WEATHER AND temperatures in the low 40s on Sunday, April 29 did not deter Chicago's faithful, as 36,637 paying customers and 1,100 uniformed servicemen came out to see the Sunday doubleheader. Up to this point in the season, the Cubs had fielded flawlessly, committing only three errors in their first nine games, but Chipman's efforts in game one were sabotaged by fielding gaffes and miscues, as Preacher Roe limited the erstwhile hard-hitting Cubs to five singles and outlasted Chipman, Stewart, Prim, and Vandenberg to win easily, 6–2. In the second game, Comellas pitched five strong innings but fell apart in the sixth, when he and Vandenberg allowed the three final Pirates runs that led to a 5–4 Pirates victory and a Pittsburgh sweep of the doubleheader. Comellas, Vandenberg, and Stewart, who pitched the ninth inning, probably deserved a better fate; the Cubs banged out 13 hits but stranded ten runners, to the great relief of Pirates starter Strincevich and his reliever, Xavier Rescigno. The huge crowd could only take solace in the fact that Cavarretta, Nicholson, Sauer, and Lowrey—the Cubs' three, four, five, and six hitters—were collectively 9-for-19 in the second game.

So the month of April ended on a sour note for the Cubs, but after playing what were considered to be the three classiest teams in the National League at the start of the 1945 season, they felt very good, indeed, about their 7–4 record, which placed them only a half game behind the surprising New York Giants. They would open May at home against Cincinnati, after which they would face a brutal six-city, 22-day road trip, not to return to Chicago again until May 23.

ON THE ROAD IN MAY

TRAVEL HARDSHIPS CAUSED the War Transportation Board to make several changes in major league scheduling during the 1945 season. The Cubs got a taste of these changes by the first week of May. With the government restricting rail travel, road trips became longer. On May 4 the Cubs would begin an arduous 17-game, 16-day road trip, starting in St. Louis and ending on the east coast. Originally scheduled to be off Monday, Tuesday, and Thursday and to play the Cincinnati Reds at Wrigley Field on Wednesday, May 2, the team had planned to travel to St. Louis by day coach for the start of their prolonged May road trip on Friday. With the Wednesday game against Cincinnati rained out, the team disembarked from the train and checked into St. Louis's Chase Hotel to begin preparing for the Saturday game against the World Champions. Meanwhile, they were faced with the prospect of five days with no baseball. The trip was made without reserve infielder Johnny Ostrowski, a fan favorite and the home run king of the Pacific Coast League, who started for the Los Angeles Angels in 1944 but had played very little with the Cubs. Ostrowski was eventually optioned back to the minors and sent to Kansas City to play for manager Casey Stengel.

THE CARDINALS' HOME was the ancient Sportsman's Park, located on the corner of Grand Boulevard and Dodier Street, two thoroughfares with more streetcar than automobile traffic. The intersection had been the site of professional baseball in St. Louis since 1872, and the present configuration of the park dated to 1909. The St. Louis Browns owned it, and the Cardinals had been paying rent since 1920 to play there. Double-decked behind the field from foul line to foul line, with bleachers in left and center field and a pavilion in right, the park had a capacity of 34,000. The center field fence was a distant 426 feet from home, the left field line was 351, and the left field power alley, 379 feet. Even so, left-handed hitters liked playing at Sportsman's Park, because the right field fence was only 310 feet away down the line and a relatively easy 354 feet down the right field power alley.[13]

If the Cubs were rusty from their week off on Saturday, May 5, the sparse crowd of 3,032 at Sportsman's Park did not seem to notice, as Derringer held the Cardinals to seven singles and a double and easily handled the World Champions, by a score of 5–1, for his fourth victory in the young 1945 campaign. Livingston got three hits, and Cavarretta and Hughes had two apiece, including a triple by Hughes, to pace the ten-hit Cubs attack. Suddenly, the Cardinals appeared vulnerable if Harry

Brecheen, Ken Burkhardt, Mort Cooper, or Max Lanier were not pitching. The Cubs had now beaten Wilks and Byerly, and the promising George Dockins of Clyde, Kansas, had surrendered four hits to the Cubs in just one inning on this Saturday afternoon game.

Unfortunately, the Chicagoans did not fare so well in the doubleheader that followed on Sunday. On that day, the Cubs could do nothing against their old nemesis, Max Lanier, while the Cardinals hit Chipman hard in the first game. The lanky lefty gave up a home run to Johnny Hopp, two doubles to Whitey Kurowski, and one double each to right fielder Augie Bergamo and catcher Del Rice, leaving in the fourth inning with a 5–1 deficit before the Redbirds sealed a 6–2 victory. In the second game, Wyse pitched a little better for the North Siders, but the Cubs' hitting short-circuited again, and Cooper pitched a complete game for a 5–1 victory. After the first game, Grimm benched outfielder Sauer, who was 0-for-8 since arriving in St. Louis but came to town with a lusty .350 batting average. He also moved Lowrey to left and put the previous year's starter, Pafko, back in center, but Pafko went 0-for-3 with a hit by pitch in four at bats. In spite of their early successes, Grimm had a minor dilemma handling the outfield. Nicholson was a fixture, and Pafko, a big contributor in 1944, was starting very slowly. Lou Novikoff and Ival Goodman were gone; Lowrey was back from the service but had irked Grimm with his salary holdout. Secory was a backup, and many thought Sauer, if given the opportunity, would blossom as a bona fide major leaguer.

Ed Sauer

Edward Sauer, the athletic, muscular younger brother of the legendary Hank Sauer, was brought up to the Cubs on September 22, 1943, after starring for the Nashville Vols. Touted as a "right-handed Bill Nicholson" (the two were almost the same size and stature), Sauer was named Most Valuable Player for 1943 in the Southern Association after pacing the Vols with a league-leading .368 average, 200 hits, 100 RBIs, 50 doubles, 30 stolen bases, and ten home runs.[14] In 1943 with the Cubs, he hit .273 in 14 games, but he hit only .220 in 23 games in 1944; over these two years, he totaled only seven doubles, with one stolen base and no home runs. Sauer might have had more of an opportunity if Pafko had not had the year he did in 1944. Ed's older, larger brother, Hank, was a promising young outfielder for Cincinnati when he went off to the military before the 1943 season. Little did anyone know in 1945 that in less than four years, Ed would be forgotten by the Cubs' faithful while Hank would be well on his way to becoming National League MVP for the Cubs, so beloved that fans would stick packages of chewing tobacco in the ivy for him and call him the Mayor of Wrigley Field.

ON MONDAY, MAY 7, the Cubs received the unwelcome news that pitcher Hanyzewski had been called to report to his Indianapolis draft board in one week for a preinduction physical. This sent a scare through the entire roster, as the federal government several months earlier had declared its intention to review the 4-F classifications for professional athletes. Ron Northey, a promising outfielder for the Phillies, Reds catcher Ray Mueller, and Braves catcher Hugh Poland had already been inducted on the basis of this change.

ED HANYZEWSKI

Hanyzewski, a handsome Notre Dame alumnus with two children, was classified 4-F due to a knee injury suffered while playing football at Washington High School in South Bend. Chicago signed him when he struck out 14 Cubs for a South Bend semipro team in an exhibition game.[15] Hanyzewski broke in with the Cubs in 1942, and by the start of the 1945 season he had appeared in 53 games for the Cubs, with frequent arm injuries limiting his appearances. When he was able to pitch, he had an exceptional repertoire, including one of the quickest fastballs in the National League. The shining moment in his career occurred early in the 1944 season, when he handcuffed the Phillies to win 5–3 and end a dismal 13-game losing streak, which triggered the firing of manager Jimmie Wilson. The Cubs were counting on Hanyzewski for the 1945 season, so the new development was another unexpected concern.

THE CUBS LEFT St. Louis for their first trip of the season to Philadelphia to visit the lowly Phillies at Shibe Park, the Phils' home since 1938, when they moved from the tiny Baker Bowl. Built in 1909 at the corner of 21st Street and Lehigh Avenue, Shibe dominated the corner with its four-story, domed rotunda, flanked by the stadium's long, three-story facade. No expense was spared in building Shibe Park, which was designed in a magnificent French Renaissance style and constructed in red brick with gray stone ornamentation. The capacity in 1945 was 33,000. Center field was an impossible 468 feet from home plate, but the foul lines in left and right were a reasonable 334 and 331 feet, respectively.[16]

Unhappy with his outfield production after the St. Louis series, Grimm benched Lowrey and Sauer, replacing them, respectively, with Pafko, who had been slumping earlier, and Secory, who had not played very much yet during the season, recovering from the leg injury he suffered in the exhibition game against the White Sox. Grimm also moved the hot-hitting Livingston up to fifth in the batting order. When the Cubs arrived in Philadelphia on May 8, many of them left the Ben Franklin Hotel immediately after checking in to participate in the V-E Day celebrations going on near the Liberty Bell. There was little to celebrate about their game the next day against the Phillies, however. Derringer, going for his fifth straight victory, was roughed up by a team that had won just three of its first 16 games, as the Cubs dropped their third straight and their fifth out of the last six, losing by a score of 5–2. The big right-hander gave up seven hits and one walk, yielding the mound to Comellas with one out in the fifth inning and the Cubs behind 5–1. Stewart finished on the mound for the Chicagoans and was effective, but the game by then was no longer in question. Livingston and Secory were the only Cubs to solve Lee's offerings, both getting two hits. Bad weather caused the cancellation of Thursday's game, so the Cubs had an entire day to ponder their three game losing streak.

The Cubs' outlook improved in the last game of the series, on Friday, however, when Wyse threw a complete game five-hitter to put down the lowly Phillies 7–1. Cavarretta, going 4-for-4, led a 12-hit attack against Philadelphia pitcher Charley Sproull and his three unlucky successors: Vern Kennedy, Charlie Ripple, and Charley Shanz. For the Cubs, Hack, Secory (hitting well for the second straight game), and the pitcher, Wyse, all had two hits. The cold afternoon affair was played in front of one of the smallest crowds of the season, 811 paid attendees. The Cubs exited Philadelphia immediately after the game to get ready for a game in Boston on Saturday against the Braves.

THE BRAVES PLAYED at Braves Field, located at the corner of Babcock Street and Commonwealth Avenue, near the Charles River. In 1945 Braves Field had the largest capacity of any National League park, with seating for 41,000, but the Braves historically drew poorly. A pavilion was located down the left field line, and the bleachers in right field were called the Jury Box because the fans seated there were very quick to pass judgment on the play of anyone unlucky enough to be in right field. The field was a perfectly symmetrical 340 feet down both foul lines, with center field only 370 feet from home plate.

Before Saturday's game, Grimm shuffled the lineup again, replacing shortstop Hughes with Schuster and center fielder Pafko with Lowrey after Pafko went hitless against Philadelphia. Things started poorly for the Chicagoans as the Braves got to Prim, the starting pitcher, for six hits and six runs in only three innings, for a 6–1 advantage. Vandenberg, Comellas, and Stewart were ineffective in relief, and the Cubs trailed 12–6 after six innings. After the Cubs scored twice and loaded the bases in the seventh, Braves manager Bob Coleman called upon his ace, Red Barrett, to face Cavarretta and save the game. Cavarretta responded with his first home run of the year, a grand slam into the Braves Field Jury Box. It marked the first game of the season in which Cubs hitters bailed out a failed pitching effort. Lowrey had a double, a triple, and a home run, and Dewey Williams had three hits and a walk. Williams, who had replaced Livingston behind the plate for the last game in Philadelphia, was becoming a pleasant surprise at the plate, going 4-for-7 with a walk in two games. In spite of Williams's contributions, Grimm sat him out for the finale on Sunday against the Braves. His replacement, Paul Gillespie, went hitless as both teams endured a 90-minute rain delay and the Braves won 3–2, with Nate Andrews besting Passeau. The first two series of the long East Coast road trip were finished; unfortunately, the Cubs found they could play no better than .500 ball against the two weakest teams in the league. As they took a New York Central night train to Manhattan to check into the Commodore Hotel, their home for the next eight days, they glumly looked forward to four games against the first-place Giants and four more against the second-place Dodgers.

THE BOTTOM FELL out, and quickly at that, as soon as the New York series started. In the Monday game on May 14, Williams's first career home run, a three-run pinch-hit shot off undefeated Giants All-Star Bill Voiselle, gave the Cubs a 5–4 lead in the ninth, which disappeared when Napoleon

Reyes tied the game in the bottom of the frame with a long homer, his second of the game, off Vandenberg. The Giants sewed it up in the tenth with two hits leading to the winning run off Prim. Chicago's first extra inning game ended as a heartbreaking 6–5 defeat.

Dewey Williams

Dewey Edgar Williams was an 18-year-old North Carolinian when he broke into professional baseball as an outfielder with Macon in the South Atlantic League in 1937 under manager Milt Stock. Moving up the ranks in the minors, he played every position except shortstop and pitcher for the Atlanta Crackers in 1940, and he was hitting International League pitching at a .313 clip as a catcher for Toronto in 1944.[17] That was the same year Stock joined the Cubs as a coach, and with the Cubs' catching corps losing Gillespie and Livingston to the war that year, Williams debuted with the Cubs on June 28 on the basis of Stock's hearty recommendation. Picked up for his catching abilities, Williams at this early stage of the 1945 season was leading the team with a .500 batting average, and he had scored five runs in only 12 at bats.

THE FOLLOWING DAY, the Giants nicked Derringer for four runs in the fifth inning and hung on as the Cubs could muster only six hits off Van Lingle Mungo and Ace Adams for another one-run defeat, 5–4. With that loss, the Cubs fell to .500, 10–10, for the first time since April 21. Voiselle came back to pitch against the Cubs in their first night game on Wednesday, May 16, and toyed with the punchless Cubs, going all the way to improve his record to 7–0 with a six-hit, 6–0 shutout. The first-place Giants shelled Cubs ace Wyse for 11 hits in five innings; the only bright spot for the Chicagoans was the fact that Pafko finally got on track with two hits. They were close to salvaging the fourth and final game at the Polo Grounds on Thursday, going into the eighth inning with a 5–2 lead behind some strong pitching by Passeau, when the Giants lit him, Vandenberg, Chipman, and Stewart for six runs in the eighth, resulting in an 8–5 victory. They lost more than the lead in the eighth when shortstop Hughes wrenched his knee making a play in short center and had to be carried off the field. Schuster replaced Hughes, who would be out for two weeks. The loss put the Cubs a distant eight and a half games behind the first-place Giants.

Moving on to Ebbets Field to play Friday night in front of a gathering of 31,334, the Dodgers' largest crowd of the young season, the Cubs were able to pound out 14 hits and 12 runs, breaking out of their offensive slump. Dodgers pitcher Lee Pfund, Wheaton College's football and basketball coach in the off-season, gave up four hits to Hack and two each to Johnson, Nicholson, Cavarretta, and the resurgent Pafko. Trouble was the Dodgers got 14 hits and 15 runs off Erickson (who started), Prim, Comellas, and Vandenberg to rally to a 15–12 victory. The Cubs, high fliers in the National League just one week earlier, were suddenly 10–13 and mired in the second division.

Several things had gone wrong for Chicago, though not all at once. Lowrey was hitting .255; Nicholson, .253; Johnson, .238; and Pafko, before he got hot Thursday and Friday, a meager .222. Grimm was encouraged when he learned that Hanyzewski once again failed his military induction physical and would soon be rejoining the staff, but Comellas, Erickson, Prim, and Stewart were pitching very ineffectively, and Vandenberg's name also came up prominently in these various losses in New York. Grimm's patience with Vandenberg, small due to his holdout to begin with, grew even smaller when the big right-hander, frustrated at how poorly he was pitching, got into an argument with the hotel detective at the Commodore, which resulted in fisticuffs, with the hotel's employee getting the worst of it.[18] Grimm did not summon the 39-year-old veteran to the mound for the next 11 days.

The resilience of the 1945 Cubs, however, began to emerge with the road trip–ending doubleheader against the Dodgers on Sunday, May 20. A crowd of 36,176 witnessed 18 innings of baseball with their local heroes never ahead as the Cubs took both games, 4–2 and 4–1. Derringer and Wyse both threw complete game victories, giving the recently ineffective bull pen a much-needed rest. Cubs hitters had no problems with either Dodgers starter, ex-Cub Curt Davis in the first game and the tough young Hal Gregg in the second, jumping on them for early leads in the first innings. Leadoff man Hack had a big afternoon, and second baseman Johnson came to life with the bat, going 5-for-8, with one hit being a triple. So the Cubs traveled home with a 12–13 record, going 5–9 on this long, tough road trip. They looked forward to two days of rest before starting a 14-game, 15-day home stand starting Wednesday, May 23, against Philadelphia, the weakest team in the National League.

BACK AT WRIGLEY

THE CHICAGOANS OPENED the home stand on a positive note, beating the Phillies 5–3 behind a complete game effort from Passeau. Johnson, Nicholson, Cavarretta, and Lowrey led the offensive attack, but the backbreaker for Philadelphia occurred in the sixth inning when the Cubs successfully executed the hidden ball trick. The legendary Jimmy Foxx, at 38 in his last season as a player and only six years away from his Hall of Fame induction, led off the sixth inning with a hit and represented the lead run after he was sacrificed to second. Cubs shortstop Schuster went to the mound to talk with Passeau, and as Foxx led off second, he was promptly tagged by the diminutive Schuster, an embarrassing mental lapse by Foxx, who fell victim to the hidden ball trick that took his struggling team out of the inning.

BILL SCHUSTER

The college-educated William Charles Schuster—at five feet, nine inches and 165 pounds, the second-smallest Cub on the roster—had played three games for the Pirates in 1937 and two for the Braves in 1939 but languished in the minors until 1943. The Buffalo native was a skilled fielder and chatterbox, who loved to talk it up in the infield, hopefully distracting his opponents out of their game. Schuster was part of the Pacific Coast League champion Los Angeles Angels in 1943, playing well at shortstop and hitting .276 with 64 RBIs. He was one of the seven Angels—the others being outfielders John Ostrowski and Andy Pafko, pitchers Red Lynn and Jodie Phipps, catcher Billy Holm, and second baseman Roy Hughes—to be called up to the Cubs after winning the Pacific Coast League title.[19] The Cubs' organization had extremely high hopes for this group and dedicated the entire last page of their September 1943 newsletter to their pictures and accomplishments. The biggest obstacle Schuster faced was his age. At the start of the 1945 season, he was already 33 years old, a little younger than Hughes but six years older than Merullo.

WEDNESDAY, MAY 23, ended with the St. Louis Cardinals strengthening their pitching staff by trading the disgruntled Mort Cooper to the Boston Braves for pitcher Red Barrett and $60,000. Cooper, who had held out with his brother after going 22–7 and allowing only two earned runs in 16 innings of

World Series work, was one of the most successful National League pitchers in the World War II years. Barrett had a lot of promise and ability, for the most part unrealized because of the mediocrity of his teammates in Boston, but had had successes against the Cubs. From Chicago's standpoint, one of their main adversaries was stronger, not weaker, after the trade.

On Thursday the Phillies' Kewpie Barrett handcuffed Chicago hitters, allowing only five hits while his teammates got six runs off Derringer, Stewart, and Erickson for a 6–3 Philadelphia victory. The game marked the second time that season that the weak Phillies beat Derringer, the Cubs' most effective starter to date, whose efforts included two victories over World Champion St. Louis. While this one loss might not be a major concern, the ground that the Cubs were losing to front-running New York was becoming one. At the end of this day, the Giants were 21–6, playing .777 baseball, off to their best start since 1907. Voiselle, their tall, dominating starter who already had two victories over the Cubs, was 7–0 and named National League Player of the Week by the *Sporting News*. On Friday, Hack, Cavarretta, and Schuster combined for ten hits, with Schuster being a perfect 3-for-3, to lead Wyse to a complete game 4–3 victory. The game was saved when center fielder Pafko raced to the 400-foot marker in deep right to make a dipped-glove, backhanded catch on Vince DiMaggio's deep liner with Coaker Triplett in scoring position. Hack, going 4-for-5 for the day, turned in another great offensive performance, which Chicago fans had come to expect.

STAN HACK

Perhaps the greatest leadoff man in Cubs history, 35-year-old Stanley Camfield Hack (from California) was in 1945 in his 14th season with Chicago and showed no signs of slowing down. He was on the team in their World Series appearances in 1932, 1935, and 1938 and had a .333 career batting average in World Series play. He had also appeared in the 1938, '39, '41, and '43 All-Star Games and had a .400 average in All-Star competition. He led the National League in stolen bases in 1938 and tied for the lead in 1939. He tied for the league lead in hits in 1940 and finished first in that category in 1941. He married Dorothy Weisel, a well-known amateur tennis star, in 1932. For years he owned a 10,000-acre ranch near Pendleton, Oregon, which he sold to a cousin in 1945; he was also an experienced pilot.[20] Hack's sunny disposition and calm demeanor earned him the nickname Smilin' Stan. In spite of the nickname, Hack found playing for the Cubs under Jimmie Wilson to be unrewarding, and he retired after the 1943 season. When Grimm replaced Wilson early in 1944, Hack was talked out of retirement rather easily.[21] His presence on the team was proving to be invaluable.

On Saturday the bats were silenced, held to only five hits by Phillies starter and ex-Cub Bill Lee, but big Paul Erickson, getting his first start of the season, threw a complete game four-hitter—good enough for a 2–1 win. The Cubs loaded the bases on two walks following catcher Len Rice's leadoff single, and Grimm had catcher Paul Gillespie bat for Erickson. Gillespie walked on a full count, forcing in the winning run. The home stand started well, with Chicago taking three out of four for a 15–14 record on the young season, but perhaps more important, getting big contributions from their bench (Rice, Schuster, and Gillespie) and a surprisingly strong pitching effort from the previously ineffective Erickson.

On Sunday, May 27, the Chicagoans began to play host to the Brooklyn Dodgers with a doubleheader starting off the four-game series. The Dodgers were still firmly entrenched in second place, largely due to an 11-game winning streak earlier in the month, but they slipped after the Cubs had beaten them twice one week earlier and by May 27 had lost seven of their last eight games. A crowd of 37,133, not including 1,100 freely admitted servicemen, saw a little of everything in a memorable seven-hour marathon of baseball.

Prim finally came into his own in the first game, surviving eight Dodgers hits and a 90-minute rain delay to gain a 6–1 victory. With a 1–0 lead in the fourth inning, Dodgers manager Leo Durocher was thrown from the game after he baited home plate umpire Bill Stewart into an argument over a called strike and then proceeded to engage in one of his legendary histrionic, play-to-the-crowd tantrums. In the sixth, both Goody Rosen and Augie Galan tried to stretch singles into doubles on long hits to center field, and both times Pafko, with the strongest throwing arm in the National League, tossed them out at second. Galan was incensed with the call and animatedly took off on second base umpire, big George Margerkurth. In their half of the sixth, Rice started the Cubs off with a single and stole second when Pafko muffed a sacrifice bunt attempt.

Pafko completely surprised the Dodgers on the next pitch, this time bunting Rice successfully to third and easily beating a wild throw to first for a bunt single, with Rice scoring on the throwing error.

At this point, a very rattled Hal Gregg walked Lowrey, whereupon Heinz Becker, pinch-hitting for shortstop Schuster, tripled over left fielder Luis Olmo's head for two more runs, more than the Cubs would need to preserve the victory. When the inning was over, Dodgers second baseman and ex-Cub Eddie Stanky, never a fan favorite in Wrigley Field, petulantly threw his glove at umpire Bill Dunn, who excused him for the afternoon. Stanky's impulsive regression cost his team more than the first game, because in 1945 any player thrown out of the first game of a doubleheader was also ineligible to play in the second game as well. The second game gave the huge crowd an even rarer experience—a tie. At 8:10 in the evening, Hack grounded out with the bases loaded in the eighth inning, at which time the umpires called the game on account of darkness.

Chicago merriment and Brooklyn misery continued on Monday. The Dodgers' 13-year nemesis, Paul Derringer, continued his mastery on the mound with a complete game nine-hit victory, 5–3. Johnson had three hits, and Sauer drove in two runs, playing outfield so Grimm could give Pafko, one of Sunday's big heroes, a day off. On Tuesday, the day before the big Memorial Day doubleheader, Grimm decided to save his frontline pitching for the Giants and let Stewart start the game on the hill to face the Dodgers' Ben Chapman. Chapman in 1945 was a 36-year-old, 14-year major league veteran who had started in the Yankees' outfield with Babe Ruth in the early 1930s and later toiled for the Senators, Red Sox, Indians, and White Sox. After the 1941 season, he took a minor league managerial position and taught himself how to pitch in his spare time. Three years later, in August 1944, the pitching-starved Dodgers called him up. In the game on Tuesday, May 29, Chapman cruised as the Dodgers won easily, 10–3. They amassed 14 hits off Stewart, Comellas, and Vandenberg, who saw his first action since his difficulties in Gotham almost two weeks earlier. In spite of this loss, the home stand was emerging as a big success, with five wins, two losses, and one tie. The hitting was coming around, the pitching in the main continued to be consistent, and the Cubs just went toe-to-toe with everyone's bitterest rivals, Durocher's Dodgers, and did not blink.

ON MEMORIAL DAY, Wednesday May 30, a standing room only crowd of 42,458, the largest gathering in Wrigley Field since 1939, saw the Cubs split a doubleheader with the league-leading New York Giants. Wyse, who started the first game, pitched tentatively and left after the second inning, having given up six hits and four runs. Prim relieved and did well enough, holding the Giants at bay while the Cubs worked up a 6–5 lead after four innings and staying through the eighth inning. After the fourth, Cubs fielding, which had been impeccable up to this point in the season, completely deteriorated. Johnson made two errors, while Cavarretta, Schuster, and Lowrey each had one, and the Giants were essentially given an 8–6 victory. The huge crowd became aggravated with their hometown heroes, and after the game, the Cubs were booed for the first time in Wrigley Field that season. Adding insult to injury for the fans was Mel Ott's record-breaking accomplishment in his first at bat. The legendary Giants hitter doubled off Wyse in the first inning, which increased his career total bases to 4,889, surpassing the 28-year record of Honus Wagner.

The crowd calmed down quickly in the second game, however, as Chipman threw a complete game three-hitter and the Cubs cruised to an 11–2 victory. This impressive offensive output came at the expense of no less than Bill Voiselle, who departed after giving up six runs in the first three innings. Voiselle had been unbeaten until just two weeks earlier and had given the Cubs difficulties in his previous appearances against them. Merullo, getting a start at shortstop, had three RBIs; his partner at the keystone, second baseman Johnson, had three hits. Center fielder Pafko had a single, a double, and a home run, while Hack, Cavarretta, and Nicholson each had two hits. They would not see New York again for one month, since the single game against them scheduled on Thursday was rained out.

SO THE CUBS rolled into June in fifth place, with a record of 18–16, six and a half games behind the Giants. They got yet another day off when the rain continued, forcing the cancellation of the Friday game at Wrigley against the Boston Braves. General manager Jim Gallagher made a roster move, returning pitcher Comellas to the Los Angeles Angels in the Pacific Coast League. Comellas had had ample opportunities but pitched effectively in only two outings. When he went AWOL from the team for a period in mid-May, his fate was sealed. Taking his spot on the pitching staff was Lon Warneke, the Cubs' pitching legend who had retired after the 1943 season. Warneke had been managing the Navy's baseball team in Camden, Arkansas, when he accepted an offer to rejoin Grimm. The 36-year-old Arkansas Hummingbird compiled a 192–120 record in 14 seasons with the Cubs and Cardinals and was instrumental in leading the Cubs to their pennant in 1932, his first full year in the majors, when he went 22–6.

The Cubs finally got to play again on Saturday, June 2, but they could not put nine good innings together and lost to the Braves 5–4. Pafko remained hot, going 3-for-5 (getting a triple and two singles), while Johnson and Livingston added two hits apiece, but Boston figured out Derringer's offerings early in the game. Relieving for Boston and saving the game was Joe Heving, a free agent picked up by the Braves who had been released by the Cleveland Indians after going 8–3 in an American League–high 63 games in 1944. The remarkable Heving, who broke into baseball in 1930, was only three months shy of his 45th birthday, betraying his status as the only active grandfather in the major leagues during the 1945 season.

The Sunday doubleheader, like the one on Memorial Day, found the Cubs beating themselves in the first game but winning decisively in the second; unlike the Memorial Day twin bill, only 9,110 fans came out in the unseasonably cold 45-degree weather. In game one, the Cubs hit safely in every inning but could never deliver a knockout punch against lefty Bob Logan, the ex-Cub (1937 and 1938) who started for Boston. The Braves got a run in the fifth and another in the sixth off the stingy Wyse, who pitched effectively but who was hurt by shortstop Merullo's and second baseman Johnson's errors, which led to both Boston runs. In spite of their errors, Chicago lost because their 11-hit attack was wasted when nobody could hit in the clutch. Nicholson had three hits, Pafko and Hack each had two, and Cavarretta added a triple, but Chicago could not string anything together. Passeau's brilliant performance gained the Cubs a split, as they beat the Braves 3–1 in the second game. Catcher Phil Masi and pitcher Jim Tobin were the only Boston batsmen with singles as Passeau threw a complete game two-hitter and was a perfect 3-for-3 at the plate. The 14-game home stand came to an end, with the Cubs going 7–4 with three rainouts, firmly entrenched in fifth place with a 19–18 record, looking up at the Cardinals, Pirates, Dodgers, and Giants but hearing footsteps behind them at the same time. Cincinnati was starting to play good baseball, in the process of winning 11 of 12, hot on the Cubs' heels, as the Chicagoans headed to St. Louis for a short three-game series.

THE COLD WEATHER that the Cubs endured at home on Sunday during their doubleheader against Boston was unexpectedly continuing in St. Louis, and the Tuesday night and Wednesday night games were canceled due to cold weather. Whether or not the games could have been played was open to question; the St. Louis franchise had a history of calling off games when they thought weather would be a detriment to the size of the crowd. Finally, on Thursday evening, the Cubs and Cards were able to play. The Cubs, getting a lackluster pitching performance from Erickson, who surrendered six hits and four runs in three innings, lost 6–4. The Cardinals starter, Jack Creel, held the Cubs hitless through the first five innings. Merullo and Heinz Becker, who played first for Cavarretta, were the most successful Cubs batsmen.

THE CHICAGOANS BOARDED their midnight train back to Chicago in sixth place, the loss having put them behind the streaking Cincinnati Reds, who awaited them in Chicago for a four-game series over the weekend at Wrigley Field. At least three clouds hung over the team's current horizon. Nicholson, who was reclassified 1-A by his Maryland draft board over the winter as part of the reexamination of 4-F ballplayers, and Chipman, who experienced the same treatment from his in Brooklyn, both faced a preinduction physical the following morning. Also, the whole team faced the fact that they had played three night games so far in the season, they had lost all three, and they had 12 more to look forward to. In the first three night games, their opponents' batting average was .365 and theirs was .252; they had also been outscored, 27–16, with 12 of those runs coming in one game.

Those sorry numbers may have been for night games, but the contest of Friday, June 8, was a day game, and the Cubs opened their short weekend home stand on a winning note, beating the Reds 7–3 in front of a small afternoon crowd of 3,446. Derringer won his seventh game of the season by handling his ex-teammates with comparative ease, their three runs coming in the seventh after a throwing error by shortstop Merullo. Merullo more than atoned for this fielding gaffe at the plate, however, being one of two Cubs to get three hits, the other being his roommate, Cavarretta. The Reds' starter, whom the Cubs solved early, was Hod Lisenbee, at 47 one of the oldest individuals to ever play in the majors and the only one still playing in 1945 who was born before the turn of the century, on September 28, 1898. Lisenbee broke into the major leagues on April 23, 1927, with the Washington Senators. He had been out of the majors since 1936, when he appeared in 19 games for the Philadelphia Athletics. The pitching-starved Reds, their staff decimated by the demands of the war, were more than happy to have him in 1945.

Earlier on Friday, Nicholson passed his preinduction physical and first baseman Becker received his notice for the same from his Dallas draft board. The chances of Nicholson being drafted at this late date, however, would be slim, since he was colorblind, was over the age of 30, had two children, and owned a farm. Becker's notice was less of a concern, perhaps, because of the significant problems he had with his feet. In spite of such speculations, these preinduction notices, necessitated by the uncertainty over the number of troops the Allied forces might need to deploy to end the war with Japan, even though victory in Europe was achieved almost a month earlier, were extremely concerning to all the teams, players, and their families during the 1945 season.

On Saturday, June 9, pitching, defense, and timely hitting helped Wyse cruise to his sixth victory of the year, with a final score of 5–1, in front of 5,236 pleased Cubs fans. Wyse scattered 11 singles and walked two, not allowing the Reds to score after the first inning. Behind second, Johnson made a great catch of a Texas leaguer off the bat of left fielder Dick Sipek, taking the air out of a potentially big first inning for the visiting Reds, and the Cubs were in control the rest of the way. Roommates Cavarretta and Merullo were the only Chicagoans without a hit; no Cub had more than one safety, and Nicholson's triple high off the curve in the right field wall was the only extra base hit of the game. Foreshadowing postseason developments, over in the American League, the Detroit Tigers won their second straight game over the Chicago White Sox, while the Boston Red Sox dusted off the New York Yankees to give the Tigers the American League lead for the first time that season. The Yankees had been in first place since May 25, but the surging Tigers put baseball on notice that they would be a major player in the American League pennant race from that day forward.

In the Sunday doubleheader against the Reds, the Cubs thrilled a crowd of 28,746 by taking both ends of the twin bill, with final scores of 10–7 and 7–4. Grimm started Prim in the first game, but the old right-hander could not get out of the first inning, yielding the mound to Stewart with only two out and a 2–0 Reds lead. Stewart lasted until the eighth, at which time Grimm, with his charges tied at 4–4, summoned Chipman and Erickson. In the bottom of the eighth, Pafko broke the tie with a two-run homer, and Derringer came in and shut down his old teammates to save the Cubs' victory. Becker went 3-for-5 with a long home run and four RBIs. Pafko matched Becker by also going 3-for-5 with a homer but had three RBIs. In the second game, Reds starter Frank Dasso and Cubs pitcher Passeau dueled each other for nine innings, as Cincinnati desperately tried to salvage one game of the series. With the Reds ahead 4–3 in the bottom of the eighth, Nicholson and Livingston hit back-to-back homers to propel a four-run inning with two out, leading to a 7–4 Cubs victory. As in the first game, Pafko and Becker figured prominently in the Cubs' offense.

Things were looking up for the Cubs as they hurriedly readied themselves for an early evening train to Pittsburgh, where they would play another dreaded night game on Tuesday and a doubleheader on Thursday. They cooled off the hottest team in baseball by sweeping the Reds. Nicholson was starting to hit for power, Pafko was starting to hit and drive in runs, and Passeau won his last two games with excellent efforts. With the four-game sweep, the Cubs moved into the first division, their record at 23–19, .005 percentage points ahead of the 25–21 St. Louis Cardinals.

WHILE THE CUBS were doing well, however, the Pirates were doing even better, and the pitching and hitting of their starter lefty Al Gerheauser was too much to prevent the Cubs from dropping their fourth night game of the year. Gerheauser scattered nine Chicago hits, while Wyse, Erickson, the little-used George Hennessey, and Stewart yielded 14, the result being a 9–3 Pittsburgh victory. Gerheauser, who would get only seven hits during the entire 1945 season, had the game of his life at the plate, with four singles in four at bats and two RBIs.

The Thursday doubleheader resembled the Cubs' futile efforts one month earlier in New York, with the streaking Pirates winning their sixth and seventh straight games, 5–2 and 6–5, to vault into first place ahead of the slumping New York Giants. Chicago never led in any of the 18 innings played, as Max Butcher and Rip Sewell, with relief help from Xavier Rescigno, held the Cubs to a two-game total of 12 singles and a double. Chipman, hit hard in the first game, gave way early to Erickson and Prim, who both pitched much better than they had been pitching, but Cubs hitters never mounted a threat against Butcher. In game two, Derringer struck out 11 and walked none but gave up 11 of Pittsburgh's 13 hits. The Cubs lost a great opportunity to make a difference in the National League pennant race by losing this doubleheader. When they went into this game, only five games separated the first-place Giants from the seventh-place Reds, but by dropping two, the Cubs fell to 23–22, firmly entrenched in fifth place and further from the first-place Pirates at the end of the day than they were from the first-place Giants when the day began. They had little time to feel sorry for themselves as an evening Pennsylvania Railroad train was waiting to take them to Cincinnati for a twi-night doubleheader on Friday, an off day Saturday, and another doubleheader on Sunday.

ANOTHER ROUND WITH THE REDS AND THE PIRATES

ONCE SETTLED INTO the Netherland Plaza Hotel in Cincinnati, the unpredictable Cubs continued their pattern of playing superbly after playing poorly. Passeau and Vandenberg, the latter officially out of Grimm's doghouse with his first start of the year, surrendered only one run to the Reds in 18 innings as the Chicagoans once again took both ends of a doubleheader, with final scores of 8–1 and 3–0. In game one, Passeau faced Vern Kennedy, who reported to the Reds one hour before game time after being released by the Philadelphia Phillies earlier that day. Passeau's teammates nicked the new Reds hurler for seven singles, two doubles, and a Cavarretta home run. Howie Fox relieved Kennedy in the eighth, when the Cubs already had the game in hand 7–1. Nicholson and Pafko went hitless while everyone else in the lineup had at least one hit, with Hack getting two and Cavarretta three.

In game two, the Cubs won their first night game of the season, as Vandenberg pitched the best game of his seven-year career, a complete game one-hit shutout. He surrendered a Texas league blooper off the bat of left fielder Al Libke that Lowrey just missed while attempting a shoestring catch in the second inning for the only Cincinnati hit of the game. Quipsters remarked that Vandenberg's first one-hitter of the season actually occurred in New York but not during a game. Cubs hitters, once again led by Cavarretta, got single runs in the first and second innings to send perennial All-Star Bucky Walters to the showers. Cavarretta, Lowrey, and Williams, who guided Vandenberg through his masterpiece from behind the plate, each had two hits. Hod Lisenbee, at 47 one of the oldest players in the majors in 1945, pitched well after he replaced Walters, surrendering no runs and only five hits; it mattered little, however. The night belonged to the erratic Cubs—and their thoughts of how good they could be if someone like Vandenberg could consistently step up and bolster the pitching staff.

HY VANDENBERG

Harold Harris Vandenberg—the 34-year-old, six–foot, three-inch, blond-haired, blue-eyed right-handed Dutchman from Abilene, Kansas— certainly had the experience to do so. The handsome Vandenberg was an enthusiastic hunter who enjoyed making his own decoys. Like so many players during the wartime seasons, Vandenberg made a career out of playing between the majors and the minors and finally getting a chance to stick in the big leagues when the war took its toll on baseball's rosters. He broke in with Bloomington in the Three I League (Indiana, Illinois, and Iowa) as a 19-year-old in 1930 and did well enough to get promoted to Minneapolis in the American Association at the end of 1931.

After three years, he moved on to Chattanooga in the Southern Association, then to Williamsport, and then to Syracuse, where he was 13–7 and got a late season call-up in 1935 by the Boston Red Sox. He gave up 15 hits in five innings for the Red Sox, who promptly sent him back to Syracuse with his 21.50 ERA. In 1936 and 1937, however, he found himself pitching 470 innings and going 30–34 for Syracuse and Baltimore in the tough International League. The New York Giants noticed, called him up in 1938, sent him down to Jersey City the same year, and repeated this exercise in 1939 and 1940. In 1941 he stayed in the International League, after the Giants sold his contract to the Cardinals, and pitched well for Rochester, leading the International League in shutouts.

His chances in the pitching-rich Cardinals farm system being slim, the Milwaukee Brewers in the American Association signed him in 1942, and Vandenberg had his best year, going 17–10 with a 3.38 ERA while working 238 innings. He decided not to play in 1943. In 1944, however, Brewers manager Charlie Grimm, promoted to come back and manage Chicago after nine games of the season, remembered the success the big workhorse had and convinced general manager Jim Gallagher to sign him. Vandenberg thrived under Grimm that year, going 7–4 and throwing 126 innings with a respectable 3.64 ERA.[22] Vandenberg, however, could irk Grimm with his escapades and the off-field activities he shared with the fun loving Paul Derringer. Then came Vandenberg's decision to skip training camp and work out "on his own" in his hometown of Minneapolis, followed by an audacious salary holdout at the start of the 1945 season, both of which aggravated the Cubs' skipper even further.[23] Vandenberg's poor early season pitching performances made the training camp decision and holdout look even worse, and after the New York City incident, Grimm was just about at the end of his rope. Then unexpectedly, the big veteran pitched a one-hitter to give the Cubs a badly needed night game win, propel them into fourth place, and narrow the gap to just three and a half games behind first-place Pittsburgh. Players like Vandenberg were the reason managers like Grimm made the money they did.

THE CINCINNATI SERIES ended with another doubleheader, scheduled for Sunday, June 17. Reds starter Ed Heusser locked up with Wyse in a tight pitcher's duel that had Cincinnati ahead 1–0 through eight innings. Heusser held the Cubs to three lonely singles through the first eight innings but tired in the ninth when he was three outs away from a win. Nicholson singled to lead off and went to third on Cavarretta's long double. Pafko's fly ball to center fielder Dain Clay was not deep enough to bring in a run, but Lowrey lined a 3–2 pitch into left field and went to second on Cincinnati's unsuccessful attempt to get Cavarretta out at the plate; the score stood at 2–1, Cubs. Livingston then delivered a clutch single to center to bring in Lowrey and give Cubs reliever Derringer an insurance run, which turned out to be unnecessary, and the Cubs had won their eighth straight over the fading Cincinnatians. Mother Nature prevented them from gaining a sweep of the doubleheader when heavy rains canceled the contest in the middle of the second inning.

So the Cubs went home, ending the short road trip with a 3–2 record, stuck in fifth place with a 26–22 record but only one game behind the league leaders in the loss column. They looked forward to two days off at home before Pittsburgh came into Wrigley Field. The Pirates were swept by St. Louis over the weekend and knocked out of first place in the tightly bunched National League race, and the Cubs had a chance to set them back even further. Brooklyn, who enjoyed a successful weekend over New York, moved to the top of the standings. The Giants, who nobody could stop through the first two months of the season, were falling on hard times. They sank from first to fourth. Bill Voiselle, their starter who was named the *Sporting News'* Player of the Week May 24 for winning his first seven games, was fined by manager Mel Ott on June 14 for giving up a home run after supposedly ignoring Ott's orders on how to pitch to Philadelphia hitters. The Giants' skipper apparently wanted to light a fire by this action, but all it seemed to do was make his club hot under the collar; New York had not won a game since the Voiselle episode. The way the league was going, if Chicago could somehow string together six or seven wins, they would be right in the thick of the race.

On Wednesday, June 20, the Cubs opened a short two-series, six-game home stand with a 6–3 win. For the second straight game, Grimm went to his starting rotation for relief help, as Passeau, who earned his sixth victory of the year, took over for Chipman in the fifth inning after the Pirates had tied the score at three all. Cavarretta's two-run homer into the right field stands turned out to be the margin of victory.

A high point for the estimated crowd of 8,000 was Pirates catcher Al Lopez's ejection by home plate umpire Babe Pinelli after Pinelli called Merullo safe when Lopez, he felt, missed the tag. Wyse pitched the Cubs into second place on Thursday as he handed the Pirates their fifth straight loss, the final score 5–4. Preacher Roe and Rip Sewell could not match Wyse, who gave up only seven hits while winning a team-high seventh victory, as Cubs hitters continued their success with 13 hits. Meanwhile, captain Phil Cavarretta kept up his torrid pace, going 3-for-4. The Cubs' first baseman was starting his charge for the National League batting title. In his last five games, Cavarretta had hit .706 with an incredible .773 on-base percentage, going 12-for-17 with five walks.

The only thing wrong with the day's events was that it marked the last time anyone would see Wyse until who knew when. After the game, he took a train to his hometown of Tulsa, Oklahoma, for a preinduction physical. The Cubs had won five straight and trailed only the Brooklyn Dodgers, whom the Cubs would visit the next week in a series the fans and the press were now anticipating would be a first-place showdown. All the Chicagoans needed was a little more success this weekend over their old nemesis, the Cardinals.

IN LINE FOR THE PENNANT?

UNFORTUNATELY, IT WAS not to be. Instead of breaking out of their mold and continuing the winning streak, the Cubs dropped three out of four to St. Louis. A touch of pennant fever came over Chicago during the warm, muggy weekend as more than 65,000 fans came out over the three days, but only those among the 44,508 on Sunday who stayed for the second game got to see a Cubs victory. On Friday two brilliant Cardinals rookies, the switch-hitting Red Schoendienst and the big right-handed pitcher Ken Burkhardt, single-handedly snapped the five-game Cubs winning streak. Schoendienst went 4-for-5, and Burkhardt held Cavarretta hitless and surrendered only five hits—two by Lowrey—for a 5–2 win.

On Saturday the Cubs solved the pitching offerings of Harry Brecheen and George Dockins for 11 hits, but all of them were singles, as the Cards prevailed again, winning 4–0. Sunday's throng saw another lopsided Cardinals win (8–2) in the first game of the doubleheader, as the newly acquired Red Barrett, who was successful against the Cubs when he pitched for Boston, harmlessly spread out 11 Cubs hits. Things got ugly early in the game when Prim drilled Cardinals right fielder Johnny Hopp in the head with a purpose pitch (thrown to send a message of caution to the opposing batters) in the first inning. The unconscious Hopp was carried off the field and taken by ambulance to Illinois Masonic Hospital, while apparently the rest of the Cardinals' batters could not wait to get even; by the fourth inning, they had rocked Prim for seven runs. Manager Charlie Grimm gambled with his pitching staff, sending in four hurlers in each of the first three games, using up 12 pitchers with nothing to show for it.

Saving the day for the Cubs and the crowd was Claude Passeau. The lanky veteran hit a three-run home run with his roommate Livingston and Merullo on base in the fourth inning and pitched all nine innings to bail out the exhausted bull pen for a 6–3 victory, his seventh of the season.

The rough weekend left the Cubs at 29–25, back in fifth place, where they were more than two weeks earlier, but only three games behind the league-leading Dodgers in the loss column and five and a half games behind them in the standings. St. Louis, Pittsburgh, and New York also stood in their way, but the Cubs were ahead of the Pirates and Giants in the loss column and had played fewer games than all three.

Statistically at this point in the season, the Cubs were actually doing much better than implied by their place in the standings. They led the league in fielding and were tied with Cincinnati for fewest errors. Only New York and Brooklyn had higher team batting averages than the Cubs' .272. Their top three starters were as good as you would find on any team: Passeau was 7–2; Derringer, 7–4; and Wyse, 8–5. Derringer may have been the most pleasant surprise of the first ten weeks of the 1945 season, winning as many games then as he had won during the entire 1944 campaign. Catching, Pafko, and Cavarretta were the other surprises. As a group, the quartet of Livingston, Williams, Gillespie, and Rice were hitting .281 with 24 RBIs; in fact, Williams, as Livingston's primary backup, led the team with a .416 average, and Livingston's batting average at .289 was bettered by only six other Cubs hitters. Pafko, after beginning so slowly that Grimm did not start him in a significant stretch of games early in the season, was tied with Nicholson for the team lead in home runs with five; only Cavarretta had more than Pafko's 32 RBIs, and Pafko's robust .294 batting average was behind only that of Williams and Cavarretta. Cavarretta himself had to be the other big surprise. After a record-setting All-Star Game performance with offensive numbers to match in 1944, the veteran Cubs first baseman was having an even bigger season in 1945, with 37 RBIs in 54 games and a .353 average.

After ten weeks, however, there were some disappointments as well. Nicholson, the National League home run and RBI champion in 1943 and 1944, had only five home runs and 31 RBIs after 54 games, numbers that factored out to only 14 and 88 over a full season. He was also hitting a very mediocre .255 thus far in 1945, after averaging .287 and .309 in 1944 and 1943. The big right fielder, who lost the 1944 National League Most Valuable Player Award by only one vote, was the only legitimate power hitter on the Cubs, and his power was sorely missed in several games.

The big starting pitching trio of Passeau, Derringer, and Wyse accounted for 22 of the team's 29 victories; but the staff's performance, excluding their success, was still very suspect. Others needed to step up to fill the fourth and fifth positions if the Cubs hoped to challenge the pitching-rich Cardinals, Giants, or Dodgers. Comellas, banished to the minors, where he had been so successful in 1944, failed to fill the bill. Prim, another minor league phenom before being promoted to the majors for the 1945 season, was only 2–4 and looked weak in many outings. Vandenberg, of whom so much was expected after he went 7–4 in 1944, had one great start but a long string of ineffective appearances. Chipman and Erickson both had some effective outings, but consistency continued to elude them. The eternally promising but equally fragile Hanyzewski was once again injured. If just two of these six could perform consistently, the Cubs would have all the pieces in place.

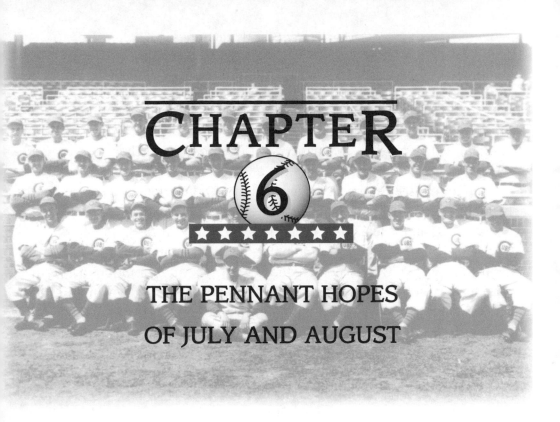

CHAPTER 6

★ ★ ★ ★ ★ ★ ★ ★

THE PENNANT HOPES
OF JULY AND AUGUST

T he Cubs, still smarting from an unsuccessful weekend in their own home against the St. Louis Cardinals, braced themselves for the heart of the season, an eight-week stretch through the middle of the August, during the dog days of summer. Their schedule from June 27 through August 21 would begin and end with long road trips in the east, broken in the middle with their longest home stand of the season. On June 26 the team traveled east for a rugged 12-day, 16-game road trip against league-leading Brooklyn, New York, Boston, and Philadelphia and gave little thought to the fact that the eight-week period would end in mid-August with an even more grueling 22-game trip to the same cities. Not in their wildest dreams did they think that this eight-week marathon would become one of the most successful stretches in their 70-year history.

AN EXHIBITION GAME against the Mitchell Field U.S. Army team was scheduled as a prelude to these contests. The trip got off to a bad start when the team learned that the severe beef and poultry shortage in New York City meant no meals would be provided at the Hotel Commodore, their quarters for games against the Dodgers and Giants.[1] On Tuesday, June 26, they easily handled the Mitchell Field team, 8–0, but the goodwill exhibition cost them two players when catcher Len Rice and shortstop Bill Schuster collided during batting practice. Both needed six stitches, and Rice was taken to Post Graduate Hospital with a possible concussion and fractured nose. Their luck turned when they got back to the Commodore and a telegram from Hank Wyse was waiting for Charlie Grimm. A relieved Grimm read that once again the draft board in Tulsa, Oklahoma, had rejected Wyse for military duty and that Wyse expected to join the team as soon as possible in New York.

From the way things went in their first game against Brooklyn, it was clear that Wyse would be needed. A crowd of 34,745 on a warm Wednesday night saw the Dodgers' Goody Rosen score the winning run on Luis Olmo's single in the bottom of the ninth off reliever Paul Erickson for a 6–5 victory. The die for the game was cast in the second inning, when Brooklyn hit Cubs starter Paul Derringer hard and scored four runs after the Cubs jumped to an early 2–0 lead. Roommates Lennie Merullo and Phil Cavarretta paced the Cubs' attack with two hits apiece as the Chicagoans sunk to six and a half games behind league-leading Brooklyn.

It was the Cubs' turn, however, in the day game at Ebbets Field on Thursday, June 28. Cubs batsmen rocked Brooklyn starter Lee Pfund for eight hits in the first five innings and jumped to a 7–0 lead. Claude Passeau started and did the best he could for six and a third innings, yielding the mound to Walt Signer with the score 9–7. Two Cubs insurance runs in the eighth negated a lone Dodgers run in the bottom of the ninth for an 11–8 Chicago victory. Once again, Cavarretta and Merullo paced the Cubs' attack, each going 3-for-5, and Andy Pafko had two RBIs. The first two games of the series illustrated the allure of night games during the World War II era. After welcoming more than 34,000 for the Wednesday evening affair, the Dodgers counted only 8,353 tickets for the Thursday afternoon confrontation.

The Brooklyn series ended with a big doubleheader on Friday, June 29, which the two teams split before a healthy crowd of 18,625. The Cubs lost another one-run affair, 5–4, in the first game but put their hosts away, 3–1, in the second. The 38-year-old Ray Prim was cruising in the first game with a 4–1 lead in the sixth inning when the oppressive heat and humidity got to him. He left the game suffering from heat stroke and was rushed to Caledonian Hospital.

In spite of Prim's absence, the Cubs still led 4–2 in the bottom of the ninth when Bob Chipman, Signer, and the Cubs' defense could not stop Brooklyn. The Dodgers hit the two Cubs pitchers hard and were helped by the Cubs' poor fielding. In the second game, Hy Vandenberg proved that he might be worth the salary raise he had held out for when he handcuffed the Dodgers on only four hits for a complete game and a 3–1 victory. In both games, Stan Hack, Andy Pafko, Peanuts Lowrey, and Dewey Williams provided the bulk of the offense. While Chicago lost two games in a series they should have won, the Friday doubleheader foreshadowed a key development, when both Prim and Vandenberg pitched effectively against the hottest offense in baseball. The Cubs' second-line pitchers were coming to life.

On Saturday, June 30, this new trend repeated itself as Erickson five-hit the Giants, a team that had beaten the Cubs in four of their first five meetings, for a complete game 5–3 victory. Pafko led the attack with a homer and two RBIs, while the keystone combination of Don Johnson and Roy Hughes (who was giving Merullo a rest from the heat) had two hits apiece. In the doubleheader ending the series on Sunday, July 1, Derringer once again stumbled in the first game, yielding 11 hits and five runs in less than four innings and losing 7–4. The only Chicago hitters who solved the Giants' hard-throwing Van Lingle Mungo were Hack, with three hits, and Cavarretta, with four. In the second game, Wyse celebrated his return to the team with a convincing complete game seven-hitter, the final score being 4–3. The game featured a 480-foot inside-the-park home run to the furthest reaches of the Polo Grounds' vast center field by Pafko.

THE CUBS LEFT for Boston feeling pretty good about themselves. In spite of a virtually meatless week in oppressively hot New York after losing two players to a freak injury in a meaningless game, they managed a 4–3 win against the Dodgers and Giants. Leaving New York City with a winning record was an accomplishment for any team. Their efforts vaulted them into the first division, firmly perched in fourth place, looking up at the Giants, Cardinals, and Brooklyn.

THE GOOD KARMA continued in the opener against the Boston Braves on Tuesday, July 3. Boston also had a lot to feel good about. They had just completed a three-game sweep against the World Champion Cardinals.

The Braves' right fielder, Tommy Holmes, was on the verge of tying Rogers Hornsby's consecutive game hitting mark and led the league with a sizzling .402 batting average. They went home from the opener shell-shocked, however, as the Cubs made 28 hits for an historic 24–2 victory. The Cubs' infield scored 16 runs, setting a major league record, as Cavarretta, Johnson, and Hack scored five times and Merullo once. Cavarretta and Pafko each had five RBIs, while Lowrey added three. Johnson and Cavarretta led the hitting attack, each going 5-for-7; Pafko went 4-for-6, Lowrey 3-for-6, Hack 3-for-4, Nicholson 2-for-4, and pitcher Passeau 2-for-6. Cavarretta raised his batting average 11 points, to .362, but gained little ground on league leader Holmes, who paced a ten-hit Boston attack by going 3-for-4. Chicago moved into second place the following day by sweeping a Fourth of July twin bill against the Braves, 5–3 and 7–6, in front of a holiday crowd of 21,159. Derringer regained his effectiveness with a complete game victory in the first game, and Vandenberg put in a second strong outing, going eight innings in game two for the victory. Derringer also pitched the ninth inning of the second game. Lowrey went 5-for-9 in the doubleheader, and Bill Nicholson hit two homers in the second game. In the race for the batting title, Cavarretta gained a little ground on Holmes by going 4-for-8 in the two games while Holmes went 4-for-9. Wyse pitched a complete game victory in the series finale on Thursday, July 5, scattering seven hits while Hack's homer off Boston starter Jim Tobin provided the winning margin in a 3–2 Chicago victory. The only high note for the Bostonians was that Holmes got a base hit and with it was only one game behind tying Hornsby's National League consecutive game hitting streak record.

THE CHICAGOANS LEFT for Philadelphia just itching to play their twi-night doubleheader Friday, July 6, against the Phillies. They now trailed first-place Brooklyn by only two and a half games but, more important, were tied with them in the loss column with 28. The Cubs were 8–3 on a tough East Coast road trip; their first trip east earlier in the season included a six-game losing streak. After hurriedly settling into the Ben Franklin Hotel, the Cubs proceeded to sweep the Phils, 11–3 and 5–1. A potent 17-hit attack, which featured six Cubs (Hack, Johnson, Nicholson, Cavarretta, Livingston, and Merullo) getting two hits apiece, helped Prim, pitching in relief of a jittery Ray Starr, gain the win. In the second game, the tireless Derringer coasted for a complete game five-hit victory. Hack, Pafko, and Lowrey provided the offensive fireworks.

The following day, it was Passeau's turn to match Derringer, and he ended up putting the Cubs only one game out of first place, winning his tenth victory, a complete game, with a 3–0 shutout. The cost for the victory would be the services of the Cubs' first-string catcher, however, as Philadelphia hurler Charley Schanz hit Mickey Livingston in the mouth with a fastball. Livingston ended up at nearby Jefferson Hospital, requiring seven stitches in his lips and cheek. After the injury, Williams and Paul Gillespie took over the catching duties in the road trip–ending doubleheader, which the Cubs swept, for their ninth and tenth victories in a row, 12–6 and 9–2. The victory in the first game, secured when Prim effectively relieved after ineffective performances by Erickson and Vandenberg, put the Cubs ahead of the Dodgers, who lost a doubleheader to St. Louis, in first place for the first time in the 1945 season. Wyse's six-hitter in the second game put a little distance between Chicago and the rest of the National League at the conclusion of the second win. The Cubs pounded the Philadelphia pitching staff for 30 hits, with every position player, except Pafko in the second game, hitting safely.

Suddenly, a lengthy East Coast trip had become a walk in the park. It had been many years since a Cubs team had gone 13–3 on an extended road trip, moving into first place on Sunday, July 8. Everyone was contributing at the plate, and the team had had 140 hits in their last ten games. Cavarretta had emerged as a major contender for the batting title, Lowrey and Pafko were driving in critical runs, and Williams and Gillespie were picking up the catching slack left by the injured Rice and Livingston. Meanwhile, Wyse, Passeau, Derringer, and Prim were all throwing the ball effectively.

PEANUTS LOWREY

The hitting star of this eastern trip was Harry Lee "Peanuts" Lowrey, who tallied a robust .373 to lead the Chicago offense into first place. The diminutive 27-year-old was born on August 27, 1918, in Culver City, California, the center of the motion picture industry in the 1920s. His grandfather's ranch in that town was used as a backdrop for the Our Gang Comedies, and Lowrey himself appeared in several films during his childhood. As an adult, he appeared in several baseball films, including *The Winning Team* with Ronald Reagan. A lithe, fundamentally sound ballplayer who could hit, Lowrey signed a contract with Moline in the Three I League (Indiana, Illinois, and Iowa) when he was 19 and worked his way up the ladder through Ponca City, St. Joseph, Tulsa, and finally the Los Angeles Angels in the Pacific Coast League, which was owned indirectly by the Cubs at that time. After Lowrey hit .311 with the Angels in 1941, Chicago invited him to spring training, and his debut with the Cubs was April 14, 1942.

In 1942 Lowrey appeared in only 27 games, playing behind Bill Nicholson, Dom Dallessandro, Lou Novikoff, and Charlie Gilbert. Lowrey split the 1942 season between the Cubs and the minors; he was sent down to Milwaukee but finished the season back in the Pacific Coast League with the Angels. While playing full time for the Cubs in 1943, he beat out Dallessandro for the center field spot, hitting .292 and finishing second in the National League in stolen bases with 13. At five feet, eight inches and 170 pounds, the baby-faced Lowrey was one of the smallest players on the team, but he was characterized by tenacity and a refusal to back down from adversity. Eddie Stanky learned that the hard way after allegedly cheating Lowrey in a card game at the Biltmore Hotel in Los Angeles early in Lowrey's career.[2]

Lowrey missed the entire 1944 season due to World War II. He was drafted into the army in April of that year and worked as an MP but was discharged, with a punctured eardrum, six months later in October. When he returned to Chicago in 1945, the Cubs were more satisfied with Pafko, who equaled Lowrey's range but had a much stronger throwing arm, in center field. Manager Charlie Grimm did not know Lowrey very well at the time, but Lowrey had a reputation as a clubhouse lawyer. Grimm entered spring training favoring Frank Secory, but Secory was injured in the April 12 exhibition game against the White Sox, and Ed Sauer got the Opening Day nod in left field. When Sauer slumped throughout the early part of the season, Grimm turned to Lowrey, and the fleet, timely hitting left fielder was proving the decision was a good one.[3]

BY EARLY JULY, the Cubs were on their way home with a ten-game winning streak, looking forward to a three-day All-Star Game break that would occur even though the All-Star classic for 1945 had been canceled. Next on the schedule was their longest home stand of the season, 22 days. Excitement once again had come to the North Side of Chicago.

The Cubs' first appointment at the start of the three-day break was an exhibition game Monday night, July 9, at Comiskey Park against the White Sox; the Sox won 6–5 in a hotly contested ten-inning affair before 47,144, the biggest Comiskey Park crowd of the season. The game netted more than $50,000 for war relief charities.

On Thursday, July 12, Wyse's devastating curve and sinker ball ended Tommy Holmes's record-breaking consecutive game hitting streak at 37 as the Chicagoans beat the Braves and Jim Tobin 6–1. Holmes, the unstoppable Boston right fielder, had hit at an atmospheric .433 clip during the streak, and many newspapers throughout the country carried pictures of Holmes and Wyse the following day. Every member of the team contributed to the Cubs' 14-hit attack on offense, including Wyse himself, who had two hits and two RBIs. In the second game, Passeau, beneficiary of the 24 runs Chicago scored against the Braves on July 3, watched helplessly as Braves hurler Nate Andrews handcuffed the Cubs on five hits, with a final score of 3–1. The crafty Passeau had won nine straight games until this setback. Livingston returned to the lineup for the first time since he was hit in the mouth on July 7 at Philadelphia. A crowd of 29,512, huge for a Thursday doubleheader, saw Passeau's winning streak end at ten games. Friday was Ladies' Day. More than 7,000 females took advantage of the occasion, and there were another 6,500 paid attendees in the crowd. Prim matched up against Johnny Hutchings. Prim and Merullo had two hits, and the Cubs' two runs were enough, thanks to Prim's complete game four-hit shutout, in a game that lasted only 94 minutes. In the series finale on July 14, unseasonably chilly temperatures in the upper 50s held down the Saturday crowd to only 6,332, but Cubs bats warmed up and scored five runs in the first inning after managing only three in their last 18 innings. Derringer lasted five innings with the Cubs up 5–4 and was replaced by Erickson. Erickson put on one of his stronger showings of the season, yielding only one run from that point forward. Gillespie's high drive in deep right field scored Lowrey with the winning run in the bottom of the eighth, but the star of the game was the surging Merullo, with a 3-for-4 day at the bat and a game-saving defensive gem in the ninth inning. The home stand started with Chicago winning three out of four, for a 45–29 record, two games ahead of the second-place St. Louis Cardinals.

Scheduled for Sunday, July 15, was a much-anticipated doubleheader against the New York Giants. Reuben Fischer and John Brewer were scheduled to face Vandenberg and Wyse. The Cubs felt some pressure to do well on this date because New York would start their aces, Van Lingle Mungo and Bill Voiselle, in the single games on Monday and Tuesday. A standing room only crowd of 43,803 came for the festivities. After falling behind 3–1 in the fourth inning, when Johnson's uncharacteristic two errors prolonged the Giants' inning, the Cubs came back with four runs of their own. Johnson, making amends for his fielding gaffes, got the inning's big hit when he doubled home Merullo and Vandenberg for two of the inning's four tallies. Vandenberg was masterful on the mound. His complete game three-hitter, exactly one month after his one-hitter against Cincinnati, featured three strikeouts and only one walk; New York's three hits were only singles. Game two provided even less drama for the huge throng. Nicholson went 3-for-5, Cavarretta hit his fourth homer of the year, Merullo went 2-for-4, and Williams tripled to lead the Chicagoans to a 7–0 lead after six innings. The Giants could do nothing with Wyse, who seemed unbeatable since rejoining the team in New York on July 2, after his military physical. They scored two consolation runs in the ninth, and the game ended in a 7–2 Cubs victory. The series ended with the Monday and Tuesday games. Passeau matched up against the intimidating Mungo, who had beaten the Cubs twice already in 1945, yielding the mound to reliever Ray Starr in the ninth with the Cubs down 3–2. Starr had no trouble with the New Yorkers in the top of the ninth. He became the winning pitcher after Lowrey tied the game with a line single; Gillespie once again came through with the game-winning hit, driving in Pafko. The Cubs were 48–29 after 77 games, the halfway point in the season. They had just won their fifth straight game and their 16th out of the last 17. They had first place all to themselves and were playing at home for the next two weeks. It did not matter that they lost the last game of the series on Tuesday, July 17, when Voiselle threw a three-hitter to spoil Erickson's five-hitter, the final score being 2–1; three weeks earlier, the Cubs had been in fifth place, and now they sat atop the National League pyramid.

On Wednesday, July 18, 42,047 fans felt as good as the Cubs players did. That was the number that came out to see a weekday doubleheader against the Brooklyn Dodgers, as Prim kept the magic going on the mound in the first game, confounding the Dodgers with his soft tosses and pitching his second shutout in five days for a 5–0 win. Helping out were Hack and Cavarretta, who paced a modest Cubs attack against Brooklyn veteran Curt Davis. But the Dodgers avoided a sweep when hurlers Lon Warneke, Signer, Chipman, Vandenberg, and Starr could not keep the Brooklyn bats in check during the second game, and the Cubs went down, 9–5. A highlight of the evening was veteran umpire Ziggy Sears's ejection of Leo Durocher for arguing a time-out call. Pitching effectively in the middle innings for the visitors was a recent call-up from St. Paul who would become one of the biggest legends in their team's history: Ralph Branca.

Thursday's game featured Wyse on the mound beating Vic Lombardi 3–1, for his 13th win. While Johnson went 3-for-4 and Pafko was 2-for-3, Wyse himself drove in the big insurance run, a base hit that brought in Williams. In the fifth inning, the Dodgers inadvertently fired the Cubs up when Dodger left fielder Luis Olmo toppled Cubs first baseman Cavarretta while running down the first base line after hitting a grounder to Merullo. Cavarretta immediately got up and charged Olmo, with first base umpire George Barr interceding before any punches were thrown or tackles attempted. The crowd of 10,578 howled with delight when a posse of Cubs, led by manager Charlie Grimm and coach Hardrock Johnson, charged the field; meanwhile, the Dodgers remained in the cool shade of the first base dugout.

The following day, Friday, July 20, Passeau was the Cubs starting pitcher. The Dodgers were ahead 10–4, but the game was suspended before its completion since the Dodgers were scheduled to depart by train at 3:50. League rules dictated that such a game would not show in the standings until it was concluded; the matchup was scheduled to resume on September 15. As a result, Brooklyn, which had come to Chicago in third place, three and a half games behind the Cubs, left town four and a half back. The Cubs could look forward next to hosting the hapless Phillies, while Brooklyn glumly awaited a weekend series in hot, humid St. Louis against the World Champion Cardinals.

The Cubs opened the four-game set against Philadelphia on Saturday with Dick Mauney, the pride of Albemarle, North Carolina, facing Derringer. The Phillies, playing without their best hitter, Vince DiMaggio, could muster only six hits off the big right-hander, and the Cubs got back on the right track, winning 5–3. Shortstop Merullo homered, Hack had two doubles, and Cavarretta had two RBIs. The following day, Prim continued Chicago's mound mastery. With 33,073 crowding into Wrigley Field for the Sunday doubleheader, Prim spread out ten Philadelphia hits for an easy 8–5 victory, with Vandenberg relieving the last three innings and striking out three while allowing only one run.

In the second game, Philadelphia rocked starter Wyse for ten hits, exploding for ten runs in the sixth inning. In that disastrous inning, Grimm replaced Wyse with Warneke; when the latter could not stop the onslaught, the little-used Signer came in. Chicago answered with three of their own runs in the bottom half of the sixth, but Philadelphia cruised to an 11–6 victory, denying Wyse a chance for his 14th victory. The best news out of the second game was another good relief showing by Vandenberg, who recorded two strikeouts while allowing no runs in the ninth inning. Chipman salvaged the last game of the series on Tuesday, July 24. The willowy left-hander pitched a complete game in searing 90-degree heat and humidity for a 6–3 victory before an afternoon crowd of 8,393. Nicholson was the big crowd-pleaser at the plate as he paced the victors with a triple and four RBIs; Pafko also tripled and drove in two. The Chicagoans, who would not see Philadelphia again until Sunday, August 12, bade a sad farewell to the Phillies after the game. The Cubs now had a record of 12–3 against the basement dwellers, and their success in this series kept St. Louis four and a half back and Brooklyn five and a half behind. The Cubs were a remarkable 24–7 against East Coast opponents in their last 31 games.

DUTY CALLED ON Wednesday, July 25, as the Cubs sacrificed an off day to play the Great Lakes Naval Station Bluejackets at Constitution Field in North Chicago, Illinois. The Bluejackets were the finest baseball team in the U.S. Navy. While they had 18-year-old Johnny Groth, the pride of Chicago Latin, starting in center field, the rest of their lineup was daunting for a service team. Red Carnett of the Cleveland Indians started at first, Pinky Higgins of the Detroit Tigers started at third, Cincinnati's Max Marshall started in left field, and recently inducted Walker Cooper, the best catcher in the National League until he was called into the service, was behind the plate. On the mound was the highest-salaried (at $50,000 plus) major leaguer during the 1940s, Navy Chief Specialist Bob Feller. The Cubs, resting many of their starters, managed only three singles off Feller and lost 1–0. A double by Hack and singles by Merullo and Nicholson were all the offense the Cubs could manage against Feller, who struck out ten.

Ed Hanyzewski tested his ever-ailing arm and pitched well for six innings before surrendering the mound to Starr, who gave up what proved to be the winning run in the eighth inning. Groth, the youngest player on the field, distinguished himself with a double while catching four fly balls. He would play with the Detroit Tigers in 1946 and enjoy a successful 15-year career that ended in 1960. Until the game against the Bluejackets, the Cubs had suffered only one shutout during 1945: a night game at the Polo Grounds against Voiselle. An overcapacity crowd of 12,000 watched the Cubs and Bluejackets put on one of the most interesting baseball exhibitions ever held during World War II.

After playing the Bluejackets, the Chicagoans were relieved to welcome the Cincinnati Reds to Wrigley Field for a five-game series scheduled from Thursday, July 26, through Sunday, July 29. While the Reds came into Chicago having beaten Brooklyn eight times, Pittsburgh seven times, and St. Louis five times, they had yet to win against the Cubs in eight contests. The Cubs' blend of timely hitting and peerless pitching resulted in a four-game sweep of Cincinnati and put major league baseball on notice that they held the inside track in the National League pennant race with a tenacious grip. Wyse beat Ed Heusser in Thursday's opener, 2–1, with a complete game victory, his 14th of the season. A Ladies' Day crowd of 20,000 saw Passeau match Wyse's efforts with a complete game five-hitter with the same score, as the Cubs pounded Reds ace Bucky Walters for 12 hits. Derringer was cruising toward an 8–0 shutout over his old team on Saturday, July 28, when he tired in the ninth and was relieved by Erickson, who shut the door with the final score 8–3, Cubs. A crowd of 44,836 pennant-frenzied Cubs fans filled every nook and cranny in Wrigley Field to see the Sunday doubleheader, when, after only two days of rest, the rubber-armed Wyse started the festivities with another complete game victory, the final score being 4–1. Game two was a squeaker with the Cubs emerging victorious, 3–2. The Reds never led in any inning in any of the five games; Friday's game was tied for two innings, as was the second game of the Sunday doubleheader. Leadoff man Hack and RBI specialist Pafko were magnificent offensively. Hack reached base 12 times and got ten hits in 20 at bats, while Pafko hit .421, going 8-for-19.

The pitching in the last game of the series, however, generated as much excitement as the Cubs fattening their lead, putting more space between themselves and St. Louis. It also overshadowed the fact that their winning percentage for July was a phenomenal .862, as they took 25 out of 29 contests. On Friday, July 27, in the middle of this crucial series, the often-scorned general manager, Jim Gallagher, got Cubs owner Philip K. Wrigley's consent to send the New York Yankees $97,000 for Chicago's starting pitcher in Sunday's final game: Hank Borowy.

HANK BOROWY

Henry Ludwig Borowy was born on May 12, 1916, in Bloomfield, New Jersey. The slender, blue-eyed right-hander had posted a 28–2 record at Bloomfield High; in one nine-inning game, he had struck out 26 of the 27 hitters he faced. In 1935 Borowy led Bloomfield to the state championship. After graduating, he accepted a baseball scholarship to nearby Fordham University, where his record of 24–1 over three seasons made him one of the most heavily scouted collegians in the country. Paul Krichell of the New York Yankees offered him an $8,000 bonus; Borowy, with nothing left to prove at the collegiate level, told him he was worth $500 more. The Yankees' organization shrugged, honored his request, and sent him directly to Newark in the International League. There, pitching in the highest level in the minor leagues, Borowy went 38–27 with a strikeout-to-walk ratio of almost 2:1.

During his major league rookie year, Borowy earned a spot in the war-depleted New York Yankees' starting rotation, where his 15–4 record and .789 win-loss percentage helped the Yankees clinch the pennant. Four of his victories were shutouts; only one American League pitcher, teammate Tiny Bonham, topped that number. Borowy's 2.52 ERA was fifth best in the league and was also lower than any ERA he posted at Newark. The hard-hitting St. Louis Cardinals rocked Borowy for six earned runs in three innings of work during the Yankees' losing World Series effort that autumn, but his revenge would come later. At the end of the season, New York raised his pay from $10,000 to $11,000.[4] In 1943 Borowy went 14–9 with three shutouts and a 2.83 ERA. That year he helped the Yanks win the World Series, pitching eight innings and earning the win at Yankee Stadium while allowing the Cardinals just six hits and two runs in the third game of the fall classic. The Yankees rewarded him with a lofty $15,000 contract for 1944, and he responded by proving his worth, going 17–12 and pitching in the All-Star Game for the American League. Only four American League pitchers finished 1944 with more victories. Borowy's 2.64 ERA that year was eighth best in the league. The only American League hurlers to post more than Borowy's 19 complete games were Detroit's Hal Newhouser and Dizzy Trout.

Throughout his career, Borowy worked hard to develop a perfectly balanced, effortless delivery, usually relying on three pitches. His fastball was "sneaky fast," reaching the plate before most hitters expected it to, and when he threw high, Borowy's fastball appeared to rise, confounding hitters even more. He mixed those fastballs with a sharp-breaking curve and one of the best sliders in the game. If he had a weakness in his first years in the majors, it was his tendency to develop blisters on his fingers, possibly resulting from his tendency to grip the ball tightly to put more movement on his pitches.

IN SPITE OF Borowy's repertoire and skill, near midnight on July 27, he cleared the American League waivers, and the Yankees sold their hot young pitcher to the Cubs. The unhappy Borowy initially told MacPhail that he would not report to Chicago, but Yankee general manager Larry MacPhail threatened to cut his pay in half the following year if he remained with the Yankees. He also told Borowy that he could become one of the most highly paid players in the game if the Cubs got into the World Series.[5] While Borowy finally decided to join the Cubs, his wife and children remained on the East Coast and never came to Chicago during the years he pitched in Chicago.[6]

If Borowy was surprised, the baseball world was incredulous: How could the Cubs, especially Jim Gallagher, possibly pull this deal off? Several theories have evolved over the years, some more plausible than others.

MacPhail's own explanation was that Borowy had outlived his usefulness. Among other things, he complained that Borowy had pitched only four complete games all season and that his last complete game had been on June 24. During the World War II era and before, it was much more common for starting pitchers to throw a full nine innings than it is today. From 1942 through 1944, Borowy started 78 games for New York and completed 46 of them. MacPhail seemed to be hiding behind a convenient pitching statistic to justify the move. The entire Yankees starting pitching staff for the same three years completed 53 percent of their starts, 249 of 462, while Borowy's percentage during this period was 59 percent. To dismiss one of the best right-handers in the American League from a team with the bull pen strength of New York for that reason is very questionable.

Three other reasons, never publicly aired, seem more plausible. In 1945 MacPhail's feud with Dodgers president Branch Rickey was still in full bloom, and strengthening the Cubs while they were five and a half games in front of Brooklyn would certainly impair a local competitor's opportunity to appear in a World Series. Another possibility was that MacPhail wanted to repay Gallagher for the generous, one-sided trades he consummated with the Cubs when he was general manager of the Dodgers. Most of the lingering bitterness in Chicago from Cubs–Dodgers trades still came from the loss of future Hall of Famer and fan favorite Billy Herman for Charlie Gilbert, Johnny Hudson, and $65,000 in 1941. The last reason casts MacPhail's motives in a more devious light and first came to Chicago's attention on Thursday, August 2, less than one week after the deal.

At that time, Colonel Edgar N. Bloomer, the head of the New Jersey draft board, directed the Bloomfield, New Jersey, selective service office to reclassify Borowy to 2-A, stating that the new Cubs pitcher was not entitled to his previous 2-B classification. The Bloomfield board met on August 7 and followed the directive. Their reasoning was that while Borowy was indeed employed during the off-season at the Eastern Tool & Manufacturing Company in 1944 and 1945 and that such employment did contribute to the war effort, he was not actually on the assembly line and hence not entitled to the safer 2-A classification. Given MacPhail's association in the military during World War II, he very well may have known, or been tipped off, about new questions regarding Borowy's draft status and felt he had a better chance to cut his losses before such an announcement was made. Borowy was never drafted into the service in spite of the change, much to the relief of the Cubs' organization.

By acquiring Borowy, the Cubs also silenced lingering criticism that Wrigley and Gallagher were reluctant to spend the money necessary to enhance the team's chances of winning the pennant. Borowy's purchase price, $97,000, was more than any team had spent for a player in years. The acquisition also added more than $17,000 to the payroll, which was the amount of Borowy's salary.[7] Perhaps only five players—the veterans Cavarretta, Derringer, Hack, Nicholson, and Passeau—commanded such high pay from Chicago in 1945.

Pittsburgh Pirates starter Max Butcher cooled off the Cubs, 1–0, in front of a healthy 17,780 fans on "Cookie Day" at Wrigley Field on Wednesday, August 1. Cubs starter Passeau, who surrendered only four hits himself, took the loss, giving him a record of 11–4 for the season. The following day, 18,535 fans saw Derringer duplicate Butcher's feat for a 1–0 Cubs victory, a sparkling three-hit shutout. Lowrey's double drove in second baseman Johnson for the game's only run, to ruin a well-pitched game by Pittsburgh's Preacher Roe. The longest home stand of the season drew to a close with Chicago posting a 17–5 record, excluding the suspended game with Brooklyn on Friday, July 20. Now came a more arduous 22-game road trip in the dog days of August to Cincinnati, Boston, Philadelphia, Brooklyn, and New York. The confident club was five and a half games in front of second-place St. Louis and six ahead of the Dodgers.

Chicago's chances looked good for Friday's twi-night doubleheader, with Wyse and Borowy facing Cincinnati's Joe Bowman and Vern Kennedy. Wyse won his 16th game as the Cubs smacked Bowman and reliever Howie Fox for 14 hits, the final score being 11–5. In the second game, the Reds had the disadvantage of facing a pitcher they had never seen before, and Borowy cruised to an easy complete game five-hitter, winning 9–1. The Cubs would have won both games if all their hitters had had the day off and only Cavarretta played. The Cubs' first baseman went 6-for-8 including a home run and drove in five runs in game one and three in game two. Lowrey also had six hits in the doubleheader, and Pafko drove in three runs. Cincinnati had now lost 15 straight games to the surging Chicagoans, but their luck ran out on Saturday. With the Cubs losing 4–3 in the top of the ninth, shortstop Merullo's long blast to left field bounced high off the wall, caroming halfway back to the infield, but the swift Merullo was out trying to stretch a sure double into a triple. Grimm, coaching at third, was incensed with the call, and his vociferous displeasure got him thrown out of the game by umpires George Barr and Tom Dunn. It was the first time in 1945 that the mild-mannered Grimm had been ejected. Vandenberg, hit hard by Cincinnati until his departure in the sixth inning, took the loss. Left fielder Al Libke drove in all four of the Reds' runs.

Both teams played yet another doubleheader on Sunday, August 5 to close out the series. Erickson benefited from the consistent hitting of the entire team and won his fifth game, 12–5. Cavarretta, held hitless by Ed Heusser on Saturday after leading the charge the previous evening, had another monster day at the plate, going 5-for-6. Hack almost matched him (4-for-5), and Merullo, picking up right where he left off Saturday, was 3-for-4 with a home run. The second game was not so easy. Joe Bowman, on one day's rest, started for Cincinnati and matched Cubs starter Passeau pitch for pitch, holding a 1–0 lead going into the sixth inning. In that frame, Lowrey and Cavarretta managed to get on base, and Grimm summoned first baseman Heinz Becker to pinch-hit for Livingston, who had already caught 15 innings for the day. Becker singled both men home for a 2–1 Cubs lead; this became the game-winning hit when both teams failed to score the rest of the way. Passeau won his 12th game, the Cubs were now 31–6 in their last 37 contests, and their lead over the Cardinals reached six full games. Needless to say, the evening trip to Boston was a very pleasant one, indeed.

AFTER THE CUBS' pennant express rolled into Boston and the team settled into their quarters at the Copley-Plaza Hotel, another surprise awaited them in their doubleheader on Wednesday, August 8, when the surprising Prim received a 16-hit endowment from the Cubs' offense. While they left too many men on base, they still beat the Braves 5–2. The offensive barrage came at the expense of Boston starter Nate Andrews, the crafty right-hander who had handcuffed the Cubs in his two previous victorious starts against them earlier in the year. In the second game, Wyse, emerging as the ace and the iron man of the staff, won a tough 2–1 decision against the great Mort Cooper in 12 innings. Once again, Merullo came through, answering the bell in the Chicago half of the 12th by driving in Pafko with a line single for the game-winning hit. An overlooked statistic in the Cubs' consistent victories was the fact that the team's record was 16–1 in their last 17 road games.

LEN MERULLO

Chicago's ascent into first place might not have occurred without the stellar play of their shortstop, Leonard Richard Merullo. The seventh of 12 children, Merullo was born on May 5, 1917, in East Boston, Massachusetts.[8] His parents were from Italy; his father supported the 14 Merullos working in a paint shop making putty. Len starred in athletics at East Boston High School and, at the age of 15, caught the eye of Ralph Wheeler. Wheeler, a sportswriter for the *Boston Herald*, operated a semipro team in the suburban Boston area out of Malden City; he was also a close friend of Charlie Grimm. When the Cubs came to Braves Field to play Boston, Wheeler would take some of his players to the park and arrange a workout for them. This is where the Cubs first saw Merullo in 1934, along with another Bostonian who would also become famous, Eddie Waitkus. Heads turned when Merullo started taking infield practice and soon showed what was the strongest arm of anyone, amateur or professional, in the park. Merullo became a project for Wheeler, who arranged for him to finish high school at St. John's Preparatory School in Massachusetts. After finishing at St. John's, Merullo won a baseball scholarship to Villanova. By his senior year, he was one of the most talented baseball collegians on the East Coast and captain-elect of the Villanova squad. Summers in college were spent playing for Cape Breton in the Northern League and also in the Cape Cod League. His acquisition by the Chicago Cubs is a classic, heart-warming Depression-era tale.

A few days before Christmas in his senior year, Merullo received a telegram from Clarence Rowland, vice president of the Cubs, inviting him to come to Chicago for a meeting with Wrigley at the Wrigley Building before his Christmas vacation—and to not discuss the visit ahead of time with anyone, family or friends. Rowland and a 23-year-old Bill Veeck, who at that time worked in the Cubs' front office, met him at Union Station and drove the star-struck Merullo down Wacker Drive directly to Wrigley's office on the top floor. Wrigley graciously told him that he thought he was a fine young man whom they would like to have as a future player. He continued talking, disclosing that he knew Merullo had 11 brothers and sisters, and reached into his desk. Then he welcomed the stunned collegian to his organization, handed him a check for $1,500, and instructed Rowland to immediately buy him a big breakfast at what is now the Hotel Intercontinental across the street and then take him to the haberdashery on the first floor of the Wrigley Building after checking him into a room. Rowland told Merullo that Wrigley wanted all his men to look their best and observed that Merullo needed new shoes and a good overcoat. Merullo said that he did not think he needed anything, but Rowland sternly told him that this was Mr. Wrigley's order. Merullo left

Chicago with a new winter coat, a felt hat to match, new shoes, and more money than his father would make in two years.

When he got home to Boston in his new clothes, his parents did not recognize him, and they were upset about not knowing where he had been. He quickly told them about his unexpected adventure and then presented the check for $1,500 to his mother. Because his parents did not read or write any English, the check meant nothing to them until Merullo's oldest brother explained that it was indeed "real money" Len had received for agreeing to be a ballplayer. From that day forward, his mother insisted that the younger Merullo boys practice baseball every day after school.

A few months later, the Yankees sent their scout, Paul Krichiel, to talk to Merullo. Krichiel, at a loss to understand why Merullo would not entertain any idea about signing, finally got him to admit that he had already signed with Chicago. Now the word was out, and Merullo was ineligible to play for Villanova his senior year. He wrote to Rowland, who wired back that he should leave college if he wished and join the team on Catalina Island for spring training. Wrigley, in an era when ethics were still of paramount importance in the business world, wrote a letter to Villanova with a check for $4,000, to cover the four years of education they had bestowed upon Merullo with the scholarship.

The young shortstop with the powerful arm worked his way from Moline in the Three I League to Tulsa, Los Angeles, and Toronto. He appeared in seven games with the Cubs in 1941 and made the team for good after spring training in 1942. He finished his bachelor's degree at Boston College in 1940 and married Jean Geggis on February 9, 1941. Merullo had a military deferment through most of World War II because the date of his marriage preceded Pearl Harbor, and because he had five brothers in the service.

The Cubs' investment in the gritty Italian kid from Boston was paying off handsomely in 1945. Chicago was five and a half games behind Brooklyn when Grimm inserted Merullo in the starting lineup permanently on July 1, and five weeks later, they were six games ahead in first place. Of the three Cubs shortstops, Merullo covered the most ground and had the most powerful arm, and he was one of the team's fastest runners. During Chicago's surge to the top, he was involved in 23 of the team's 34 double plays and hit .290. Merullo's salary in 1945 was a princely $9,000, and the Cubs were getting more than their money's worth.[9]

CUBS BATS FELL silent and cost them two losses against Boston at Braves Field, on Thursday, August 9, and Friday, August 10. In a game featuring a pitching matchup between two of the biggest names in the 1930s, Big Bill Lee, the pride of Plaquemine, Louisiana, overwhelmed the team he previously led to greatness in 1935 and 1938 with a six-hit 7–3 victory over Derringer. Lee helped pitch Chicago to a pennant in 1935, going 20–6 and leading the National League in winning percentage. He duplicated the feat in 1938, winning 22 and losing 9, while posting the league's best ERA, 2.66. Short of catchers in 1943 and thinking Lee was washed up, general manager Jim Gallagher traded him to Philadelphia for Livingston.

On Friday, Al Javery and Don Hendrickson walked ten Chicago batters, but they got only three base hits and lost 2–1, as Borowy took his first loss in a Chicago uniform, which was also his first unimpressive outing since he arrived. The graceful right-hander yielded 11 hits while allowing four walks; Tommy Holmes's home run in the seventh proved to be the difference in the ball game. In the last two games against a mediocre Boston pitching staff, the Cubs had made only nine hits, and suddenly, the Cardinals were only four and a half games behind. In the finale of the Boston series on Saturday, August 11, as would happen so many times in the season, another pitcher rose up to become the stopper: Claude Passeau. The gentleman farmer from Mississippi was four outs away from a perfect game when Boston catcher Phil Masi singled with two outs in the eighth inning. Then the little-used Morrie Aderholt added another single in the ninth, but the final outcome was never in doubt, with the Cubs winning 8–0 in a 14-hit attack. Instrumental in the win were Cavarretta and Hack, with two hits apiece, but just as in Sunday's second game in Cincinnati, Grimm summoned a little-used player from the bench to step to the forefront. Catcher Len Rice answered the call with his best game of the season, going 3-for-5 at the plate and guiding Passeau to the closest he would ever come in his career to a perfect game. More good news awaited the team in the clubhouse when they read the Western Union ticker—Giants 10, Cardinals 1—as Chicago ended another road series five and a half games ahead of St. Louis. The spotlight in this series was also on another race, the one for the National League batting title between Boston's Holmes and Chicago's Cavarretta. Holmes, whose batting average started to ebb after his record-setting consecutive game hitting streak, led the league with a .365 average after Saturday's game. Cavarretta was now close behind at .360.

The baseball world took note of Passeau's accomplishment, two two-hit victories in the same season. Lost in the excitement was the fact that he also had the longest winning streak of any pitcher in the majors, nine games, from May 23 until July 12. More than any other pitcher, Passeau was the mainstay and stopper on the Chicago staff during the World War II seasons.[10]

CLAUDE PASSEAU

Claude William Passeau graduated with a bachelor of science degree from Millsaps College in 1932, was signed by the Detroit Tigers, and broke in at Decatur, Illinois, in the Three I League.[11] The following year, he moved up the Tigers' chain and played at Beaumont in the Texas League, rooming with future Tigers slugger Rudy York. The Tigers gave up on Passeau in 1934, but he was picked up by Charleston in the Middle Atlantic League, where he went 10–7. In 1935 Passeau caught fire for Des Moines, then in the Western League, when he went 20–11, struck out 239, and walked 73 in 244 innings. Before the season was over, he was called up by the Pittsburgh Pirates; he made his major league debut during the last weekend of the season, on September 29, 1935. The Pirates sent him, along with catcher Earl Grace, to the Philadelphia Phillies for catcher Al Todd on November 21, 1935.

The trade to baseball's version of purgatory was actually a break for the tall right-hander, who got to pitch a lot and hone his craft. From 1936 through 1939, he was the Phillies' first or second starter and the winningest pitcher on a team that, in those years, lost an average of almost 100 games per season. In 1937 Passeau led the major leagues in innings pitched with 292. On May 29, 1939, Chicago paid dearly to pry him away from Philadelphia, giving up outfielder Joe Marty, pitcher Ray Harrell, and the fireballing Kirby Higbe to obtain him. Passeau responded by leading the National League in strikeouts while going 15–13. From 1940 through 1944, Passeau was the ace of the staff, compiling an 83–59 record during five seasons of playing for an under-.500 team and posting a sparkling 2.84 ERA over the same period. During those years, he was also one of the best-hitting pitchers in the major leagues, with 15 home runs in his career, including a grand slam in 1941 against Brooklyn.

Passeau's military deferment was the result of a number of factors. For one thing, the fingers on his left hand were partially closed, the result of a gunshot accident he suffered at age 16.[12] In addition to his physical deformity, he was eligible for deferment because he was married before Pearl Harbor Day, had two sons, and was a tung oil farmer in Luceford, Mississippi, during the off-season.

Although he never played baseball in high school, Passeau was a fierce, old-school competitor who relied mainly on a fastball and one of the best sliders in the major leagues. He specialized in keeping batters off-balance, not necessarily with pitch selection but by working fast and, like so many other successful pitchers of his era, throwing wherever he chose. Passeau had absolutely no qualms about brushing batters back or hitting them, especially if they had been successful against him the previous time up. Consequently, Passeau was a pitcher who always seemed to have a psychological edge over the batter, whoever it was. For the 1945 season, Passeau was paid handsomely for contributions over the years and value to the pitching staff. His $17,000 salary was in the same league with Cavarretta, Hack, and Nicholson; only the newly acquired Borowy, with more than half of his salary already paid by the Yankees, earned more. Passeau had certainly shown he was worth it, and his two-hitters against Boston on June 3 and August 11 foreshadowed the even greater success he would have in the World Series.

WITH MORE THAN half of the long road trip completed, the Chicagoans were eager to visit the cellar-dwelling Phillies in Shibe Park. Hack's three timely hits, Erickson's solid pitching, and a two-out relief stint in the ninth by Borowy led to a hard-fought 4–3 victory.

PAUL ERICKSON

Paul Walford Erickson was born on December 14, 1916, in Zion, Illinois. A blond, blue-eyed, six-foot, three-inch, 200-pound Swede, he was quickly tagged Li'l Abner by his teammates.[13] Erickson was an excellent athlete in high school and was signed with Ponca City in the Western Association in 1937. After he was traded to St. Joseph in 1939, he led the league in strikeouts, fanning 198 batters in 212 innings. Later Erickson was promoted to the Tulsa Oilers in the Texas League, where he struck out 136 batters and walked 77 in 196 innings while posting an excellent 2.62 ERA. The Cubs, impressed with his record, invited him to spring training at Catalina Island in 1941, and on June 29, 1941 he debuted in the majors, 40 miles south of his hometown.

During his first season he surrendered only one home run in 141 innings. Erickson was well liked by his teammates and roomed with pitcher Bob Chipman during the 1945 season.

The big man cast an intimidating shadow on the mound and threw an equally daunting fastball. He often used both to his advantage. In a grudge game against Brooklyn early in his career, he intentionally loaded the bases with 12 straight brushback pitches. His other money pitch was a big curveball. When Erickson could get his curveball over the plate, he could dominate a game. He threw a two-hitter against Pittsburgh on June 11, 1944, and a three-hitter against St. Louis on September 10. His problem was that there was never a guarantee that he would have command of both pitches at the same time, and when his curve flattened out and his fastball was not in the strike zone, Erickson had difficulties. This situation characterized his season in 1944. In spite of some brilliant performances, he ended the year with a 5–9 record and averaged almost one walk every two innings.

Erickson worked as a milkman in the Edgewater and Rogers Park neighborhoods of Chicago during the off-season and also after spring training began in 1945. Grimm wanted him at French Lick, and many in the press thought he was holding out for more money. This would only remain speculation, however, because the team had a policy of keeping such matters private. With Hanyzewski unavailable, Erickson's emergence as the team's pure power pitcher was proving invaluable.

THE TEAM WAS concerned, however, at what the August 12 victory might cost them. In the third inning, Erickson struck out Philadelphia second baseman Fred Daniels, but the ball got away from catcher Gillespie. Gillespie's hurried throw to first was off the mark, and in making the catch, Cavarretta collided with the scampering Daniels, badly bruising his right shoulder. Cavarretta continued playing for two more innings but was then taken to Jefferson Hospital. Cavarretta, who had not missed a game all season, was ordered not to play for an indefinite period of time. Suddenly, Chicago lost its best hitter, team captain, and cleanup hitter.

PHIL CAVARRETTA

Phillip Joseph Cavarretta was born on July 17, 1917, in Chicago and began making a name for himself in the city's baseball circles while in high school.[14] At Lane Technical High School, Cavarretta pitched to two straight city championships while playing under local baseball legend Percy Moore. In the summer he played for Moore's American Legion squad, sponsored by the National Tea Company, and in 1933 he led the team to the national title in Newark, New Jersey. Times were hard in the Cavarretta household during the Depression, and in the spring of his junior year, he told Moore that he would have to drop out of school to get a job to help out at home. Moore knew Chicago Cubs manager Charlie Grimm and arranged for Cavarretta to try out with the Cubs. During those years, open tryouts were more common than they are today, but individual evaluations such as Cavarretta's were more of a rarity. Still, on a chilly spring day in 1934, Cavarretta came early to Wrigley Field and pitched about 15 minutes of batting practice. He was then invited to do some hitting. No less a figure than Lon Warneke, the ace of the staff in 1933, who went 18–13 with a 2.00 ERA, pitched to him, but the lithe teenager lined drives into the outfield and then took a Warneke offering into the right field bleachers. Chicago signed him and sent him to Peoria in the Central League.

Cavarretta, who had spent almost no time in his life out of the city and away from his family, was homesick but settled in on Peoria's baseball diamond very well, hitting for the cycle in his first game. When the Central League folded under the financial pressures of the Depression after Cavarretta had played in only 34 games, he was reassigned to Reading, Massachusetts. The distance exacerbated his loneliness, but he had the athletic ability to overcome it, hitting .308 with 33 doubles and settling in at first base. He was called up to finish the season with the Cubs, hitting .381 in seven games. In the first game he started for Chicago, he homered off Whitey Wistert to lead the Cubs to a 1–0 victory.

Grimm, the player-manager in 1934, was 38 at the time, and his playing days at first base were behind him. He felt that Cavarretta was a natural heir apparent and worked with Cavarretta on his fielding. Cavarretta started 146 games for Chicago in 1935, hitting .275 with 12 triples and eight home runs. At the age of 18, he was the Cubs' starting first baseman in the World Series against Detroit, exactly 17 months after he had been thinking about leaving high school to look for work. In November of the following year, he married Loranye Clares.

By 1945 the only Chicago player with more seniority was Hack. While the Cubs valued Cavarretta's abilities, they were not always above misusing his talents. In 1942 manager Jimmie Wilson unsuccessfully tried to convince him to give up first base and become a pitcher because the team was short of left-handers. That year Chicago had Babe Dahlgren, who also played first. Fortunately, this change never took place. Wilson's desire, however, was perhaps excusable; Cavarretta was blessed with an extremely strong throwing arm. On September 5, 1943, the team organized some competitions with Pittsburgh between the two games of a doubleheader. Cavarretta easily won the baseball-throwing contest with a 385-foot toss. It would have been fascinating if the same competition were scheduled the following year, when the rifle-armed Pafko was a rookie on the team. The power that Cavarretta generated from his 180 pounds, however, was remarkable. When batting, he held the bat behind his body, parallel to the ground at waist level, and had one of the quickest swings of anyone during his era. As World War II drew to a close, that swing seemed perfect at times. Always a tough out, Cavarretta would often go on short streaks in which he was almost impossible to retire. He was one of the offensive stars in the 1944 All-Star Game. When Grimm shuffled the lineup and put Cavarretta in the cleanup spot on June 28, 1945, he responded with one of those streaks, going 12-for-17 with five walks for a .772 on-base percentage. If he could stay ahead of Tommy Holmes by the end of 1945, the Cubs would have their first batting champion since Heinie Zimmerman in 1912.

THE STRENGTH IN Chicago's bench, however, made Cavarretta's absence much less noticeable, and this fact became clear in the second game against the Phillies on August 12. Becker played an errorless first base while recording ten putouts, and he got three hits in five at bats. Becker's bench mate (catcher Rice) and slugger Nicholson also had three hits apiece as the Cubs smothered the hapless Phils 12–6. Wyse cruised to his 18th win of the season. The high point for the 17,994 Phillies fans occurred before the game even started. A ceremony welcoming back Philadelphia pitcher Hugh Mulcahy, the first major leaguer to voluntarily enlist in the service, took place at home plate to the cheers of the long-suffering Philadelphia faithful. While Chicago was sweeping the tailenders, St. Louis and Brooklyn split a hard-fought doubleheader, putting the Cubs at their high water mark for the season, in first place by six and a half games.

LEN RICE

The contributions of little-used reserve catcher Leonard Oliver Rice could not be overlooked. Rice, the only major leaguer ever born in Lead, South Dakota, grew up in Oakland, California, and distinguished himself as one of the most talented high school athletes in the Bay Area in the 1930s. His athletic career was often interrupted by serious injuries. The six foot, 175 pounder was a talented running back in high school who lost a kidney to a serious injury suffered on the gridiron. He excelled at both track and baseball, winning many sprint competitions, and was signed by the St. Louis Cardinals and assigned to Grand Island of the Class D Nebraska State League as a catcher. Rice had two serious back injuries in his first years in the minors, and the Cardinals eventually cut him. He hooked up with Lincoln, Nebraska, and worked his way up the minor league chain, playing at Ogden, Tucson, Columbia, and finally, Syracuse in the Class AA International League. At Tucson, Rice caught 123 of 124 scheduled games. He had a good year in 1943 at Syracuse, and after being invited to the Cincinnati Reds' spring training camp in 1944, he made their major league roster. Veteran Ray Mueller had a lock on the Reds catching job, and Rice played only ten games for the Reds, with no hits in four at bats. Cincinnati sent him back to Syracuse, where he hit .290 with ten doubles, four triples, and nine stolen bases in only 82 games. Rice's triples and stolen base totals proved that he could still run well. His play behind the plate was equally impressive; he allowed only five passed balls and caught 28 runners attempting to steal. The Cubs took notice and purchased his contract from Cincinnati at the beginning of spring training in 1945. Already carrying three catchers at the time, general manager Jim Gallagher saw Rice as more than just another substitute behind the plate. Here was a catcher with a good arm who could hit, and even more unusual, he could run. Rice's performance in the last two games validated Gallagher's hunch.[15]

TWO OF THE older pitchers in the majors matched up in the Monday afternoon game on August 13 when 39-year-old Derringer faced 39-year-old Dick "Kewpie" Barrett from Montoursville, Pennsylvania. Not even this chronological curiosity intrigued the beleaguered Philadelphia fans, however, as a crowd of just 1,004 came out and saw Derringer go the distance for his 13th win of the season, with a final score of 4–1. Johnson and Lowrey contributed two hits apiece. Once again, however, the offensive star—with a triple, a double, a single, and two runs scored—was Becker, the affable 30-year-old German.

HEINZ BECKER

Heinz Reinhard Becker was born on August 26, 1915, in Berlin, Germany. His family left their war-torn homeland in 1922, emigrating to Venezuela.[16] Becker's father had been a brewer in Germany, but once the family arrived in South America, he bought some cattle and established a ranch. In 1925, when Becker was ten, the family sold their property and moved to Dallas, Texas. As Becker grew into his six–foot, two-inch, 200-pound frame, his rapidly developing athletic ability drew the attention of several scouts. He began his career at the Class D level of the minors in 1938. By 1942 he was one of the most feared hitters in the Class AA American Association, leading the Milwaukee Brewers with a .326 average and 61 RBIs in just 101 games. Invited to spring training by the Cubs, he made the squad and debuted in the major leagues on April 21, 1943. Becker appeared in only 24 games and had trouble with National League pitching, going 10-for-69 for a .145 average, and returned to Milwaukee. Charlie Grimm, managing the Brewers at the time, did not give up on the 29-year-old returnee. Grimm's faith in the big first baseman paid off; hitting .346 with 26 doubles, nine triples, and ten home runs, Becker was the offensive powerhouse on a team that went 102–51. When Grimm left Milwaukee to manage Chicago, he remembered Becker's abilities and made sure that he was invited back for spring training in 1945. From the way baseball's only German-born major leaguer with the blue number "7" on his back was handling National League pitching, it turned out to be a good decision.

A physical condition prevented Becker from getting to the big leagues sooner and playing more when he arrived. He suffered from bunions and ankle problems from two different ankle fractures that did not heal correctly.[17] His feet were in such poor condition that they affected his ability to play in the field. Becker's flat feet kept him out of the military during World War II, and the painful bunions prevented him from any chance he had of being any more than an occasional fielder. Becker spent more time than any of the other players with trainer Andy Lotshaw just to continue playing. All the effort was obviously worthwhile; his contributions to the team while the injured Cavarretta recuperated prevented the Cubs' offense from missing a beat.

THE PHILLIES FOUND a way to double their attendance on Tuesday, August 14—simply schedule a night game on Victory in Japan Day. They should have known that it would also give them a better chance of winning, given the Cubs' record in night games up to this date. Sure enough, the lights went on, and 39-year-old left-hander Oscar Judd, whom the Phillies picked up on waivers from Boston on May 31, baffled Cubs hitters, yielding only six hits for a 2–1 victory. His mound opponent, Prim, pitched even better, allowing only four hits, but one of them was a home run to the Phillies' promising young catcher, Andy Seminick, who had also homered the night before. There seemed to be something about the Chicagoans being in the City of Brotherly Love at times of extreme military significance. Their first loss of the season to the Phillies took place during the V-E Day celebrations, and what would be their last loss to Philadelphia occurred on V-J Day. Their lead was down to five and a half games, and they boarded a chartered bus to New York's Commodore Hotel to play Brooklyn the next day. On the bus they got two good pieces of news: The food shortage at the Commodore was over, and Cavarretta felt well enough to play against the Dodgers.

Grimm held Cavarretta out of the first game in Brooklyn on August 15, possibly because he had premonitions that he simply would not need him. In a game reminiscent of their offensive bombardment at Boston in early July, the Chicagoans hammered three Dodgers pitchers for 19 hits in a 20–6 pasting, which left Durocher and his crew nine and a half games out of first. Borowy was the recipient of the Cubs' offensive largesse in his first appearance in New York since his dismissal from the Yankees. The Cubs led 15–4 after four innings, at which time Grimm had some fun with his defensive lineup, playing three different second basemen (Johnson, Hughes, and Schuster) and acquiescing to Hughes's request to spend a couple innings at first base. Three Cubs—Hack, Lowrey, and Gillespie—had three hits each; Pafko and Nicholson each drove in three runs. Once again, the hitting star emerged from the bench, his three hits yielding six RBIs: Paul Gillespie.

PAUL GILLESPIE

At six feet, three inches and 195 pounds, Paul Allen Gillespie, of Sugar Valley, Georgia, was the biggest of the four Chicago catchers in 1945.[18] Breaking in with Class D Brownsville as a catcher in 1938, he was traded to Lake Charles, Louisiana, the following year. The staff at Lake Charles was more impressed with his hitting than his catching and moved him into the outfield. This experiment lasted only one year, and he was back behind the plate in 1940. He continued to toil in the minors, working his way up to Elmira, Knoxville, Salina, and Tulsa. In 1942 he had a strong season both batting and catching for the Tulsa Oilers, with whom the Cubs had a contractual agreement for players, and he earned a September call-up to Chicago. The left-handed hitting catcher made the most of his opportunity, homering over the right field fence against New York at the Polo Grounds on September 11, 1942, becoming the first Cub in history to homer his first time at bat. His entire first month in the majors was an auspicious one; in only 16 at bats, he hit two homers and drove in four runs. Gillespie, however, was used to making grand entrances. In his first game for Salina in 1941, he managed a single, a double, and a triple.

Concerned about his military status with World War II raging, Gillespie enlisted in the Coast Guard after the 1942 season, received a medical discharge in September 1944, and returned to Chicago for nine games also in September 1944. Manager Charlie Grimm liked his size and his power, and the 25-year-old was a lock to make the team at French Lick in 1945. He also became one of the team's pacesetters in the style and fashion department. Impressed with the clean-cut appearance of a waiter with a crew cut he saw in Boston during the team's visit in early July, Gillespie got the same haircut. Within a few weeks, six other players—Cavarretta, Chipman, Hack, Nicholson, Rice, and Ed Sauer—followed suit with similar haircuts.[19] The big catcher enjoyed a cigar after a game and was the only player to wear glasses off the field.[20] Gillespie did not have Livingston's experience, Rice's speed, or Williams's throwing arm, but none of these catchers approached Gillespie's left-handed power, which he put on grand display in these important August games.

THE FOLLOWING AFTERNOON, on Thursday, August 16, Brooklyn manager Durocher managed to get tossed from the game by plate umpire Ziggy Sears for arguing a call on a pitch to Luis Olmo. Durocher seemed to save most of his ire for Dodgers–Cubs games in 1945; three of his four ejections were in games against the Cubs. The tactic fired up his recently humiliated team, as the Dodgers spread out nine hits to win a close one, 2–1. Lefty Tom Seats handcuffed the league-leading Chicagoans, allowing seven hits in nine innings, with Johnson and Pafko both getting two of them while Wyse took the loss. Another tense game occurred Friday, when Passeau faced Hal Gregg, the ace of the Dodgers' pitching staff. Pafko's big home run proved to be the difference as the Cubs boosted their lead to six games. Saturday, August 18, was their final game in Ebbets Field for the 1945 season. Derringer completely dominated the sinking Brooklynites with a decisive 7–3 win, for his 14th victory. Lowrey and Nicholson had two hits apiece, while Johnson, Becker, and Pafko each had three. Both Nicholson and Pafko drove in two runs as well.

The significance of Chicago taking three out of four in the toughest park in the National League could not be overlooked. The Cubs' dominant play all but eliminated Brooklyn from pennant contention. They were ten and a half games behind the front-running Chicagoans. The successful series also left St. Louis six and a half behind. The pennant hinged upon the Cubs' performance against the Cardinals, with whom they still had 12 games remaining. Four games in the Polo Grounds against the Giants were all that remained in the 19-day road trip. They entered that series with a glittering 13–5 record since leaving home.

Don Johnson

With the season that Cavarretta, Pafko, Lowrey, Hack, and so many pitchers on the team were having, the day-to-day accomplishments of Donald Spore Johnson were often overlooked. The 34-year-old second baseman, however, was used to it. The Chicago organization overlooked him for more than ten years, not needing a second baseman through the 1930s and early '40s with future Hall of Famer Billy Herman around. After Herman was traded, Johnson once again was overlooked in favor of Eddie Stanky. He finally cracked the Cubs' major league roster in 1943, appearing in ten games, and beat Stanky out for the starting job in 1944, allowing Chicago to trade Stanky for a badly needed left-handed pitcher, Bob Chipman. Johnson thrived under Grimm's guidance, making the National League All-Star team in 1944, his first full season in the majors.

Johnson was also the only player on the team whose father had been a major leaguer and the only one with a link to the Black Sox scandal. Ernie Johnson, his father, broke in with the Chicago White Sox in 1912, a year after Don was born, and later played with St. Louis's Federal League franchise and with the Browns. When Judge Landis banned Black Sox shortstop Swede Risberg for life, the White Sox had a big hole to fill at short and signed Don's father for the 1921 season. He ended a ten-year major league career with the New York Yankees in 1925, appearing in the World Series. His son was turning out to be a big reason why Chicago would appear in the fall classic in 1945.

A HUGE CROWD of 48,310 showed up on Sunday, August 19, to see the fourth-place Giants try their luck against the hottest team in the major leagues. None of them left with any doubt about why Chicago sat on top of the standings. In the first game, the crafty Prim, enjoying the best two months of his long career, surrendered only one lonely single in the last four innings, while the timely hitting of Merullo, Lowrey, and Becker manufactured two runs in the ninth inning for a 3–1 victory.

RAY PRIM

For Raymond Lee Prim—the best pitcher ever to call Salipta, Alabama, home—it was his ninth win of the year. Nicknamed Pop because of his 39 years and graying hair, Prim was born a right-hander on December 30, 1906, but as a young boy suffered a severe burn to his right hand, which caused the tendons to tighten. In the years that followed, he determinedly taught himself to pitch left-handed. After breaking into the majors with the Washington Senators in 1933, he played sparingly for two years before he was traded to the Philadelphia Phillies, where he pitched in 29 games. A long stint in the minors followed. In 1945 he made the Cubs on the strength of an excellent 1944 season at Los Angeles in the Pacific Coast League, when he went 22–10, had a 1.70 ERA, 17 shutouts, and 139 strikeouts, and surrendered only 40 walks in 286 innings. After a slow start in the beginning of the 1945 season for Chicago, Prim began pitching in the majors with the same effectiveness he displayed the year before on the West Coast, becoming the most pleasant surprise of the 1945 Cubs pitching staff.[21]

IN THE SECOND game, the Giants had even less of a chance to win, facing Borowy for the first time. In a game that was never in doubt, the newest member of the Cubs won his fourth game in five attempts since leaving the Yankees, with a final score of 8–0. The best pitching staff in the National League held the hard-hitting Giants to one run in 18 innings and had allowed but eight runs in the last 45 for a 1.60 team ERA.

Chicago was now 74–38 for a .681 winning percentage, by far the best in the major leagues. With 42 games left in the season, they were seven and a half ahead of second-place St. Louis, an amount that would be their biggest lead of the season. They slipped in the last two games of the road trip on Monday, August 20. Wyse failed for the second time to win his 19th game, and the Cubs were unable to hit the intimidating Van Lingle Mungo for another night game loss (9–3) on Monday evening. On Wednesday the Giants, determined to remain in the first division, pecked away at a two-run deficit and got the best of Passeau with a two-run ninth inning, the final score being 4–3. The long road trip ended with the Cubs having a 15–7 record. The Cubs were exactly where they had been when it started: in first place, five and a half games ahead of St. Louis.

CHICAGO ENDED THE 61-game second phase of their season with a record of 45 wins and 15 losses, with a suspended game against Brooklyn to be completed in September. The period began with an eastern road trip, in which they went 13–3, and ended with the just completed, prolonged eastern excursion, where they went 15–7. In between was their longest home stand of 1945, in which they went 17–5–1. Chicago marched into first place with a 15-game winning streak in July. They had scored 20 or more runs in two road games.

The factors contributing to the .750 winning percentage during this period were numerous. Five Cubs regulars hit over .300: Hack, .372; Cavarretta, .370; Johnson, .334; Lowrey, .305; and Pafko, .303. Cavarretta, Nicholson, Lowrey, and Pafko each drove in more than 40 runs in the 61 games, with Pafko emerging as the team's RBI leader with 48. While not putting up the numbers of some of his fellow regulars, Merullo contributed many key hits, and his hustle on the bases and in the field were critical ingredients to the team's success. The performance of several second stringers was another contributing factor. Becker played magnificently when he replaced the injured Cavarretta, hitting .340. Infield handyman Hughes batted .318. Gillespie hit .292 and got some key, game-winning hits. Another catcher, Rice, hit .280.

The purchase of Borowy not only put the team on notice that management was indeed serious about winning the pennant but also gave Grimm a top-drawer starter whose presence added a great deal of versatility to how he could use the pitching staff. After Borowy's arrival, Grimm settled on a starting rotation of Wyse, Borowy, Passeau, and Derringer, with lefty Prim emerging as the fifth starter. Wyse emerged as the iron man of the staff and had 18 wins two weeks before Labor Day. The fiercely competitive Passeau won nine straight in one stretch. Derringer's effectiveness and consistency resembled his glory years in Cincinnati. The biggest surprise was the ancient Prim, whose soft-tossed offerings confounded opposing hitters and netted him one of the lowest ERAs in the league. Chipman, Erickson, and Vandenberg, creators of some pitching masterpieces from May through July, were a little too erratic to be fully trusted in a starting rotation in the thick of a pennant race. But the left-handed Chipman could now be used in critical relief roles, and the two power pitchers, Erickson and Vandenberg, would have fresher arms through September. Backed by the best fielding Chicago fans had seen in years, Cubs pitching emerged as the class of the National League.

There were two worries, however: one minor and one major. First-string catcher Livingston, showing the effects of some serious injuries, was hitting only .215. As the catcher with the most complete package of skills on the team, Livingston would be needed for the stretch. A bigger issue was Nicholson. While his RBI production during this second phase of the season was a healthy 43 in 61 games, his batting average was down to .257, and he had only five home runs. These were not the numbers the Cubs expected from their chief power hitter, especially after he led the league in homers and RBIs the two previous seasons. Nicholson's lack of production gave the team a weakness they were not expecting, the loss of the long ball threat.

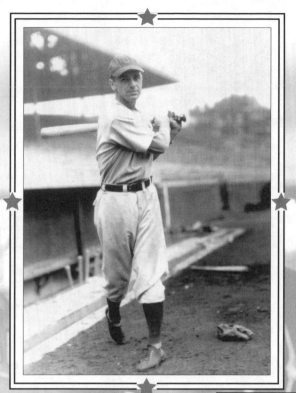

Second baseman DON JOHNSON, who broke into the majors as a 31-year old rookie in 1943, made the National League All-Star team in 1944 and hit .302 while batting second in 1945. When Johnson was nine, his father, Ernie, came to the White Sox to play shortstop after the South Siders' roster was decimated following the Black Sox scandal.

The handsome fireballer ED HANYZEWSKI was a Notre Dame alumnus beset with arm trouble throughout his career.

HANK BOROWY is captured
here at the end of an
effortless, graceful pitching
delivery. After Chicago
acquired him from the
Yankees in late July he went
11–2 and sealed Chicago's last
pennant.

Starting catcher MICKEY
LIVINGSTON went from
harrowing World War II
experiences in 1944 to being
one of the offensive heroes of
the 1945 World Series just ten
months later. The 31-year old
South Carolinian had a ten-
year major league career, five
of which was with the Cubs.

Six-time All-Star PAUL
DERRINGER, one of the most
dominant pitchers of his time,
ended his 15-year, 223-victory
career by going 16–11 for the
Cubs in 1945. The right-handed
Derringer combined pinpoint
control, fierce competitiveness,
and an intimidating nature
when on the mound.

The handsome PAUL ERICKSON,
pictured here in a freshly-
laundered home uniform, was a
legendary athlete growing up in
nearby Zion, Illinois. The big
right-hander could frighten
opposing batters with his blazing
fastball and occasional wildness.

After being discharged by the Coast Guard, powerful catcher PAUL GILLESPIE rejoined the Cubs in time for the 1945 pennant. Gillespie was an experienced backstop who brought a strong left-handed bat into the lineup behind Livingston and Williams during Chicago's last pennant.

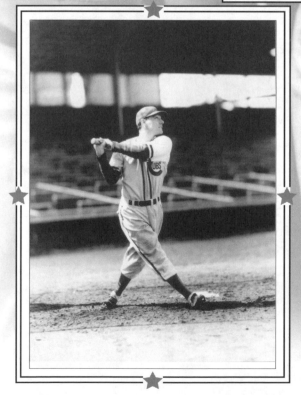

Chicago native PHIL CAVARRETTA, National League Batting Champion and Most Valuable Player in 1945, was only 28 when the 1945 season started, but was already an 11-year veteran.

Manager CHARLEY GRIMM *(r)* shares a portrait with the venerable STAN HACK *(l)*. Grimm was loved by his players for his no-nonsense but caring demeanor and loved by the fans both for his histrionics in the third base coaching box and because his Cubs teams usually won.

Perhaps the two most important Cubs of the World War II era, roommates STAN HACK *(l)* and BILL NICHOLSON *(r)*, are seen here in a classic pose at the step of the Cubs' dugout. Both players were four-time All-Stars; third baseman Hack was one of the best leadoff men of his time and Nicholson became the premier National League power hitter during World War II.

Speedster BILL SCHUSTER, whom Charlie Grimm relied upon to play second, short, and third base, stretched the 1945 World Series to seven games with his sprint from first base on Stan Hack's double in game six.

An effective mixture of intelligence and intimidation helped pitching mainstay CLAUDE PASSEAU, a graduate of Millsaps College, become a four-time All-Star and one of baseball's premier pitchers during World War II.

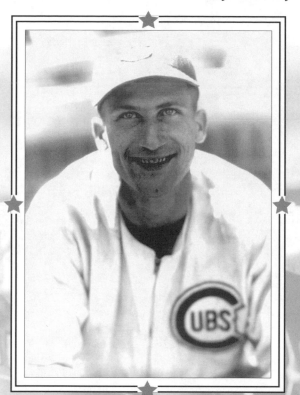

Catcher DEWEY WILLIAMS was one of the Cubs' leading hitters for the first few months of the 1945 season and possessed one of the most respected arms of any catcher in his era. His five-year major league career ended in 1948.

The major league career of outfielder ED SAUER, a key contributor off the bench in 1945, spanned four years, 11 fewer than his more famous brother Hank.

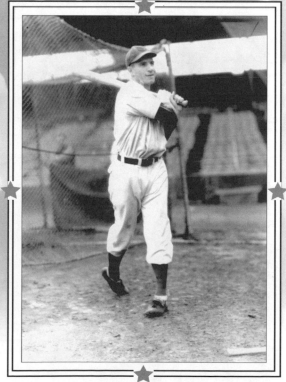

Muscular outfielder FRANK SECORY's clutch pinch-hits throughout the 1945 season proved invaluable. After his five-year career as a major league player ended, Secory became an umpire, working in the National League from 1952 through 1970.

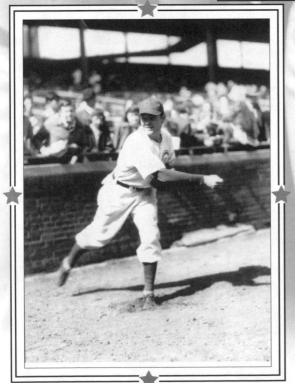

27-year old HANK WYSE went 22–10 while pitching over 278 innings for the 1945 Cubs after going 16–15 the year before and in spite of a back injury that forced him to wear a corset while pitching many of the season's games.

Big HY VANDENBERG pitched excellently for the Cubs in 1944 and 1945 while periodically trying manager Charlie Grimm's patience in the process.

Shortstop LEN MERULLO shares a moment with his son Boots in the dugout before the start of the fourth game of the 1945 World Series. Merullo starred at Villanova while teammate Hank Borowy was pitching for Fordham. Merullo later became a successful major league scout. *(Photo from the collection of Len Merullo.)*

LEN RICE was a true athletic rarity as a catcher who could *really run*. The ex-football and track star's major league career was cut short by injuries.

The diminutive left fielder PEANUTS LOWREY was a former childhood actor in Hollywood whose baby-faced appearance masked a tough-as-nails demeanor. In spite of his size, Lowrey could hit for power and became one of Chicago's RBI leaders. When his playing days were over, he coached for several major league teams.

39-year old lefty RAY PRIM
pitched masterfully for the
Cubs in 1945. Prim's major
league career began with the
Washington Senators in 1933
before he toiled from 1936
through 1944 in the minors.
His excellent pitching for the
Los Angeles Angels in the
Pacific Coast League in 1944
led to his promotion the
following year. Some felt there
would not be a pennant for
Chicago in 1945 without him.

ANDY PAFKO
accepts good wish-
es from three of his
five brothers, Ed,
Mike, and Jon,
before the fourth
game of the 1945
World Series. As
youngsters the
Pafko boys changed
the clocks on the
family farm so they
would have an
extra hour of day-
light for baseball
when their chores
were done.

HEINZ BECKER was a great
hitter whose major league
career was shortened
by chronic ankle and
foot problems.

Fleet-footed shortstop
ROY HUGHES made a
miracle recovery from a
freak accident that prolonged
his playing career.

1945 CHICAGO CUBS

TOP ROW: Ed Sauer, Don Johnson, Frank Secory, Heinz Becker, Paul Derringer, Hy Vandenberg, Ed Hanyzewski, Paul Gillespie, Ray Starr, Bob Chipman, Hank Wyse, trainer Andy Lotshaw.

MIDDLE ROW: Len Merullo, Jorge Comellas, Johnny Ostrowski, Andy Pafko, Dewey Williams, Mickey Livingston, Peanuts Lowrey, Len Rice, Ray Prim, Mack Stewart.

FIRST ROW: Bill Schuster, Stan Hack, Roy Hughes, coach Roy Johnson, manager Charley Grimm, coach Red Smith, coach Milt Stock, Bill Nicholson, Claude Passeau, Phil Cavarretta.

All photographs (except Len Merullo's) are from the
George Brace Collection. George Brace and his mentor,
George Burke, started capturing baseball players on film in
1929, beginning what would become one of the world's most
famous collections of baseball photographs. Brace continued
photographing nearly every major league player, as well as
other celebrities that passed through Chicago, through the
1993 season. He documented over 10,000 players during that
time. His daughter Mary has maintained the collection since
his death in 2002.

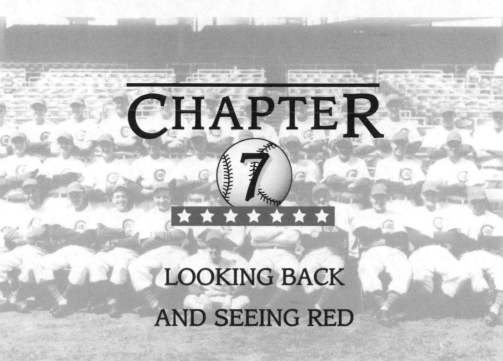

CHAPTER 7

LOOKING BACK
AND SEEING RED

T he Cubs began the last phase of their season on Thursday, August 24 with a three-day home stand against the St. Louis Cardinals, the only team with a realistic chance of challenging them for the pennant. The Cubs would be strengthened by the return of Phil Cavarretta, whose shoulder injury had kept him out of the last 12 games, with the exception of a pinch-running assignment in the team's 2–1 defeat at Brooklyn on August 16. Chicago started the series five and a half games ahead of St. Louis. The first game featured a classic pitching matchup, with Hank Borowy facing off against longtime Cubs nemesis Harry Brecheen. Both pitchers went the distance, with Borowy allowing only four hits, but Brecheen allowed only three for a 1–0 Cardinal victory before 44,733 tense fans at Wrigley Field.

The next day, Ray Prim, 7–1 in July and August, faced Cardinals rookie Ken Burkhardt, who had thrown shutout victories in his last three outings, and the Cards proved superior once again, beating the Chicagoans 3–1 with 31,671 enduring the disappointment. Prim, who had no record against St. Louis from his previous outings, gave up three runs in the second inning and was replaced by Hank Wyse in the sixth. Wyse held the Cardinals scoreless from that point on, but the Cubs did not score off Burkhardt until their single tally in the eighth inning. Andy Pafko was the only Cubs batter to have his way with the tough Cardinals rookie, going 3-for-4 for the day.

The sweep was finalized on Sunday, when Red Barrett, whom the Cardinals had acquired in a trade with Boston for the unhappy Mort Cooper at the start of the season, became the National League's winningest pitcher, with an easy 5–1 win over the Cubs. Barrett's 19th victory of the year was marred only by Dewey Williams's eighth-inning home run and Cavarretta's two hits; Paul Gillespie and Peanuts Lowrey claimed the other two of the Cubs' five hits. The cheers of 42,998 could not buoy the sinking Chicagoans, whose lead over St. Louis had sunk to a mere two and a half games, with nine games still left between them. The pitching was certainly good enough, but key batters who had carried the team through their hot July and August hit poorly in the weekend series. Stan Hack went 0-for-12; Don Johnson, 1-for-12; Lowrey, 3-for-12; and Bill Nicholson, 2-for-10. The team's five-game losing streak left a bitter taste as they boarded an overnight Pennsylvania Railroad train on Monday for Pittsburgh.

Earlier that day, the Cubs had posed for World Series pictures and held a workout at Wrigley Field. Once the team was settled after practice, manager Charlie Grimm dropped a bombshell and released Tuesday's starting lineup early. Penciled in at first was Heinz Becker, Cavarretta was slated for right field, and Nicholson, slugging king of the National League in 1943 and 1944, was on the bench. The last time Nicholson had been out of a Cubs starting lineup was in 1942, and he was not at all happy about this development. But numbers did not lie, and the statistics were all on Grimm's side. Nicholson's power productivity had been down all season. During the current five-game losing streak, the big hitter had gone just 3-for-18, and the hits making up his .166 batting average consisted of singles on August 21 against New York and on August 25 against St. Louis and a double in the August 26 loss to St. Louis.

In spite of the ruffled feathers over Nicholson's benching, the trip to Pittsburgh could not have gone better. The Cubs won their first night game of the year when Borowy, with help from Len Rice and Lowrey, easily handled the Pirates, 6–3. Key to the Cubs' victory were a Lowrey homer plus three RBIs, while Rice, filling in admirably behind the plate, added another two hits to lead the Cubs' attack. On Wednesday, Grimm put Nicholson back in right field and moved Becker to first when Cavarretta complained that he simply could not play with his sore shoulder.[1] After Cavarretta was ordered to Chicago for a week's rest, the clutch-performing Becker led the Cubs' offense with two hits and one RBI, while Prim and Hy Vandenberg pitched brilliantly for the 2–0 Cubs shutout. After the game, the Western Union ticker in the clubhouse reported that Cincinnati had just beaten St. Louis for the second straight game, increasing the Cubs' lead to a much more comfortable four and a half games. They would need every one of them after the weekend series that was to follow.

GOING INTO THE huge weekend series in St. Louis as they prepared to play the World Champions, Grimm sensed the team was tight. To ease the tension, Grimm—along with traveling secretary Bob Lewis, trainer Andy Lotshaw, and coach Red Smith—came up with a plan to loosen up the troops on their off day, Thursday, August 30, before the series began.

During the season, Grimm lived not far from Wrigley Field, in an apartment near Addison Street and Lake Shore Drive, but his permanent residence was a farm near Union, Missouri, about 30 miles outside of St. Louis. Grimm called the superintendent of schools and arranged to have a school bus meet the train from Boston at the station and then transport the team to his place for a day of barbecue, beer, and outdoor recreation. He invited the press but swore them to secrecy, and the event never reached the Chicago papers. Long after dark, a head count was taken as the players boarded the bus to get to their hotel. Everyone was accounted for except Paul Derringer, who was eventually found lying in a cluster of rose bushes.[2]

Grimm's country soiree may have loosened up the ball club, but the Cardinals tightened the pennant race in the first game of the series on Friday evening, and once again, Brecheen did most of the squeezing, as Wyse failed once again to gain his 18th win, even though the Cubs held a rare lead over the Cardinals when Ed Sauer, who replaced Nicholson in right field, knocked out a home run in the first inning. The Chicago press ripped the Cubs' infield the next day, with head shaking over the team's tentative and error-prone play. Another problem Grimm had to confront was the breaking down of one of his best substitutes, Becker, whose chronic foot problems had left him virtually crippled after all the playing he had done over the previous three weeks. Jim Gallagher responded by buying the contract of Reggie Otero from the Los Angeles Angels. The 30-year-old native of Havana singed Pacific Coast League pitching all summer, hitting .344 and striking out only six times in 302 at bats. Sparsely built at five feet, eleven inches and 160 pounds, Otero had equally impeccable fielding, making only four errors in more than 700 chances.

The tentative Chicagoans gave it away on Saturday night, wasting another great effort by Claude Passeau, but staged a small rally in the ninth to tie at 2–2. Passeau easily retired the first two Cards in their half of the ninth, and Chicago geared up for an extra inning game when Red Schoendienst hit a weak ground ball to Roy Hughes (who had replaced Lennie Merullo after Frank Secory pinch-hit for him in the seventh inning) at short. The sure-handed Hughes picked a terrible time to fumble a grounder. Johnny Hopp came up next. As if to pay back the Cubs for the beaning he had suffered at their hands earlier in the season, Hopp tripled Schoendienst home with the winning run, the final score being 3–2. Chicago's last victory over St. Louis had been more than two months earlier, on June 24, when Passeau had carried the team almost single-handedly with his pitching and by hitting a three-run homer.

With two victories under their belts, and the Cards only two games out, St. Louis fans smelled blood, and 36,701 of them came out to see the Sunday doubleheader. The crowd was the largest for St. Louis baseball since 1939. Borowy drew the start in the first game against the little-used Cardinals right-hander Glenn Gardner. Manager Billy Southworth had no choice but to start Gardner, because the Cardinals, like most major league teams, had back-to-back doubleheaders on Labor Day weekend. Borowy was magnificent, with only center fielder Babe Adams, catcher Kenny O'Dea, and second baseman Emil Verban able to hit him safely. But the slumping Cubs batters had just as much trouble with Gardner, whom they had not seen before. With the score standing at 1–1 in the top of the tenth inning, Gardner struck out Nicholson, but Becker drew a walk and was replaced by the fleet newcomer Otero. Pafko doubled high off the left field wall, and the Cardinals then intentionally walked Lowrey to get to

Merullo. Grimm put in the hard-hitting, left-handed swinging Gillespie to pinch-hit; Cardinals skipper Southworth countered by removing the tiring Gardner and replacing him with George Dockins, the pride of Clyde, Kansas. Grimm then called Gillespie back to the bench and replaced him with the little-used Secory. After taking the first pitch for a strike, Secory ripped Dockins's second offering to the bottom of the wall in right-center, his first double of the season and the biggest hit of his career.

FRANK SECORY

Frank Edward Secory, the pride of Mason City, Iowa, was born on August 24, 1912, and had his major league debut with the Detroit Tigers on April 28, 1940. The Tigers sent him back to the minors after one game, but in 1942 he came up for a brief period with the Cincinnati Reds. Secory impressed Grimm when he played for the Milwaukee Brewers in the American Association and posted an excellent season in 1944, hitting nine home runs and 19 doubles in only 88 games for a .290 average. Later that season, he was called up to the Cubs and continued to impress at the plate during 22 games, hitting .321 and four homers, with 17 RBIs and eight stolen bases. The affable Secory was well liked by his teammates, and his big hit in St. Louis validated the faith Grimm had placed in him over the previous three years.

SECORY'S CLUTCH PERFORMANCE guaranteed that Chicago would leave St. Louis in sole possession of first place, but their performance against St. Louis ace Red Barrett in game two raised questions about whether they deserved it. The Cubs' anemic offense managed only one hit off the winningest pitcher in the National League, and they wasted a strong six-hitter by Prim to lose 4–0. Merullo got the only hit, a single, off Barrett but was out when he tried to stretch it into a double. Giving up no walks and with some help from his fielders in cutting down the aggressive Merullo, Barrett faced the minimum 27 batters. Chicago left St. Louis with a lead of two games and a few percentage points, with a record of 77–47. The Cardinals, at 76–50, were now firmly entrenched in second place, six games ahead of Brooklyn, but the Cards had won 13 of their 17 contests against Chicago. The Cubs went home to play a Labor Day doubleheader against Cincinnati; St. Louis stayed put, hosting Pittsburgh in their own holiday twin bill.

THE CUBS' LABORS and their luck on Labor Day both proved to be very fruitful, as a huge and hopeful crowd of 43,161came to see two games against the Cincinnati Reds. Pafko provided all the cushion that Derringer would need for his 15th victory of the season with a first-inning grand slam home run off Reds ace Ed Heusser. It was a huge victory for Derringer against his old teammates. Ineffective in his last two outings against Pittsburgh on August 30 and St. Louis on August 26, Derringer would be needed by Chicago for this September stretch run.

ANDY PAFKO

Enough could not be said about the Cubs' affable second-year center fielder, Andrew Pafko. The youngest starter on the 1945 Cubs, Pafko was born on February 25, 1921, in Boyceville, Wisconsin, a small town in the rolling countryside between Eau Claire and Minneapolis. His parents, first-generation Slovaks, had raised six athletic sons on the family farm. In high school, Pafko excelled at football and baseball, but his athletic career nearly came to a tragic end when a church heater exploded, blinding him and burning one side of his face. A friend rescued him but later died from injuries suffered in the blaze. Medical treatment eventually restored Pafko's vision, and he was able to resume his athletic endeavors.

Mother and father Pafko knew little about sports, and in 1940, when Andy tried out for his first professional team—Eau Claire in the Northern League—he never told his parents. Perhaps it was for the best. The sturdy 19-year-old fared poorly at Eau Claire, hitting only .209 in 20 games, but the following year, he made the Green Bay squad in the Wisconsin State League, where he hit .349 in his first year. Also that year, Pafko won a throwing contest when he hurled a ball from home plate out of the Green Bay stadium. Pafko's efforts in 1941 landed him a spot with Macon in the Sally League in 1942, where he led the league with 18 triples, hit .300, and had 12 assists. For his efforts with the bat and his strong throwing arm, Pafko earned $150 a month in 1942, twice his Green Bay salary. In 1943 the Chicago organization promoted him to its highest minor league club, the Los Angeles Angels, and doubled his pay again. That year, Pafko put together one of the best seasons in the Pacific Coast League's history, leading the league in runs scored, hits, total bases, and RBIs and winning the batting title with a .356 average.

Once Los Angeles was eliminated from the Pacific Coast League playoffs, Pafko was called up to finish the last 13 games of the 1943 season with the Cubs. The 22-year-old had never been to Chicago, and when he got off the Santa Fe passenger train at Dearborn Station, it was raining. Hoping the game would be called off so he could get acclimated to the big city, Pafko took a cab to Wrigley Field, knocked on the clubhouse door, and was greeted by third baseman Hack, who said, "Welcome to the big leagues, Andy." By the end of the day, everyone in the park knew his name, as he drove in four runs with a single and a double against the Philadelphia Phillies. Like many ballplayers of his era, Pafko never set foot in a major league park until he played a game in one.

When the 1944 season started, the 23-year-old rookie won the starting position in center field, where he appeared in 128 of the Cubs' 154 games and hit .269. As the 1944 season progressed, it became clear that most teams were unfamiliar with his defensive abilities. Before the season was over, Pafko would be credited with 24 assists, most of them in the first half of the season, because by midsummer the rest of the league was afraid to run on him or to test his arm, which was the best in a Cubs outfield, some in the media said, since Hall of Famer Kiki Cuyler played in Chicago.

Like most of the unmarried players during World War II, Pafko lived at the Sheridan Plaza Hotel, usually walking the mile and a half from the hotel to Wrigley Field and back. Pafko neither smoked nor drank, and he made a point of always arriving an hour early to the park. Perhaps the straightest arrow on the team, he recalls that manager Grimm once teasingly asked him, "Hey Pafko, when are you gonna give me something to worry about?" Whether holding base runners in check, flagging down long drives in center field, or driving in runs in clutch situations, Pafko continued to quietly prove that there was nothing in him for anyone to worry about.[4]

IN GAME TWO, Vandenberg, getting the starting assignment because there were still five games scheduled in four days, handcuffed the Reds for a 7–1 victory over Vern Kennedy. Nicholson, another veteran who would be sorely needed in September and whose effectiveness had been lacking, propelled the Cubs' offense with a big two-run homer. Their good fortune came in the form of the Pittsburgh Pirates. Longtime Cardinal nemeses Preacher Roe and Fritz Ostermueller teamed up with Xavier Rescigno to defeat St. Louis at Sportsman's Park, 6–5 and 6–2. The Cardinals' pennant express had been derailed, at least temporarily, and the Cubs ended Labor Day four games in front in the National League.

On their off day September 4, the Cubs were encouraged with the news that Hi Bithorn, the fireballing right-hander of Danish and Puerto Rican extraction who went 18–12 with a 2.60 for them in 1943, had just received his discharge papers from the Navy. The excitement centered on the fact that Bithorn went 4–1 against St. Louis in 1943, and one of his wins was a two-hitter. Chicago still had five games scheduled against the Cardinals, and the dream was that somehow Bithorn could be ready when the team traveled to St. Louis on September 18. St. Louis ended the day only three and a half games back, defeating the Pirates 8–3.

Another doubleheader at Wrigley Field occurred on September 5, with the Chicago hosting New York, as the Cubs began their longest home stand of September, 15 games. Once again, the Cubs' bench strength paved the way, this time to two victories. Hughes replaced Johnson at second base, handled ten chances errorlessly, and led the Cubs' attack by going 5-for-9 in the twin bill. The hot-hitting Otero, a starting third-stringer with Cavarretta and Becker out, had an equally productive afternoon, with three RBIs while going 3-for-7. A happy 25,769 fans cheered Prim on to his 11th victory of the year in game one, and in the second game, Passeau beat the Giants for the first time that season, with a final score of 10–2. Their short five-game lead over the Cardinals at the end of the doubleheader was reduced to four and a half when Boston had as much trouble with Brecheen as the Cubs had had lately and lost 4–2. The following game on Thursday was a happy repeat of Wednesday's affairs. Borowy pitched his ninth complete game since joining the Cubs, and Nicholson hit a two-run homer in the fifth inning for a 6–1 victory, the Cubs' third victory over the fireballing Bill Voiselle. Wyse, however, failed to win his 19th on Friday, as newcomer Sal Maglie, recently called up from the Jersey City Giants, shut out the Cubs on six hits by a score of 2–0. The offense remained cold on Saturday, September 8, their last game of the year against the Giants. Derringer and Giants hurler Harry Feldman both had shutouts going through eight innings. Derringer, tiring in the ninth inning, allowed three runs. With two runners on and no outs, he hurt his own cause when he was so surprised at the lead-footed Ernie

Lombardi's bunt that he did not bother to field it. Two more Giants hits followed, and the game was over after the Cubs went down peacefully without scoring in their half of the ninth. The Giants left Chicago victorious. The Cubs ended the day three and a half games ahead of St. Louis, with nine games left on the home stand. Otero was one Chicago ballplayer sad to see the Giants leave; he had two hits off Maglie on Friday and another two off Feldman on Saturday.

THE BRAVES CHECKED into the Edgewater Beach on Saturday, September 8, and readied themselves for a Sunday doubleheader at Wrigley Field. They would have been better off simply staying in the grand old hotel on Sunday morning, as the Cubs tied the major league record set by the St. Louis Cardinals in 1944, winning their 17th doubleheader of the season, 9–1 and 4–0. Cavarretta played for the first time since August 28, and Pafko returned to the lineup after being held out of the last two games against the Giants. Lowrey led the hitting attack with two doubles and four RBIs, while Prim and Passeau stymied the Braves' hitters. Prim coasted with nine runs behind him but pitched well enough not to need them, limiting the Braves to only five hits. Passeau was even better, not allowing a Boston safety until the fifth inning and shutting them out with a sparkling three-hitter. The Cubs would need both victories. St. Louis won a doubleheader of their own, beating the fading New York Giants in St. Louis 5–4 and 3–2.On Monday, September 10, good relief pitching by Vandenberg and Paul Erickson went to waste. Grimm pulled starter Bob Chipman in the second inning, but from that point forward, the two relievers held Boston scoreless. Once again, however, the Cubs had a hard time against a rookie pitcher they had never seen before. Newcomer Ed Wright held the Chicagoans to seven scattered hits, three of which were in the infield, for a 2–0 Cubs loss. In St. Louis, the Giants dropped their third straight to the World Champions and cut the Cubs' lead to only two and a half games with a 2–1 victory over Voiselle. The following afternoon Borowy continued to keep the wolves at bay in the last game of the series with Boston, gaining his eighth win since joining the Cubs and his tenth complete game with a 5–4 victory. Nicholson fueled the offense with his 13th homer of the year, a two-run shot into the left field bleachers with Pafko aboard at first base. Hack, Cavarretta, and Pafko had eight of the Cubs' ten hits, and Pafko got his 92nd and 93rd RBIs of the season. The crowd gasped in disbelief, however, when Grimm pulled Nicholson in the ninth, sending Secory to pinch-hit for him against reliever Bob Logan. Nicholson had struck out in the seventh, and the Cubs had a rally going in the ninth when the move was made. Secory made Grimm's move look good when he coaxed a walk out of Logan, at which time Grimm sent Ed Sauer up to hit for Gillespie, who singled past third for the winning run. The move characterized the way Grimm liked to manage, substituting speed and contact hitting for power hitting, and it paid off in this game. Without the managerial moves, St. Louis could have been a game closer, because they beat the Giants for their sixth straight win, by a score of 6–5. At the end of the day's proceedings, the Chicagoans still clung to a two and a half game lead.

In the race for the batting title, Borowy gave teammate Cavarretta a big boost by holding Boston slugger Tommy Holmes hitless in four at bats, leaving the Cubs' first baseman seven points ahead of his nearest rival, .358 to .351. Cavarretta's sportsmanship in his quest for the title surfaced in the Tuesday game. Holmes hit a bounding smash to Merullo, who, at deep short, made a good play just getting to the ball but then threw it away as he hurried to get the speedy Holmes at first. The official scorer ruled it an error, feeling that a good throw would have forced Holmes out. Cavarretta made a point of talking to him after the game, however, to tell him that Holmes had the play beaten all the way and should get credit for a base hit. The scorer changed his ruling, keeping the race for the batting title a little closer.

Next up for Chicago was a three-game set against the Philadelphia Phillies, whom they had beaten 16 times in 20 attempts. The Cubs gave starting pitcher Wyse a four-run lead in the third inning, and Wyse protected it for the full nine innings to win his 19th game, a 4–0 shutout. Pafko continued to be the engine in the offensive machine, driving in three runs with a double high off the center field wall in the third inning. Philadelphia starter Kewpie Barrett paid him back, hitting him squarely with a pitch his next time up; word was getting around the league about Pafko and how dangerous he was becoming with men in scoring position. Rain canceled the Thursday affair, and with fewer dates for makeup games available on the September schedule, a doubleheader was arranged for Friday. The Phillies got to Derringer in the seventh inning of the first game, scoring two decisive runs off the tiring right-hander, while the Phillies' starter, the ever-crafty Andy Karl, held Cubs batsmen in check. Derringer became the first pitcher in the National League to lose three games to Philadelphia in 1945. Passeau put an end to such nonsense in the second game, beating the Phillies for the third time this season and earning his 17th win, by a score of 6–0.

Cubs fans went home intent on cheering for Brooklyn, an improbable occurrence given their own bitter rivalries with the Cubs but necessitated by their chance to knock off the Cardinals in an evening doubleheader in St. Louis. Furious that the games were not canceled due to the cold rainy weather, Brooklyn manager Leo Durocher telephoned National League president Ford Frick. If the games were played, the Dodgers would have to leave past midnight in day coaches to make it in time for their Saturday battle at Wrigley Field. Frick would have none of it—the schedule remained, and the band from Brooklyn rose up and soundly thrashed the World Champions 7–3 and 6–1. The Cardinals now had 15 games left to play and were three and a half games behind Chicago.

Brooklyn came to Wrigley Field to end Chicago's long home stand with single games on Saturday and Monday and a doubleheader on Sunday, September 16. Before the scheduled games could begin, both teams had to complete the suspended game from July 20. The Dodgers had had a comfortable lead, 10–4, in the ninth inning when it was stopped; now, almost two months later, they added two runs to make it an official victory, 12–5. Borowy faced Tommy Seats in the scheduled Saturday matchup but was taken out and replaced by Vandenberg after six innings with the Dodgers up 3–2. This was the first game since his arrival that Borowy did not go all nine innings. The Cubs exploded for five runs in the seventh, and Vandenberg was doing an admirable job on the mound until the ninth. With Chicago ahead 7–4 in the ninth, Brooklyn got to him, scoring two runs and rallying. Grimm replaced Vandenberg with one out and the bases loaded, bringing in Claude Passeau. After getting Frenchy Bordargary on a pop-up for the second out, Passeau struck out ex-Cubs great Babe Herman, who was pinch-hitting for rookie shortstop Tommy Brown; the final score was Cubs 7, Dodgers 6. Lowrey went 4-for-5 with a double and a triple and two RBIs, while Nicholson was 2-for-4 with a single and a triple. The fuzzy-cheeked Brown helped the Cubs with two crucial errors at shortstop, which prolonged Cubs rallies, one on a ball hit by the recently called-up Johnny Moore. Fans could be excused if they thought they were watching a father-and-son game when the play occurred. Moore, born in 1902, was 43 and one of the oldest players in the majors, and Brown, age 17, was the youngest. The Cubs needed all the help they could get—also that Friday, St. Louis handled Philadelphia and their pitching ace Andy Karl, 3–1.

A crowd of 40,187 came Sunday to see the twin bill, and they liked what they saw. The amazing Prim was magnificent in the first game, confounding Dodgers hitters all day while the Cubs got just enough offense to win, 3–2. Young Ralph Branca pitched well himself, but a big single by Lowrey in the bottom of the sixth drove in what stood to be the winning run. Most of the crowd watched the big scoreboard in center field as much as the action on the field. During the break between games, a huge roar went up when all the numbers were removed from the Phillies' and Cardinals' lines and the final read Philadelphia 4, St. Louis 3. Down 3–2 with two men out and two on in the ninth inning, Phillies player-manager Ben Chapman inserted himself in the lineup and lined a two-RBI single off Cardinals ace Red Barrett, dealing the Cardinals a severe blow in their pennant pursuit.

In game two for the Cubs, Wyse, becoming the first Cubs pitcher to win 20 games since Passeau in 1940, handcuffed Brooklyn on just five hits, the Cubs winning by a score of 4–0. The top of the Chicago order provided almost all the offense against Dodgers starter Tommy Seats and the two that relieved him. Leadoff man Hack was 2-for-4, and the second hitter, Johnson, was 3-for-4 with two RBIs. With the twin victories, Chicago set a new major league record by winning their 18th doubleheader of the season, eclipsing St. Louis's total of 1944 by one. The Cubs at this point had also lost three doubleheaders and split ten. A split is what the Cardinals managed at the day's end, beating Philadelphia handily in their second game, 10–3.

The final game of the season between the two teams was on Monday, September 17, and the Dodgers had an easy time against the listless Chicagoans, winning 4–0. Diminutive Sandy Herring, the pride of Altus, Oklahoma, whose major league career started in 1929 with Detroit, pitched one of the best games of his career, allowing only three lonely singles. Passeau deserved a better fate, pitching well himself but not getting any support. With the game well in hand, Brooklyn manager Durocher proved that some things never change, getting thrown out of the game again—the fourth time that year—for insulting plate umpire Babe Pinelli. As all Cubs fans were expecting, St. Louis easily put down the Phillies, 7–3. The stage was set for Chicago's biggest series of the year.

Immediately after the loss to the Dodgers, the Cubs went to Union Station to board a late afternoon Pennsylvania Railroad train to take on St. Louis in three critical night games. The formula was simple: get swept and there is a tie for first; win just one and remain up two games; win two games and leave them four out with just more than a week left in the season. Whether the team was tired or not, the numbers proved that the bats were fatigued. While Brooklyn's pitching was nothing to sneer at, the heart of the Chicago lineup was doing almost nothing at the plate. Cavarretta, Pafko, and Nicholson collectively hit .181 (8-for-44) in the big series against the Dodgers. Now they faced an even tougher Cardinals staff. Another obstacle was that all three contests were night games; Chicago was 3–7 for the season when playing under the lights.

THE CUBS CAME ready in game one and jumped on Cardinals ace Red Barrett for two runs in the first inning. St. Louis answered with a lone tally in their half of the first, and Passeau had a 2–1 lead going into the sixth inning. The Cardinals pushed two across in the sixth, and Barrett got stronger in the late innings, with the result being a 3–2 Cubs loss. Hack, Pafko, and Gillespie, each with two hits, had six of the seven safeties; Cavarretta was 0-for-4, Nicholson was 0-for-3. The Cardinals were two games out with two night games against the Cubs to go. Grimm reluctantly benched Nicholson for the rest of the series, putting Secory in right field.

Wednesday night's affair was the most nerve-racking game of the season for both teams. Grimm replaced Hack and Nicholson with Hughes and Secory, respectively, wanting as many right-handed hitters in the lineup as he could get. On the mound, Borowy and Cardinals starter George Dockins were in complete command through seven innings, locked in a classic 0–0 pitchers' duel. In the bottom of the eighth, the Cardinals scratched a run off Borowy and were three outs away from being a game out of first place. Dockins made quick work of Hughes for one away, but Johnson hit a smash to third baseman Whitey Kurowski and reached first safely. Grimm replaced Johnson (whose ankle injury had shelved him in early September), sending Ed Sauer in to run for him. Lowrey's perfectly placed sacrifice bunt got Sauer to second, but Cavarretta fouled out to the catcher, Del Rice, and suddenly two were out. Pafko, who already had two of the Cubs' four hits, came up and, on Dockins's second offering, hit a frozen rope into right field, bringing home Sauer with the tying run. Borowy quick put out the side in the bottom of the ninth, and the Cubs were in extra innings.

The tenth inning began with a walk by catcher Mickey Livingston. Then Dockins fumbled Bill Schuster's bunt, and the Cubs had runners on first and second with nobody out. Grimm immediately replaced Livingston with the swifter Johnny Ostrowski, as Borowy came up and bunted in front of the plate. Then Dockins made a critical mistake, panicking and throwing to third, thinking he could get Ostrowski, who beat the throw to load the bases with nobody out. St. Louis manager Billy Southworth then replaced the badly rattled Dockins with his young ace, Ken Burkhardt, and Grimm sent Nicholson in to pinch-hit for Hughes. The slugger came through with his biggest hit of the season, a single to the gap in right, easily scoring Ostrowski and Schuster and sending Borowy to second. Hack, entering the game in the ninth, flew out to center fielder Johnny Hopp but hit the ball deep enough to allow Borowy to get to third. Burkhardt, still fuming about the bad pitch he threw to Nicholson, took his frustration out by trying to pick Borowy off third base. His wild throw landed in the box seats, and the Cubs were up 4–1. The game ended that way when the dispirited Redbirds went down in order in the bottom of the tenth inning. The Cubs would now leave St. Louis at least two games ahead.

The big series ended with the Cubs facing their old nemesis, Harry Brecheen. Once again, Grimm stacked his lineup with right-handed hitting against the crafty lefty; Cavarretta was the only left-handed hitter in the Cubs' lineup. Chicago's hitters displayed their customary form against the Cardinals' lefty, wasting a very good pitching effort by Prim and getting shut out 2–0 on six lonely hits. Brecheen, the best ballplayer to ever call Broken Bow, Oklahoma, his home, had won 28 games in the last two seasons—seven of them against the Cubs. Chicago left St. Louis on Friday at noon, getting a full night's rest at the Chase Hotel after their tense, draining series with the Cardinals. They were in first place, but the lead was down to two games; both teams had eight games left, and the Cubs' magic number was seven; any combination of Chicago wins and St. Louis losses equaling that amount meant the pennant was theirs.

THE CARDINALS' LONG September home stand continued against Cincinnati on Saturday, September 22. Chicago's Saturday game was rained out, and St. Louis moved a half game closer to the Cubs when Red Barrett won his 23rd game of the year (and his 21st for the Cardinals), 9–4. Grimm surprised the press by stating that he was delighted his boys were rained out and that St. Louis had to play a game. The rainout, he explained, gave his pitching staff an extra day of rest and would allow him to enter the last week of the season with his Big Four—Wyse, Passeau, Borowy, and Derringer—in a perfect sequence without having to use a secondary starter. He also felt that the unexpected second day of rest would give his team an edge over the Cardinals, because they had to play on Saturday, and that this tradeoff was worth losing a half game in the standings.

On Sunday, September 23, Chicago had another doubleheader scheduled against Pittsburgh while St. Louis hosted Cincinnati in another single game. The Cubs welcomed 43,755 fans into the park, several thousand with standing room only tickets, in what turned out to be Pafko's biggest day of the season. Before the game, Pafko received a watch and a matching luggage set from the Chicago Slovak Goodwill Club. Presiding over the ceremony were the Honorable Thomas J. Bowler, Clerk of the Superior Court, and Reverend J.J. Pelikan, Pafko's minister at the Trinity Slovak Lutheran Church. They praised the young man for being such an upstanding member of Chicago's Slovak community and pointed out to the fans that he had hit .500 in the big series in St. Louis, going 6-for-12 in the three night games. Pafko's evening nearly reached fairy tale proportions in the third inning. With his team trailing 3–0 against the tough Preacher Roe, Pafko came up with the bases loaded and took Roe's third delivery deep into the left field bleachers for a grand slam home run. The Cubs got two more runs in the inning, Wyse pitched shutout ball the last six innings, and the Cubs had a big win, 7–3.

Bad weather canceled the second game of the doubleheader, and St. Louis won another match with the Reds, 9–6, so in spite of the feel-good atmosphere at Wrigley Field, the Cubs were still only a game and a half ahead in first place. The National League immediately ordered the Cubs and Pirates to play both games the following day, Monday, September 24, but heavy rains made that impossible, too. It may have been just as well; the Cardinals were off on Monday before their crucial Tuesday and Wednesday matchups with the Cubs at Wrigley Field, and they would have had a huge advantage facing the Cubs well rested while their hosts had played a doubleheader the day before. The Cubs' world was tense, to say the least. The team had been in first place for 79 consecutive days. In the next 48 hours, they had to face Harry "the Cat" Brecheen and Red Barrett, two hurlers who together had beaten them eight times this season and suffered only one loss. The lone Chicago win, ironically, was not even against the Cardinals; the Cubs beat Barrett in Boston on Saturday, May 12, by a score of 13–12 before he was traded to St. Louis. Brecheen would face Borowy on Tuesday, and Passeau and Barrett were the starters for Wednesday's game.

The tension both teams felt at the beginning of Tuesday's game was glaringly apparent as the sure-handed Hack booted a ball at third, giving the Cardinals two runs in the first inning. The inning would have been bigger if Pafko had not thrown out Kurowski at third after Emil Verban's single. But Chicago came right back as Hack and Johnson started the Cubs off with base hits and the nervous Brecheen made a critical error, bringing in two Cubs runs. In the fifth the visitors nudged another run across to regain the lead. Borowy led off the seventh with a single and got to second when Hack drew a walk; then Johnson drove Borowy in with a big hit. When Red Schoendienst booted the ball in the outfield, he reached second, and Hack got to third. Brecheen, rattled at this point, intentionally walked Lowrey to get to Cavarretta, who was on the verge of winning the National League batting title. Cavarretta, who had done nothing against St. Louis the previous week, singled sharply to center, sending Hack home for a 4–3 Cubs lead. At that point, Southworth came out and replaced the frustrated Brecheen with Lefty Dockins. Pafko welcomed Dockins, the pride of Clyde, Kansas, knocking his second pitch deep into the well in the left field corner, scoring Johnson and Lowrey. Next, Dockins nervously faced Nicholson but retired him with a short fly ball to right fielder Hopp, not deep enough to allow Pafko to move up.

Southworth returned to the mound and replaced the crestfallen Dockins with Ken Burkhardt, who induced Livingston to pop out to first baseman Ray Sanders, as the seventh inning ended with the Cubs leading 6–3.

In the first half of the eighth, St. Louis came roaring back for what would be the best inning they would have all year against Borowy. They had scored two runs and had only one out, with the tying run on base, when Grimm decided he had had enough of Borowy and called Prim in from the bull pen. Cavarretta made a rare error at first to put the winning run on base, and Prim reached back for something extra as he calmly retired Hopp and Buster Adams to put out what could have been a pennant-losing fire. In the ninth inning, Prim picked up right where he left off, retiring the dangerous Kurowski and Ray Sanders for two out, yielding a scratch single to Verban, and then easily retiring shortstop Marty Marion . . . and preserving Chicago's pennant in the process.

The next day the *Chicago Tribune* printed a photograph of the jubilant Pafko, Cavarretta, Borowy, and Prim singing in the Cubs' clubhouse. Close to a thousand fans lined the concourse and the ramp outside the clubhouse, cheering and hoping to catch a glimpse of their heroes as they exited the stadium. The Cubs were now two and a half games up on their rivals, and could be no worse off than one and a half games ahead after their final match up against the cardinals on Wednesday, September 26. The Cardinals had only five games left, one fewer than Chicago, and their time was running out.

THEIR TIME MAY have been running out, but St. Louis was certainly not out of fight or desire, as 42,289 Cubs fans found out on Wednesday, when the Cardinals nicked Passeau for two runs in the third and knocked him out of the game with three in the fifth, taking the lead from Chicago, 5–3. A parade of pitchers followed the Cubs' starter: Prim, Vandenberg, Lon Warneke, Ed Hanyzewski, Ray Starr, and Chipman. The Cubs, hitting Red Barrett better than they had since he came to St. Louis, narrowed the gap with two more runs in the sixth and were down 6–5 when the bull pen caved in as Warneke, Hanyzewski, and Starr gave up eight hits and five runs in the seventh inning and St. Louis stayed alive, on top now by a score of 11–6. A furious Grimm protested the game to the National League office, claiming that in the middle of the Cardinals' rally, Ray Sanders had passed Kurowski in the base paths. The crucial game turned out to be one of the few contests all season in which the Cubs' bull pen utterly failed in a must-win game. The Cardinals slugged 18 hits, and the loss had to happen, even though the Cubs finally got even with their season-long nemesis, Red Barrett, and got 11 hits themselves. After the game, the Cubs' general manager announced to the press that the four National League World Series games, scheduled for October 7, 8, 9, and 10, were completely sold out, should they be played in Chicago. The team had begun accepting mailed ticket requests two days earlier on Monday, September 24, and a corps of 100 clerks processed the last requests during the game against the Cardinals that afternoon. Grimm was confident and defiant in the somber Cubs locker room, vowing that St. Louis would never catch up.

Although Chicago had not yet won the pennant, ticket scalpers were already making huge profits in Chicago. The Cubs' ticket prices for World Series games were $7.20 for a box seat and $6 in the grandstand, but scalpers were getting $50 for box seats and $25 for a grandstand ticket. Scalpers who had not received their tickets from the team through the mailing got them from others who had, after paying a hefty premium themselves. The following week, Cubs owner Philip K. Wrigley, angry about the situation, wrote an open letter to all Cubs fans.

As both teams left Union Station after the game, the Cardinals heading to Pittsburgh and the Cubs to Cincinnati, St. Louis's itinerary for the last four days of the season was as follows: Thursday night, a makeup game in Pittsburgh; Friday, an off day to travel to Cincinnati; Saturday, a single game in Cincinnati; and Sunday, a doubleheader in Cincinnati. Chicago's schedule was similar, but how it became so was very complicated.

THE CUBS' ORIGINAL schedule for the last weekend of the regular season had featured a pair of games at Cincinnati on Thursday, September 27 and Friday, September 28, an off day on Saturday, and a season finale at Pittsburgh on September 30. A problem, however, lay in the fact that only one of the three games originally scheduled against Pittsburgh at Wrigley Field—a single game on Saturday, September 22 and a doubleheader on Sunday, September 23—had been completed. The National League's solution was to radically alter the schedule for this last weekend. Instead of playing single games in Cincinnati on Thursday and Friday, Chicago would play a doubleheader in Cincinnati on Thursday, September 27. That way they would be off on Friday, when they would travel to Pittsburgh. The doubleheader that was never played the previous weekend at Wrigley Field was transferred to Pittsburgh. The Cubs and Pirates would play a doubleheader on Saturday, September 29, and a single game on Sunday, September 30. While the two pennant contenders would be facing the same teams as they ended the year, Chicago had a big advantage that was little discussed: Over the season, St. Louis had much more trouble than Chicago had with Pittsburgh and Cincinnati. Going into Thursday's game, the Cardinals were 12–9 against the Pirates and 10–9 against the Reds, or 22–18 overall for the season. Chicago's overall record with those two teams was 30–9; they were 11–8 against the Pirates and 19–1 against the Reds. The results of the four teams' pairings on Thursday, September 27, followed this precedent perfectly.

A tiny crowd of 3,370 came out hoping to see the Reds ruin Chicago's pennant dreams. As the games started, Cincinnati, picked by many to compete for the pennant when the year began, instead was firmly entrenched in seventh place, six games behind Boston and 14 ahead of Philadelphia. Pitching for them in the twin bill would be Ed Heusser, with an 11–15 record (1–3 thus far against Chicago), and Vern Kennedy, with a 5–11 record to date (0–5 against Chicago). Grimm sent out Wyse, 4–0 against Cincinnati and the Cubs' winningest pitcher, and Derringer, also 4–0 against his old team, whom he always relished defeating.

Everything went right for the Chicagoans in their first game Friday afternoon, as their play resembled their July and August performances. With the score tied 0–0 in the sixth, Hughes, starting in place of Merullo, drew Heusser's first walk of the game, making it to second on Wyse's sacrifice. Then Hack flew out to Hank Sauer in left field, but Johnson got the Cubs' second hit of the game, a double, to drive in Hughes. Lowrey then homered, hitting a ball that almost landed on York Street beyond the left field wall. After Cavarretta singled and Pafko doubled, Heusser got too careful with Nicholson, walking him and filling the bases. Gillespie came up and hit a deep line drive to right field; big Al Libke's spectacular catch prevented Chicago from scoring three more, and the side was out. Wyse pitched one of his best games of the year in his biggest game of the year. He walked only one batter, struck out two, and gave up but three hits, a single and a double to the Reds' little shortstop Eddie Miller and a single to catcher Al Lakeman. The jubilant Cubs won a big one, 3–1.

The second game proved to be more of a contest. In the first inning, Hack led off with a single and Hughes drew a walk; the Cubs had Reds starter Vern Kennedy in trouble with nobody out. Lowrey sacrificed the pair to second and third. Then Cavarretta boomed a triple off the right-center field screen, and it was 2–0, Cubs. But Cincinnati came right back in the second inning against Derringer, as first baseman Mike McCormick and Hank Sauer both hit sharp singles. Next, Miller grounded out to Cavarretta, moving the runners up, and Lakeman singled to tie the game. In the fourth, Chicago regained the lead with singles by Gillespie, Derringer, and Hack. The Cubs got two more in the sixth when Nicholson walked, Gillespie was hit by a pitch, and Merullo sacrificed them up a base. Derringer followed with a groundout, and it looked like the Reds were out of the inning when Hack bounced weakly to first base. Kennedy ran over to cover the base and booted McCormick's toss, with Nicholson and Gillespie coming in to score. The Reds came back with two in the eighth when Hack overthrew first base while fielding a bunt by Dain Clay. The Cubs had a nervous 5–4 lead going into the ninth inning but got two more insurance runs in their half of the ninth, and the fired-up Derringer won his fifth game of the season over his old teammates, with a final score of 7–4, and upped his season record to 16–11.

The elated Chicagoans hurried back to the Netherland Plaza Hotel and tuned the radios to the night game in Pittsburgh. The magic number was down to two. If the Pirates could beat the Cards, the magic number would be down to one, and the Cubs would be assured a tie. They had reason to celebrate soon after the game started, as the Pirates jumped all over George Dockins in the first inning for three runs, sending him to an early shower. Preacher Roe, who had beaten the Cardinals twice while losing only once earlier in the season, dominated the game. The slim lefty from Ashflat, Arkansas, surrendered only three hits, the game was over in less than two hours, and the Cardinals went down meekly, 5–2. Symbolizing St. Louis's feelings after the game, a light rain fell as they glumly prepared for a dreary trip to Cincinnati.

On the afternoon of Friday, September 28, the Cubs settled into the Schenley Hotel near Forbes Field and could not wait for the Saturday doubleheader to begin. Borowy would start against 37-year-old Fritz Ostermueller, whom the Cubs had beaten the two previous times they faced him. Vandenberg would face Rip Sewell in the second match.

Hack opened the game with a double and got to third when Hughes, playing because Johnson had injured his neck colliding with the second base umpire in Thursday's first game, beat out a bunt. The Cubs had runners on the corners with nobody out for the middle of the batting order when Al Gionfriddo caught Lowrey's fly ball in center field deep enough for Hack to score easily. Pittsburgh immediately tied the game in their half of the first on a double by Gionfriddo and a single by right fielder Johnny Barrett. In the fifth inning, Merullo broke the tie when he scored from second after shortstop Frankie Gustine threw the ball past Babe Dahlgren at first base. But the Pirates fought back in the sixth as catcher Bill Salkeld drew Borowy's fourth walk of the game and went to second on Bob Elliott's single. Later, Gustine's sacrifice bunt failed when Borowy threw to third to get Salkeld. With a full count, Borowy walked Dahlgren to load the bases. Then Frankie Colman batted for Pete Coscarat and hit a sacrifice fly to Pafko, with Elliott scoring the tying run after the catch. Ostermueller, the pitcher, beat out a grounder to deep short to score Gustine to make the score 3–2, Pittsburgh. The Cubs tied it in the top of the seventh when Borowy beat out a bunt, Hughes walked to put him on second, and Lowrey got a clutch single to left-center, scoring the streaking Borowy. Hughes was out at the plate when he tried to catch the Pirates napping before the play was over.

With the game tied 3–3 going into the ninth, a tiring Ostermueller walked Hack to start the inning. Hughes singled sharply to right field, and they both moved up on Lowrey's perfect bunt. Needing a double play, the Pirates walked Cavarretta, loading the bases, to get to Pafko, who already had two hits and an RBI. Noting the success Pafko had had with Ostermueller all afternoon, Pirates manager Frankie Frisch took him out and summoned right-hander Nick Strincevich. As he had done so many other times during the season, Pafko, falling away from an inside curve that he was not going to take with two strikes, made as much contact as he could and hit a deep drive to Johnny Barrett in right field for his biggest RBI of the season, making it 4–3, Cubs.

The Pirates, however, were not finished. With one out, Gionfriddo on second, and Barrett on first, Grimm changed pitchers, taking out Borowy and bringing in a lefty, Chipman. Chipman did his job, inducing Jim Russell to ground out to Hughes at second with the runners moving up and the winning run on second. Then Grimm surprised everyone by removing Chipman and replacing him with a right-hander, big Paul Erickson. Frisch, meanwhile, sent right-handed hitting Tommy O'Brien, Pittsburgh's best pinch hitter, with a .335 average, to bat for Salkeld. Erickson got a quick strike on O'Brien, who took the second pitch for ball one. The Cubs' hurler, wanting to get something extra on his already intimidating fastball, threw so hard that his cap flew off on the next pitch, which was high and inside. O'Brien ducked and catcher Dewey Williams, who had replaced Gillespie two innings earlier, desperately put his glove up in the air to prevent a wild pitch. The wall behind the catcher in Forbes Field was 120 feet away, the longest distance of any major league park, and a wild pitch could score two runs with the pennant in the balance. Whether it was divine intervention or sheer luck, O'Brien could not get his bat out of the way, and it deflected the wild pitch for a foul ball. The unsettled O'Brien now had two strikes on him. Williams, with nerves of steel, signaled for Erickson to throw a curve. With one of the better fastballs in the league, Erickson could dominate when his curveball was working and he could use it effectively, but he had had trouble with it all year and rarely used it as his out pitch. Erickson went along with the call and broke one off close to the outside corner. O'Brien, completely crossed up with the pitch, took a defensive half-swing. Erickson's 53rd strikeout of the year became the biggest of his career, as the Cubs won their 16th championship. There were many men of the hour, but the biggest tip of the hat could go to Hughes. The 11-year veteran, comfortable with his role as an infield substitute at age 34, had been an emergency starter since Johnson had sprained his neck. Hitting in the crucial second spot in the lineup, Hughes was 3-for-4 with a walk and figured prominently in every inning the Cubs scored. The Cubs' bench, the best in baseball in 1945, was a huge reason for this championship season.

After the victory, the humid visitors' clubhouse at Forbes Field was a scene of utter jubilation. Trainer Andy Lotshaw was at the door hugging each player as he came in, telling anyone who would listen that this was his sixth pennant with the team since he had started 25 years ago and that each one was better than the last. Erickson, walking on air, was the life of the party.[5] Hack and coach Hardrock Johnson hugged, clasped hands, and danced an endless jig.[6] Warneke, whose strong right arm helped carry Chicago to pennants in 1932 and 1935, was thrilled that the team had won for Gallagher, Grimm, and all the younger players and elated that he had been part of it again in the sunset of his career. The diminutive William E. Benswanger, president of the Pirates, came to offer his congratulations and was the recipient of some uncalled-for and impolite high jinks from Derringer, which did not go over well at all with the Cubs' brass.[7] Grimm, the manager, was perhaps the most grateful of the bunch. "My boys, my boys," he kept saying as he hugged each player. Emotionally, he told the press to ignore him, not to ask him anything, and to talk only to his players, exclaiming, "They're the guys that won it!" He did allow that when he saw the ball bounce off O'Brien's bat, he knew they had it won.[8]

In the anticlimactic second game, Grimm started Ostrowski at third, Schuster at second, and Secory in left field. Before the game was half over, Ed Sauer replaced Lowrey in center, Otero went to first for Cavarretta, Rice replaced Gillespie behind the plate, and Cy Block played third. The Cubs got five runs off Rip Sewell in the fifth, with Sauer's double and Gillespie's home run being the big hits. Vandenberg and Warneke shut out the indifferent Pirates on five hits, the final score being 5–0.

Between games, Grimm announced that he would be throwing a big victory party that evening at the Schenley Hotel, where the team stayed. The Cubs happened to clinch the pennant on Grimm's 23rd wedding anniversary; ironically, his wedding had also been in Pittsburgh back in 1922. His wife, Lillian, was in town, spending the weekend with him as well. Toward the end of the celebration, she silenced the happy lot and asked if she could make a request. She wondered if every player would not mind removing his necktie and passing it over to her. After her request was honored, with her arms full of cravats, she thanked the young men and announced that over the winter, she would make a quilt out of them. It would be her husband's 23rd anniversary present. The room fell silent with everyone smiling.[9]

ON SUNDAY, SEPTEMBER 30, the Cubs wearily trudged to Forbes Field for the final game of the year, still showing the aftereffects of their victory party the night before. Grimm had fun making the lineup card. He let Merullo lead off for the first time and put recent call-up Block at second, Lowrey in left, Cavarretta at first, Pafko in center, Nicholson in right, Ostrowski at third, Williams behind the plate, and Chipman on the mound. Before the game was over, Secory replaced Lowrey in left, catcher Livingston gave Cavarretta a rest at first, Sauer went to center, catcher Gillespie replaced Nicholson in right, and Erickson pitched the last three innings. Grimm's goal was to give his regulars some more at bats before the World Series, allow Cavarretta, who batted four times with a single and a double, to safely protect his upcoming batting title, and give some valuable playing time to those on the bench he would rely on in the fall classic. In this, the final regular season game, Merullo distinguished himself in the leadoff spot with two hits in five at bats, while Williams's triple and Ostrowski's two doubles paced the offense, which tallied five times in the fifth inning for a 5–3 Cubs win.

Cavarretta went into the game at .354, 175 hits in 494 at bats; Tommy Holmes was at .350, 220 hits in 628 at bats. Cavarretta added a point to his average by going 2-for-4; Holmes, however, got to play a doubleheader against the Giants that Sunday. The amazing Holmes, having one of the best years at the plate of any player in history, added three points to his average by going 4-for-6 in game one against Giants hurler Don Fisher. If Holmes could go 3-for-3 against Sal Maglie in the second game, he would finish the season with an average of .356, and the title would be his. The second game was called on account of darkness at unlit Braves Field in the seventh inning, and Holmes was hitless in two at bats, and Cavarretta was the National League batting champion. He was the first Chicago Cub to win a batting championship since the great Heinie Zimmerman hit .372 in 1912.

Nobody really cared anymore, but the Cardinals won two games against Cincinnati on Saturday and their final game of the season on Sunday. And over in the American League, the Detroit Tigers, needing one win to eliminate the surprising Washington Senators for the pennant, beat the St. Louis Browns 5–3 on a grand slam home run in the bottom of the ninth off the Browns' ace, Nelson Potter. Cubs loyalists were quick to point out that Detroit's record of 88–65 was the lowest winning percentage by a pennant winner in history.

The Chicagoans took an overnight train back to Chicago after the game. Their schedule was full on Monday, October 1. They would arrive to a cheering throng at Union Station at 8:40 a.m. Later in the morning, the team was expected at Wrigley Field to try on new uniforms, vote on dividing up their shares from the World Series revenue, and pose for photographs by the press. Everyone on the team viewed these activities as labors of love.

THE REST OF THE NATIONAL LEAGUE

THE 1945 SEASON ended very quietly for the rest of the National League. The Cardinals had a winning record against every team in the league and had a tremendous record against Chicago, whom they beat 16 times in 22 games. They had much more trouble with Boston and Pittsburgh and had an overall record of only 5–11 in extra inning games. Whitey Kurowski, Buster Adams, switch-hitting rookie Red Schoendienst, Marty Marion, and the newly acquired Red Barrett had tremendous seasons, but St. Louis missed Enos Slaughter and Stan Musial. In spite of their noble, season-long pursuit of first place all season, the Cardinals were one of three National League teams to never be at the top of the standings, in spite of finishing with an excellent 95–59 mark.

For all his faults, Durocher kept a war-decimated Brooklyn team close to the top of the league throughout the entire season. At the end of the year, he was relying on two teenagers and had an infielder, Mike Sandlock, starting at catcher. Eighteen-year-old Hal Gregg emerged as the ace of the staff, getting one win for each of his years in an amazing season, and 17-year-old shortstop Tommy Brown became the youngest player in history to hit a home run. In spite of their consistent play, the Dodgers could not come through in big games against Chicago and St. Louis, and they settled into third place at 87–67.

Pittsburgh, picked to challenge for the pennant before the season began, had a seven-game winning streak in mid-June to take over first place but then lost five straight and fell out of serious contention when Chicago had their epic stretch in July and August. The Pirates cemented fourth place by taking 14 out of their first 17 games in September but only managed three wins in their last ten games, finishing up at 82–72. They got great performances from pitchers Preacher Roe and Nick Strincevich, while Bill Salkeld's contributions at and behind the plate were without peer.

The hard-hitting New York Giants were the scourge of the league at the start of the season, going 25–7, paced by their great young pitcher Bill Voiselle, who won his first eight starts. Things fell apart for New York, however, during a long western road trip in the middle of the season, and before the swoon was over, the Giants had endured 25 losses in 33 games. Voiselle won only six of his last 20 starts, and the only dependable hurlers were Van Lingle Mungo and Harry Feldman. First baseman Phil Weintraub, right fielder–manager Mel Ott, left fielder Danny Gardella, and catcher Ernie Lombardi collectively hit 68 home runs, an amount eclipsed by only five of the 16 major league teams in 1945, but it was not enough to warrant even a first-division finish. New York finished fifth with a record of 78–74.

The Boston Braves were one of two teams to change managers during the season, when they dismissed Bob Coleman and brought in his associate Del Bissonette. They started the year very poorly, but the heavy hitting of Chuck Workman, Butch Neiman, and Tommy Holmes and a stretch of good pitching helped their record hover around the .500 mark until mid-July. At that point, they won only two games in a two-week stretch, and Coleman was dismissed. The 27-year-old Holmes had one of the greatest seasons in history in 1945. He finished first in five offensive categories: total hits, home runs, slugging average, total bases, and doubles. Holmes was second in RBIs, third in runs scored and home run percentage, and fourth in stolen bases. He also set an unrecorded record that will almost certainly never will be broken, striking out only nine times in 636 at bats, an unheard-of ratio for anyone with his power production. The affable right fielder helped keep Boston's fans from thinking about how 1945 was their 11th straight year in the second division; they finished a distant sixth, 18 games below .500, at 67–85.

The Cincinnati Reds won 11 of 12 games between late May and early June but could not put together a stretch of three wins after that time. Picked by many all season to contend for the pennant, no team disappointed more in 1945 than Cincinnati, which suffered from weak hitting and never recovered from the number of pitchers they lost to World War II. They set a record by losing 21 of 22 contests to Chicago and finished with a seventh-place record of 61–93.

Not too much was expected of the Philadelphia Phillies in 1945, and even less was expected when they managed only six wins during the first four weeks of the season. They eventually fired manager Freddie Fitzsimmons and replaced him with Ben Chapman, obtained in a trade with Brooklyn; Chapman stayed on the roster as a player-manager. The Phillies lost 16 in a row in one stretch; the pitching of Andy Karl and the offensive play of first baseman Jimmy Wasdell and center fielder Vince DiMaggio provided what little enthusiasm the team could muster. DiMaggio set a new major league record by hitting four grand slam home runs in one season. The Phillies finished dead last, 15 games out of seventh place, with a record of 46–108. The team set two new records for futility: 17 seasons finishing in last place and 13 seasons with 100 or more defeats.

CHAPTER 8

★ ★ ★ ★ ★ ★ ★ ★

BRING ON THE TIGERS

I n October 1945 the United States, still adjusting to the end of World
War II, eagerly embraced the cultural rituals that seemed to take on a
new importance now that the country could shed the hardships of the
war. Major league baseball had already experienced the change. In 1945
the majors recorded a total of 11,375,185 paying customers, eclipsing
their previous high of 10,281,891 in 1940. The 1945 World Series, it was
predicted, would benefit from the game's popularity immensely. If the
series between the Detroit Tigers and Chicago Cubs lasted six or seven
games, it would easily become the richest World Series ever played. The
record at the time was the 1940 classic between Detroit and Cincinnati,
and with Chicago being the National League entry this time around, the
industry rubbed its hands together, smug in the knowledge that Wrigley
Field's capacity was about 10,000 more than Cincinnati's Crosley Field.

Soothsayers all over the nation felt the series would be close, with
most of them thinking Chicago would capture the title in six games. The
Chicago Daily News hired Hall of Famer Rogers Hornsby to analyze the

matchup in a featured series before the first game.[1] He picked Chicago, thinking they were a team with better balance and a deeper pitching staff. The Cubs also had a bench that proved itself through the season, both in the field and at the plate, in many crucial games. Hornsby noted that Chicago successfully held off a five-week charge at the end of the season by what was generally thought to be the strongest team in 1945, the St. Louis Cardinals. The Cubs had the stronger infield, with Phil Cavarretta, Don Johnson, and Stan Hack all considered superior to Detroit's first baseman Rudy York, second baseman Eddie Mayo, and third baseman Jimmy Outlaw. Andy Pafko's offensive and defensive capabilities overshadowed those of the Tiger's center fielder Roger "Doc" Cramer, but with Bill Nicholson's decline at the plate, the dangerous Roy Cullenbine earned Detroit an equal rating in right field. For all of Peanuts Lowrey's contributions to Chicago's pennant, nobody considered him superior to Detroit's recently discharged power-hitting left fielder, Hank Greenberg. The Cubs, however, got the nod at catcher. Detroit's Paul Richards had a keen understanding of the game and was a great handler of pitchers, but Cubs starting catcher Mickey Livingston had many of the same attributes and was more of an offensive threat. The Cubs' deep catching corps also contributed to their superiority behind the plate.

Detroit had two of the best starting pitchers in baseball in the lanky Hal Newhouser, who finished the 1945 season with a record of 25–9, and the intimidatingly fast Virgil Trucks, who received his discharge from the Navy just before the World Series began. Their starting corps dropped off after that, but Frank "Stubby" Overmire was difficult to hit for batters unfamiliar with him, and Paul "Dizzy" Trout, who had won 18 and lost 15 for the Tigers, was a big contributor to their first-place finish and a dominant American League pitcher in 1943 and 1944.

Nonetheless, Chicago's starters, the critics felt, eclipsed them. Hank Borowy was pitching magnificently and had a history of dominating the Tigers when he pitched for New York in the American League. In 12 starts against Detroit, the graceful right-hander sported a 9–3 record. Claude Passeau gave no quarter to opponents when he pitched and, like Overmire, was not easy to solve for those hitters unfamiliar with him. Hank Wyse was coming off the best year of his career, and the perplexing lefty Ray Prim presented a completely different look on the mound than his fellow starting pitchers, as well as great control and a baffling array of pitches for free-swinging hitters. Chicago also had the stronger bull pen. Manager Charlie Grimm had World Series veteran Paul Derringer available, as well as hard throwers like Paul Erickson and Hy Vandenberg and the finesse lefty Bob Chipman. Tigers relievers Al Benton, Jim Tobin (whom the Cubs had seen for years in the National League), Leslie Mueller, and Zeb Eaton were not their equals.

Chicago White Sox manager Jimmy Dykes, however, saw things differently. Claiming more expertise because his team had played both the Cubs and Tigers several times in 1945, Dykes predicted that the Cubs would find the hard-throwing Trucks unhittable and that lefties Newhouser and Overmire would also be hard on Chicago. Overmire, he explained, was extremely underrated and had a tremendous repertoire of effective pitches. Dykes did not mention, however, that his contests against Detroit were authentic and that his games against the Cubs were exhibitions in which Grimm played his frontline players sparingly.

ON MONDAY, OCTOBER 2, the Cubs boarded a late afternoon New York Central Limited in Chicago's sooty LaSalle Street Station to open the World Series in Detroit with three games beginning on Wednesday, October 3. While in Chicago, they posed for pictures, tried on their new uniforms, and voted on how to divide up World Series revenue shares. Pictures of Chicago's heroes, dressed up in their traveling suits and ties, appeared in all the major newspapers. When they rolled into downtown Detroit, the first crisis of the 1945 World Series occurred.

THE WIVES REVOLT

DETROIT WAS THE industrial capital of the Allied powers during World War II, and its population swelled during the war due to the insatiable need for personnel in its heavy industries and smaller manufacturing concerns. Hotel space, difficult to find in Detroit all through the war, was even worse with the World Series coming to town. The Cubs' entourage settled into three downtown hotels: the Book–Cadillac, the Statler, and the Detroit Leland. Grimm settled into his quarters at the Book–Cadillac and opened a telegram from St. Louis Cardinals manager Billy Southworth.

The gracious Southworth congratulated him on his championship and simply stated how proud he was to have Grimm's team represent the National League in the series. His good feelings were interrupted by a late night telephone call.[3]

All of the Cubs players and sportswriters whose wives accompanied their husbands on the trip were taken to a docked passenger steam ship, the Greater Detroit, which was to be their quarters during their stay in the Motor City. The rooms were extremely small cabins, and the wives protested vehemently. The Cavarrettas, Lowreys, Merullos, Nicholsons, and Wyses were among those assigned to the boat. Grimm took the call and beckoned traveling secretary Bob Lewis, who huddled with Mr. Jerry Moore, the manager of the Fort Shelby Hotel. At 2:00 a.m. Tuesday, the "wives' revolt" was finally quelled; everyone assigned to the boat checked in to the Book–Cadillac Hotel. It was a good thing that the team was not scheduled for a workout at Briggs Stadium until 2:30 that afternoon.

At noon that Tuesday, October 2, the team assembled at the corner of National and Michigan avenues in the heart of downtown Detroit for a picture and media session before their 2:30 workout. Coaches Hardrock Johnson and Red Smith pitched batting practice while Wednesday's starter, Borowy, briefly loosened up. Left-handed hitters Cavarretta, Nicholson, Paul Gillespie, and Heinz Becker liked what they saw when they looked down the first base line, a low fence only 325 feet away, significantly closer and lower than Wrigley Field's. Right-handed hitters noticed that the left field foul pole, at 340 feet from the plate, also was comfortably closer than their home field's was. A long fly hit high enough would have an even greater chance of being a home run because the outfield's second deck actually hung over the outfield, ten feet closer to home plate. Center field, however, was another story, with the fence 440 feet from the plate and a flagpole on the field about 20 feet away. With short lanes down the lines and a big pasture in center field, Briggs Stadium reminded many in the National League contingent of the Phillies' home, Shibe Park.[4] Borowy, Cavarretta, Hack, Roy Hughes, Passeau, and Lon Warneke were the only Cubs who had previously played in the park. Borowy last experienced Briggs Stadium on June 23, when he was still with the Yankees. Passeau still had bitter memories about pitching there when the Tigers hosted the 1941 All-Star Game. Hughes, previously an

American Leaguer with the Cleveland Indians and St. Louis Browns, had last appeared at Briggs in 1938. Cavarretta, Hack, and Warneke all participated in the last Cubs–Tigers fall classic for Chicago in 1935. If Mother Nature was taking sides before the fall classic, it appeared she favored the Chicagoans. When the Tigers took the field at 4:30 for their workout, a cold, autumnal drizzle fell from the gray skies.

GAME ONE: DETROIT, WEDNESDAY, OCTOBER 3

IN THE MORNING of the first game of the World Series, Wednesday, October 3, the Associated Press polled the 80 writers in Detroit to cover the series to see which team they felt would win the fall classic. Forty-five writers picked Detroit and 35 picked Chicago.[5] All the Detroit writers picked the Tigers and all the Chicago writers picked the Cubs. A big reason the Tigers won the poll was based upon the fact that Newhouser, the Detroit starter who dominated all American League hurlers in 1945, would be available for two starting assignments. Newhouser was starting the first game, and based on his peerless pitching performances, Cubs fans indeed had reason to worry. A 24-year-old left-hander, excluded from the World War II draft due to a heart condition,[6] Newhouser grew up in Detroit and attended Wilbur Wright Preparatory School before leaving to pitch for Alexandria in the Evangeline League in 1939. The Baseball Writers' Association of America awarded him the Most Valuable Player award in 1944 when he posted a 29–9 record. Newhouser started 36 games for Detroit in 1945 and led all American League pitchers in nine important categories. He was first in wins and winning percentage, going 25–9 for a .735 mark. He also led every pitcher in his league with a 1.81 ERA, complete games (29), shutouts (8), innings pitched (an amazing 313.1), fewest hits allowed per game (6.86), strikeouts (212), and strikeouts per game (6.09). Tigers manager Skip O'Neill submitted the following batting order: Jimmy Webb, shortstop, .200 average for the season; Mayo, second base, .285; Cramer, center field, .275; Greenberg, hitting cleanup and playing left field, .311; Cullenbine, right field, .277; York, first base, .264; Outlaw, third base, .272; Richards, catcher, .256; and Newhouser, pitcher, coming into the series with an incredible .257 batting average.

Grimm changed the Cubs' lineup somewhat from what he usually had during the season. Hack (.323 for the year) led off, followed by

Johnson (.302) and Lowrey (.283). Cavarretta (.355, highest in the majors) batted cleanup, Pafko (.298) hit fifth, and Nicholson (.243) was hitting sixth. Grimm had Livingston (.254) starting at catcher and hitting seventh, Hughes (.261) starting at shortstop, and Borowy (.171) pitching and hitting last. The weather was cloudy and frigid, the perfect setting for a great pitchers' duel.

The Chicagoans, however, quickly ignored the weather. After baseball commissioner Happy Chandler, throwing lefty, tossed out the ceremonial first ball, Hack started the World Series by bouncing out weakly to Outlaw at third base. Johnson followed with a single and stole second easily. Lowrey flied out to center field, and Cavarretta legged out a roller to Mayo at second, with Johnson scampering to third. Chicago had two outs and two men in scoring position when catcher Richards could not handle a Newhouser offering, and Johnson scored on the passed ball, moving Cavarretta to third. Newhouser, nervous now with the dangerous Pafko at bat, intentionally walked him to get to Nicholson, with two out and two on. The big right fielder hit a rocket off the right field wall, tripling in Cavarretta and Pafko. Livingston drove in Nicholson with a sharp single, silencing the pro-Tigers crowd of 54,637. Livingston tried to steal on the thoroughly flustered Newhouser but was thrown out by Richards. Things were looking good for Chicago—with only a half inning gone, they were up 4–0.

Borowy experienced an uncomfortable first inning as well. Webb and Mayo both singled to center, but Cramer bounced into a double play, Hughes to Johnson to Cavarretta. Borowy, not himself, filled the bases when he walked Greenberg, pitching around him, and was too careful with Cullenbine, who also walked. Suddenly, the bases were loaded with two out. York bailed him out, popping a rising fastball up to Cavarretta for the third out. This did not seem to be a first inning pitched by two of the most dominating hurlers of the era.

The Cubs made more noise in the third inning. Johnson got a double when his drive to center just eluded the diving Cramer. Lowrey moved him up to third with a sacrifice bunt, and Cavarretta singled him home. Pafko came up and hit a deep drive between Greenberg and Cramer in left-center, driving in Cavarretta with his double. Livingston got his second hit, singling home Pafko. The bewildered O'Neill trudged to the mound and replaced the fading Newhouser with Benton. Livingston, thinking he could surprise the new pitcher, was thrown out stealing. The score was Cubs 7, Tigers 0.

If the Tigers were not thoroughly dispirited at this point, they certainly were after batting in their half of the third. Cavarretta made a spectacular grab on Webb's sharp one-hop liner and flipped to Borowy for what 50 years later would be the series' first fielding gem. Borowy then struck out Mayo and walked Cramer. Not wanting to challenge Greenberg, he hit him with a purpose pitch. The dangerous Cullenbine came up with two men on, overswung at a Borowy offering, and popped out to Johnson. The Tigers had big chances in two of the first three innings but remained behind, 7–0.

The Cubs' fielding superiority surfaced again in the fifth inning, when Mayo led off with a single to left. Cramer popped out to Livingston behind the plate for the first out, but Greenberg followed with a sharp line single to center. At this point, it seemed apparent that if Detroit had scouting reports on the Cubs' center fielder, Mayo had not paid attention. He foolishly dashed around second, steaming toward third, and was originally reported to be out by a good seven feet when the rifle-armed Pafko delivered a perfect throw to Hack.[7] Briggs Stadium went from deafening delirium to complete silence in a matter of seconds, as Chicago nonchalantly trotted off the field.

The Cubs put some seasoning on the salad in the seventh inning when Cavarretta's rocketing line shot off a Tobin fastball landed deep into the right field bleachers for the first home run of the 1945 World Series. Pafko then singled to center and easily stole second off the infuriated hurler. Nicholson, whose bat the Cubs badly needed in this series, came through again, singling home Pafko. The game, for all intents and purposes, was over: Cubs 9, Tigers 0.

Borowy went the distance, giving up only six hits, for his tenth career win against the Tigers in 13 starts. He became the first major league pitcher to have won a World Series game in both leagues since Jack Coombs, who won game three of the 1916 series pitching for the Brooklyn Dodgers. Cubs trainer Andy Lotshaw told the press he deserved some credit for the win, explaining that he found two huge paving bricks, which he steamed and then submerged in scalding water when the Cubs were on the field. When Borowy left the mound and returned to the dugout as the Cubs came up to bat, he put one brick under Borowy's feet and the other wedged behind Borowy's right arm to keep him warm and limber.[8] Grimm cautioned against making too much of the game, saying that Newhouser was a tremendous pitcher who they just happened to hit hard and that if Cavarretta had been called out in the first inning, it could have been a very different game.

The steamy, silent Tigers locker room offered no excuses. Greenberg said they simply played a bad game, that Borowy was not at his best, but he settled down once he was up by seven runs. Mayo admitted he had underestimated Pafko, and when he saw the throw coming in, he was stunned and realized he did not have a chance. Newhouser vowed to show the baseball world what he could do the next chance he got.[9] The Chicago victory marked the first time in nine years that a National League team had won the first game of the World Series.

THE DETROIT TIGERS' autumn gift from the military, the recently discharged Trucks, drew the starting assignment in game two against Chicago's Wyse. Trucks had one of the liveliest fastballs in the majors, and in his two years pitching in the Navy, he lost only one game, a close decision to the Army All Stars at the Pearl Harbor Navy Base. Trucks, of Irish and Native American descent, had previously pitched against Wyse in the Texas League, throwing for Beaumont when Wyse threw for the Tulsa Oilers. The 28-year-old, born in Birmingham, Alabama, was also an accomplished basketball player.

GAME TWO: DETROIT, THURSDAY, OCTOBER 4

MANAGER O'NEILL SUBMITTED the same lineup for game two that he had the day before, and the only change Grimm made was starting Gillespie in place of Livingston. Grimm's move was a surprise, as Livingston had gone 2-for-4 in the first game of the fall classic.

Trucks presented no problems to the Chicagoans in the first inning. Hack, leading off, beat out a slow roller to short. Johnson bunted him to second, and Lowrey got all of a Trucks fastball, lining it hard to left for a single. Grimm waved Hack around third, but Greenberg charged the ball and cut down Hack, trying to score, with an excellent peg to the plate. Cavarretta quietly ended the inning when he grounded out to first base. The Tigers had no success whatsoever against Wyse through the first three innings.

In the fourth, after Lowrey grounded out to short, Cavarretta hit a tremendous double deep into right-center field. Trucks got the second out when Pafko also grounded out to short, with Cavarretta holding at second. Nicholson continued to come through in the clutch, however, lining a sharp single over second and driving in Cavarretta with the first run of the game. The inning ended when Gillespie flied out to center fielder Cramer. The Tigers made their first hit of the game off Wyse when Cramer singled to center to lead off the fourth. Greenberg came up and rolled weakly to Hack, who threw him out at first while Cramer streaked safely into second. Wyse then became too careful with Cullenbine and walked him. With men on first and second and only one away, Wyse was in trouble for the first time in the game with the dangerous York up. York flied out to Pafko; Cramer, remembering Pafko's exploits in the field the day before, wisely held at second. Outlaw then grounded out to Johnson, who flipped the ball to Hughes at short, forcing Cullenbine. The Tigers lost out on a big chance to break the game open.

In the fifth inning, Hack doubled to center field with two out, but Johnson ended the inning when he grounded out to Mayo at second base. Wyse continued to cruise for a while in the Tigers' fifth, getting Richards to fly out to Pafko and Trucks to pop out to Johnson at second. With two away and little going on, the Tigers started to connect. Webb singled sharply to left and Wyse walked Mayo; there were two on and two out. Cramer produced the first Detroit clutch hit of the series, a single over Hack's head at third, which scored Webb. The game was tied and Wyse had to face Greenberg with two men still on base. The big slugger got hold of one of Wyse's few flat curveballs and hit a three-run homer deep into the left field stands. At the end of five innings, the Tigers led for the first time in the series, 4–1.

In the sixth, after York opened the inning with a drive that Pafko caught at the back of the warning track in left-center field, Grimm called the bull pen and ordered Erickson to warm up. Wyse retired Outlaw and Richards with little difficulty, but Grimm, not liking how Detroit's power men were beginning to tee off on the Cubs' starter, sent Erickson to the mound in the seventh. Erickson got in a jam that inning after striking out Trucks, which started when Webb got a scratch infield hit with one away, Cramer singled, and Greenberg walked as Erickson gingerly pitched around him. A deep fly out to Nicholson by Cullenbine ended the threat, and Erickson had no problems in the eighth inning.

Trucks, however, had no problems with Chicago's hitters in the last four innings of the game, and the Tigers knotted the World Series, a game apiece, with one game left at Briggs Stadium before the show moved to Chicago. A standing room only crowd of 53,636 (Briggs Stadium's capacity in 1945 was 52,954) loudly cheered their local heroes when Trucks struck out Becker, pinch hitting for Erickson, to end the game.

The celebrations in the noisy Tigers clubhouse centered around Greenberg and Trucks, who hugged each other for an extended period of time while press photographers from across the nation snapped their picture. Trucks gave all the credit to Greenberg, but Greenberg disagreed, saying that Trucks won the game by silencing Chicago's lively hitters. Both emphasized that it would now indeed be a competitive series, and Greenberg added that he hoped the press mob would be in their den the next day, after the third.[10]

GAME THREE: DETROIT, FRIDAY, OCTOBER 5

PASSEAU TOOK THE mound for the Cubs on Friday, October 5, standing between Detroit and its second victory. Starting for Detroit was the 26-year-old "Stubby" Overmire, a native of Moline, Michigan, a pugnacious, tricky left-hander whose nickname came from his bulldog physique; Overmire was barely five feet, seven inches tall and weighed 170 pounds. Overmire was a 1941 graduate of Western Michigan State Teachers' College and spent only two years in the minors before joining the Tigers pitching staff in 1943. He went 9–9 with a 3.88 ERA in 1945 but walked 46 and struck out only 34.

Both pitchers gave up only one hit through the first three innings. Lowrey laced an Overmire curve for a hard single to left in the first inning, and Cavarretta followed with a walk. Overmire escaped early trouble by inducing Pafko to ground out for a fielder's choice to end the inning. In the second, York managed a clean single off Passeau after two were out for the Tigers' first hit.

In the fourth inning, Lowrey batted for the second time and just missed a home run, hitting a long drive off the left field fence for a double. Cavarretta sacrificed him to third and Overmire lost Pafko, walking him on four pitches. Nicholson drove in Lowrey with a single, sending Pafko to second. After Livingston flied out to Cramer, Pafko scored on Hughes's base hit. In the seventh, O'Neill took Overmire out of the game and replaced him with Benton. Livingston greeted him at the plate with a double high off the right field wall, and he scored after being sacrificed to third by Passeau's sacrifice fly. The Cubs' half of the inning ended with them on top 3–0.

The game was essentially over after the fourth inning, as Passeau tamed every Tigers hitter after York's lonely second-inning single. To the dismay of 55,500 highly partisan Tigers fans, funereal in their silence as they left the park after the game, the tough, lean right-hander had just pitched the best game in the history of the World Series for a 3–0 shutout. The only other base runner for Detroit other than York was Webb, who walked to lead off the sixth inning; like York, he never got to second base, erased on a force at second when the next hitter grounded into an easy double play. His one-hitter was the first in World Series play since 1906, when another Cubs pitcher, Ed Ruelbach, one-hit the Chicago White Sox, winning 10–1. Because Passeau threw a shutout, the media declared his effort the greatest in the history of the fall classic.

Passeau deflected the praise from the press, directing it to his outfielders, who made nine putouts during the contest. Knowing that he had written history, he asked where the ball he pitched to the last batter was. Catcher Livingston, who recorded the final historic out when Webb popped up behind the plate, took it out of his pocket and presented it to his happy roommate. The Tigers had little to say but issued no excuses. O'Neill simply said that Passeau was able to repeatedly make perfect pitches, especially when he was behind in the count, and that there was little any hitters would have been able to do against him. Catcher Richards said that Passeau threw him nothing but sliders all through the game, but they were the best sliders he had ever seen.[11] Cullenbine, who had 18 home runs and 92 RBIs during the season but was still waiting for his first

World Series hit, agreed with Richards and quietly explained that he simply could not make any contact off any of Passeau's offerings.

The elated Chicagoans bade adieu to the Motor City, happily boarding a special express, along with other National League personnel, that departed from downtown Detroit at 4:30 p.m. A second train would depart immediately after that, containing the Tigers and American League officials. A third express, containing all the members of the national media, left after the Tigers' train.

AT 10:15 P.M. CHICAGO time, the Cubs pulled into Union Station, where about 200 individuals were waiting for them on the sooty platform in the dark train shed. The crowd formed an aisle and cheered as the smiling players walked through into the station.

A TICKET QUANDARY IN CHICAGO

AT ABOUT THE same time that the Cubs were boarding their special train to Chicago, a line with 500 hopeful fans began queuing up for the 5,000 bleacher and 2,500 standing room only tickets that the team made available for what would be the first World Series game in Wrigley Field since game four of the fall classic on October 6, 1938. Bleacher seats for the World Series were $1.20 apiece, and standing room tickets were $3.60. Within two hours, the number of fans swelled to 5,000, and 60 police officers from the nearby Town Hall Chicago Police station supervised the crowd with a wary eye for trouble, bracing themselves for an all-night vigil, because the box office would not open until 8:00 a.m. When they were not looking, some of the youngsters in the line were offering their place to latecomers for as much as $15, twice the cost of a box seat ticket. No standing room tickets would be sold until all the bleacher seats were sold.[12]

The issue of how to dispense the tickets fairly had become a thorn in owner Philip K. Wrigley's side. Wrigley was incensed that ticket scalping, legal at the time, was rampant and that transactions for tickets at inflated prices were even going on in Chicago's best hotels. As a show of sympathy to Cubs fans unable to buy tickets and those upset with the scalping, Wrigley stayed in Chicago instead of going to Detroit to see the first three games, intent on working out some sort of a plan. He told the press that staying away was the least he could do. He was intent on seeing that the remaining tickets were sold to deserving fans, answering as many letters of complaint sent to him that he could. On Thursday, October 4, he decided to submit to the major Chicago newspapers a letter addressed to every fan upset with the ticket situation, paying each paper to ensure its inclusion.[13] The letter, entitled "We're Burned Up, Too," read as follows:

> The Cubs went to a lot of trouble and extra expense to engage outside office space and a large force of bank tellers and clerks to try and do an extra good job of distributing evenly and fairly the comparatively limited supply of World Series tickets, the sale of which, because the proceeds go into a special account of the Commissioner of Baseball, have to balance out to the penny; to say nothing of settling up with Uncle Sam for the exact tax on the printed price of each ticket. However, once the tickets are in the hands of the public, there is nothing to prevent individuals from selling their seats at a neat profit through scalpers. Unfortunately, there are always a few people who prefer a quick profit to anything else. We all know this to be true, but as we said to start with—we still do not like it.
>
> —The Chicago National League Ball Club [14]

THE CHICAGO NATIONAL LEAGUE BALL CLUB

WHILE INDIVIDUALS COULD not be arrested for selling the tickets for more than the printed price, it was illegal to not pay the government the tax due from the sale of the ticket. Nigel D. Campbell of the Internal Revenue Service told the media that 25 federal tax agents were assigned to check on the sale of tickets by scalpers throughout the Chicago Loop and that charges would be pressed against anyone not paying the tax.

Wrigley also stayed in Chicago to supervise the preparation of Wrigley Field for the four-game series. The stadium received a thorough cleaning, and extra help was on hand to hang bunting and ready the playing field. An additional 4,000 folding chairs were added to the box seat section for the four games. The Cubs also arranged for the Andy Frain ushering crew to become familiar with a new device to assist in crowd control, the Handie-Talkie. Known more commonly today as a walkie-talkie, these new portable radios were supplied by the Galvin Manufacturing Company (later renamed the Motorola Corporation), which was eager for the product's demonstration in such a highly visible setting.[15]

GAME FOUR: CHICAGO, SATURDAY, OCTOBER 6

THE CHICAGO CUBS took the field for the fourth game of the series to the thundering cheers of 42,923 excited Chicago fans while Prim warmed up his 38-year-old left arm on the mound. Cubs fan Peter Gladu proved to be many years ahead of his time when he removed the small ceiling cover in his attic and sat on the steeply sloped roof of his home at 3709 N. Kenmore for a free view of the historic proceedings.[16] Chicago would be facing 30-year-old Trout for the first time in the season. Trout tied for the most American League victories in 1943, when he went 20–12. He followed that up by going 27–14 in 1944, leading the league in ERA (2.12), complete games (33), and shutouts (7). When Trout was on his game, he could be one of the toughest pitchers in the major leagues to hit. Fifteen of Grimm's neighbors came to the game from Union, Missouri, along with his 16-year-old son, Bill. Three of Pafko's brothers—Ed, John, and Mike—were also at the game. Their little brother made them proud, making a great diving grab of Mayo's line drive with one away in the first, as Prim set the Tigers down in order. Neither team had a base hit until Cubs catcher Livingston singled to left off Trout in the third inning, but the Cubs did nothing else in the rest of that frame. The Tigers came alive in the fourth inning. After Hack tossed out Webb, Mayo patiently worked Prim to a full count and then drew a walk. Cramer singled to Nicholson in right field, bringing up Greenberg, who had struck out in the second inning. Greenberg singled to left to drive in Mayo and send Cramer to second. The switch-hitting Cullenbine followed with a double down the left field line, scoring Cramer and sending Greenberg to third. A nervous Grimm, not liking how hard Prim was being hit, brought Derringer in from the bull pen. Following Grimm's instructions, Derringer purposely walked York to set up the double play. Then Derringer induced Outlaw to hit a grounder to second, but all the Cubs could get was a force at second base while Greenberg scored and Cullenbine scampered safely into third. The weak-hitting catcher Richards then singled to center to score Cullenbine. Derringer, upset with Richards's at bat, now faced Tigers pitcher Trout. Trout grounded to Hughes to end the inning. Detroit had a 4–0 lead and had knocked Prim out of the game.

The Cubs answered in their half of the fourth with two singles, by Johnson and Lowrey, and suddenly the crowd was back in the game.

Cavarretta, Pafko, and Nicholson were coming up with nobody out. Cavarretta struck out on a 3–2 count, and Pafko grounded out to second base, sending Johnson and Lowrey to second and third. Nicholson was up and the crowd was on its feet. They sat down dejectedly when Trout struck out Nicholson.

In the sixth inning, Johnson again got things going, with a triple down the right field line. Lowrey came up with a man on third and nobody out; he grounded out to Outlaw at third, but first baseman York noticed that Johnson had strayed too far off third during the proceedings. He threw quickly to third to nab Johnson, but his errant throw got away from Outlaw, and Johnson scored the first Chicago run, unearned because it resulted from York's throwing error. The Cubs ended the inning quietly when Cavarretta flew out to Greenberg in left field and Pafko flied to Cramer. The Cubs made a little noise in the last half of the ninth but nothing came of it. Third baseman Outlaw made the play of the game, stopping Lowrey's smash down the line and throwing him out at first. Cramer pulled down Cavarretta's deep drive at the base of the wall in center field. When Nicholson popped out to catcher Richards, the World Series was tied at two games apiece.

THE LOQUACIOUS TROUT had plenty to say after the game. Downplaying his catcher's claim that it was the best game Trout had pitched in three years, Trout was eager to tell the press about his first encounter with the Chicago team. In 1934 Trout, then a high school phenom from Terre Haute, Indiana, showed up to impress the team and asked to pitch batting practice. After they rejected his request, he explained that he had walked four miles to get to the park after arriving by train and asked if they would at least get him something to eat. The response, he said, was a blank stare. Dejected, he went back to Terre Haute, later ignoring the interest the Cubs had in him after successful seasons at Indianapolis in the American Association and instead signing with Detroit.[17] Trout died in 1972, twelve years before his son Steve starred on the mound in the 1984 playoffs in Wrigley Field . . . pitching for Chicago.

The Chicago clubhouse was very quiet after the game. Grimm defensively pointed out that the Cubs themselves got some pretty good pitching in the game from Prim, but he never explained why he felt it necessary to remove Prim in the fourth inning. Cubs hitters simply pointed out that they had a difficult time picking up Trout's fastball throughout the entire contest. There was some optimism in the fact that longtime Tiger tamer Borowy would pitch for them on Sunday, but that was tempered by the fact that they themselves had to bat against Newhouser.[18]

GAME FIVE: CHICAGO, SUNDAY, OCTOBER 7

AN EVEN BIGGER crowd, 43,463, showed up for Sunday's game, bracing themselves for what they assumed would be the best pitching duel of the World Series. Both pitchers had things under control until the third inning. After Borowy struck out Newhouser, he walked Webb, and Mayo singled him around to third. Borowy then threw a mistake pitch to Cramer, who slammed a high drive to the deepest part of center field. Pafko sprinted to his right and made a marvelous catch, though the ball was hit deep enough to easily drive in Webb, who jogged to the plate after tagging up at third. A relieved Borowy now had to face Greenberg. The big slugger hit a similar smash to right-center, but the amazing Pafko once again was equal to the task. Covering an even further distance to his left, he snared Greenberg's long drive in full sprint, saving Borowy from what could have been a disastrous inning. The combative Chicagoans came back in their half of the third, however. After Livingston was retired by Newhouser on a weak ground ball toward first and Merullo struck out, Borowy dropped a double down the left field line. The flustered Newhouser, upset at giving up an extra base hit to the weak-hitting Cubs pitcher, then surrendered a single to leadoff man Hack, which drove in Borowy to tie the game. Newhouser collected himself as Johnson came to bat. With Johnson in the batter's box, Newhouser fired to first and picked off the inattentive Hack to retire the side.

The game was still tied at one when Detroit came up in the sixth. Cramer singled to center and made it safely to second when the ball went past Pafko for an error. Greenberg doubled down the left field line and drove in Cramer. Cullenbine hit a weak roller to the right of first base but beat the racing Cavarretta to the bag for an infield single, and the alert Greenberg sprinted safely to third on the play. York then lined a single to center to drive in Greenberg. Grimm, after trudging to the mound to remove the disgusted Borowy, summoned Vandenberg from the bull pen. Outlaw successfully sacrificed the two Tigers runners to second and third. Catcher Richards, the eighth hitter in manager O'Neill's lineup, was intentionally walked to load the bases, with Newhouser, the pitcher, coming up. In a critical at bat that changed the face of the 1945 World Series, Vandenberg could not find the plate and walked the surprised Newhouser on four pitches, pushing Cullenbine across the plate. Webb hit a ground ball to Johnson at second, which the Cubs could not turn for a double play, and York scored while Richards took third. The impatient Grimm had seen enough of Vandenberg and played the percentages, bringing in southpaw Chipman to face the left-handed hitting Cramer. It worked. Cramer grounded out to Johnson at second base, but the damage was done. The Cubs had four more chances against Newhouser but trailed 5–1.

Chicago went down quietly in the sixth, and Derringer came in to pitch against Detroit in the seventh. The Tigers got a gift double when Greenberg's pop-up fell between the sprinting Merullo and Lowrey. Cullenbine, intent on sacrificing Greenberg to third, was safe at first when Derringer errantly threw too late to Hack at third trying to nail Greenberg. York sent a fly ball to medium deep center field, which Pafko caught for the first out. Neither Greenberg nor Cullenbine dared to move after seeing Pafko's arrowlikc peg to the plate. Outlaw came up and hit another fly to Pafko, this one deep enough to score Greenberg and make it 6–1, Detroit. Hack easily threw out Richards at first to end the inning.

Chicago was determined in their half of the seventh. After Newhouser struck out Johnson, Lowrey singled to short center, and Newhouser, being cautious with Cavarretta, walked him. Pafko's grounder to Newhouser resulted in a force play at second, retiring Cavarretta for the second out, with Lowrey scampering to third. Nicholson rapped a grounder to Outlaw at third, but the hustling Pafko beat the throw to second, allowing Lowrey to score. Livingston came up and smashed a long drive to right field, bringing the crowd to its feet for the anticipated three-run homer, which would make the score 6–5. The ball hit deep on the warning track and bounced into the bleachers for a ground-rule double. Pafko scored, but Nicholson was allowed to advance only to third. Dewey Williams, hero of so many regular season games with the bat, pinch-hit for Merullo. Newhouser was able to strike him out, preventing any further damage, as the game went into the eighth inning with Detroit ahead 6–3.

Derringer put the Tigers down in order in the eighth, and Cubs fans got excited once again when Frank Secory, batting for Derringer in the bottom of the eighth, singled past second baseman Mayo. Hack grounded out to Newhouser, however, then Johnson was out on a close play at first when he surprised the Detroit infield with a bunt, and Lowrey popped out behind the plate to end any hopes the Cubs had going into the ninth inning.

Erickson came in to pitch for Chicago and hit Cramer in the leg with a fastball; Cramer defiantly tried to shrug it off but was noticeably limping when he went to first base. Greenberg got even with Erickson, hitting his third double of the game, which sent Cramer to third base. Cullenbine then got hold of another Erickson fastball and doubled, easily scoring Cramer and also sending Greenberg across the plate. York followed and hit a screaming line drive to Hack at third for the first out. Bill Schuster, who had replaced Merullo at short after Williams pinch-hit for him in the seventh, threw out Outlaw after fielding his ground ball. Richards weakly tapped a ground ball to the mound, and Erickson threw him out at first. Two more runs for Detroit made it 8–3, with the Cubs coming to bat in the bottom of the ninth.

Three outs were all that was between the Detroit Tigers and a 3–2 lead in the World Series. Cavarretta started the ninth with a gift double when Cramer could not handle his fly ball to center field. After Newhouser struck out Pafko, Nicholson singled Cavarretta home, and Cubs fans allowed themselves to do some hoping. Livingston, one of Chicago's offensive surprises in the series, came to bat. The Cubs' catcher lofted a fly to Cullenbine in right field, deep enough to excite the crowd, but not long enough to do any damage, and Cullenbine made the catch. Schuster, the Cubs' last hope, popped out behind the plate to Richards. Detroit had their third victory in the series, and like Chicago, they had now won two World Series games on the road.

Some members of the print media got on the Cubs after the game. Arch Ward pointed out in his column In the Wake of the News that "so many of the Cub players are going pheasant hunting after the series that the clubhouse looks like an arsenal. . . . Apparently the boys are equipped to hunt any kind of game except Tigers." An irritated Grimm tartly proclaimed that the Cubs "just got the hell kicked out of them" but also said that Newhouser's changeup pitch was the best he had ever seen. Cavarretta explained that the Newhouser that Cubs hitters saw the previous Wednesday was the same one they saw today, except that in this, his second game, all his curveballs were strikes. Borowy was at a loss to explain what happened, claiming his fastball and curveball was as good as they were when he dominated Detroit in the first game, but that this time the Tigers were not fooled and were more patient. Chicago's back was to the wall as they thought about game six, when Detroit would once again have to face Passeau, while they themselves had to deal with Trucks.

The Chicago sports pages on that Monday were bleak. On Sunday the Chicago Bears had lost their second game of the season, 17–0, to the Cleveland Rams. James J. Carroll, betting commissioner of St. Louis, revised an earlier prediction and named the Tigers as the favorites to win the World Series. The watch commander at the Town Hall Chicago Police station reported that three ticket scalpers were charged with disorderly conduct for attempting to sell $1.20 bleacher seats for game six for $10 each. Chicago really needed a good outing from Passeau that afternoon.

Interestingly, the most famous legend from the 1945 World Series occurred after this game, but was not reported in sports sections of the *Chicago Daily News*, *Herald American*, *Sun*, or *Tribune*. A saloon keeper named William (Billy Goat) Sianis brought his pet goat, Sonovia, to the fourth game of the World Series after buying two box seat tickets. He was promptly confronted by Andy Frain ushers, who quickly escorted the goat out of the ballpark. After the Cubs lost the fourth and fifth games to the Tigers, Sianis placed a hex on the Cubs and sent Philip Wrigley a simple telegram: "Who smells now?"[19]

GAME SIX: CHICAGO, MONDAY, OCTOBER 8

BOTH TRUCKS AND Passeau had their way in the pivotal sixth game through the first four innings. Mayo, the second hitter of the game, gave the Cubs a scare by smashing a fat Passeau offering to the right field fence, where Nicholson made the catch. In the second, after Passeau walked Cullenbine, York doubled between Pafko and Nicholson in right-center, sending Cullenbine to third. Passeau intentionally walked Outlaw to face the weak-hitting Richards with the bases loaded. The tall right-hander could not find the plate, walking Richards to force in the game's first run.

Passeau regained his composure and got Trucks on a pop-up and Webb on a grounder to Johnson at second. The Cubs tried to answer that run in their half of the second when Pafko singled sharply to open the inning. Livingston grounded to Mayo at second, and Mayo threw to Webb at shortstop to force Pafko. Webb's throw to first was wild, however, and Livingston raced to second. When he was called out by umpire Bill Summers, he leaped to his feet and charged Summers, vehemently protesting the call. Summers held his ground, gestured to Livingston to end his complaint, and the fuming catcher retreated to the dugout.

The Cubs finally figured out Trucks's offerings in the bottom of the fifth. The combative Livingston singled sharply to center. Hughes then dropped a bunt and beat it out for a hit when York lost his footing at first base. Passeau failed in two sacrifice bunt attempts and grounded weakly to Trucks, who ill-advisedly threw to third too late to force Livingston, and Chicago had the bases loaded with nobody out. Hack's clutch single scored both Livingston and Hughes, and the alert Hack made it to second when Richards had difficulty fielding the relay to the plate, the throw arriving after Hughes had slid safely home. Suddenly, the Cubs were ahead 3–2, and 41,708 fans cheered in deafening appreciation. Trucks, clearly rattled over the turn of events, induced Johnson to ground out to Mayo at second, with both runners holding their bases. He was too cautious with the dangerous Lowrey, however, and walked him to load the bases. Up came National League batting champion Cavarretta, and every seat in Wrigley Field was empty, the big crowd standing in noisy anticipation. Cavarretta did not disappoint; he stroked a clean single to center, easily driving in Passeau and Hack and sending Lowrey to second. Manager O'Neill came to the mound and took the ball from the infuriated Trucks, summoning right-hander George Caster to the mound for his first World Series appearance. Caster proved up to the task, as Pafko popped out to Outlaw and Nicholson struck out. Things were looking up for the North Siders; they led 4–1 and had knocked the fireballing Trucks out of the game.

The Tigers' half of the sixth inning was one of those moments in baseball when a freak occurrence turned the tide of history. Cullenbine led off with an infield single and stole second while Passeau was striking out York. Outlaw came up and hit a hard smash right back to the mound, which Passeau partially deflected with his bare hand and then picked up, throwing him out at first. Passeau stared at his hand and called time. The umpires granted an extended time-out while Passeau hurriedly dashed to the dugout to get his hand treated. The fingernail on his middle finger had partially torn off, but after conferring with Grimm and trainer Lotshaw, he went back in to pitch. Infielder Bobby Maier pinch-hit for Richards and hit another hard shot right at Passeau, which he also deflected but this time threw too late to first, Maier being credited with an infield single. Big Johnny McHale then pinch-hit for Caster, the pitcher, and Passeau, in obvious pain, somehow managed to strike him out.

The Cubs rewarded their gallant pitcher's heroics with another run in their half of the sixth. With Tommy Bridges and Bob Swift coming in as the new Detroit battery, Livingston, seemingly on a mission, doubled to left field. Hughes followed with another double down the right field line, Livingston scoring easily to make it 5–1, Chicago. Bridges then picked Hughes off base for the first out. Passeau came up, gamely trying to bat with a badly injured finger, and somehow hit a hard line drive, which Mayo speared at second base. Hack grounded out to end the inning.

Detroit manager O'Neill, ready to use his whole team in pursuit of victory, put in Charlie Hostetler to pinch-hit for Webb. Hostetler reached first when Hack fumbled his grounder at third base. Mayo grounded out weakly to Cavarretta, with Hostetler taking second. Cramer then sharply singled to left. Hostetler lost his footing after he rounded third, fell down, and was nailed at the plate on a good throw from Lowrey in left field to Livingston, while Cramer scampered in to second. Passeau, laboring at this point, walked Greenberg. Cullenbine then singled to center, scoring Cramer, while Greenberg could only get to second. Passeau signaled to the Chicago dugout, and Grimm came to the mound. Both of them were staring intently at Passeau's injured hand when Grimm patted him on the back and summoned Wyse to the mound. Grimm had hoped to start Wyse in the hoped-for game seven. A thundering ovation arose as Passeau, one of the toughest, fiercest competitors of his era, trudged to the dugout. York greeted Wyse with a single, which scored Greenberg, but Outlaw grounded out to Johnson. The high theatrics ended with Chicago still ahead, 5–3. Everyone was too involved with the game to analyze the implications of Passeau's replacement by Wyse and what it would mean in a seventh game. In reality, at that moment, it did not matter; Chicago had to win this afternoon, and then they would face that predicament.

The Chicagoans continued their fight in the bottom of the seventh. After Johnson struck out, Lowrey beat out a slow roller to shortstop. Bridges, worried about facing the dangerous Cavarretta, walked him. Pafko blasted the longest drive of the game, which the crowd thought was a homer when it left his bat, but which Greenberg hauled down with his back against the ivy. Bridges, nervous but relieved that Pafko's shot stayed in the park, walked Nicholson, filling the bases. At this point, the Tigers' hurler had no confidence left and walked Livingston to force in a run. O'Neill called Benton in from the bull pen, and Hughes rudely greeted him with a line drive off his shin, a hard infield single that scored Cavarretta from third. Wyse came up and struck out. The score stood at 7–3, Cubs, and only six outs stood between them and a seventh World Series game.

The Tigers, fully cognizant of their situation, went to work against Wyse in the eighth. Catcher Swift drew a walk to lead things off. O'Neill sent Hub Walker up to pinch-hit for the pitcher Benton, and Walker got the most important hit of his career, a double past Cavarretta, sending Swift over to third. The sure-handed Hack then made his second error of the game, botching Joe Hoover's easy grounder, allowing Swift to score; there was nobody out, runners were on first and second, and nobody was being fooled by Wyse's offerings. Mayo blooped a single to center, which scored Walker, but Mayo was thrown out at second when he tried to stretch his hit into a double. Grimm trudged to the mound, took Wyse out, and replaced him with another starter, lefty Prim. Cramer came up against Prim and smashed a screaming drive to left field, where Lowrey made one of the best catches of the series for a spectacular putout. Facedown in the turf after the great play, Lowrey had no chance to throw out Hoover (who tagged up after the catch) at the plate. With two out, the score 7–5, and a runner on first, the Cubs' lead hung in the balance with Greenberg coming to the plate. Prim made him look bad on a couple of strikes, but Greenberg, waiting patiently for his pitch, stretched the count to 3–2. Prim fired a low strike out of a three-quarters delivery and Greenberg was ready, lofting a long fly ball to left that Lowrey did not give up on until he ran against the ivy wall. He looked up desperately and saw the ball bounce off the screen above the left field catwalk for a game-tying two-run homer. Livingston angrily gestured for a new ball and went out to settle the crestfallen Prim, who was already getting third baseman Hack's counsel. Prim managed to retire Cullenbine on an easy grounder to short, but after eight innings, it was a brand-new game, with momentum swinging over to the Tigers.

O'Neill, wanting to end the series, gambled and called Trout to the mound. Like Grimm, he was using a potential starter for the seventh game in a relief role in the sixth game, but unlike Grimm, if he were successful, he would not have to worry about the next game's pitcher. Trout walked Hack to start the eighth inning. Hack got to second on Johnson's sacrifice and to third on Lowrey's grounder to second. Cavarretta came up with the crowd full of anticipation, but all the batting champ could do was fly out to Greenberg in left field. Grimm pulled out all the pitching stops in the top of the ninth, bringing Borowy in to pitch. With one out, Outlaw and Swift singled. When Trout grounded weakly to Hughes at short, Outlaw gambled, breaking from third to try to score the go-ahead run. Hughes's throw to catcher Livingston forced Outlaw into a hasty retreat; Livingston fired to Hack, who tagged him out. Hoover then harmlessly popped out to Cavarretta. The Tigers gambled and lost; at the time, they did not know how much the gamble would eventually cost them.

Pafko led off the Cubs' ninth and roused the crowd with a long double down the left field line. Trout, however, struck out Nicholson and induced pinch hitter Gillespie to ground out. Grimm sent the dangerous Becker to pinch-hit for shortstop Hughes, and O'Neill ordered Trout to intentionally walk him, knowing that with his foot ailments, Becker would be a liability at first. Grimm countered by sending in the athletic Cy Block to run for Becker. It was all for naught when Borowy lifted a lazy fly ball to Cramer in center field.

The tenth and 11th innings were probably the quietest of the game. The sun finally broke through for the first time on the chilly afternoon, and the classic shadow lines on the field symbolically kept the hitters in the shade and the pitching mound in full illumination. Cramer hit a harmless single in the tenth but was rubbed out when Greenberg bounded into a double play. Hack singled to open the Cubs' tenth but was eliminated when Detroit turned Lowrey's grounder into a twin killing. In the 11th

Borowy and Trout both enjoyed three up, three down innings.

Things heated up, however, in the 12th. Borowy had no trouble with Swift, who was retired on a lazy fly ball to Lowrey in left field. Trout came up but popped out weakly behind the plate, Williams making the catch. Hoover then singled to left field with Mayo striding to the plate. Hoover, intent on getting something going, broke for second with Mayo at the plate. Williams fired a perfect throw to Merullo, and the ball was waiting in Merullo's glove when Hoover started to slide. Playing for keeps, Hoover went into Merullo with spikes high, hoping to knock the ball out of Merullo's glove. Merullo easily hung on but paid for his efforts; his left forearm was bleeding where Hoover spiked him. Williams led off the Cubs' 12th against Trout by grounding out to Mayo at second. Secory pinch-hit for Merullo, who was unable to hit with a badly cut left arm, and rapped a sharply hit line drive past Trout for a clutch single to center field. Grimm sent the fleet Schuster in to run for Secory. Borowy came up and struck out. Then it was Hack's turn at bat. He took Trout's first pitch, which was outside, for a ball. Trout then snapped two quick strikes past him. The next pitch was another Trout fastball, and Hack was looking for it. He hit a frozen rope that shortstop Hoover had no chance on but which Greenberg immediately charged. He went to one knee to field it as the ball made its second bounce, about five feet in front of him. All of a sudden, he reflexively lifted his left arm and shoulder as the bounce turned out to be a wild one, with the ball caroming five feet in the air over his shoulder. Schuster, with the play in front of him as he rounded second, found another gear and streaked around third so quickly that he was within 15 feet of the plate when Greenberg finally retrieved the ball. The crowd went delirious, and the Cubs, many clad in stadium coats, sprang joyously out of the dugout to mob both Schuster and Hack. Trout, confounded by the unfortunate turn of events, slowly trudged off the field with the rest of the disconsolate Detroiters. In rapidly darkening Wrigley Field, the big clock atop the center field scoreboard read 5:58—it had been three hours and 28 minutes since the first pitch, a new record for the longest World Series game ever played. The seventh game of the World Series would now be held on Wednesday, October 10. Both teams could certainly use the off day in between.

The euphoric Cubs clubhouse was all noise and bedlam. Grimm embraced veteran Hack, who went 4-for-5, including a single with the bases loaded in the fifth and the clutch double that made possible the first seventh game of a World Series in Wrigley Field history. While Merullo was getting stitches placed on the two bad cuts on his forearm, Hack, Schuster, and Borowy posed endlessly for pictures.[20] Grimm lavished praise on Borowy's great effort, and Borowy said his control was the best it had been since the series began. Hack thought the pitch that he artfully lined to left was a curveball, tailing away, and his only thought on contact was how well he had connected. Passeau's middle finger was completely black and blue from the smash that tore off the nail, and he told the press that he had a terrible time controlling the ball with the injury. The discussions about who should pitch game seven were lively and raucous, with Grimm changing his mind several times during the debate but not settling on anyone. Passeau's injury forced him to go deep into the starting rotation, but this was not the time to brood.

It was the time to brood in the Tigers' locker room.[21] Cullenbine cursed the scorers for giving Greenberg an error for letting Hack's hit get behind him. Greenberg spoke to no one until he was out of the shower, and then he simply pointed out that the ball was traveling so fast after the high bounce that he had no chance to stop it. O'Neill complained that luck did not go his team's way, especially in the seventh inning, when Hostetler fell rounding third, denying Detroit a run that could have prevented any need for extra innings. Unlike Grimm, he unequivocally announced a starting pitcher for game seven on Wednesday: his peerless workhorse, Newhouser. Greenberg's error was changed, and Hack was given credit for a double when the three official scorers, H.G. Salsinger of Detroit, Martin J. Healey of St. Louis, and Edward Burns of Chicago met later that night. Burns explained that the error was initially given because Greenberg unnecessarily charged the ball, and if he had held back, its bounce would not have mattered. Upon further review, they noted that Schuster had broken with the pitch and was well past second when the ball reached left field. Schuster's position on the base paths made Greenberg's charge essential to prevent the speedy Schuster from going to the plate.[22]

MOST TICKETS HAD been distributed for a game seven, and the Chicago Cubs' offices were busy all night, readying for an onslaught of eager purchasers who would swarm the 28 ticket windows at 8:00 a.m. on

Tuesday. Wrigley himself supervised the arrangements, intent upon getting tickets to loyal fans he had heard from who had been shut out of the first three games in spite of their loyal attendance during the leaner World War II seasons. He vowed he would distribute tickets in person, if it were necessary. By nightfall several hundred fans were already queued up for an all-night vigil while the temperature sunk to the low 40s. The complete complement of Andy Frain ushers were on hand, as were extra police officers from the nearby Town Hall Chicago Police station. Fans lit fires in several metal trash cans to keep warm while sympathetic policemen looked the other way.[23]

GAME SEVEN: CHICAGO, WEDNESDAY, OCTOBER 10

IN NAMING A starting pitcher, Grimm gambled and decided to give the last dance to the one that brought him. Borowy would start game seven, his third start in the World Series, starting on less than two days' rest. He vowed that he felt fine. Unfortunately for Chicago, his pitches looked fine to the Tigers. Webb led off the game and worked the count to 3–2 before he singled sharply to Nicholson in right field. Mayo hit the ball into the same spot on the first pitch he saw, sending Webb to third. Cramer then singled to Lowrey in left, and the Tigers had the lead with two on and none out in the first inning. Grimm then made the biggest mistake of the series. He hurriedly walked to the mound and asked a baffled and completely surprised Borowy for the ball. Borowy did not immediately leave; he waited until Grimm was through giving instructions to new pitcher Derringer and had started back to the dugout, so as not to walk with him. Hack, fully aware of the great pitcher's feelings at the time, patted Borowy on the back and supportively squeezed his shoulder with his glove. The crowd was on its feet, honoring the graceful right-hander, who in only two months of work did as much as anyone else on the team to make the World Series appearance possible.[24]

The choice of Derringer by Grimm at this time was a questionable one. Perhaps Grimm was thinking about 1940, when Derringer, then one of the most dominant pitchers in baseball, beat Detroit twice in the World Series, handcuffing their powerful lineup repeatedly while he helped lead Cincinnati to their first World Series victory.

Grimm's mistake soon became apparent to the 41,590 fans in

attendance. After Greenberg successfully sacrificed the runners to second and third, Derringer intentionally walked Cullenbine. Things looked up when York popped a Derringer curveball up to Hack for an easy second out. The crowd fell silent, however, when Derringer, who pitched 18 years in professional baseball before he ever walked in a run, walked Outlaw on four pitches, forcing Mayo across the plate. The weak-hitting Richards followed with a sharp double down the left field line, clearing the bases for a 5–0 Tigers lead. Newhouser made the final out, a weak tap to second baseman Johnson, as the Tigers batted around in the first inning.

Chicago collected themselves and immediately went to work on Newhouser after he struck out Hack to start the bottom half of the first. Johnson doubled deep into left-center field, and Lowrey surprised everyone in the park by laying down a perfect bunt. The surprised Newhouser fumbled the ball, and Lowrey was safe on the error. Cavarretta singled sharply to right, easily scoring Johnson and sending Lowrey to third. Pafko then hit a shot to Webb at shortstop, which he turned for a double play.

The crowd felt better and was encouraged when Derringer retired Webb and Mayo to begin the second inning. Cramer then singled and Greenberg walked, as Livingston and Derringer vehemently protested umpire Art Passarella's call. Derringer, rattled at this point, then walked Cullenbine and York, forcing Cramer across the plate. Grimm came to the mound and brought in Vandenberg to replace Derringer, who glared at Passarella as he glumly retreated into the dugout. Vandenberg retired the side when Outlaw weakly grounded out back to him.

The Cubs made it 6–2 in the fourth, and the Tigers were lucky they only scored once. Lowrey just missed a home run, flying deep to Cullenbine in right-center. Cavarretta then singled and came home on Pafko's long triple to center field. With one away, Nicholson came up, and the anxious crowd stood in hopeful anticipation. Newhouser got him out on a weak tap back to the mound, and the bubble burst when Livingston, a great clutch hitter all through this series, suffered the same fate, as Pafko died at third.

Erickson replaced the highly effective Vandenberg in the sixth and continued to stymie the Tigers, striking out the late-swinging Greenberg on one of his blazing fastballs to end the inning. The Tigers got to the big blond hurler in the seventh, however, when Richards, having the game of his life, doubled for the second time, driving in Cullenbine, who had previously walked on a full count. The Cubs had nine outs left and were losing 7–2.

Offensively, the Cubs were having no success whatsoever against Newhouser. Lowrey's single in the sixth inning and Livingston's in the seventh were all Chicago could muster against him in the middle frames. The Cubs' pinch hitters, so effective throughout the season and in several appearances in the World Series, had as much trouble with the tall left-hander as the regulars did. Ed Sauer batted for Vandenberg in the fifth and struck out. Secory suffered a similar fate in the seventh, not swinging at a low pitch well wide of the plate, which umpire Passarella incredibly called strike three.

After Secory batted for Erickson, Grimm gambled again and put the injured Passeau on the mound, even though he had Wyse, Chipman, and Prim healthy and ready. Thanks to his severely bruised pitching hand, Passeau lacked his usual pinpoint control, and he walked Webb and gave up a double to Mayo, which drove Webb in all the way from first. Mayo got to third on a ground out to second by Cramer and scored Detroit's ninth run when Greenberg's fly to Lowrey was deep enough to score him after he tagged up.

Chicago desperately tried to answer the bell against Newhouser in their half of the eighth. Lowrey singled to left after Johnson was retired and went to third when Cavarretta singled. Pafko then struck out, bringing up Nicholson. Detroit had to change catchers in the middle of Nicholson's appearance when a foul tip broke Richards's little finger—eight innings too late, in Chicago's estimation. Nicholson finished his at bat by doubling to center, driving in Lowrey and sending Cavarretta to third. Livingston came up, but Newhouser, bearing down, managed to strike him out. The Cubs had now left seven men on base through eight innings; Newhouser seemed to pitch his best when Chicago posed a threat.

Grimm finally used Wyse in the ninth inning, and he had no trouble with York, Outlaw, and Swift. The Cubs refused to die quietly in the bottom of the ninth, as Hughes led off with a sharp single up the middle. Grimm gave catcher Clyde McCullough, recently discharged from the military, a World Series at bat, having him pinch-hit for Wyse. McCullough did what probably any major leaguer who had not played in three years would have done against Newhouser—he struck out. Hack lifted a lazy fly to Cramer for the second out, and Johnson lined a sharp one-hopper, which Webb made a good play on to force Hughes at second and end the game. The Tigers—inferior to their opponents in hitting, fielding, and pitching depth—rode on the backs of two of the biggest stars of the era to win the World Series for the second time in their history, four games to three.

THE DISAPPOINTED CUBS were not emotional in the clubhouse, because the game really had ended in the first inning. Grimm said that Detroit deserved to win but they were not the better team; they had a fresh, rested pitcher in Trucks, an effective but erratic starter who came through for them in Trout, and the best workhorse in the majors, Newhouser. He congratulated Borowy on all his efforts but did not discuss his handling of the pitching staff in the fateful seventh game. Hack hurriedly packed to take a United Air Lines flight back home to California, a novel enough mode of travel in 1945 to warrant a mention by the press. Derringer and Vandenberg packed up to go pheasant hunting. Cavarretta mentioned that he was staying in Chicago and looking forward to seeing some football games. Grimm himself would leave for his farm in Missouri the next day.[25]

In the ecstatic Tigers clubhouse, O'Neill said that Richards's double in the first inning sealed the game early, and he noted that his team had five heroes: Greenberg, Newhouser, Richards, Cramer, and Webb. Richards said that Newhouser had the best stuff he had seen through the first five innings and did not use it all after that because the game was out of reach.[26]

EACH DETROIT PLAYER earned $6,123 for winning the World Series, and the Cubs' losing shares were $4,277 apiece, roughly the average major league pay for an entire season in 1945. The 1945 World Series was the most lucrative in history, $270,125 above the previous revenue record set in 1940 between Detroit and Cincinnati. With the series attendance reaching an all-time high of 333,457, and $100,000 paid by Mutual Broadcasting Corporation for nationwide radio rights, the new revenue record was expected. It was a lucrative series for just about everyone involved. Parking lot personnel got away with charging a dollar for a parking space. Hot dog vendors averaged $60 a day for the four World Series games at Wrigley Field.

The play on the field was also pretty unique. Twenty-one new World Series records were set, and 18 were tied. Newhouser broke Walter

Johnson's record of 20 strikeouts by fanning 22 Cubs. Hack and Cavarretta were the hitting stars of the series, hitting .367 and .423, respectively, each getting 11 hits, one short of the World Series record. The tremendous clutch hitting of Livingston was also a factor. Livingston hit .364, topped only by his teammates Hack and Cavarretta and better than every Tiger except Cramer. The Cubs set a record for most runs scored by a losing World Series team (32). Pafko set a new record for most chances successfully handled by an outfielder (27), and Hack set a new mark for most putouts by a third baseman (12).

Members of the Baseball Writers' Association of America were equally impressed by some of the individual efforts by players from both teams, and their voting on the ballots for the Most Valuable Player Award reflected those feelings. Cavarretta won the award in the National League and Newhouser in the American. Seven other Cubs and eight other Tigers got votes for the award. Pafko finished fourth in National League voting, while Borowy was sixth, Wyse seventh, and Hack eleventh. Passeau, Johnson, and Lowrey also received votes. Mayo was the runner-up for the award in the American League; Richards finished tenth, and Cullenbine, Greenberg, Trout, Benton, Cramer, and York also received votes.

THERE WERE FIVE main reasons why Detroit—a slower, poorer fielding, and weaker hitting team with less pitching depth—was able to overtake their stronger opponents. First, Chicago could not come up with the long ball. Cavarretta's home run at Briggs Stadium in the first game was the only round-tripper the Cubs had in the entire series; throughout the season, key home runs by Lowrey, Pafko, Nicholson, Williams, Gillespie, and Merullo often provided the winning runs in the late innings of many games. These hits were absent in the fall classic. Another reason was the resurgence of Detroit starter Trout. Trout's performance was so erratic through the month of September that manager O'Neill became reluctant to use him. Trout came back to pitch masterfully in game four and posted an ERA of 0.66 over 13 innings in the World Series. Another factor, enjoyed by both teams, was the roster additions made possible by the military discharges of veteran players. During the season, the Tigers welcomed Greenberg back from the Army and would not have overtaken Washington to win the pennant without him. Right before the series,

Trucks returned from the Navy. With Trucks back, Detroit suddenly had a third starter with a long history of success, one who stymied Chicago in game two. The Cubs were replenished by the military discharge of McCullough, their first-string catcher when he entered the Navy, and Hi Bithorn, their ace in 1943. Trucks and Greenberg had the advantage of playing baseball throughout their military tours of duty and were fit and ready when they rejoined Detroit. In the series, Grimm was only able to use McCullough once, as a pinch hitter (who struck out), and Bithorn was overweight and in no condition to pitch upon his return to Chicago.

The other two reasons centered around bad luck and bad planning. Passeau had allowed only two hits, one an infield single, when Outlaw's smash injured his hand in the sixth inning. The injury to Passeau's finger forced him out of the game in the following inning and forced Grimm to use his three best starters—Wyse, Prim, and Borowy—in relief. Passeau, who dominated Detroit in game three, most likely would have been able to continue effectively well past the middle of the seventh inning (when he came out) had he not been injured. Grimm compounded the bad luck with bad planning—his starting pitching decision for the seventh game. Wyse had faced only six batters in Monday's sixth game and, with the exception of that short stint, had had four days of rest since his last start, on October 4. Vandenberg, who gave up only one hit in six innings of work during the series, would have been another viable option. Williams, who warmed up Vandenberg in the bull pen in the late innings of the sixth game, said that Vandenberg's stuff was simply fantastic and he should have started game seven. Grimm compounded the mistake by giving up too soon on Borowy and unwisely using Derringer as his first reliever in the fateful seventh game.

Edward Burns in the *Chicago Tribune*, however, had the simplest and most straightforward reason for Chicago's loss. If Detroit was indeed one of the most mediocre teams to ever reach the World Series, they still had two of the greatest players in the game performing peerlessly for them: Greenberg and Newhouser. The great performance of these two was enough to carry the rest of the Detroit team to the title. If Chicago had had such a dominant hurler and power hitter, like the Paul Derringer of 1940 and the Bill Nicholson of 1943 or 1944, respectively, then perhaps the outcome would have been different.

CHAPTER 9

COMPARING 1945 TO 2003

Any review of the statistics for the 1945 National League offers a quick explanation of how the Chicago Cubs won their tenth pennant of the twentieth century: They simply fielded, hit, and pitched better than any other team in the league. Throughout baseball history, the team with the best pitching has often finished first. Less often does a team capture the pennant by dominating the league in hitting. Finishing first but leading the league in fielding only is even less common. It is extremely rare for a team to finish first in all three categories. Of the 89 pennant-winning teams in the American and National leagues through 1945, this feat had only been accomplished five times: by the New York Giants in 1904, the Chicago Cubs in 1906, the Philadelphia Athletics in 1910, the St. Louis Cardinals in 1944, and the Cubs again in 1945.

In 1945 the Cubs committed 16 fewer errors than any other team in the National League and finished with a fielding average of .980, three percentage points better than the St. Louis Cardinals, who at .977 placed second, and higher than any American League team. Only one team, however, completed fewer double plays than the Cubs' 124: the New York Giants, with only 112. This should be read not as a condemnation of Chicago's infield as much as an illustration of the ways in which fielding and pitching are interrelated. In 1945 Chicago's pitchers allowed far fewer walks and hits than any other pitching staff in the major leagues, so the infield had many fewer chances to complete a double play. Meanwhile, the Cubs' catching quartet allowed only five passed balls, second in the league to Boston's four. Three Cubs starters that year boasted higher fielding averages than anyone else in the National League at their position: Stan Hack at third, Peanuts Lowrey in left field, and Andy Pafko in center field. Right fielder Bill Nicholson finished second in the league in this category, while Phil Cavarretta at first base and Don Johnson at second were third.

At the plate, the team hit .277, for the best hitting average in the majors. Their National League domination at the plate, however, was not as decisive as their prowess in the other two categories. The team's .345 on-base percentage was second best in the league; only two teams made more base hits, and only two teams took more walks. Three teams finished ahead of the Cubs in doubles, but only two had more triples. The team's weakest offensive showing was in home runs. Chicago's meager total of 57 earned the Cubs a tie with Brooklyn for the fifth best in the league, but the figure is misleading, because the two teams with the lowest totals, Cincinnati and Philadelphia, hit 56 apiece, while the two best, New York and Boston, had 114 and 101, respectively. With slugger Nicholson missing his home run swing, the Cubs' biggest weakness was in power hitting. Four teams scored more runs, but no team executed as many successful sacrifice hits.

If pitching wins pennants, however, Chicago most certainly deserved the National League flag in 1945. The Cubs that year had the lowest team ERA, an excellent 2.98, and allowed only 532 runs in 154 games, 51 fewer than any other team. Chicago's hurlers also allowed the fewest bases on balls and the fewest hits, and they finished the highest number of complete games. Only one staff (Brooklyn) totaled more strikeouts, only one (St. Louis) had more shutouts, and two (St. Louis and Pittsburgh) had fewer wild pitches.

The Cubs' 98 victories were a result of an extremely well-balanced lineup of individuals who experienced better years at their positions than the players at the same positions on the other teams. No first baseman had a better year with the bat and the glove than Cavarretta, who won the batting title and had the third-highest fielding percentage of all first basemen. Meanwhile, Johnson's .302 average topped all second basemen, and only two others eclipsed his fielding average. Johnson also led the league in sacrifice hits, with 22 to his credit. Hack's .975 fielding average was tops among third basemen in the major leagues, and the same was true for his .323 batting average. Over in left, Lowrey led the National League in fielding percentage, and he boasted the third-highest batting average among left fielders as well. Center fielder Pafko, in his second year in the majors, claimed the highest fielding percentage, the third-highest batting average, and the most RBIs, by far, of anyone playing his position.

Finishing in the middle bracket among National League shortstops for hitting and fielding were Len Merullo and Roy Hughes, but only one shortstop, Eddie Miller of the Cincinnati Reds, hit more home runs than Merullo, and no team in baseball got more clutch game winning hits out of the shortstop position than Chicago got from this duo. In comparison to his past accomplishments, Nicholson had an off year. Seven National League right fielders hit for a better average, and three had more home runs, but still, only one had a better fielding percentage. Chicago's catching quartet of Livingston, Gillespie, Williams, and Rice were also a mixed bag. Collectively, they held the fourth-highest batting average for catchers and the second-highest number of home runs, but in fielding, they tallied the second-worst percentage.

THE 1945 CHICAGO Cubs won consistently at home and on the road. No team approached their records of 49 and 26 in home games and 49 and 30 while playing on the road. The team also set a major league record by winning 20 doubleheaders in one season. And they tied a record held by three other teams—including themselves in 1909—by beating one team, the Cincinnati Reds, 21 times in 22 games. Lastly, a quaint record, long forgotten with their ensuing decades of losing seasons, was also set by the 1945 Chicago Cubs: They won their 16th pennant in their 70-year history, establishing an all-time major league record for championship seasons by breaking the tie at 15, which they had shared with the New York Giants.

CHICAGO'S PERFORMANCE IN the pennant-winning year of 1945 offers some interesting comparisons to the heartbreaking division-winning season of 2003. Any comparison, though, must take into account the ways in which the game has changed during those 58 years. For one thing, today's major league teams play 162 games during the season, compared to 154 in 1945. In general, the eight extra games do not need to be factored in except where statistical differences between the two seasons appear slight. What is worth considering, however, are the ways in which fielding, hitting, and pitching have changed. In fielding the changes have been minor, but hitting and pitching have seen significant changes.

Strikeouts and home runs are the most obvious examples. In 2003 the Los Angeles Dodgers' home run total of 124 was the lowest for any major league team. With that total in 1945, the Dodgers would have led the majors by ten. In 1945 National League hitters knocked out 577 homers in 616 games for an average of .93 home runs per contest. In 2003 hitters blasted 2,708 home runs in 1,296 games for an average of 2.1 per game. While home runs are far more prevalent today, singles, doubles, and triples were more common in 1945. In 1945 the typical National League fan would see an average of 17.5 total hits, excluding homers, by both teams in nine innings. By contrast, the average number of hits other than homers in 2003 was 15.75. The league's total season batting averages reflect the changes: It was .265 in 1945 and .261 in 2003. Along with home runs, strikeouts are also more than twice as prevalent in the major leagues today as they were in 1945. One reason is that power pitchers are more common today than they were in 1945, and contact hitting, with the exception of a few players, is a neglected art. In 1945 National League batters struck out 3,865 batters in 616 games for an average of 6.3 strikeouts per game. In contrast, the 16 National League teams in 2003 played 1,296 games, with 17,066 batters striking out for an average of 13.2 strikeouts per game.

Two offensive categories partially dependent on speed, stolen bases and triples, offer an interesting contrast between the play of the World War II era and today. In 2003 National League players stole 1,293 bases for an average of 2.1 per game, while in 1945 the average was .85 per game, or not even half as many. In 1945 base stealing was about as common as home run hitting. Hitting triples, however—considered by some to be the most exciting feature of baseball—was more prevalent in 1945 than it is today. Interestingly, this phenomenon has less to do with the speed of the players than with the stadiums they played in. In the 1940s many outfields were much larger than they are today. For instance, the center field fence in the Polo Grounds was 490 feet from home plate, and the distance in Shibe Park was 468 feet. Elsewhere, Forbes Field's center field wall was 457 feet from the plate, while at Sportsman's Park the distance was 425 feet. In the 1940s a ball hit hard into the outfield gap afforded the hitter a much better chance of tripling than it would today in the smaller outfields in contemporary ballparks.

Pitching, as the statistics on strikeouts reveal, was a vastly different endeavor in 1945 than it is today. In the World War II era, complete games by starting pitchers were much more the norm than they are today. At that time, team rosters were not structured with long relief men, setup men, or closers. While it is true that several teams had pitchers they preferred to reserve for late innings, by and large, relief pitchers were also secondary starting pitchers or else they were hurlers taken out of the starting rotation to pitch key innings at the end of certain games. In 2003 the 16 National League pitching staffs together registered only 99 complete games, while in 1945 the Cubs led the National League with 86 complete games and the St. Louis Browns led the majors with 91. In 1945 the Philadelphia Phillies finished dead last in the major leagues in complete games, yet they managed 31; in contrast, the Oakland Athletics of 2003 led all of major league baseball in complete games pitched with barely half that total, 16. Amazingly, the prevalence of bases on balls is almost identical for the two seasons. In 1945, 4,151 National League batters walked in 616 games for an average of 6.74 per game, while 2003 saw 8,778 walks in 1,296 games for an average of 6.77. With variations in so many key aspects of the game evolving in the 58 years between the 1945 Cubs and the 2003 team, the most accurate means of comparing the two lies in measuring performances against competitors as well as directly between themselves.

WHILE THE 1945 Chicagoans fielded better than any team in the major leagues, the 2003 Chicago Cubs finished eighth out of 16 National League teams in that category. The 2003 team, however, committed 15 fewer errors in eight more games and had 37 more double plays than the 1945 squad. This seeming discrepancy is explained by the fact that the 1945 team's strikeout total was 541, while the 2003 team's total was 1,257. Thus, in 2003, Cubs fielders handled more than twice as many balls which the opposition hit into fair territory as their 1945 counterparts did.

Unlike the 1945 team, which finished first in the major leagues in hitting, the 2003 Cubs finished 11th out of 16 teams with a .259 average, 18 points behind the 1945 Cubs. Their on-base percentage was .323, better than only three of the 15 other National League teams, while 12 teams scored more total hits and 13 drew more walks. In doubles, the 2003 Cubs were seventh, and in triples they finished 13th. The 1945 squad's excellence in these categories has already been mentioned: They finished second in on-base percentage, third in total hits and walks, fourth in doubles, and third in total triples. While there is no doubt that the 2003 team had more power, hitting 172 home runs in 162 contests (1.06 per game) compared to the pennant-winners' 57 homers in 154 games (.37 per game), the 1945 team, amazingly, still scored 735 runs, or 11 more than the 2003 team, in eight fewer games.

Comparing the two teams offensively reveals that the 1945 Cubs had a decisive edge in nine of 13 significant categories. In 1945 Cavarretta's .355 batting average won the National League batting title and was the highest percentage in the major leagues. In 2003 Mark Grudzielanek led the Cubs with a .314 average. In 1945 Cavarretta's on-base percentage of .449, first in the National League, was far superior to Grudzielanek's team-leading .366 in 2003. Also in 1945, Hack scored 110 runs—more than any other Cub—while Sammy Sosa led the 2003 Cubs with 99. Hack's 193 hits for the 1945 Cubs were tops for his team and third in the National League; in 2003 Moises Alou led the squad with 158.

Sosa's 286 total bases give the 2003 team its first advantage over 1945, when Cavarretta led the pennant winners with 249. Grudzielanek's 38 doubles were also better than Cavarretta's 34 and gave him the fifth-highest National League total for 2003. In triples, however, Pafko hit 12, five more than Corey Patterson's seven for 2003. Pafko also had more RBIs than any 2003 Cub; his 110 were third best in the 1945 league. Not far behind Pafko that year were Cavarretta with 97 and Lowrey with 89. In 2003 the Cubs' top RBI producers were Sosa (103), Alou (91), and Alex Gonzalez (59).

Although the 1945 Cubs were only slightly behind their 2003 counterparts in total bases and doubles, there is no comparison between the number of home runs the two teams hit: In 1945 the team, led by Nicholson, hit 57; in 2003 Sosa led the Cubs to a total of 172. Nicholson's contribution to the 1945 effort was 13, while in 2003 Sosa blasted 40. The 2003 team was also stronger in steals. In 1945 the Cubs stole 69 bases, while in 2003 they had 73 steals. In walks, however, the 1945 Cubs outperformed their 2003 counterparts. In 1945 the Cubs had 554 walks and were third best in the league, while in 2003 they managed only 492 and finished 14th out of 16 teams. Individual strikeout records tell a similar story. In 1945 no Cub struck out more than Nicholson, who fanned 73 times. Yet four Cubs on the 2003 team struck out more than that, and Sosa struck out the most, 143 times, almost doubling Nicholson's count. Interestingly, Hee Seop Choi struck out almost as many times as Nicholson (71) while appearing in 74 fewer games. The two teams' sacrifice totals reveal how neglected the sacrifice hit is in modern baseball. In 1945 All-Star second baseman Johnson led the Cubs with 22; in 2003 a weak-hitting pitcher, Shawn Estes, led the team with nine.

In a position-by-position comparison between the two teams, the 1945 team is superior at five positions: catcher, first base, shortstop, third base, and center field. Two positions, second base and left field, are very close, with the edge going to the 2003 team, while in right field, the 2003's team advantage is more obvious. The 1945 catching quartet hit .264 with 68 RBIs, while the three Cubs catchers in 2003 hit .231 with 53 RBIs. A comparison of the most frequent starting catchers comes out the same: Mickey Livingston exceeded 2003's starting backstop, Damian Miller, in every offensive category, was equally adept at handling pitchers, and was a better runner. In spite of the excellent season Eric Karros and Randall Simon had at first base in 2003, there is little comparison between them and Cavarretta and Heinz Becker. Cavarretta, captain of the team in 1945, won the batting title and was named Most Valuable Player in the National League. For his part, Becker hit for a higher average than Simon and had six more RBIs while playing six fewer games. Shortstop Merullo of the 1945 Cubs had a higher batting average and far fewer strikeouts than Alex Gonzalez did in '03, but he drove in fewer runs and had fewer home runs, no triples, and 18 doubles. Hack, perhaps the best third baseman in team history, put up far better numbers than Mark Bellhorn or Aramis Ramirez in every offensive and defensive category except home runs and RBIs. It is unfair in some ways to even mention the two categories in which Hack fell short, because he was a leadoff hitter, one of the best of his era, while Bellhorn and Ramirez are power hitters. In center field a similar exception could be made. The 2003 Cubs are at a disadvantage at this position because of Patterson's unfortunate injury in the middle of the season, which cut an excellent year short. While his replacement, Kenny Lofton, played superbly, Pafko exceeded both of them together in triples and RBIs and nearly matched them in home runs. Pafko also struck out half as many times as Patterson in almost twice as many games and led the National League outfielders in fielding percentage, with one of the most fearsome throwing arms of his era.

At second base, 2003's Grudzielanek had a slightly better year than Johnson's excellent showing in 1945. While the two could be considered equal in the field, Grudzielanek hit .314 and posted an on-base percentage of .366, while Johnson hit .302 with a .343 on-base average. Deciding between Alou's efforts in 2003 and Lowrey's in 1945 is more difficult, as both had excellent seasons. In the field, the fleet-footed Lowrey had more range, but Alou possessed a stronger throwing arm. At the plate, it was almost a wash: Lowrey hit .283, while Alou hit .280. A breakdown of their efforts shows that Lowrey hit seven home runs, struck out only 27 times, and got 48 walks, while Alou hit 22 homers but struck out 67 times and walked 63 times. In RBIs, Lowrey and Alou tied at 91 apiece. Alou had 35 doubles and one triple; Lowrey had 22 doubles and seven triples. In right field, however, the 1945 and 2003 Cubs were not nearly so close. Although a comparison between Sammy Sosa and the Bill Nicholson of 1943 or 1944 might be a coin toss, Sosa's 2003 performance was more significant than Nicholson's in 1945. While Nicholson was a far better fielder, finishing second at his position in the National League, and had a more accurate throwing arm, Sosa, even with his reduced offensive numbers in 2003, exceeded Nicholson's off year at the plate in 1945. In Nicholson's defense, he walked 92 times and struck out 73, clearly a better showing than Sosa's 62 walks and 143 whiffs. But Sosa drove in 15 more runs than Nicholson, 103 to 88, in eight more games. A telling statistic, in which the two appear much closer than one might think, is on-base percentage. The difference between them in 2003 and 1945 is .002: Sosa had .358 and Nicholson had .356.

The pitching staff of the 2003 Chicago Cubs received a tremendous amount of national attention as the season progressed, and Cubs hurlers became the primary component in their division championship. Poor pitching was always a key factor in the Cubs' losing seasons over the last five decades, and suddenly Chicago had a pitching staff that finished second in the National League in complete games (13), shutouts (14), and hits allowed (1,304). They also finished third in team ERA (3.83) and fourth in runs allowed (683).

The starting rotation in 2003 was Kerry Wood, Mark Prior, Carlos Zambrano, Matt Clement, and Shawn Estes. Among the group were two of the most dominating young strikeout artists in baseball: Prior, with an 18–6 record and 2.43 ERA, and Wood, 14–11 with a 3.20 ERA. In 2003 Wood had two shutouts and Prior had one. Meanwhile, the intense young Zambrano pitched well and became the workhorse of the staff, pitching 214 innings, winning 13 and losing 11, with a 3.11 ERA and one shutout. Clement had the best season of his career thus far. He seemed virtually unhittable in several of his 14 wins, including one shutout, but he also was ineffective in some of his 12 losses, which accounted for his ERA of 4.11. The fifth starter and only lefty in 2003, veteran Estes, was erratic but had some impressive outings as well, posting an 8–11 record and 5.73 ERA with one shutout. Wood led the staff with four complete games, while Zambrano and Prior each had three, Clement two, and Estes one. For all their successes, however, the 2003 pitchers paled in comparison to the 1945 Cubs' starting rotation, and in spite of the excellent contributions of setup men like Mike Remlinger and Kyle Farnsworth and classy closer Joe Borowski, the remainder of the 2003 pitching staff did not contribute nearly as much as the 1945 team's second-line pitchers did.

The 1945 Cubs' team pitching statistics, the class of the National League, were discussed earlier. Their domination of the league was due in large part to the starting rotation Cubs opponents faced: Hank Wyse, Claude Passeau, Paul Derringer, Ray Prim, and, after July 28, Hank Borowy. Wyse ended the 1945 season with a record of 22–10 and an ERA of 2.68. He had 23 complete games and two shutouts. Against Pittsburgh on April 28, he threw a one-hit game; on July 12 against Boston, he threw a three-hit game; and in Cincinnati on September 27, he threw a second three-hitter. Wyse, meanwhile, posted the second-highest number of wins, winning percentage, complete games, and total innings pitched (278) in the National League. He was also fourth in fewest walks per nine innings and opponents' on-base percentage. Passeau had one of the best years of his distinguished career, going 17–11 with a 2.46 ERA and a National League best of five shutouts. Passeau pitched a two-hit game on August 11 against Boston. In 1945 no pitcher in the major leagues surpassed Passeau's string of nine consecutive victories, a feat he accomplished between May 23 and July 12. Passeau's ERA and complete game total were third best in the National League, his winning percentage was the fourth highest, and his victory total, opponents' batting average, and strikeout-per-game ratio all ranked fifth. Passeau saved the best game of his career when he made history in the 1945 World Series with a one-hit shutout. The veteran Derringer had his best year since 1940 in 1945, his last year in the major leagues. Derringer went 16–11 with a 3.45 ERA and one shutout. On August 2 he threw a three-hitter against Pittsburgh. Prim, invited to spring training after excelling in the Pacific Coast League in 1944, went 13–8 with an ERA of 2.40 and two shutouts. His brilliant relief effort the last week of the season against St. Louis kept Chicago in first place. The soft-tossing left-hander's ERA was the lowest in the National League among pitchers who were in the league all season; this qualification gave him the ERA crown and took it away from teammate Borowy. Prim also finished first in fewest hits allowed per game, fewest walks allowed per game, opponents' batting average, and (what would obviously follow) opponents' on-base percentage. Midseason-acquisition Borowy was 10–5 for the New York Yankees when Chicago acquired him in late July. With the Cubs he went 11–2 with a 2.13 ERA, had 11 complete games in 14 starts, and had one shutout. Borowy made history when he became the second pitcher in major league history to win 20 or more games while pitching in both major leagues in the same season. His .846 winning percentage with Chicago was the best in the major leagues by more than 100 points. On August 24 he lost a three-hit game to St. Louis, his only loss to St. Louis in four starts. Without Borowy's effectiveness against the Cardinals, Chicago would not have won the pennant.

Chicago's second-line starters in 1945 were also near perfect at times. Hy Vandenberg, 7–3 with a 3.49 ERA, pitched a one-hitter on June 15 against Cincinnati and a three-hitter a month later, on July 15, against New York. Meanwhile, Paul Erickson went 7–4, posting a 3.32 ERA; he four-hit Philadelphia on May 26 and got the pennant-clinching strikeout with the winning run on base in Pittsburgh on the second-to-last day of the season. Lefty Bob Chipman, 4–5 with a similar 3.50 ERA, pitched three-hitters on April 22 against Pittsburgh and on May 30 against New York.

In 1945 the Chicago Cubs won 98 games and lost 56, a winning percentage of .636, finishing 49–26 at home and 49 and 30 on the road. In comparison, the 2003 Cubs won 88 and lost 74, a winning percentage of .543, and ironically also finished with identical home and road records, 44–37. The 1945 Cubs had the winningest season in the majors; the 2003 had the fifth-best regular season in the National League and the tenth-best in the majors. The 1945 Cubs' record was so good that they would have finished first in any division in the major leagues in 2003. The record of the 2003 Cubs, applied to the 1945 major league season, would have earned them third place in the American League and fourth place in the National.

VOLUMES HAVE BEEN written about how baseball changes through the years and how difficult it is to precisely compare a team from one era to a team from another. Yet the fielding, hitting, and pitching superiority of the 1945 Cubs, the superior performance against the competition in their pennant-winning season, and the noteworthy individual accomplishments of the players makes clear that the 1945 Chicago Cubs had a better season in nearly every way than the 2003 Chicago Cubs did. They were, after all, the last team to bring a National League pennant to Chicago.

CHAPTER 10

LOSING BECOMES THE NORM

The 1946 Chicago Cubs were ready, willing, and eager to defend their National League pennant when spring training began, but few baseball experts expected them to go far. Most observers liked the St. Louis Cardinals, and the few who did not, liked the Brooklyn Dodgers. The reason had to do with the end of World War II. In the fall of 1945, the only Cubs still in the military were catcher Clyde McCullough, pitcher Hi Bithorn, and the young Eddie Waitkus. In St. Louis, however, with the war's end, the team welcomed back Stan Musial and Enos "Country" Slaughter, two future Hall of Famers. In Brooklyn 1946 brought several prominent players back into the fold, including shortstop Pee Wee Reese, third baseman Cookie Lavagetto, left fielder Pistol Pete Reiser, and pitchers Kirby Higbe and Hugh Casey. The Chicagoans clearly had their work cut out for them.

Through the early months of the season, the Cardinals and Dodgers alternated in first place. The rest of the league hoped that some competitive balance would return in late May, but hopes faded when the upstart Mexican League, a newly developed professional league south of the border, raided American and National League rosters and signed several top American major leaguers.[1] The league was funded by Mexican millionaire Jorge Pasquel, and the inducement to play for greater compensation outweighed the threat of a five-year ban for players who broke contracts with the major leagues. In spite of Commissioner Happy Chandler's threats to place defectors under the five-year ban, the historically penurious St. Louis Cardinals suffered heavy losses when key players ignored the threat and jumped to the new league anyway. Among the defectors was starting pitcher Max Lanier, who checked out after a 6–0 start with St. Louis. Fred Martin and Lou Klein soon followed. Meanwhile, the Dodgers lost two starters: catcher Mickey Owen and outfielder Luis Olmo. As bad as they were, the roster raids could have been even worse for the Cardinals. Pasquel and his agents made tempting offers to Musial, Slaughter, Whitey Kurowski, and Terry Moore, but luckily for the Cardinals, the men chose to remain in St. Louis.

On July 2, 1946, Brooklyn was seven and a half games ahead of the league, the biggest lead they would have all season. By mid-July, when they went to St. Louis, their lead had slipped to four and a half. Then the Cardinals swept them in a four-game series at Sportsman's Park, and one of the best pennant races in history was on. The rivalry continued until the last weekend of the season, when the Cardinals took the flag with a 98–58 record, two games ahead of the Dodgers.

Ending the season in third place were the Cubs, who at 82–71 finished 14 games out of first. One bright spot was the performance of rookie Waitkus, who hit .304 and displaced Phil Cavarretta at first base. Cavarretta was shifted to right field and slugger Bill Nicholson to the bench. Another rising star was 26-year-old lefty Johnny Schmitz, the pride of Wausau, Wisconsin, who emerged as the team's best pitcher following his discharge from the Navy. Schmitz went 11–11 with some tough losses but led the league in strikeouts and posted a shimmering 2.61 ERA. Injuries decimated Chicago's chances, however, and manager Charlie Grimm shuttled players in and out all summer as regulars Stan Hack, Andy Pafko, Don Johnson, Mickey Livingston, and McCullough went down.

By 1946 some of the contributors to Chicago's glory days were gone forever. Paul Derringer was among the first to go. Tired of his antics, the

Cubs did not offer him a contract after the World Series; instead, he went to Indianapolis in the Class AAA American Association, where he lost his pinpoint control and went 9–11, walking five times as many men as he struck out. Hy Vandenberg faced a similar fate. Chicago's most obstinate holdout in 1945 was not invited to return; instead, he joined Derringer in the American Association but appeared in only 12 games for the Milwaukee Brewers. Meanwhile, Ed Hanyzewski hooked up with Nashville in the Class AA Southern Association but played only ten games. The Cubs sold Roy Hughes to the Philadelphia Phillies. Seven others—Ed Sauer, Lloyd Christopher, Len Rice, Paul Gillespie, Cy Block, Reggie Otero, and Bill Schuster—returned to the Pacific Coast League, which, though not the big show, was the most prosperous, passionately followed baseball organization at the Triple A level.

The rest of the 1945 Cubs returned for the1946 season. Heinz Becker continued to hit well but did not play a single game at first base. In May 1946, the Cubs traded him to Cleveland for first baseman Mickey Rocco. Pitcher Hank Borowy continued with the Cubs through the 1948 season. In December 1948, he was traded to the improving Philadelphia Phillies, along with Waitkus, for two pitchers: Monk Dubiel and the 39-year-old Dutch Leonard. Cavarretta continued with the team through 1953, serving as player-manager from 1951 to 1953, when he was fired for telling owner Philip K. Wrigley that he did not think the 1954 team would be competitive. Cavarretta ended his 22-year career in 1955, filling in for the Chicago White Sox after his dismissal by Wrigley. In 1950 Chicago sold Bob Chipman's contract to the Boston Braves for cash, where he ended his 12-year career in 1952. The Philadelphia Phillies claimed Paul Erickson off the waiver wire in 1948, but he stayed with the Phillies less than two months before they put him on waivers and the New York Giants claimed him; a month later, New York sold him to the Pittsburgh Pirates in a cash transaction, and it was there that he ended his eight-year career.

Four-time All-Star Hack ended his magnificent career in 1947 but came back to manage the Cubs from 1954 through 1956. Another All-Star, Johnson, left the team in 1948 after appearing in just six games. In the middle of the 1947 season, the Cubs put Livingston on waivers, and he was picked up by the New York Giants, who used him as a backup through 1948, his last year in the majors. Peanuts Lowrey remained a

Chicago mainstay until 1949, when he was sent to Cincinnati along with the recently acquired Harry Walker for Frankie Baumholtz and Hank Sauer. Lowrey accomplished little for the Reds, but his career revived when Cincinnati sold him to the St. Louis Cardinals, where he racked up some excellent years and became one of the best pinch hitters in the National League. In 1955 Lowrey ended his 13-year playing career with Philadelphia but coached in the majors from 1960 through 1981, including five seasons back at Wrigley.

Lennie Merullo developed back problems and retired after the 1947 season but continues as a successful major league scout. In 1989 Merullo joined an elite group of athletes when his grandson Matt launched a six-year career as a White Sox catcher. In the history of major league ball, there have been only nine grandfather-grandson combinations. In contrast to Merullo, Nicholson, the Cubs' greatest power hitter in the 1940s, never regained his form. In November 1948, the Cubs traded him to Philadelphia for Harry Walker, who had won the batting title the year before, playing for St. Louis and Philadelphia. Nicholson achieved a measure of success with the Phillies before his 1953 retirement, but he did not learn until the end of the 1950 season that he suffered from diabetes, which explains why his power hitting declined so precipitously after 1944. Johnny Ostrowski stuck with the Cubs through 1946 and came back briefly with the Boston Red Sox in 1948, ending his career in his hometown with the White Sox in 1949.

The young Pafko continued to excel with the Cubs and remained the team's most productive and popular player until 1951, when Cubs management traded him, along with Schmitz, Rube Walker, and Wayne Terwilliger, to the Brooklyn Dodgers for Bruce Edwards, Joe Hatten, Eddie Miksis, and Gene Hermanski. The 1951 trade was typical of Cubs management's inability to get value from other teams in the postwar era. Three others who finished their playing days as Cubs included the great Claude Passeau, who retired from the majors in 1947; the invaluable Ray Prim, who retired after appearing in only 14 games for the Cubs in 1946; and Frank Secory, who appeared in 33 games in 1946 before retiring at the end of the season. In 1952 Secory became a National League umpire in 1952 and worked in that capacity until 1970.

Lon Warneke was another 1945 Cub who continued past his playing days in the majors as an umpire. His retirement from league play came at the conclusion of the 1945 season, when he ended his impressive 15-year career with a 193–121 record; he continued as an umpire in the National League from 1949 to 1955. Dewey Williams stayed with the Cubs through 1947 and ended his major league career in 1948 with Cincinnati. After his playing days were over, he remained active in baseball and established the ManDak (Manitoba and North Dakota) League. Hank Wyse had a successful season with the Cubs in 1946 but was released after the 1947 season and was picked up by the Philadelphia Athletics, with Chicago getting nothing in return. In spite of long-standing back problems, Wyse continued to pitch until 1951, when he went from Philadelphia to the Washington Senators.

The three players who would have undoubtedly helped the Cubs in 1945 had they not been at war did not stick with the Cubs very long after their return, regardless of their levels of success. In January 1947, the Cubs sold Bithorn to Pittsburgh, receiving nothing but cash in return. Five years later, on January 1, 1952, Bithorn died in mysterious circumstances in El Monte, Mexico. The major league stadium in San Juan, Puerto Rico, is named in his honor. McCullough, one of the best catchers in the National League immediately after World War II, left for Pittsburgh in December 1948, when he was traded, along with Cliff Chambers, for Cal McLish and Frankie Gustine. That same month, Waitkus went to Philadelphia, along with Borowy, in the trade that brought Dubiel and Leonard to Chicago. The handsome, multilingual Waitkus, pride of Boston Latin High School, experienced a life-changing injury when he was shot by a deranged female admirer in the Edgewater Beach Hotel in the spring of 1949. His shooting, rehabilitation, and successful return to baseball became the inspiration for Bernard Malamud's *The Natural*, which was made into a movie of the same name.

WHEN ALL WAS said and done, the Cubs, one of professional sports' most storied and successful organizations during the first 70 years of its existence, became one of baseball's most consistent failures in the 60 years following World War II. The team's third-place finish in 1946 would be the last time they would finish in the first division for 21 years. After 1946 Chicago would not a see a winning season until 1963, when they went 82–80 but still finished seventh in a newly expanded ten-team

National League. In those 17 seasons without a winning record, the Cubs ended only one year, 1952, with a .500 record (of 77–77), their best showing in the 18-year stretch following World War II. This was the same organization that had posted five first-place finishes for the previous 21 years and had been involved in pennant races in 13 of them—the same organization that finished last only once in its 70-year history and finished last in the National League only once before 1945. Over the next 20 years, the Cubs would tally eight last-place finishes and would add six second-to-last finishes. What happened?

The decline of the Chicago Cubs during the second half of the twentieth century was chiefly the result of five developments. Of these, only one—the war's effect on the Cubs' farm system—was beyond the franchise's control. The other four—the team's lateness in developing a farm system, their poor record with recruits, management's impatience with slow-developing talent, and a series of disastrous trades—were Chicago's responsibility. In 1940 Wrigley, upset with the team's unexpected fifth-place finish, replaced Charles "Boots" Weber as the general manager. Weber, who began in 1934 following the death of William Veeck Sr. a year earlier, was the architect of the Cubs' pennant-winning rosters in 1935 and 1938. Making few decisions without Wrigley's council, Weber engineered successful trades with other major league clubs and signed young prospects who became excellent contributors. His replacement after only one fifth-place finish demonstrates how much young Wrigley cared about winning. As Weber's replacement, Wrigley named a *Chicago Herald-American* sportswriter, Jim Gallagher.

Gallagher's organizational ideas were sound. He noted how successful the St. Louis Cardinals and New York Yankees had become with their extensive farm systems and convinced Wrigley that the era of buying good talent from minor league teams was coming to a close. Because so many minor league organizations either had working agreements with specific major league teams or were owned by them outright, buying from the minors offered limited prospects. In 1941 Gallagher convinced the Cubs' organization that they, too, would have to develop a farm system if they were to remain competitive. Shortly thereafter, the Cubs took total control of the Los Angeles Angels and established working agreements with six other minor league teams.

Gallagher referred to this as the heart of his "five-year plan," a phrase the press had fun with but which reflected the amount of time he felt their minor league teams would need to develop legitimate major league players.

Gallagher's thinking was both right and wrong. The Cubs did need to develop a farm system; perhaps the only team as slow as Chicago to reach this stage of development was the Pittsburgh Pirates. Other teams without a farm system simply could not afford one. In hindsight, Gallagher's thinking regarding the five-year plan also seemed correct. Twelve contributors to Chicago's 1945 pennant were products of minor league teams the Cubs had established working relationships with under Gallagher's watch. If anything, the plan reached fruition a year early.

Gallagher was mistaken, however, in estimating how successful a team could be just relying on its own farm system, and his timing proved poor, as World War II wreaked havoc on the minor leagues and military conscription negated any chance a team might have of slowly bringing along a talented player. Branch Rickey, the mastermind of the farm system concept, was aware of this; during the war, he made a point of signing prospects too young for the draft. Gallagher also ignored the fact that to fill a need to put them over the top most teams relied on trades with other major league teams or on big purchases of key players from other major league rosters. But his biggest weakness was in the trade market; more often than not, other general managers fleeced him in player transactions. What little the Cubs got for their players on the 1945 pennant-winning team is proof of that.

Gallagher's shortcomings in trade-making became evident early in his career. In May 1941, he sent future Hall of Famer Billy Herman to Brooklyn in exchange for Johnny Hudson, Charlie Gilbert, and $65,000. A fixture at second base on three pennant-winning Cubs teams, Herman was replaced by the young Lou Stringer. Before the close of the year, Herman would help lead Brooklyn to a pennant, while the light-hitting Stringer did little in 1941 and led all second basemen in errors in 1942. Perhaps to his credit, Gallagher was the general manager when Borowy was acquired in 1945, but the acquisition did not start with him; it started with the impatient general manager of the Yankees, Larry MacPhail, whose unhappiness with Borowy's high salary and uncertain draft status caused him to abandon the star.

After the war, the Becker-for-Rocco trade typified Gallagher's inability to gauge the trading market. While Becker, in spite of his ailments, continued to play first and hit well for the Indians, Rocco never played a game for the Cubs. All Gallagher could get for popular slugger Nicholson in 1948 was Harry Walker, who played in only 42 games for the Cubs. Meanwhile, postwar starting catcher McCullough was an All-Star for the National League in 1948, yet the following December, Gallagher traded him to Pittsburgh for Frankie Gustine and Cal McLish. Gustine played a total of 76 games for the Cubs and hit .226, while McLish's Cubs career ended after 38 appearances and a 5–11 record. Waitkus was another All-Star in 1948, hitting .304 and .292 in his first two full seasons as Chicago's first baseman. A week after McCullough's departure, Waitkus was packed up with Borowy and sent to the Philadelphia Phillies; in exchange, Gallagher received pitchers Dubiel and Leonard. The Cubs got very little in this deal, as Dubiel went 14–21 with Chicago and Leonard, 26–30. In fairness to Gallagher, the Lowrey-for-Baumholtz-and-Sauer trade proved fortuitous, with Baumholtz posting several strong seasons through the mid-1950s and Sauer becoming a postwar Chicago legend. But getting nothing from the Philadelphia Athletics for pitching mainstay Wyse sullied Gallagher's reputation.

Cubs fans would not have reacted as bitterly to these developments if the farm system had continued to produce, but unfortunately, it did not. It certainly was not for lack of trying. After World War II, Wrigley spent heavily to develop players. In 1946 Chicago owned or was affiliated with 20 minor league organizations, the same number as the New York Yankees. Only Rickey's Brooklyn Dodgers, with 25, had more. Poorer teams could not compare: The Washington Senators had six, while the Chicago White Sox and Cincinnati Reds had eight apiece. The Cubs did not skimp on scouts either. In 1946 the Cubs had 45 scouts working for them, more than any team in the majors. In comparison, the Yankees had just 20. A large scouting staff was another item the poorer teams could not afford: The St. Louis Browns had 11, the Philadelphia Athletics had six, and the Washington Senators had only three.

Unfortunately, the size of the farm system and scouting department turned out to be no guarantee that the Chicago organization would produce top-quality players. Of the 73 rostered players at the Cubs' Triple

A Los Angeles team and their two Double A squads in Nashville and Tulsa, 66 never played a single inning of major league baseball, and the seven who became major leaguers either had very brief careers or were traded before they blossomed. During his time with the Cubs, Sal Madrid appeared in only eight games, and Fred Richards in ten. Clarence Maddern lasted longer but still managed to play in only 30 games over three seasons. Hank Schenz saw action in 166 games over four years. Cliff Chambers, who went 2–9 for Chicago in 1948 and was traded the following season to Brooklyn, racked up several effective years on the mound after he left, especially with the St. Louis Cardinals. Hard-throwing Russ Meyer, a free spirit nicknamed the Mad Monk, was sold to Philadelphia after going 10–10 for a last-place Cubs team in 1948. Gallagher should have known that a .500 season for a starting pitcher on a last-place team is very good, but he let him go anyway. In 1949 Meyer went 17–9 for the Phillies and played on the National League All-Star team, and he started for the Phillies in their pennant-winning 1950 season. The only minor leaguer who made a significant contribution to the Cubs from their high minor league roster after World War II was pitcher-outfielder Hal Jeffcoat, who played for Chicago from 1948 until 1955, when he was traded to Cincinnati.

The Cubs' very poor record of player development contrasted starkly to the scouting and minor league organizations of other major league teams that were much smaller yet much more productive. The Philadelphia Phillies are a case in point. When the team was taken over by the Carpenter family during World War II, one of the first things the new owners did was hire Herb Pennock, who had been in charge of the Boston Red Sox minor league system, to establish a farm system for the Phillies. In 1946 the Phillies had 13 scouts, 32 fewer than the Cubs, and connections with 11 minor league teams, compared to the Cubs' 20. Their top minor league team in Utica, New York, was playing in the Class A Eastern League, while the Cubs had two teams each at the Class A and AA level, as well as one Triple A team. Yet between 1948 and 1954, Chicago finished last or second to last eight times, sixth once, and fifth once. During that same period, Philadelphia came in sixth only once, fifth in four seasons, fourth twice, and third twice, and they won the National League pennant in 1950. The Phillies' third-place 1949 team and pennant-winning squad the following year were so well fortified with young players from the team's minor league system that the youngsters became known as the Whiz Kids. Meanwhile, Chicago learned the hard way that in terms of player development, the size of their farm system and level of spending were not as important as knowledge and experience.

In spite of Chicago's poor showing after World War II, Cubs fans remained loyal and continued to come to the ballpark in significant numbers until the 1953 season. The only year between 1946 and 1952 in which the Cubs did not draw a million fans was 1951. Wrigley's loyalty to Grimm, however, was more short-lived and ended early in the 1949 season. After finishing last in 1948 for only the second time in their history, the Cubs under Grimm started 1949 with 19 wins and 31 losses, and Wrigley moved Grimm "upstairs," taking him out as manager and naming him to a team vice presidency. While Grimm kept the position briefly and then decided to manage in the minors, Wrigley brought in Frankie Frisch, who had had tremendous success managing the St. Louis Cardinals' Gashouse Gang teams from 1933 through 1938 and had managed last in Pittsburgh in 1946. Wrigley apparently felt that Grimm's laid-back, player-friendly approach needed to go, and nobody would ever accuse the autocratic, brusque Frisch of having similar qualities. The new manager finished the year with a 42–62 record, and the Cubs found themselves in last place again. The following year, after a seventh-place finish but only a three-win improvement, Wrigley kept Frisch but fired general manager Gallagher.

Wrigley replaced Gallagher with Wid Matthews, a longtime Brooklyn Dodgers executive under Rickey whose specialty was minor league development. In spite of the change, the Cubs' farm system fared no better under Matthews, but his downfall was inexperience and his inability in making successful trades, the other key part of his job.

What little good feeling Chicago fans had toward Matthews quickly disappeared on June 15, 1951. In a trade with the Brooklyn Dodgers that reminded Chicagoans of the worst fleecings that Gallagher ever endured, he traded Pafko, Schmitz, Walker, and Terwilliger for catcher Bruce Edwards, outfielders Gene Hermanski and Eddie Miksis, and pitcher Joe Hatten. At the time Pafko left, he was the most popular ballplayer in Chicago. A big contributor to their glories in 1945, Pafko had become one of the most complete center fielders in the game, consistently hitting for average and power, with perhaps the most respected throwing arm in the league. He also made the National League All Star team four consecutive years, 1947–1950. In 1950, he had led the team with eight triples and 36 home runs, and few outfielders could match him defensively. His baseball achievements notwithstanding, Pafko was one of the few players identified as a Chicagoan. He had owned property and lived in the Kelvyn Park neighborhood, went to church there, and, several years before, had married his wife there.

In the aftermath of the trade, Edwards, the key to the deal, became a sore-armed catcher and played sporadically in 105 games over the next three seasons. Meanwhile, Hatten pitched his way to a 6–10 record in Chicago, while Hermanski played an average outfield and hit .258 over three years. Miksis played six years with the Cubs with productivity that paled in comparison to Pafko's. Pafko, meanwhile, started in the Dodgers' "rifleman outfield" of the 1950s, aided by the strong arms of Duke Snider and Carl Furillo. He went to the World Series once with the Dodgers and twice with the Milwaukee Braves, ending his distinguished career in 1959 when he retired.

AFTER THE INFAMOUS trade, Matthews faced a barrage of criticism from the entire baseball world. Some called the transaction the worst in baseball since Babe Ruth left the Yankees for the Red Sox three decades earlier. In the Pafko trade and in others, Matthews proved no more competent at judging talent than his predecessor, Gallagher. The trade, and the poor seasons the team endured, could not have come at a worse time in terms of the city's baseball landscape.

The White Sox, one of the major league's most dormant franchises in the previous 30 years, were in the dawn of their greatest decade in history. Their new manager, Paul Richards, had an exciting, competitive team in 1951, with first baseman Eddie Robinson, second baseman Nellie Fox, shortstop Chico Carrasquel, outfielder Minnie Minoso, and pitcher Billy Pierce. With the sure-handed Carrasquel and the exciting Minoso, the Sox captured Chicago's minority baseball audience before the Cubs knew it existed. Their successful run reminded many of the Cubs of the late 1920s and '30s. In the 17 seasons between 1951 and 1967, the Sox missed a first-division finish only once, going 85–77 for a fifth-place finish in 1962. Throughout those years, there were storied pennant races with the New York Yankees and Cleveland Indians, and in 1959, the Sox won the pennant for the first time in 40 years. The Cubs, in contrast, completed the worst decade of their history in the 1950s and did not return to the first division until Leo Durocher's young team appeared in 1967. Between 1947 and 1966, the Cubs saw only one winning year, 1963, when they went 82–80, which was only good enough for a seventh-place finish in the expansion-weakened ten-team National League. To Wrigley, the unthinkable had happened: Chicago had become a White Sox town. To the dismay of Cubs fans, Wrigley did not seem to care.

From 1951 through 1967, the White Sox outdrew the Cubs at the box office in every season. In 1959, '61, '62, and '64, Sox attendance was almost double that of the Cubs. In 1960 White Sox attendance was almost two and a half times the Cubs' total. During those years, the Sox billed themselves as a team of speed, base running, fielding, pitching, and pennant races. When Bill Veeck took over the team, fans discovered an expanded entertainment experience, featuring not only a ball game but also fireworks, free giveaways, and an exploding scoreboard. The team began scheduling far more night games than daylight affairs but often sold out their afternoon games on Saturdays and doubleheaders on Sundays. The Cubs, meanwhile, became the team that played in "beautiful Wrigley Field," with advertisements urging fans to come out, have a picnic in the sunshine, and watch Ernie Banks hit a home run.

In spite of the White Sox's domination in the 1950s, at least part of the Cubs' popularity today is tied to their hidebound traditions of the postwar era. Throughout those years, Cubs afternoon home games were televised locally throughout the season, while Sox night games rarely were. During those years, the White Sox rarely played weekday afternoon games. But because the Cubs had no lights, every contest was a matinee. Legions of baby boomers, following baseball almost like a religion in the 1950s, grew up coming home from school in time to follow the last few innings of the Wrigley Field game on television. Indeed, children's shows on WGN were not aired until the game was over. For thousands of children, a televised Cubs game became a part of the happy ritual of returning home from school. When the youngsters' inevitable request to go to a game in person came up, it was an easy request for a parent to honor. Afternoon games meant no change in meal plans and no alteration in a child's evening routine. The park itself was extremely accessible, and its North Side neighborhood location seemed more amiable than the gray, industrial environs of Comiskey Park. It is impossible to understate the countless youngsters in the 1950s and '60s who grew up with the Cubs; the games were televised more often, they were on the air when children could see them, and when a youth achieved a moderate measure of independent mobility, he could go to the games very easily by himself.

A large fan base and wide recognition, however, do not guarantee success on the field. The Chicago Cubs' lateness in developing a farm system, their inability to make it productive after World War II, their impatience with young players who did not immediately produce at the major league level, their tardiness in considering talented African-American ballplayers, and the inability of the front office to improve the team through trades were all reasons why the team's fortunes in the last half of the twentieth century proved such a stark contrast to the first half of the 1900s. In spite of their failures—or indeed, perhaps because of them—the Cubs managed to keep the most loyal following of any organization in athletic history. Imagine what the Chicago Cubs would be like, and how their followers would respond, if only they could repeat what they achieved in 1945. . . .

NOTES

CHAPTER 2:
WORLD WAR II'S EFFECTS ON MAJOR LEAGUE BASEBALL

1. Hearings Before the Subcommittee on the Study of Monopoly Power of the Committee on the Judiciary, United States House of Representatives, 82nd Congress, First Session, Part 6, Organized Baseball, U.S. Government Printing Office, Washington, D.C., 1951. (Hereinafter referred to as House Judiciary Hearings, 1951.)
2. Ibid.
3. John Thorn et al., *Total Baseball*, p. 2,514.
4. Ibid.
5. Ibid.
6. Richard Goldstein, *Spartan Seasons*, pp. 19–20.
7. William B. Mead, *Even the Browns*, p. 87.
8. Ibid., p. 89.
9. House Judiciary Hearings, 1951.
10. Mead, p. 93.
11. House Judiciary Hearings, 1951.
12. Goldstein, p. 12.
13. "Draft Threat Softened by McNutt Ruling," *Chicago Tribune*, March 22, 1945.
14. Thorn et al., p. 2,517.
15. Goldstein, p. 100.
16. Thorn et al., p. 2,517.
17. Baseball Notes, *Sporting News*, April 13, 1944.
18. Mead, p. 66.
19. Goldstein, p. 20.
20. Ibid., p. 124.
21. House Judiciary Hearings, 1951.
22. Goldstein, p. 14.
23. House Judiciary Hearings, 1951.
24. Mead, p. 94.
25. Ibid., p. 43.
26. Goldstein, p. 146.
27. Ibid., pp. 131–132.
28. Ibid., p. 133.

CHAPTER 3:
THE NATIONAL LEAGUE DURING WORLD WAR II

All references regarding team revenues, profits, losses, and financial information are from the House Judiciary Hearings, 1951. All references regarding attendance figures are from Thorn et al., *Total Baseball*, pp. 104–109.

1. Mead, p. 226.
2. Bill James, *The New Bill James Historical Baseball Abstract*, p. 100.
3. David Nemec et al., *The Baseball Chronicle*, p. 214.
4. Bill Gilbert, *They Also Served: Baseball & the Home Front*, p. 221.
5. Nemec et al., p. 222.

6. Goldstein, p. 103.
7. Nemec et al., p. 220.
8. J.G. Taylor Spink, *Baseball Register* (1945), p. 16.
9. Leslie M. O'Connor, *Official Baseball 1945*, p. 84.
10. James, p. 295.
11. Goldstein, p. 170.
12. O'Connor (1945), preface.
13. Goldstein, p. 204.
14. "Vince DiMaggio to Phils in Trade for Gerheauser," *Chicago Sun-Times*, April 1, 1945.
15. Goldstein, p. 143.
16. Nemec et al., p. 224.
17. Ibid., p. 227.
18. O'Connor (1945), preface.
19. Goldstein, p. 214.
20. Bill Veeck, *Veeck: As in Wreck*, p. 39.
21. Ibid., p. 71.
22. Paul M. Angle, *Philip K. Wrigley: A Memoir of a Modest Man*, p. 60.
23. Charlie Grimm, *Jolly Cholly's Story: Baseball, I Love You*, p. 160.
24. Baseball Notes, *Sporting News*, January 11, 1945.
25. O'Connor (1945), preface.
26. Jules Tygiel, *Past Time: Baseball as History*, pp. 99–100.
27. Nemec et al., p. 200.
28. Interview with Andy Pafko, May 7, 2004.
29. Goldstein, pp. 10–11.
30. Mead, p. 122.
31. Nemec et al., p. 227.
32. O'Connor (1945), preface.
33. Goldstein, p. 213.
34. O'Connor (1945), p. 91.
35. Tygiel, p. 106.
36. Nemec et al., p. 201.
37. Tygiel, p. 107.
38. Nemec et al., p. 208.
39. Kirby Higbe, *The High Hard One*, p. 151.
40. Mead, p. 106.
41. Higbe, p. 170.
42. Goldstein, p. 161.
43. Ibid., p. 216.
44. O'Connor (1945), preface.
45. Ibid., p. 96.
46. Branch Rickey testimony, House Judiciary Hearings, 1951.
47. Mead, p. 43.
48. House Judiciary Hearings, 1951.
49. Nemec et al., p. 208.
50. Gilbert, p. 71.
51. Mead, p. 201.
52. Ibid., p. 200.
53. bid., p. 121.

CHAPTER 4:
SPRING TRAINING AT THE FRENCH LICK SPRINGS HOTEL

1. "Red Smith to Serve as Cub Scout, Coach," *Chicago Tribune*, March 1, 1945.
2. In the Cubs' Dugout, *Chicago Cubs News*, August 1, 1945.
3. Peter Golenbock, *Wrigleyville*, p. 298.
4. O'Connor (1945), p. 93.
5. "Cubs' Dauntless Dozen Hold 3 Hour Drill in French Lick," *Chicago Tribune*, March 12, 1945.
6. "Roy Hughes Fights His Way to Stardom and Wins a Home," *Chicago Cubs News*, August 2, 1944.
7. Lawrence Katz, *Baseball in 1939: The Watershed Season of the National Pastime*, p. 48.
8. Richard J. Tofel, *A Legend in the Making*, p. 202.
9. Looping the Loops, *Sporting News*, September 27, 1945.
10. "Majors Slash Spring Games to Save Miles," *Chicago Tribune*, March 16, 1945.
11. "Cubs and Reds to Play in French Lick," Chicago Sun, April 4, 1945.
12. Interview with Dr. Robert McMillan, May 14, 2004. In 1945 radium treatments ("x-ray therapy") were an accepted medical intervention for a myriad of afflictions, from acne to thyroid problems. The rest involved in Passeau's rehabilitation undoubtedly was more effective than the treatments, unless he had a bone spur growing into a muscle or connective tissue, which was not reported to be the case.
13. The Barber Shop, *Chicago Daily News*, April 5, 1945.
14. "Up to Gallagher to Move Next, Says Vandenberg," *Chicago Daily News*, April 9, 1945.
15. Correspondence from Len Merullo, January 18, 2004, and interview with Andy Pafko, May 7, 2004.
16. "Tenants Buy Flat Building to Save Homes," *Chicago Tribune*, March 4, 1945.
17. Classified Advertisement section, *Chicago Herald-American*, April 14, 1945.
18. Correspondence from Len Merullo, February 6, 2004.
19. All references to cinematic and other cultural diversions are from the Arts section, *Chicago Tribune*, April 15, 1945.
20. Ibid.

CHAPTER 5:
APRIL THROUGH JUNE: WIN SOME, LOSE SOME

1. Grimm, p. 160.
2. Angle, p. 109.
3. Ibid., p. 63.
4. "Wrigley Field Bleachers & Scoreboard Get New Coat of Green," *Chicago Cubs News*, April 13, 1944.
5. "Livingston in front as Cubs' #1 Backstop," *Sporting News*, April 26, 1945.
6. James, p. 830.
7. House Judiciary Hearings, 1951.
8. O'Connor (1945), p. 250.
9. "Mr. Chipman Goes to Town in Cubs' Livery," *Sporting News*, August 9, 1945.
10. O'Connor (1945), p. 249.
11. "Careful Hill Pace Made Wyse Cub Ace," *Sporting News*, July 26, 1945.
12. Spink (1945), p. 128.

13. O'Connor (1945), p. 244.
14. Down in the Dugout with the Cubs, *Chicago Cubs News*, April 13, 1944.
15. Looping the Loops, *Sporting News*, September 27, 1945.
16. O'Connor (1945), p. 251.
17. "Some Facts About the Cubs," Official American League and National League World Series Program, 1945, p. 8. (Hereinafter referred to as 1945 World Series Program.)
18. Golenbock, p. 311.
19. Down in the Dugout with the Cubs, *Chicago Cubs News*, April 13, 1944.
20. In the Wake of the News, *Chicago Tribune*, October 10, 1945.
21. "Cub Notes," *Sporting News*, June 7, 1945.
22. Spink (1945), p. 123.
23. "It's Up to Gallagher . . . , " *Chicago Daily News*, April 9, 1945.

CHAPTER 6:
THE PENNANT HOPES OF JULY AND AUGUST

1. In the Wake of the News, *Chicago Tribune,* June 17, 1945.
2. Interview with Len Merullo, September 3, 2002.
3. 1945 World Series Program and *Sporting News*, July 19, 1945.
4. All salary information on Hank Borowy is from the Baseball Hall of Fame Library, Cooperstown, New York.
5. "MacPhail Talks About Borowy Trade," *Chicago Tribune*, October 2, 1945.
6. Interview with Mrs. Henry L. Borowy, May 7, 2004.
7. "MacPhail Talks . . . ," *Chicago Tribune*, October 2, 1945.
8. Interview with and correspondence from Len Merullo, September 3, 2002; January 17, 2004; February 6, 2004; and March 20, 2004.
9. Ibid.
10. O'Connor, *Official Baseball* 1946, p. 53.
11. Interview with Claude Passeau, March 5, 2002.
12. "Looping the Loops," *Sporting News*, September 27, 1945.
13. Interview with Paul Erickson, March 16, 2002.
14. "Phil Cavarretta Doing It All," *Sporting News*, May 31, 1945.
15. "Some Facts About the Cubs," 1945 World Series Program, p. 8.
16. Ibid.
17. "Looping the Loops," *Sporting News*, September 27, 1945.
18. "Some Facts About the Cubs," 1945 World Series Program, p. 3.
19. In the Cubs' Dugout, *Chicago Cubs News*, August 1, 1945.
20. "Looping the Loops," *Sporting News*, September 27, 1945.
21. "Some Facts About the Cubs," 1945 World Series Program, p. 3.

CHAPTER 7:
LOOKING BACK AND SEEING RED

1. Reports varied on the extent of Cavarretta's shoulder injury; it was referred to as both a "sprain" and a "separation."
2. Grimm, p. 168.
3. O'Connor (1945), pp. 93, 288, 295.
4. Interviews with Andy Pafko, March 12, 2002, and May 7, 2004.

5. The Barber Shop, *Chicago Daily News*, October 1, 1945.
6. Photograph in the Sports section, *Chicago Tribune*, September 30, 1945.
7. Correspondence from Len Merullo, February 6, 2004.
8. "'My Boys!' Is Grimm's Proud Victory Cry," *Chicago Tribune*, September 30, 1945.
9. The Barber Shop, *Chicago Daily News*, October 1, 1945.

CHAPTER 9:
BRING ON THE TIGERS

1. "Cubs in 6—Hornsby," *Chicago Daily News*, October 1, 1945.
2. The Barber Shop, ibid.
3. In the Wake of the News, *Chicago Tribune*, October 3, 1945.
4. O'Connor (1945), p. 257.
5. "Tigers by a Shade!" *Chicago Tribune*, October 3, 1945.
6. Goldstein, p. 220.
7. Lew Fonseca, writer and producer, *The World Series of 1945*. This, the "official film" (produced by Chicago Film Studios) of the 1945 World Series, shows Pafko's throw reaching Hack perfectly on one short bounce and Mayo actually making it a closer play than reported. Hack waved to Pafko after the play as a means of acknowledging the strong toss.
8. "A Paving Brick Helps Cubs Win!" *Chicago Tribune*, October 4, 1945.
9. In the Wake of the News, ibid.
10. "Greenberg and Trucks Draw Tigers' Post-Game Applause," *Chicago Tribune*, October 5, 1945.
11. "Passeau's One Hit Shutout Stuns Detroit," *Chicago Tribune*, October 6, 1945.
12. "Bleacher Fans Keep All-Night Vigil at Gates," ibid.
13. "Wrigley Shuns Series to Address Ticket Crisis," *Chicago Tribune*, October 5, 1945.
14. Angle, pp. 112–113.
15. "Wrigley Field All Dolled Up for Big Series," *Chicago Tribune*, October 5, 1945.
16. Photograph in the Sports section, *Chicago Tribune*, October 7, 1945.
17. "Trout Recalls Time the Cubs Rejected Him," ibid.
18. In the Wake of the News, ibid.
19. David Fulk and Dan Riley, *The Cubs Reader*, p. 46.
20. Correspondence from Len Merullo, February 6, 2004. To this day, Merullo does not feel that the spiking he experienced was intentional, and he is understandably proud of his World Series scars.
21. In the Wake of the News, *Chicago Tribune*, October 10, 1945.
22. Fonseca, film. *The World Series of 1945* does not show Schuster's position on the base paths at the time Hack hit the pitch. It is clear from the film, however, that Greenberg did charge the ball but the extremely high bounce made it impossible for him to field it, because the ball was still traveling at a very high rate of speed when it reached him. Contrary to some reports, the ball did not hit a divot or a turf bruise left from a football game; the Chicago Bears' first Wrigley Field home game in 1945 was not until Sunday, October 13 (which they lost to the Chicago Cardinals, 16–7). The *Tribune's* front page on October 10, 1945, had an article entitled "Scorers Clear Greenberg of Crucial Error."
23. "7th Game Ticket Fans Besiege Cubs' Park," Sports section headline, *Chicago Tribune*, October 10, 1945.
24. Fonseca, film. Description of what appears in the film *The World Series of 1945*.

25. "Five Run First Inning Blasts Chicago Hopes," *Chicago Tribune*, October 11, 1945.
26. In the Wake of the News, ibid.

CHAPTER 10:
LOSING BECOMES THE NORM

1. J.G. Taylor Spink, *Official Baseball Guide* 1947, p. 195.

BIBLIOGRAPHY

BOOKS

Angle, Paul M. *Philip K. Wrigley: A Memoir of a Modest Man*. Chicago: Rand McNally, 1975.

Brown, Warren. *The Chicago Cubs*. Carbondale, Illinois: Southern Illinois University Press, 2000.

Fulk, David, and Dan Riley. *The Cubs Reader*. Boston: Houghton Mifflin Company, 1991.

Gilbert, Bill. *They Also Served: Baseball & the Home Front*. New York: Crown, 1992.

Gold, Eddie, and Art Ahrens. *The New Era Cubs 1941–1945*. Chicago: Bonus Books, 1985.

Golenbock, Peter. *Wrigleyville*. New York: St. Martin's Press, 1996.

Goldstein, Richard. *Spartan Seasons*. New York: MacMillan, 1980.

Grimm, Charlie. *Jolly Cholly's Story: Baseball, I Love You*. Chicago: Henry Regnery, 1968.

Higbe, Kirby. *The High Hard One*. New York: Viking Press, 1967.

James, Bill. *The New Bill James Historical Baseball Abstract*. New York: The Free Press, 2001.

Katz, Lawrence. *Baseball in 1939: The Watershed Season of the National Pastime*. Jefferson, North Carolina: Banner Books, 1991.

Leventhal, Josh. *Take Me Out to the Ballpark*. New York: Black Dog & Leventhal Publishers, 2000.

Mead, William B. *Even the Browns*. Chicago: Contemporary Books, 1978.

Nemec, David et al. *The Baseball Chronicle*. Lincolnwood, Illinois: Publications International, 2001.

O'Connor, Leslie M., ed. *Official Baseball 1945*. New York: A.S. Barnes, 1945.

———. *Official Baseball 1946*. New York: A.S. Barnes, 1946.

Spink, J.G. Taylor. *Baseball Register*. St. Louis, Missouri: C.C. Spink & Son, 1945.

———. *Official Baseball Guide 1947*. St. Louis, Missouri: C.C. Spink & Son, 1947.

Thorn, John et al. *Total Baseball*. New York: Total Sports, 1999.

Tofel, Richard J. *A Legend in the Making*. Chicago: Ivan R. Dee, 2000.

Tygiel, Jules. *Past Time: Baseball as History*. New York: Oxford University Press, 2000.

Veeck, Bill. *Veeck: As in Wreck*. Chicago: University of Chicago Press, 2001.

Wolff, Rick, ed. *The Baseball Encyclopedia*. New York: MacMillan, 1990.

OTHER SOURCES

NEWSPAPERS

Chicago Daily News, April 5, April 9, and October 1, 1945.

Chicago Herald-American, April 14, 1945.

Chicago Sun, April 1 and April 4, 1945.

Chicago Tribune, March 1 through October 13, 1945.

Sporting News, April 13, 1944; January 11, April 26, May 31, June 7, July 19, July 26, August 9, and September 27, 1945.

MAJOR LEAGUE PUBLICATIONS AND FILMS

Chicago Cubs News, April 13 and August 2, 1944; and April 13, August 1, and September 27, 1945.

Fonseca, Lew, writer and producer. *The World Series of 1945*. Chicago: Chicago Film Studios, producer, 1945. The "official film" of the 1945 World Series.

Official American League and National League World Series Program, 1945.

INDEX

Italicized page numbers indicate photographs.

Teams are listed under their home city.

ABOUT THE AUTHOR

C harles N. Billington is a licensed clinical social worker with 30 years of experience in mental health. After graduating from St. Olaf College in Northfield, Minnesota, he received his master's degree from the University of Illinois in Chicago. He has worked as an administrator, psychotherapist, and consultant. Most recently he has worked with the senior citizens.

A three-sport athlete in high school who played baseball at the collegiate level, he combined his background in sports and his interest in history with his work with seniors to write about the Chicago Cubs' last World Series. The fascinating

Photo by Elizabeth Daniel.

recollections of two elderly baseball players who came to him for assistance became the inspiration for the work.

Charles grew up in the Chicago area and lives in the north suburbs with his wife of 25 years and two children. His hobbies include boating, playing the piano, and playing outfield in the Chicago North Men's Senior Baseball League.

OTHER LAKE CLAREMONT PRESS BOOKS

FINDING YOUR CHICAGO ANCESTORS: A BEGINNER'S GUIDE TO FAMILY HISTORY IN THE CITY AND COOK COUNTY
by Grace DuMelle
No matter where you live, if you have Chicago ancestors, this is the book to have. Investigating ancestry and family history in the City of Big Shoulders can be daunting without this step by step guide to genealogy. Written especially for beginners, you'll find techniques and resources that save time and frustration–everything from operating a microfilm reader to playing by bureaucrats' rules. The book uses a unique approach of answering one question per chapter so you don't have to wade through a lot of preliminaries to launch or continue your search. As seen in *Chicago Magazine*.
1-898121-25-9, March 2005, softcover, 329 pp., illustrations, $16.95

CHICAGO'S MIDWAY AIRPORT: THE FIRST SEVENTY-FIVE YEARS
by Christopher Lynch
Training ground of heroes and daredevils. Transportation hub to the nation. Heart of a neighborhood. Outpost of glamour. Crossroads of the world. Birthplace of the major airlines. Contemporary success story. Learn why Midway Airport may be Chicago's most overlooked treasure and the country's most historic airport with this collection of oral histories, historic narrative, and fascinating photos. As recommended in the *Chicago Sun-Times* and several aviation magazines.
1-893121-18-6, Jan. 2003, oblong, larger format softcover, 201 pp., 205 historic and contemporary photos and artifacts, $19.95

THE HOOFS AND GUNS OF THE STORM: CHICAGO'S CIVIL WAR CONNECTIONS
by Arnie Bernstein, with foreword by Senator Paul Simon
Put Chicago's Civil War history into your hands with this comprehensive popular history/guidebook that shows you familiar memorials, old gravesites, and everyday streets in fresh perspective. While America's Civil War was fought on Confederate battlefields, Chicago played a crucial role in the Union's struggle toward victory. *The Hoofs and Guns of the Storm* takes you through a whirlwind of nineteenth-century people, places, and events that created the foundation for modern-day Chicago. Recommended by top Civil War historians, authors, and Civil War round tables!
1-893121-06-2, Sept. 2003, softcover, 284 pp., 82 photos, $15.95

GREAT CHICAGO FIRES: HISTORIC BLAZES THAT SHAPED A CITY
by David Cowan
As Chicago changed from agrarian outpost to industrial giant, it would be visited time and again by some of the worst infernos in American history—fires that sparked not only banner headlines but, more importantly, critical upgrades in fire safety laws across the globe. Acclaimed author (*To Sleep With the Angels*) and veteran firefighter David Cowan tells the story of the other "great" Chicago fires, noting the causes, consequences, and historical context of each. In transporting readers beyond the fireline and into the ruins, Cowan brings readers up close to the heroism, awe, and devastation generated by the fires that shaped Chicago.
1-893121-07-0, Aug. 2001, oblong, larger format softcover, 167 pp., 80 historic photos, $19.95

THE CHICAGO RIVER: A NATURAL AND UNNATURAL HISTORY
by Libby Hill
Hill presents an intimate biography of a humble, even sluggish, stream in the right place at the right time—the story of the making and perpetual re-making of a river by everything from geological forces to the interventions of an emerging and mighty city. Winner of the 2001 American Regional History Publishing Award (1st Place, Midwest) and the 2000 Midwest Independent Publishers Association Award (2nd Place, History), and nominated for best public works book of the year.
1-893121-02-X, Aug. 2000, softcover, 302 pp., 78 maps and photos, $16.95

THE GOLDEN AGE OF CHICAGO CHILDREN'S TELEVISION

by Ted Okuda and Jack Mulqueen

Behind-the-Scenes Stories of the Golden Age of Chicago Children's Television as Told by the People Who Lived It! At one time every station in Chicago—a maximum of five, until 1964—produced or aired some programming for children. From the late 1940s through the early 1970s, local television stations created a golden age of children's television unique in American broadcasting. Though the shows often operated under strict budgetary constraints, these programs were rich in imagination, inventiveness, and devoted fans. The mere mention of their names brings smiles to the faces of Midwestern Baby Boomers everywhere: *Kukla, Fran, & Ollie, Super Circus, Garfield Goose, Bozo's Circus, Mulqueens' Kiddie-A-Go-Go, BJ & Dirty Dragon, Ray Rayner and Friends*, and a host of others. Discover the back stories and details of this special era from the people who created, lived, and enjoyed it—producers, on-air personalities, and fans. As seen in *Chicago Magazine*.

1-893121-17-8, June 2004, softcover, 251 pp., 78 photos, $17.95

REGIONAL TRAVEL & GUIDEBOOKS BY LOCALS

THE STREETS & SAN MAN'S GUIDE TO CHICAGO EATS

by Dennis Foley

Tongue-in-Cheek Style and Food-in-Mouth Expertise Certified by the City of Chicago's Department of Lunch. Quickly becoming a cult classic among city workers! Streets & San electrician Dennis Foley shares his and his co-workers' favorite lunch joints in all reaches of the city. Enjoy Chicago's best mom-and-pop eateries at fast-food prices and never eat in chain restaurants again! Warning: requires a sense of humor, a sense of adventure, and a large appetite. As seen in the *Chicago Tribune, Chicago Sun-Times*, and many more.

1-893121-27-5, June 2004, softcover, 117 pp., 83 reviews, 23 detours, 25 coupons, $12.95

A COOK'S GUIDE TO CHICAGO: WHERE TO FIND EVERYTHING YOU NEED AND LOTS OF THINGS YOU DIDN'T KNOW YOU DID, 2ND EDITION

by Marilyn Pocius

Chef Marilyn Pocius takes food lovers and serious home cooks into all corners of Chicagoland in her explorations of local foodways. In addition to providing extensive information on specialty food and equipment shops (including gourmet stores, health food shops, butchers, fishmongers, produce stands, spice shops, ethnic grocers, and restaurant supplies dealers), Pocius directs readers to farmers markets, knife sharpeners, foodie clubs, cooking classes, and culinary publications. Her special emphasis on what to do with the unfamiliar items found in ethnic supermarkets includes "Top 10" lists, simple recipes, and tips on using exotic ingredients. A complete index makes it easy to find what you need: frozen tropical fruit pulp, smoked goat feet, fresh durian, sanding sugar, empanada dough, live crabs, egusi seeds, mugwort flour, kishke, and over two thousand other items you didn't know you couldn't live without! Recommended in the *Chicago Sun-Times, Chicago Tribune*, and many others.

1-893121-47-X, May 2005, softcover, approx. 300 pp., $15.95

A NATIVE'S GUIDE TO CHICAGO, 4TH EDITION

by Lake Claremont Press, edited by Sharon Woodhouse

Venture into the nooks and crannies of everyday Chicago with this one-of-a-kind, comprehensive budget guide. Over 450 pages of free, inexpensive, and unusual things to do in the Windy City make this the perfect resource for tourists, business travelers, visiting suburbanites, and resident Chicagoans. Called the "best guidebook for locals" in *New City's* "Best of Chicago" issue!

1-893121-23-2, Nov. 2004, softcover, 468 pp., 22 photos, 10 maps, $15.95

A Native's Guide to Northwest Indiana

by Mark Skertic

At the southern tip of Lake Michigan, in the crook between Chicagoland and southwestern Michigan, lies Northwest Indiana, a region of natural diversity, colorful history, abundant recreational opportunities, small town activities, and urban diversions. Whether you're a life-long resident, new in the area, or just passing through, let native Mark Skertic be your personal tour guide of the best The Region has to offer. With regional maps, chapters on 31 communities, and special sections on antiques, boating, gaming, golf courses, the lakeshore and dunes, shopping, theater, and more. As seen in *Lake Magazine*.

1-893121-08-9, Aug. 2003, softcover, 319 pp., 62 photos, 5 maps, $15

GHOSTLORE AND HAUNTED HISTORY

Chicago Haunts: Ghostlore of the Windy City

by Ursula Bielski

Bielski captures over 160 years of Chicago's haunted history with her distinctive blend of lively storytelling, in-depth historical research, exclusive interviews, and insights from parapsychology. Called "a masterpiece of the genre," "a must-read," and "an absolutely first-rate-book" by reviewers, *Chicago Haunts* continues to earn the praise of critics and readers alike.

0-9642426-7-2, Oct. 1998, softcover, 277 pp., 29 photos, $15

More Chicago Haunts: Scenes from Myth and Memory

by Ursula Bielski

Chicago. A town with a past. A people haunted by its history in more ways than one. A "windy city" with tales to tell . . . Bielski is back with more history, more legends, and more hauntings, including the personal scary stories of *Chicago Haunts* readers.

1-893121-04-6, Oct. 2000, softcover, 312 pp., 50 photos, $15

Creepy Chicago: A Ghosthunter's Tales of the City's Scariest Sites

by Ursula Bielski, illustrated by Amy Noble

Chicago's famous phantoms, haunted history, and unsolved mysteries for readers ages 8–12. *Chicago Haunts for kids*!

1-893121-15-1, Aug. 2003, softcover, 19 illustrated stories, glossary, tips for young ghosthunters, 136 pp., $8

Muldoon: A True Chicago Ghost Story: Tales of a Forgotten Rectory

by Rocco A. Facchini and Daniel J. Facchini

Poverty, crime, politics, scandal, revenge, and a ghost: Fresh out of the seminary in 1957, Father Rocco Facchini was appointed to his first assignment at the parish of St. Charles Borromeo on Chicago's Near West Side. Adjusting to rectory life with an unorthodox, dispirited pastor and adapting to the needs of the rough, impoverished neighborhood were challenges in themselves. Little did he know that the rectory and church were also being haunted by a bishop's ghost! These are the untold stories of the last days of St. Charles parish by the last person able to tell them. Called "The hot new read among Chicago priests" in the *Chicago Sun-Times*. Recommended by Catholic and secular publications alike.

1-893121-24-0, Sept. 2003, softcover, 268 pp., 44 photos, $15

ORDER FORM

Wrigley Field's Last World Series   _____ @ $16.95 = _____
Finding Your Chicago Ancestors   _____ @ $16.95 = _____
The Golden Age of Chicago Children's Television   _____ @ $17.95 = _____
A Native's Guide to Chicago, 4th Edition   _____ @ $15.95 = _____
Literary Chicago   _____ @ $15.95 = _____
The Chicago River   _____ @ $16.95 = _____
Great Chicago Fires   _____ @ $19.95 = _____
Chicago's Midway Airport   _____ @ $19.95 = _____
The Hoofs & Guns of the Storm   _____ @ $15.95 = _____
Graveyards of Chicago   _____ @ $15.00 = _____
A Cook's Guide to Chicago, 2nd Edition   _____ @ $15.95 = _____

_____   _____ @ $ ___ = _____

_____   _____ @ $ ___ = _____

Subtotal: _____
Less Discount: _____
New Subtotal: _____
8.75% Sales Tax for Illinois Residents: _____
Shipping: _____
TOTAL: _____

Name _____

Address _____

City _____ State _____ Zip _____

☐ *Add me to the LCP monthly Customer e-mail newsletter list.*

Please enclose check, money order, or credit card information.

Visa/MC/Disc/AmEx# _____ Exp. _____

Signature _____

Discounts when you order multiples copies!
2 books — 10% off total, 3-4 books — 20% off,
5-9 books — 25% off, 10+ books — 40% off

—Low Shipping Fees—
$2.50 for the first book and $.50 for each additional book, with a maximum charge of $8.

Order by mail, phone, fax or e-mail.
All of our books have a no-hassle, 100% money-back guarantee.

4650 North Rockwell Street
Chicago, Illinois 60625
773/583-7800
773/583-7877 (fax)
lcp@lakeclaremont.com
www.lakeclaremont.com